FAVORITE RESTAURANT RECIPES

FAVORITE RESTAURANT RECIPES

500 Unforgettable Dishes from the R.S.V.P. Column of **Bon Appétit**

THE KNAPP PRESS

Publishers

Los Angeles

Bon Appétit is a registered trademark of
Bon Appétit Publishing Corp. Used with permission.

Published in the United States of America in 1982
The Knapp Press
5900 Wilshire Boulevard, Los Angeles, California 90036
Copyright © 1982 by Knapp Communications Corporation
All rights reserved
Distributed by The Viking Press
625 Madison Avenue, New York, New York 10022
Distributed simultaneously in Canada by Penguin Books Canada Limited

Library of Congress Cataloging in Publication Data
Main entry under title:
Favorite restaurant recipes.
Includes indexes.
1. Cookery, International. I. Bon appétit.
TX725.A1F32   1982   641.5'14   82-8954
ISBN 0-89535-100-5   AACR2

10 9 8 7 6 5 4 3 2 1

PRINTED AND BOUND IN THE UNITED STATES OF AMERICA

BILL OF FARE

INTRODUCTION   vii

TO START   2

BEVERAGES   20

FROM THE TUREEN   28

SALAD BOWL   50

SAUCES AND CONDIMENTS   62

FROM THE SEA   68

POULTRY   94

MEATS   114

LIGHT ENTRÉES   138

VEGETABLES   156

BREAD BASKET   166

FINISHING TOUCHES   180

DINER'S DICTIONARY   226

INDEX OF RECIPES   236

INDEX OF RESTAURANTS   243

INTRODUCTION

Dining deliciously is a popular subject here at *Bon Appétit*. And what dishes are more memorable than those created by the men and women for whom cooking is both an art and a livelihood?

Hundreds of *Bon Appétit* readers write to us every month requesting recipes for the restaurant dishes they love most. A few years ago, we started reprinting our readers' letters and the requested recipes in a monthly column called R.S.V.P. That column has become one of the most popular features in our magazine.

Now our editors have compiled more than 500 of these recipes here in FAVORITE RESTAURANT RECIPES. This is a unique cookbook: Its sources are small cafes and grand palaces of *haute cuisine*, unsung cooks and three-star master chefs. Each recipe comes with a double recommendation: from an enthusiastic reader and from our staff and the test kitchens of *Bon Appétit*.

Just as we have selected only the most special recipes for you, so have we made certain that they will be easy to prepare at home. We've taken care to ensure that all ingredients and equipment are readily available. Where necessary, we've streamlined or rewritten the recipes to make them practical for the home kitchen.

For your convenience, the recipes are organized by the part they play in a meal. In the chapter on appetizers, for example, you'll find an Avocado Mousse from the elegant Leith's Restaurant in London side by side with Salmon Ceviche from The Waterfront in San Francisco and the Vegetarian Chopped Liver served by Homowack in Spring Glen, New York. Among the 48 recipes for main-course poultry dishes are the Salmis of Duck Legs and Thighs that André Daguin serves at his acclaimed restaurant in Auch, France, along with the Buttermilk Pecan Chicken featured at the Patchwork Quilt Country Inn in Middlebury, Indiana. And there are equally diverse chapters on soups, salads, seafoods, meats, vegetables, sauces, desserts, drinks. . . .

What makes all these recipes so successful, we have found, is not exotic ingredients, professional cookware, or the deft hand of a professional chef. Rather, it's the ingenious small, personal touches, the unusual combination of textures and tastes, the surprising spice —the chef's special secret—that make them truly unforgettable. We are delighted to be able to bring these very special recipes to you.

Bon Appétit

FAVORITE
RESTAURANT
RECIPES

TO START

They are called *antipasti* in Italy, *zensai* in Japan, and *vorspeisen* in Germany. In Spain there are *tapas*, in Russia *zakuski*, and in Mexico *antojitos*. And in France, of course, there are *hors d'oeuvre*. Whatever the name, appetizers are enjoyed around the world—and no more anywhere than in the United States, where eclectic restaurateurs offer diners a dazzling array of before-the-meal delicacies of every possible national origin.

Some interesting customs have grown up around appetizers. In Madrid, where eating is even more popular than bullfights, there is a sort of ritualized pub crawl called a *chateo*. Friends go from cafe to cafe to sip Sherry and sample the tiny fried or marinated morsels called tapas. Since some cafes and taverns offer as many as sixty different kinds of tapas, the chateo can easily become an extended affair, and some Madrileños even find that they have to forego one of their five "official" meals. . . .

In Czarist Russia, the tidbits known as zakuski were often served as a meal before the meal; waiters brought tray after tray of appetizers from the kitchen, and patrons washed them down with liberal draughts of wine and vodka. After the revolution, immigrants brought this tradition to Paris, where the French adapted it and gave birth to the appetizer buffet, or *hors d'oeuvre a la russe*—a "small dinner" composed entirely of appetizers. (The Italians will tell you that they have been doing this for centuries, and the Swedes make the same claim for their marvelous *smörgasbord*.)

Whether they are hot or cold, simple or elegant, French or Japanese, appetizers are meant to whet the appetite, not satisfy it. But the ones that follow—ranging from dips to terrines to escargots —are so delicious that you will probably be tempted to "have just one more." And one more after that.

Salade de Champignon et Avocat au Crème Fraîche et Vinaigre Framboise from Ernie's in San Francisco (see page 8).

BAVAROIS DE POISSON
(Fish Mousse with Fennel Butter Sauce)

DÉJÀ-VU
PHILADELPHIA, PENNSYLVANIA

8 servings

> 2 cups full-flavored fish stock
> 1 teaspoon fennel seeds
> ½ pound pike, sole or flounder fillets, skinned
> 2 teaspoons unflavored gelatin
>
> 2 cups whipping cream
> 1 teaspoon salt
>
> Lettuce leaves
> Beurre Blanc Fennel Sauce*

Line bottoms of 8 ¾-cup ramekins or soufflé dishes with parchment paper; butter paper. Set aside.

Bring fish stock and fennel seeds to boil in medium saucepan over medium-high heat. Boil stock 3 minutes. Let cool to room temperature.

Strain mixture into medium saucepan. Stir in fish and gelatin and cook over medium-high heat until mixture is reduced by ⅓ and fish flakes easily, about 3 to 5 minutes. Transfer mixture to processor or blender and puree about 3 minutes. Transfer puree to large bowl. Set in larger bowl filled with ice cubes, stirring puree constantly until room temperature. Remove bowl from ice bath and set aside.

Combine cream and salt in medium bowl and beat until soft peaks form. Fold whipped cream into puree. Spoon mixture evenly into prepared dishes or ramekins. Refrigerate overnight.

To serve, arrange lettuce leaves on 8″ salad plates. Unmold each serving into center of each plate. Gently remove parchment paper. Spoon Beurre Blanc Fennel Sauce over each mousse and serve immediately.

*Beurre Blanc Fennel Sauce

Makes ½ cup

> 6 black peppercorns
> 2 tablespoons fennel vinegar**
> 2 tablespoons dry vermouth
> 1 large shallot, chopped
> ½ cup (1 stick) well-chilled butter, cut into 16 pieces

Combine peppercorns, fennel vinegar, vermouth and shallot in small heavy saucepan and cook over medium-high heat until reduced to glaze, about 3 to 5 minutes. Remove pan from heat. Whisk in 2 pieces butter 1 piece at a time and stir until mixture is smooth. Place pan over low heat and whisk in remaining butter in same manner. Serve at once.

**For fennel vinegar, combine ¼ cup white wine vinegar and 1 teaspoon fennel seeds in small saucepan and bring to simmer over medium heat. Let simmer 5 minutes. Strain thoroughly before using.

CAPTAIN'S CHAIR CHEESE DIP

THE CAPTAIN'S CHAIR
HYANNIS, MASSACHUSETTS

Dip can be prepared 1 day ahead. Serve with crudités or crackers.

Makes 3 cups

> 1 16-ounce carton small curd cottage cheese
> ½ pound cream cheese, room temperature
> ¼ pound bleu cheese, crumbled
> ½ cup (1 stick) butter, melted
> 3 tablespoons beef stock base
> 2 teaspoons sweet paprika

Combine first 3 ingredients in large bowl and mix well. Blend butter, stock base and paprika in another bowl. Add cheese mixture and stir until thoroughly combined. Turn into serving bowl and refrigerate.

SALSA CALIENTE
(Hot Sauce)

TORTILLA FLATS AT THE WHARF
LAHAINA, MAUI, HAWAII

Makes about 2 cups

> 1 16-ounce can crushed tomatoes
> 1 3-ounce can green chili salsa
> 2 tablespoons vinegar
> 1 to 2 jalapeño peppers or to taste, chopped
> 6 green onions, chopped
> 1 tablespoon hot pepper sauce or to taste
> Salt

Combine tomatoes and salsa in medium bowl. Add vinegar and stir until well mixed. Let stand about 15 minutes. Add remaining ingredients and blend thoroughly. Cover and refrigerate for at least 24 hours before serving.

BRANDADE DE MORUE
(Codfish Mousse)

LA RIVE
CATSKILL, NEW YORK

"This extraordinary dish is a specialty of Marseilles."
—Linda Palmieri, Kingston, New York

6 to 8 servings

> 1 pound potatoes, peeled and cut into 1-inch cubes
> 1 pound fresh cod fillets
>
> ¾ cup mayonnaise
> 1½ to 2 large garlic cloves, crushed
> Salt and freshly ground white pepper

Place potatoes in 3- to 4-quart saucepan and lay fish over top. Add water to cover fish completely. Cover, bring to slow boil and simmer until potatoes are cooked. Pass fish and potatoes through food mill (do not use processor), adding just enough cooking liquid to moisten. Cover and chill.

Combine mayonnaise and garlic in small bowl. Blend into chilled mixture. Season with salt and pepper to taste. (Flavors intensify if allowed to remain covered in refrigerator several hours.) When ready to serve, taste and adjust seasoning as needed.

SALMON CEVICHE

THE WATERFRONT RESTAURANT
SAN FRANCISCO, CALIFORNIA

8 servings

   2 **pounds salmon fillets, cut into ½-inch pieces**
   2 **cups fresh lemon juice**

   2 **medium tomatoes, seeded and diced**
   1 **medium red onion, diced**
  ½ **cup olive oil**
  ⅓ **cup fresh lime juice**
   2 **whole canned green chilies, rinsed and diced**
   1 **tablespoon chopped cilantro**
   2 **garlic cloves, minced**
  ½ **teaspoon cumin**
    Dash hot pepper sauce

Combine salmon and lemon juice in bowl. Cover and refrigerate overnight, stirring occasionally.

Drain salmon well and mix with remaining ingredients. Chill before serving.

MAQUEREAUX AU VIN BLANC
(Mackerel in White Wine)

L'AIGLON
NEW YORK, NEW YORK

8 servings

   4 **large onions, sliced**
   4 **1½-pound fresh mackerel fillets**
  12 **ounces (1½ cups) dry white wine**
1¾ **cups fish stock**
   1 **cup dry sherry**
  ¼ **cup fresh lemon juice**
  ¼ **cup light olive oil**
  ½ **teaspoon whole black peppercorns**

  ½ **teaspoon salt**
  ¼ **teaspoon thyme**
   3 **bay leaves**
    Lemon wedges (garnish)

Arrange ¾ of onion slices in large skillet. Place mackerel fillets on top and cover with remaining onion slices. Add wine, stock, sherry, lemon juice and oil and sprinkle evenly with seasonings.

Gently poach over direct heat 10 minutes or just until fish loses its translucency. Cool in liquid. Carefully transfer fillets to serving platter. Top with onion slices. Cover completely and refrigerate.

Strain poaching liquid. Return to skillet and boil until reduced by ½. Cool. Transfer to small container and refrigerate.

Serve fish and sauce cold, garnished with lemon.

AQUAVIT HERRING TORE WRETMAN

OPERAKÄLLAREN
STOCKHOLM, SWEDEN

4 to 6 servings

   4 **fillets of salt herring or matjes herring**

Brine

   5 **tablespoons plus 1 teaspoon white vinegar**
  ¼ **cup water**
  ¼ **cup sugar**
   4 **whole cloves**
   1 **slice lemon peel (about ½x2 inches)**
  ¾ **teaspoon (scant) crushed allspice**
  ½ **teaspoon (scant) cracked black pepper**
  ½ **teaspoon (scant) caraway seeds**
  ½ **teaspoon (scant) aniseed**

Garnish

  ¾ **onion, thinly sliced**
  ⅔ **lemon, peeled and thinly sliced**
  ⅓ **tart apple, peeled, cored and cut into large julienne**
1⅓ **teaspoons juniper berries, lightly crushed**
   3 **tablespoons Aquavit**

If using salt herring, soak overnight in cold water to cover; rinse and pat dry. If using matjes herring, rinse lightly and pat dry.

Combine all ingredients for brine in small saucepan and bring to boil. Remove from heat and let cool.

Cut herring fillets into 1-inch pieces. Layer in large glass jar or bowl with all garnish ingredients except Aquavit. Add Aquavit to brine and strain into jar. Cover tightly and marinate in refrigerator 1 to 2 days before serving.

Can be refrigerated 1 week.

INTER-CONTINENTAL PATE

HOTEL INTER-CONTINENTAL
WAILEA, MAUI, HAWAII

"An exceptionally creamy pâté prepared with chicken livers and many different herbs."
—Bill Gardiner, Vancouver, British Columbia

Makes about 4½ cups

    3 tablespoons (⅜ stick) unsalted butter
    2 small white onions, chopped
    1 tablespoon dried rosemary
  1½ teaspoons salt
  1½ teaspoons freshly ground white pepper
  1½ teaspoons ground thyme
    ½ teaspoon dried basil
    ½ teaspoon nutmeg

    1 pound 3 ounces chicken livers, washed, trimmed and patted dry

  1¾ cups (3½ sticks) unsalted butter, room temperature
  1½ hard-cooked eggs
    2 tablespoons Cognac
    2 tablespoons dry sherry
    1 tablespoon chopped fresh parsley

Preheat oven to 400°F. Melt 3 tablespoons butter in large ovenproof skillet over medium heat. Add onions, rosemary, salt, pepper, thyme, basil and nutmeg; sauté until onion is soft, about 10 minutes.

Add chicken livers to skillet and saute until browned, about 5 minutes. Transfer skillet to oven and bake until livers are cooked through, 5 to 8 minutes. Remove from oven; cool completely.

Mix 1¾ cups butter in processor until light and fluffy. Add liver mixture, eggs, Cognac, sherry and parsley and puree until smooth. Transfer to serving dishes or crocks. Chill until firm, about 2 hours or overnight.

PATE MAISON

CASA VIEJA
CORALES, NEW MEXICO

"A couple of years ago, while attending a convention in New Mexico, I spent a lovely evening at Casa Vieja in Corales. I have never forgotten the wonderful Pâté Maison."   —C.J. Estelle, Billings, Montana

Makes 1 9x5-inch loaf

    2 quarts water
    2 teaspoons peppercorns
    2 teaspoons whole cloves
    3 bay leaves
      Few sprigs parsley

  2½ pounds very fresh chicken livers

    2 cups (4 sticks) butter, softened
    1 small onion, finely chopped

    1 large garlic clove, minced
    1 tablespoon salt
    2 teaspoons dry mustard
    ½ teaspoon nutmeg (freshly ground if possible)
      Dash hot pepper sauce
    ¼ cup brandy

Combine first 5 ingredients in a 4-quart saucepan. Bring to a boil and simmer 10 minutes. Strain.

Add chicken livers to liquid. Cook just below simmering point until liquid is clear and rosy and livers are done, about 10 minutes. Drain livers and pass once through meat grinder. Set aside.

In large mixing bowl, blend together remaining ingredients except brandy. Add liver and mix until smooth. Stir in brandy.

Line a 9x5-inch loaf pan with aluminum foil. Pack pâté into pan. Chill thoroughly before serving.

Note: Flavors will develop more fully if pâté is allowed to chill overnight.

MOUSSE DE TOMATES AUX OEUFS DE CAILLE
(Tomato Mousse with Quail Eggs)

TAILLEVENT
PARIS, FRANCE

6 servings

  3½ pounds tomatoes, cut into wedges
    ¼ pound carrots, chopped (about ¾ cup)
    1 small onion, chopped (about ¼ cup)
    1 celery stalk, cut into medium slices
    1 shallot, minced
    1 garlic clove
    1 bouquet garni (½ teaspoon dried thyme, ½ teaspoon dried tarragon and 10 sprigs fresh parsley)

      Salt and freshly ground pepper
    1 tablespoon plus 2 teaspoons unflavored gelatin

  24 quail eggs
    1 cup whipping cream
      Very finely shredded lettuce
  24 pieces olive julienne or truffle julienne
    2 cups Tomato Coulis*
  48 small shrimp, cooked, shelled and deveined
  30 small fresh parsley sprigs

Combine tomatoes, carrots, onion, celery, shallot, garlic and bouquet garni in large saucepan. Cover and cook over low heat, stirring frequently, until thick, about 1 hour. Uncover and continue cooking until almost all moisture has evaporated and mixture is thick puree, about 15 to 20 more minutes.

Discard bouquet garni. Press puree through fine sieve or food mill. Taste and season with salt and pepper. Transfer 1 cup puree to small saucepan. Sprinkle gelatin over top to soften. Place over low heat and stir until gelatin is completely dissolved. Add ½ cup puree and blend well. Transfer mixture to large bowl and set aside to cool completely; do not refrigerate.

Simmer quail eggs 10 to 12 minutes, cool and shell. Whip cream in large bowl until soft peaks form (should not be stiff). Fold whipped cream into puree. To serve, spoon mousse into pastry bag fitted with No. 9 sawtooth edge tip. Pipe into nest pattern on 6 serving plates. Lightly line inside of nest with lettuce. Arrange 4 quail eggs at right angles on each nest. Lay 1 slice of olive or truffle across each egg. Spoon Tomato Coulis around each nest. Arrange 4 pairs shrimp in Coulis directly below quail eggs. Garnish center of each pair of shrimp and center of nest with sprig of parsley. Serve immediately.

*Tomato Coulis

Makes 2 cups

- 1½ to 2 cups peeled, seeded, chopped and drained tomatoes
- ½ cup light olive oil
- 2 to 3 tablespoons red wine vinegar
  Salt and freshly ground pepper
  Tarragon

Puree tomatoes in processor. Add oil, vinegar, salt, pepper and tarragon to taste and mix until well blended. Set coulis aside at room temperature until ready to use.

STEAK TARTARE

ALPENHOF
JACKSON HOLE, WYOMING

6 to 8 servings

- 1 pound beef tenderloin that has been frozen 3 days, thawed in refrigerator
- 6 anchovy fillets
- 3 egg yolks
- 4½ teaspoons brandy
- ¾ teaspoon Dijon mustard
- ¼ to ½ teaspoon Worcestershire sauce
- 3 drops hot pepper sauce
- 1 tablespoon minced onion
- 1 teaspoon drained minced capers
- 1 teaspoon minced dill pickle
- 1 teaspoon minced fresh parsley
- ½ teaspoon Spanish paprika
- ½ teaspoon salt or to taste
- ¼ teaspoon freshly ground pepper
  Minced fresh parsley (garnish)

Finely hand chop chilled beef.

Mash anchovies in medium bowl. Add egg yolks, brandy, mustard, Worcestershire sauce and pepper sauce and mix well. Stir in onion, capers, pickle, parsley and paprika. Add raw beef, salt and pepper and blend thoroughly. Transfer to chilled serving plate and garnish with minced parsley.

LA GROTTA CARPACCIO

LA GROTTA RISTORANTE ITALIANO
ATLANTA, GEORGIA

"The beef 'cooks' in a marinade of oil, vinegar and herbs." —Candace Peters, Atlanta, Georgia

6 servings

- 1¼ pounds beef tenderloin, trimmed of all fat and membrane and flash frozen to facilitate slicing
- ½ cup chopped shallots
- 1 tablespoon Dijon mustard
- 1½ teaspoons chopped fresh parsley (preferably Italian)
- 1 teaspoon dried sage
- 1 teaspoon dried rosemary
- 1 teaspoon dried basil
- ½ cup red wine vinegar
  Juice of 1 lemon
- 1¼ cups olive oil
  Salt and freshly ground pepper

Slice beef into paper-thin slices and set aside.

Combine shallots, mustard and herbs in medium bowl. Stir in vinegar and lemon juice. Add oil in slow steady stream, whisking constantly. Season to taste with salt and pepper. Layer meat in shallow dish, alternating with marinade to coat completely. Cover and refrigerate about 6 hours or overnight. To serve, arrange overlapping slices on salad plates.

AVOCADO MOUSSE

LEITH'S RESTAURANT
LONDON, ENGLAND

4 servings

- 2 avocados
- 1½ teaspoons unflavored gelatin
- 1½ teaspoons fresh lemon juice
- ¼ cup mayonnaise
- 1½ to 2 teaspoons grated onion
- ½ teaspoon Worcestershire sauce
- ½ teaspoon salt
- ¼ teaspoon freshly ground pepper
- ¼ teaspoon paprika
- 4 drops hot pepper sauce
- 2 to 3 tablespoons sour cream

  Cucumber slices (garnish)

Puree avocados in food processor or blender. Soften gelatin in lemon juice and add with remaining ingredients except sour cream and garnish. Mix well. Turn into serving bowl. Whip sour cream lightly with fork and spread over mousse to prevent discoloration. Refrigerate until set.

Serve cold garnished with cucumber slices.

SALADE DE CHAMPIGNON ET AVOCAT AU CREME FRAICHE ET VINAIGRE FRAMBOISE
(Mushroom and Avocado Salad with Crème Fraîche and Raspberry Vinegar Dressing)

ERNIE'S
SAN FRANCISCO, CALIFORNIA

4 servings

- ½ **pound very large mushrooms or 4 fresh shiitake mushrooms, very thinly sliced**
- ½ **avocado, peeled and very thinly sliced**

Dressing

- 2 **cups Crème Fraiche***
- ¼ **cup (scant) Raspberry Vinegar** or red wine vinegar
  Salt and freshly ground white pepper
  Watercress sprigs and tomato roses (garnish)

Arrange mushroom and avocado slices on individual salad plates.

Combine ingredients for dressing and pour around salad. Garnish with watercress and tomato roses.

*Creme Fraiche

Makes 2 cups

- ⅔ **cup sour cream**
- 1⅓ **cups whipping cream**

Combine ingredients and heat to 110°F. Let stand at room temperature until thickened, about 8 hours.

**Raspberry Vinegar

Makes 2 cups

- 12 **fresh or unsweetened frozen raspberries**
- 2 **cups red wine vinegar**

Combine ingredients and let stand at room temperature for at least 1 week before using.

TEXAS CAVIAR

THE BEEF BARRON
LAS VEGAS, NEVADA

Makes about 7½ cups

- 1 **pound black-eyed peas**
- 2 **cups Italian salad dressing**
- 2 **cups diced green pepper**
- 1½ **cups diced onion**
- 1 **cup finely chopped green onion**
- ½ **cup finely chopped jalapeño peppers**
- 1 **2-ounce jar diced pimiento, drained**
- 1 **tablespoon finely chopped garlic**
  Salt and hot pepper sauce to taste
  Lettuce leaves

Soak peas in enough water to cover for 6 hours or overnight. Drain well. Transfer peas to saucepan. Add enough water to cover. Place over high heat and bring to boil.

Let boil until tender, about 40 minutes; do not overcook. Drain peas well. Transfer to large bowl. Blend in dressing and let cool.

Add all remaining ingredients except lettuce and mix well. To serve, line individual plates with lettuce and spoon salad over.

RAISED GARLIC BALLS

JOHNNY LOUNDER'S RESTAURANT
PITTSBURGH, PENNSYLVANIA

Makes 66 to 68 balls

- ½ **cup plus 2 tablespoons milk**
- 2 **tablespoons (¼ stick) butter or margarine**
- ¼ **teaspoon salt**
- 1 **tablespoon (1 package) active dry yeast**
- 2 **to 2¼ cups all purpose flour**
- 1 **egg**
- 1 **to 1½ tablespoons garlic powder**
- 1 **tablespoon sugar**
  Oil for deep frying
  Garlic salt

Generously oil large bowl and set aside. Pour milk into small saucepan and heat until scalded. Transfer to mixing bowl and add butter and salt. Cool to lukewarm. Add yeast and let stand 5 minutes. Mix in 1 cup flour, beating with wooden spoon until smooth. Blend in egg, garlic powder and sugar. Beat in remaining flour and knead by hand on lightly floured surface until smooth and elastic, or mix in flour with heavy duty electric mixer fitted with dough hook, beating until dough pulls away from sides of bowl, about 3 to 5 minutes. Transfer to oiled bowl, cover with damp towel and let stand in warm place until doubled in volume, about 45 minutes.

Turn out on lightly floured working surface. Roll or pat to ½-inch thickness. Use small round cutter (about 1-inch diameter; center of doughnut cutter works well) to shape dough. Place on lightly floured baking sheet and let stand 15 minutes.

Meanwhile, heat oil to 350°F. Deep fry garlic balls several at a time until golden brown. Drain on paper towels. Sprinkle with garlic salt and serve at once.

THE CELEBRATED GRAND CENTRAL
OYSTER BAR & RESTAURANT

Of all the daily arrivals at Manhattan's teeming Grand
Central Station, the oyster is king. At the stand-up
"commuters' ramp" outside the Oyster Bar entrance,
you can choose from Blue Points and giant Box oysters,
creamy Malpeques and Maine Belons, salty Cotuits and
tiny Olympias, Chincoteagues, Kents, Apalachicolas and
the Long Islands. Order them by the piece or pick your
favorite for a stew or one of the famous seafood pan
roasts made before your eyes.

If there's time, eat in the restaurant proper. Here, since
the station opened in 1913, nearly every American president and numerous celebrities have feasted on chowders,
seafood stews, endless varieties of fish and shellfish and,
of course, oysters.

In 1975, under the aegis of restaurateur Jerome Brody,
the Grand Central Oyster Bar & Restaurant was pains-
takingly restored and refurbished. The spacious dining
rooms, luncheon counters and sit-down bar serve 2,000
diners a day.

Each morning before dawn, expert seafood buyer
George Morfogen inspects and purchases the day's offer-
ings at the massive Fulton Fish Market at the tip of Manhattan Island. By 7:30 A.M. he is back at the restaurant,
checking in the delivery of the fish and supervising their
handling and storage in the quarters below.

This cavernous space houses the huge "fish butchery,"
with its refrigerator trays holding freshly cut steaks and
fillets ready for cooking. Three massive cauldrons hold
simmering fish stock and Manhattan and New England
clam chowders. In the commercial size bakery, nearly
1,400 biscuits are baked at a time and all of the wondrous
desserts are prepared by a Swiss pastry chef.

MARINATED SCALLOPS AND
MUSSELS ON AVOCADO

OYSTER BAR & RESTAURANT
NEW YORK, NEW YORK

4 servings

  ½ **pint mussels, steamed, shelled
     and chilled**
  ½ **pound bay scallops, poached and chilled**
  1 **cup Mustard Vinaigrette***
  2 **ripe avocados, halved, pitted and peeled
     Finely chopped parsley (garnish)**

Toss mussels and scallops in Mustard Vinaigrette
until lightly coated with dressing. Marinate 4 hours
or overnight. Fill avocado halves with seafood mixture and garnish with parsley.

***Mustard Vinaigrette**

Makes 1 cup

  6 **tablespoons olive oil**
  6 **tablespoons peanut oil**
  2 **tablespoons white vinegar**
  2 **tablespoons dry white wine**
  1 **to 2 teaspoons Dijon mustard or to taste**
  1 **teaspoon salt**
  1 **teaspoon finely chopped parsley**
  ½ **teaspoon oregano**
  ½ **teaspoon Worcestershire sauce**
  1 **garlic clove, minced**
  1 **small onion, minced
     Dash Tabasco sauce
     Freshly ground white pepper**

Combine all ingredients in a bowl and whisk
together until dressing is opaque and creamy.

CEVICHE

LA CASITA
BERKELEY, CALIFORNIA

6 to 8 servings

- 1½ pounds fresh saltwater fish or shellfish (preferably sea bass, red snapper, clams or scallops), cut into 1-inch cubes
- 1 cup fresh lime juice
- 1 medium white onion, sliced into rings and blanched
- 1 large tomato, peeled and diced
- ¼ cup cilantro or parsley leaves
- ¼ cup olive oil
- 3 jalapeño chilies en escabeche, drained, seeded and chopped
   Salt
   Lettuce leaves
   Lime slices (garnish)

Place fish in glass or ceramic dish. Add lime juice and toss gently. Cover and refrigerate at least 4 hours, turning fish once. Add onion, tomato, cilantro, olive oil, chilies and salt and stir gently. Cover and refrigerate 4 hours. To serve, arrange on lettuce leaves and garnish with lime slices.

MUSHROOM MARINADE

FOREST RESTAURANT, HARRAH'S HOTEL/CASINO
LAKE TAHOE, CALIFORNIA

Marinates 1 pound mushrooms

- 2½ cups salad oil
- 1 cup white vinegar
- 1 bunch chives, chopped
- 1 bunch green onions, finely chopped
- 2½ tablespoons sugar
- 1½ tablespoons salt
- 1 tablespoon fresh lemon juice
- 1 tablespoon finely minced garlic
- 2 teaspoons Worcestershire sauce
- 2 teaspoons bottled browning sauce
- ⅛ teaspoon prepared mustard
- 1 pound fresh mushrooms, washed and patted dry

Whisk all ingredients except mushrooms in deep bowl until well combined. Add mushrooms. Cover and marinate in refrigerator at least 4 hours or, preferably, overnight.

This marinade also works well with sliced zucchini, cauliflower or broccoli.

SOPAIPILLAS

VILLA DE DON PERALTA
TAOS, NEW MEXICO

"Villa de Don Peralta is an unpretentious little place, and has the most delicious sopaipillas I have found in New Mexico."
—Mrs. A. J. Ostheimer, Honolulu, Hawaii

6 servings

- 2 cups flour
- ½ teaspoon salt
- 1 tablespoon baking powder
- 1 tablespoon lard (not vegetable shortening)
- ⅓ cup (approximate) warm water
- 3 cups oil for frying

Mix flour, salt, baking powder and lard. Add warm water a little at a time until mixture is slightly moistened. Knead dough until soft but not sticky. Cover and let stand. Heat oil to about 360°F.

When oil is hot, roll out dough on lightly floured surface to a thickness of about ⅛ inch. Cut into 3-inch triangles or squares and drop into hot oil. Fry, turning once, until golden brown.

GREAT MEXICAN NACHOS

THE GREAT MEXICAN FOOD AND
BEVERAGE COMPANY
TAMPA, FLORIDA

6 servings

   Oil
- 12 corn tortillas
- ½ pound cheddar cheese, grated
- ½ pound Monterey Jack cheese, grated
   Nacho Sauce*

Preheat oven to 400°F. Heat oil in deep fryer or large saucepan to 350°F. Meanwhile, cut tortillas into eighths. Add to oil in batches (do not crowd) and fry until crispy and lightly browned, about 1 to 2 minutes. Remove chips with slotted spoon and drain on paper towels.

Arrange chips on ovenproof platter(s) and sprinkle with cheeses. Spread Nacho Sauce thinly over top. Bake until cheese is melted.

Nacho Sauce

Makes about 2 cups

- 2 cups tomato puree
- 1 green onion, finely chopped
- 2 tablespoons finely chopped onion
- ½ teaspoon minced fresh garlic
- ½ teaspoon freshly ground pepper
- ½ teaspoon dried oregano

Puree all ingredients in processor or blender.

VEGETARIAN CHOPPED LIVER

HOMOWACK
SPRING GLEN, NEW YORK

Makes about 4 cups

    1 tablespoon butter
    ½ cup chopped onion
    4 hard-cooked eggs, coarsely chopped
    2 cups toasted walnut pieces
    ½ cup cooked lentils
    ½ cup tomato herring or sardines in
       tomato sauce
    ¼ cup plus 1 tablespoon mayonnaise
       Salt and freshly ground pepper
       Sugar

Melt butter in small skillet. Add onion and sauté until golden brown. Transfer to processor or blender and add eggs, nuts, lentils, herring and mayonnaise. Mix until smooth. Season with salt, pepper and sugar to taste.

BEIGNET AU FROMAGE

BASTILLE BRASSERIE PARISIENNE
CHICAGO, ILLINOIS

"The restaurant deserves an A+, especially for the Beignet au Fromage—a crispy golden-brown wedge oozing with melted cheese."
                              —Ann Barrett, Rockford, Illinois

6 servings

       Oil for deep frying
    1 egg
    ½ cup milk
       Salt and freshly ground pepper to taste
    6 2-inch wedges firm Brie, rind removed
    3 cups fresh French breadcrumbs
    3 apples, sliced

Pour oil in large skillet to depth of 2 inches and heat to 350°F. Combine egg, milk, salt and pepper. Dip each Brie wedge in egg mixture, then coat thoroughly with crumbs. Fry a few at a time until crisp and brown on both sides. Serve immediately with apple slices as an accompaniment.

GRUYERE CHEESE FRITTERS

OLD BRIDGE HOTEL
HUNTINGDON, CAMBRIDGESHIRE, ENGLAND

"While in England, we had a delightful dinner at the Old Bridge Hotel. There was a most unusual appetizer called Gruyère Cheese Fritters."
                              —Bea Farias, Sacramento, California

Makes about 40 fritters

    1 egg white
    1 pound Gruyère cheese, grated
    2 tablespoons chopped parsley
    ¼ teaspoon grated nutmeg
    ½ teaspoon paprika

    ¼ cup flour
    1 egg
    2 tablespoons milk
    ¾ cup breadcrumbs

       Oil for deep frying

Whisk egg white until foamy. With hands, mix in cheese, parsley, nutmeg and paprika until well blended. Chill 2 to 3 hours.

Mix together flour, egg and milk. Shape cheese mixture into 1-inch balls and dip in egg mixture, then in breadcrumbs. Refrigerate overnight.

Heat oil to 350°F. Fry balls approximately 3 to 5 minutes. Drain on paper towels; serve immediately.

FUNDIDO

THE RED ONION
CALIFORNIA

2 servings

    ½ teaspoon lard or bacon fat
    ⅓ cup well-drained canned tomatoes
    ½ small onion, coarsely chopped
    1 mild green chili, minced
    3 sprigs cilantro, minced
    1 garlic clove, minced
    ⅛ teaspoon sugar
    ⅛ teaspoon salt

    ¾ cup cheese sauce (homemade or
       commercial)
    2 ounces chorizo (Mexican sausage),*
       broken into pieces
    ¼ cup grated Monterey Jack cheese
       Tortilla chips

Heat lard in medium skillet over medium-high heat. Add next 5 ingredients and sauté until tender. Stir in sugar and salt.

Bring cheese sauce to simmering point in top of double boiler. Meanwhile cook chorizo in small skillet. Remove with slotted spoon, drain and add to cheese sauce. Stir in tomato mixture and Jack cheese and heat through. Serve hot with tortilla chips.

*Chorizo is available at Mexican markets or specialty food stores.

CHEESE STICKS

RISTORANTE TORINO
ATLANTA, GEORGIA

Makes 2 dozen appetizers

    Oil for deep frying
1 **pound mozzarella cheese, cut into
    ¼x¼x2½-inch sticks**
1 **cup flour**
    Salt and freshly ground pepper
6 **eggs, lightly beaten**
3 **cups breadcrumbs**
    Freshly grated Parmesan cheese
    Marinara sauce

Heat oil for deep frying to 375°F. Dredge cheese sticks in flour seasoned with salt and pepper to taste. Dip into beaten eggs, coating well. Cover with breadcrumbs, then roll in palm of hand so crumbs adhere. Dredge once again in crumbs and roll in palm of hand to make firm crust. Fry until deep golden brown. Be careful not to overcook or cheese will lose its shape. Drain on paper towels. Sprinkle with Parmesan cheese and accompany with marinara sauce for dipping.

CRAB RANGOON

TRADER VIC'S
SAN FRANCISCO, CALIFORNIA

Makes 2½ to 3 dozen

 ½ **pound fresh crabmeat, drained
    and chopped**
 ½ **pound cream cheese, room temperature**
 ½ **teaspoon A-1 sauce**
 ¼ **teaspoon garlic powder**
2½ **to 3 dozen won ton wrappers**
 1 **egg yolk, well beaten**

    Oil for deep frying
    Chinese mustard and/or red sauce

Combine crabmeat with cream cheese, steak sauce and garlic powder in medium bowl and blend to a paste. Place heaping teaspoon on each won ton. Gather four corners of won ton together at top. Moisten edges with egg yolk and pinch or twist together gently to seal.

Heat oil in wok, deep fryer or electric skillet to 375°F. Add won tons in batches and fry until golden brown, about 3 minutes. Remove with slotted spoon and drain on paper towels. Serve hot with Chinese mustard and/or red sauce for dipping.

CROSTINI

TINO'S
NEW YORK, NEW YORK

6 to 8 servings

 ¼ **cup (½ stick) unsalted butter**

 6 **anchovy fillets, mashed**
 3 **ounces (6 tablespoons) dry white wine**

 3 **tablespoons olive oil (or more)**
 6 **slices white bread, crusts trimmed
    Flour**
 6 **egg yolks, lightly beaten
    Fresh breadcrumbs**

Melt butter in small skillet over medium heat. Add anchovies and wine and stir until well blended. Set aside and keep warm.

Heat oil in large skillet over medium heat. Dip bread in flour, shaking off excess. Dip into yolks, then coat completely with crumbs. Cut slices in half. Add to skillet in batches and fry until both sides are golden brown, adding more oil if necessary, about 2 to 3 minutes per side. Serve immediately topped with warm anchovy sauce.

BLANC DE FOIE GRAS AUX HUITRES
(Custard of Foie Gras and Oysters)

HOTEL DE CRILLON
PARIS, FRANCE

6 servings

1½ **pounds chicken livers (preferably light
    colored), trimmed
    Milk**
1½ **tablespoons Cognac**

 1 **cup plus 1 tablespoon milk**
 2 **tablespoons port**
 5 **eggs**
    Salt and freshly ground white pepper

Sauce Champagne

 2 **tablespoons (¼ stick) unsalted butter**
 2 **large shallots, chopped**
 ⅓ **cup Champagne**
 2 **tablespoons white wine vinegar**
 1 **tablespoon oyster liquor**
 ½ **teaspoon minced fresh parsley**
 3 **tablespoons whipping cream**
 1 **cup (2 sticks) unsalted butter, cut
    into pieces
    Salt and freshly ground white pepper**

24 **oysters, drained (reserve liquor for
    sauce) and poached in court bouillon**
 2 **large leeks (with small portion of
    green), well washed, cut julienne and
    steamed (garnish)**

Combine chicken livers in medium bowl with enough milk to cover. Gently stir in Cognac. Cover and refrigerate overnight.

Preheat oven to 350°F. Generously butter 6 ¾-cup soufflé dishes. Bring 1 cup plus 1 tablespoon milk to boil in small saucepan over medium-high heat and reduce to ¾ cup; let cool. Meanwhile, warm port briefly in small cup over low heat. Remove from heat and ignite, shaking cup gently until flame subsides. Drain chicken livers well and pat dry. Transfer to processor. Add boiled milk and port. With machine running, add eggs through feed tube one at a time, mixing until smooth. Season with salt and pepper to taste. Strain mixture into bowl. Divide evenly among prepared molds.

Transfer molds to shallow baking pan. Add enough boiling water to pan to come halfway up sides of molds. Bake until knife inserted in centers of molds comes out clean, about 40 minutes. (Let custard cool 3 to 4 minutes before unmolding.)

For sauce: Melt 2 tablespoons butter in small saucepan over medium-low heat. Add shallots and sauté until tender; do not brown. Stir in Champagne, vinegar, oyster liquor and parsley. Increase heat and cook until mixture is reduced to 1½ tablespoons. Blend in cream and cook 1 minute. Remove from heat and whisk in 1 cup butter one piece at a time, making sure each piece is incorporated before adding next. Season with salt and pepper to taste.

To serve, spoon some of sauce onto individual plates. Invert molds over sauce and top with additional sauce. Arrange warm oysters around molds. Garnish with leek julienne and serve immediately.

CRAB PUFFS

THE SEASONINGS CAFE
CLINTON, NEW JERSEY

8 servings

    4 egg whites, room temperature
    ¾ teaspoon cream of tartar
    1¼ cups mayonnaise
    8 ounces crabmeat, flaked
    1 tablespoon freeze-dried chives
      Freshly ground pepper
      Ground red pepper

    16 slices bread, well toasted (crusts trimmed) and halved diagonally
      Paprika (garnish)

Beat egg whites in large bowl until foamy. Add cream of tartar and continue beating until very stiff. Combine mayonnaise, crabmeat, chives and peppers in another bowl. Fold into whites, blending well.

Preheat broiler. Arrange toast triangles on large baking sheet. Top each piece with 1 heaping tablespoon crab mixture. Sprinkle with paprika. Broil 4 to 5 inches from heat source until puffed and golden brown, 3 to 5 minutes. Serve immediately.

CRAB LORENZO

ARTHUR'S
DALLAS, TEXAS

6 to 8 servings

    4 large mushrooms, finely chopped
    3 shallots, finely chopped
    1 garlic clove, finely chopped
    ¼ cup (½ stick) butter
    ½ cup flour
    3 cups half and half

    2 tablespoons chopped fresh chives
    1 large bay leaf
    1 tablespoon Worcestershire sauce
    ¼ cup white wine
      Salt and pepper
    ¾ pound crabmeat

    6 to 8 slices French bread, toasted
    1½ cups hollandaise sauce
      Chopped parsley (garnish)
      Lemon slices (garnish)

Sauté mushrooms, shallots and garlic in butter until transparent. Remove from heat and mix in flour. Over low heat, slowly stir in half and half. Cook until smooth, about 3 to 4 minutes.

Add chives, bay leaf, Worcestershire sauce, wine, salt and pepper to taste, and bring to boil. Simmer 30 minutes. Remove bay leaf. Add crabmeat and cook 3 to 4 minutes.

Arrange toast slices on heatproof platter. Spoon hot crabmeat mixture over toast. Cover with hollandaise sauce. Broil until lightly browned, about 1 to 2 minutes. Garnish with parsley and lemon.

CLAMS GOURMET

THE DOLPHIN INN
TAYLORS POINT, BUZZARDS BAY, MASSACHUSETTS

8 servings

    1 pound Monterey Jack cheese, shredded
    3 6½-ounce cans chopped clams, drained
    2 tablespoons finely chopped parsley
    2 tablespoons chopped chives
    2 garlic cloves, finely minced
      Dash ground red pepper
      Dash freshly ground black pepper
    8 slices pumpernickel

Combine cheese, clams, parsley, chives, garlic and peppers and mix until well blended. For each serving, place bread slice in 4-ounce soufflé dish or au gratin pan. Divide clam mixture among dishes. Broil until golden brown and bubbly. Serve immediately.

BAKED OYSTERS

NIMBLE'S
LAHAINA, MAUI, HAWAII

6 to 8 servings

24 **fresh large oysters, shucked and drained**
   Oyster Sauce*
2 **pounds fresh spinach, blanched,**
   squeezed to remove as much moisture as
   possible and chopped
12 **strips bacon, cooked until crisp, drained**
   and crumbled
   Freshly grated Parmesan cheese
   Paprika

Preheat oven to 375°F. Grease 2-quart shallow baking dish (or use 6 to 8 individual ovenproof dishes). Place oysters in single layer and top with Oyster Sauce, then spinach and crumbled bacon. Sprinkle liberally with Parmesan, covering spinach completely. Dust lightly with paprika. Bake uncovered until cheese begins to brown and bubble, about 12 to 15 minutes.

*Oyster Sauce

Makes about 2½ cups

2 **cups mayonnaise**
¼ **cup chili sauce**
2 **tablespoons Dijon mustard**
½ **teaspoon paprika**
3 **to 4 dashes hot pepper sauce**
   Fresh lemon juice to taste
   Salt and freshly ground pepper to taste

Combine all ingredients.

CANAPE ROBAIRE

ROBAIRE'S
LOS ANGELES, CALIFORNIA

Robert Robaire recommends a Riesling to accompany the canapé.

2 servings

   Bouquet garni
5 **to 6 jumbo shrimp**

1 **tablespoon shredded pimiento**
3 **tablespoons hollandaise sauce**
1 **cup grated Swiss cheese**
1 **large slice sourdough bread, 1 inch**
   thick

Place bouquet garni in a pot of cold water and bring to a boil. Drop in shrimp and boil until shrimp turn pink, about 4 minutes. Shell, devein and cut into thick pieces.

Preheat oven to 375°F. In bowl, mix shrimp, pimiento, 2 tablespoons hollandaise sauce and cheese. Spread mixture evenly over bread. Top with remaining hollandaise. Bake 15 minutes. If not brown, may be briefly broiled. Serve piping hot.

SHRIMP RUFEL

EMBASSY CLUB
DES MOINES, IOWA

"The shrimp with mushrooms, garlic and herbs would make an interesting main dish."
                              —*Didi Filmore, Des Moines, Iowa*

6 servings

6 **tablespoons (¾ stick) butter**
3 **garlic cloves, minced**
18 **large shrimp, shelled, cleaned and**
   halved lengthwise
2 **cups sliced mushrooms**
1½ **cups whipping cream**
6 **tablespoons sweet sherry or port**
1 **tablespoon dried basil**
1 **tablespoon dried tarragon**
2 **tablespoons brandy**
   Toast points

Melt butter in saucepan over medium heat. Add garlic and sauté briefly, about 2 to 3 minutes; do not brown. Add shrimp and sauté just until they begin to color. Remove shrimp. Add mushrooms, increase heat and sauté briefly. Remove with slotted spoon. Add cream, sherry and herbs and simmer until sauce is reduced and slightly thickened. Return shrimp and mushrooms to pan and heat through. Warm brandy in small saucepan, pour over sauce and flame. Spoon over toast points and serve immediately.

SHRIMP TOAST

DRAGON INN
OVERLAND PARK, KANSAS

Makes 48 appetizers

   Oil
1 **pound uncooked shrimp, shelled and**
   deveined
¼ **cup whole water chestnuts**
2 **green onions (white part only)**
1½ **teaspoons dry white wine**
1 **teaspoon vegetable oil**
½ **teaspoon salt**
½ **teaspoon freshly ground pepper**

12 **slices sandwich bread, crusts trimmed**

Pour oil into deep fryer or skillet to depth of 2 inches and heat to 350°F. Mix shrimp, water chestnuts and onion in processor or grinder until very fine. Add wine, vegetable oil, salt and pepper and mix well.

Spread mixture evenly over bread slices. Fry bread in batches until golden brown, about 5 minutes; drain on paper towels. Cut each slice into 4 strips. Serve immediately.

ESCARGOTS

THE SUN DIAL
ATLANTA, GEORGIA

"The most magnificent escargots my husband and I have tasted." —Donna Combs, Atlanta, Georgia

6 servings

  1 **cup (2 sticks) butter, softened**
  2 **tablespoons chopped shallots**
  2 **tablespoons chopped garlic**
  2 **tablespoons champagne or white wine**
  1 **tablespoon Worcestershire sauce**
  1 **tablespoon chopped fresh parsley**
  1 **teaspoon brandy**
  1 **teaspoon lemon juice**
  ½ **teaspoon salt**
    Pinch pepper
 36 **snails and shells**

Mix, but do not whip, all ingredients except snails. Heat mixture in large skillet. Add snails and simmer 10 to 15 minutes, allowing liquid to cook into snails.

Preheat oven to 350°F. Put small amount of butter mixture into bottom of each shell. Insert snail using end of fork. Top with additional butter mixture. Continue until all shells are filled, placing them in flat baking dish as they are completed. Pour remaining butter mixture over snails and heat until bubbling, about 10 minutes.

ESCARGOT EN CROUTE

HARRISON'S
INDIANAPOLIS, INDIANA

4 to 6 servings

Butter Mixture

  1 **cup (2 sticks) butter**
  ½ **bunch fresh parsley, finely chopped**
  7 **to 9 garlic cloves, minced**
  1 **shallot, minced**
  2 **tablespoons dry white wine**
 1½ **teaspoons Worcestershire sauce**
  1 **teaspoon fresh lemon juice**
  1 **teaspoon Pernod**
  2 **anchovy fillets, minced**
  ¼ **teaspoon hot pepper sauce**
    Salt and freshly ground pepper

  2 **tablespoons (¼ stick) butter**
 24 **to 36 snails, washed**
  ¼ **cup diced onion**
  6 **tablespoons dry white wine**

  4 **to 6 sheets puff pastry dough, cut slightly larger than escargot dish**
  1 **egg**
  2 **tablespoons water**

For butter mixture: Whip butter in mixing bowl. Add next 9 ingredients with salt and pepper to taste and mix well. Set aside.

Melt 2 tablespoons butter in medium skillet. Add snails, onion and wine and sauté until liquid evaporates. Set aside and let cool.

Place one snail in each hole of escargot dish. Generously cover with butter mixture. Place 1 sheet of puff pastry dough over each escargot dish. Trim dough and seal around edge of dish. Beat egg with water and use to brush dough. Chill until ready to bake, at least 20 minutes.

Preheat oven to 375°F. Bake until pastry rises and is golden, about 20 to 30 minutes.

Remaining butter mixture can be refrigerated as long as 2 weeks and used when garlic butter is needed.

BROILED DUCK BREASTS

RESTAURANT ANDRE DAGUIN, HOTEL DE FRANCE
AUCH, FRANCE

These thin slices of duck meat are the perfect accompaniment to cocktails.

8 servings

  2 **whole meaty duck breasts, halved, skinned and trimmed of excess fat, wings removed**

Dry Marinade

  2 **medium shallots, minced**
  2 **bay leaves, crushed**
  5 **garlic cloves, unpeeled and halved**
  4 **teaspoons coarse salt**
  1 **tablespoon minced fresh parsley**
  1 **teaspoon freshly cracked white peppercorns**
  ¼ **teaspoon dried thyme leaves**

    Freshly ground pepper

Bone breasts in whole pieces.

For marinade: Combine remaining ingredients except pepper in shallow tray and blend well. Roll breasts in marinade and place on wide shallow platter. Cover with plastic wrap and refrigerate 2 days, turning breasts once each day to season evenly.

Preheat broiler. Place rack 4 inches from heat source. Wipe breasts to remove excess seasoning and any moisture that may have collected. Discard marinade. Place breasts skinned side down on broiling rack and broil 2 minutes. Turn and broil 2 minutes more for rare or 3 minutes for medium.

Transfer to carving board and thinly slice meat diagonally. Sprinkle with pepper. Roll each slice and fasten with toothpick. Serve immediately.

ARTICHOKES ALLA ROMANA

TAVOLA CALDA DA ALFREDO
NEW YORK, NEW YORK

"The most superbly prepared artichokes I've ever tasted."
—Debbie Wilpon, New York, New York

6 servings

> 6 **medium artichokes**
> 1 **lemon, halved crosswise**
>
> 2 **cups consommé**
> 1½ **cups olive oil**
> 1 **cup chopped fresh parsley**
> 1 **tablespoon chopped fresh garlic**
>   **Salt and freshly ground pepper**

Slice tops from artichokes. Remove tough outer leaves and cut off stems to make flat base. Trim off thorny tips using scissors. Rub cut edges with lemon halves. Drop artichokes and lemon into large pot filled with enough boiling salted water to cover. Cover partially and parboil 10 minutes. Remove artichokes with slotted spoon and turn upside down to drain. When cool, gently spread artichoke leaves; remove fibrous chokes from center with spoon.

Preheat oven to 400°F. Combine consommé, oil, parsley, garlic and salt and pepper to taste in bowl. Place artichokes upright in baking dish and pour consommé mixture evenly over top. Bake artichokes until outer leaves begin to turn copper color, about 25 to 35 minutes. Baste artichokes and broil until tops brown, about 3 minutes. Serve in soup plates with remaining liquid.

RAMEKIN FORESTIERE

THE COUNTRY FRENCHMAN
GREELEY, COLORADO

12 servings

Ramekin

> ½ **cup (1 stick) butter**
> 4 **cups finely minced mushrooms**
> ½ **cup finely minced shallots**
>
> 1 **tablespoon fresh basil or 1½**
>   **teaspoons dried**
> 1 **tablespoon fresh tarragon or 1½**
>   **teaspoons dried**
> 2 **large eggs, lightly beaten**
> 1½ **cups chopped ham**
> ½ **cup breadcrumbs**
>   **Salt and pepper to taste**

Sauce

> 2 **cups milk**
> ½ **cup chicken stock**
> ½ **cup whipping cream**
> ¼ **cup (½ stick) butter, melted**
> ¼ **cup flour**

> 1 **tablespoon chopped fresh tarragon or**
> 1½ **teaspoons dried**
>   **Salt and pepper to taste**

Preheat oven to 350°F. Melt butter in 10- to 12-inch skillet. Sauté mushrooms until all liquid is absorbed. Add shallots and sauté 2 to 3 minutes.

Combine herbs, eggs, ham and breadcrumbs. Add mushroom mixture and season with salt and pepper. Place in 12 buttered ⅓-cup ramekins. Place in 2 7x11-inch baking dishes half filled with water. Bake in preheated oven 45 minutes.

For sauce: Combine milk, chicken stock and cream in 1½-quart saucepan. Bring to boil, stirring constantly. Combine butter and flour to form a roux. Add some of liquid to roux, then gradually add to remaining liquid. Cook over medium heat, stirring constantly, until thick and smooth. Add tarragon and season with salt and pepper. Serve sauce over hot ramekins.

CHINGALINGAS

CANTINA LOS TRES HOMBRES
KINGS BEACH, CALIFORNIA

"This dish became so popular, it is now a featured entree in the dining room."
—Peter Stocker, Kings Beach, California

Makes about 60 appetizers

> 1 **3- to 4-pound chicken**
> 1 **teaspoon salt**
> 1 **garlic clove**
> 1 **bay leaf**
>
> 1 **tablespoon lard or vegetable shortening**
> 1 **small onion, minced**
> 1 **green bell pepper, seeded and diced**
> 1 **garlic clove, minced**
> 2 **tomatoes, diced**
> 1 **teaspoon concentrated chicken soup**
>   **base or chicken bouillon granules**
>
> 12 **6- to 8-inch flour tortillas**
>
>   **Oil for deep frying**
>   **Guacamole and sour cream (garnish)**

Combine chicken, salt, garlic and bay leaf in large saucepan or Dutch oven with enough cold water to cover and bring to boil over high heat, skimming foam from surface. Reduce heat and simmer until chicken is tender, about 1 hour.

Remove chicken from broth and let stand until cool enough to handle. (Save broth for another use.) Shred chicken with fork or fingers, reserving pieces of skin, and set aside.

Melt lard in large skillet over medium heat. Add onion and bell pepper and sauté until softened, about 5 minutes. Add minced garlic and sauté briefly. Stir in shredded chicken, tomatoes and soup base. Reduce heat and simmer until almost all liquid is evaporated, about 15 to 20 minutes.

Meanwhile, finely chop chicken skin in processor or with sharp knife. Sauté in medium skillet over medium-high heat until browned and crisp, about 10 to 15 minutes. Discard fat; add skin to chicken mixture, blending well. Continue cooking, stirring occasionally, for about 5 minutes.

Steam tortillas until soft. Place about ¼ cup chicken mixture at bottom edge of 1 tortilla and roll up, tucking in ends. Secure flap with wooden pick. Repeat with remaining tortillas.

Heat oil to 375°F. Add chingalingas in batches and fry, turning once, until golden brown, about 3 to 4 minutes per side. Drain on paper towels. Discard picks. Slice each roll into 5 pieces. Serve warm with guacamole and sour cream.

EGG ROLLS

THE PHOENIX
ST. PAUL, MINNESOTA

"A unique egg roll . . . one of the best I've ever tasted."
—Nathalie Cunningham, St. Paul, Minnesota

Makes 24 rolls

- **14 ounces pork, finely ground**
- **1½ cups finely chopped carrot**
- **½ cup finely chopped onion**
- **½ cup finely ground chicken**
- **3½ ounces cellophane noodles,* soaked in warm water, then cut into 2-inch lengths**
- **3 eggs, lightly beaten**
- **½ cup fish sauce* or soy sauce**
- **1 teaspoon garlic powder**
- **1 teaspoon freshly ground pepper**

- **24 egg roll skins***
- **1 quart (4 cups) water**
- **1 teaspoon brown sugar**

   Oil for deep frying

Combine pork, carrot, onion, chicken, noodles, eggs, fish sauce, garlic powder and pepper in medium bowl and mix well.

Separate egg roll skins and lay out on work surface. Combine water and brown sugar and use to lightly moisten wrappers. Divide filling among wrappers, placing in center. Fold in sides. Roll up, pressing edges to seal.

Heat oil in deep fryer to 350°F. Fry rolls a few at a time until golden brown.

*Available in oriental markets.

Egg rolls can be fried ahead and reheated until crisp in 200°F oven with door ajar, about 10 minutes.

SAUERKRAUT BALLS

CARMASSI'S
PITTSBURGH, PENNSYLVANIA

Makes about 30 to 40 balls

- **½ pound cooked turkey**
- **½ pound cooked ham**
- **½ pound cooked beef**
- **3 eggs**
- **1 cup sauerkraut, squeezed dry and finely chopped**
- **½ cup cheese sauce or pasteurized process cheese spread**
- **1 small onion, minced**
   Salt and freshly ground pepper
- **½ to 1 cup dry breadcrumbs or cracker meal**

   Oil for deep frying

Using meat grinder, coarsely grind turkey, ham and beef together and place in mixing bowl. Add eggs, sauerkraut, cheese sauce, onion, salt and pepper to taste and combine thoroughly. Roll into 1- to 1½-inch balls, then in breadcrumbs or cracker meal.

Heat oil to about 400°F and deep fry balls, a few at a time, until golden brown, about 20 to 40 seconds.

CAPTAIN JON'S HOT VEAL PATE

CAPTAIN JON'S
TAHOE VISTA, CALIFORNIA

6 to 8 servings

- **8 bacon strips**
- **¼ pound ground lean veal**
- **¼ pound ground lean pork**
- **¼ pound ground pork back fat**
- **2 ounces ground chicken livers**
- **2 garlic cloves, crushed**
- **2 tablespoons tawny port**
- **1 tablespoon brandy**
- **12 green peppercorns**
- **1 teaspoon onion puree**
- **½ teaspoon dried thyme**
   Pinch allspice
   Pinch ground cloves
   Salt and freshly ground pepper

Preheat oven to 325°F. Line bottom of 1-pound (about 7x3 inches) loaf pan with 4 strips of bacon. Combine remaining ingredients except bacon and mix well. Turn into loaf pan and cover with remaining bacon. Set in large shallow baking dish and add boiling water to come halfway up sides of pan.

Bake until meat thermometer inserted in center registers 160°F, about 1½ to 2 hours. Drain off excess fat, then cool slightly. Cover and chill 24 hours. To serve, discard bacon and cut loaf into slices ½ inch thick. Warm in 350°F oven until just heated through, about 5 to 10 minutes.

FRENCH-FRIED EGGPLANT

THE BLACK ANGUS COUNTRY INN
GLENMOORE, PENNSYLVANIA

6 to 8 servings

    1 large eggplant, peeled
      Flour

    2 eggs
    1 cup milk
    ¾ cup breadcrumbs
    ¼ cup freshly grated Parmesan cheese
    1 teaspoon onion salt
    1 teaspoon salt
    1 teaspoon white pepper

      Oil for deep frying
      Salt

Cut eggplant into ½-inch rounds, then into 2x½-inch strips. Dust lightly with flour, shake off excess and set aside.

Combine eggs and milk in medium bowl and blend until smooth. In another bowl, mix breadcrumbs, Parmesan, onion salt, salt and pepper. Dip eggplant strips into egg mixture, then coat completely with seasoned breadcrumbs. Shake off excess and place in single layer on baking sheet. Chill thoroughly (at least 2 hours or overnight).

Heat oil to 375°F. Fry eggplant strips a few at a time until golden, about 3 minutes. Drain on paper towels, sprinkle with salt and serve immediately.

BATTER-FRIED MUSHROOMS

HOLLYMEAD INN
CHARLOTTESVILLE, VIRGINIA

"A superb way to start a meal."
      —*Mrs. Paul Eldridge, Chevy Chase, Maryland*

6 to 8 servings

    2 cups all purpose flour
    1 tablespoon salt
    1½ teaspoons garlic powder
    1 teaspoon baking powder

    1½ cups beer

      Oil for deep frying
    36 to 48 medium to large whole mushrooms

Combine flour, salt, garlic powder and baking powder in medium bowl. Add beer and whisk until smooth. Cover and chill 30 minutes. Whisk again, then let stand in refrigerator until ready to use. (Batter can be prepared 1 day ahead if desired.)

Heat oil to 375°F. Holding stem, dip each mushroom into batter, covering cap completely. Fry in batches until golden brown. (Allow oil to return to 375°F before adding next batch.) Drain mushrooms thoroughly on paper towels.

BLACKROCK CASTLE MUSHROOM BOUCHEE

BLACKROCK CASTLE
CORK, IRELAND

6 to 8 servings

Pastry Cups

      Puff pastry dough made with 4 cups flour
    1 egg, beaten
    1 tablespoon water

Mushroom Filling

    ½ cup (1 stick) butter or margarine
    1½ pounds fresh mushrooms, sliced
    ½ cup finely diced onion
    ¼ cup finely diced green pepper
    ¼ cup finely diced red pepper
    ¾ cup flour
    2 cups hot chicken stock
    ¼ cup dry white wine
    1 egg yolk
    ½ cup whipping cream
      Salt and pepper
      Parsley sprigs (garnish)

For Pastry Cups: Roll out puff pastry dough ¼ inch thick. With a 3-inch pastry cutter, cut out 32 circles. With a 2-inch cutter, cut holes in centers of half the disks to form rings. Combine egg with water. Brush rings and disks with egg mixture. Place rings on top of disks. Seal cups by pressing down gently on them. Prick center of each cup with fork. Place on cookie sheets about 1 inch apart. Refrigerate for ½ hour until firm to touch.

Preheat oven to 425°F. Bake cups until puffed and golden, about 20 to 25 minutes.

For Mushroom Filling: Melt butter in large skillet. Add mushrooms, onion, green and red peppers and cook until tender but not brown. Mix in flour. Gradually add hot chicken stock and cook until thickened. Stir in wine. Simmer 20 minutes. Blend in egg yolk and cream. Season with salt and pepper to taste. Pour hot mixture into pastry cups. Garnish with parsley sprigs.

CHAMPIGNONS FARCIS AUX CRABES

LES QUATRE AMIS
NORTHFIELD, MINNESOTA

6 servings

    24 large white mushrooms
    4 tablespoons freshly grated Parmesan cheese
    8 ounces cream cheese

4 ounces Alaskan king crabmeat, drained,
   rinsed and refreshed by tossing with
1 tablespoon fresh lemon juice
2½ tablespoons olive oil
2 tablespoons chopped fresh parsley
1½ tablespoons breadcrumbs
   Juice of ½ lemon
1½ teaspoons minced shallot
1½ teaspoons Cognac
1 teaspoon Dijon mustard
1 teaspoon salt
½ teaspoon freshly ground pepper

**Garlic butter, minced fresh parsley and
lemon wedges (garnish)**

Preheat oven to 425°F. Lightly butter large baking
sheet. Remove mushroom stems.

Combine 2 tablespoons Parmesan and next 11
ingredients in medium bowl and beat with electric
mixer about 5 minutes. Fill mushrooms, forming
½-inch dome on top of each. Arrange on baking
sheet and bake 10 minutes. Remove from oven and
sprinkle with remaining 2 tablespoons Parmesan.

Preheat broiler. Run mushrooms under broiler until
Parmesan melts and is golden brown. Remove from
oven and garnish with garlic butter, parsley and
lemon wedges.

HAYSTACK BAKED STUFFED MUSHROOMS

NEEDLE IN A HAYSTACK
MONTGOMERY CENTER, VERMONT

*"The one-woman kitchen presented such a creative
selection of food, we returned to dine a second time.
Especially outstanding was a stuffed mushroom appetizer
containing sliced almonds."*
—Lauren and Glen Howard, Washington, D.C.

6 servings

18 medium mushrooms
½ small onion
2 garlic cloves, crushed
3 tablespoons oil
3 tablespoons (⅜ stick) butter
¼ cup toasted sliced almonds
1½ teaspoons dried parsley flakes
1½ teaspoons Worcestershire sauce
½ teaspoon dried basil
½ teaspoon paprika
4 to 6 tablespoons dry sherry
4 to 6 tablespoons breadcrumbs

**Freshly grated Parmesan cheese
Butter
Freshly ground pepper**

Remove stems from mushrooms and set caps aside.
Combine stems, onion and garlic in processor and
chop finely. Heat half of oil and butter in small
saucepan. Add mushroom stem mixture and sauté
over medium-high heat 4 to 5 minutes, adding more
oil and butter if needed. Add almonds, parsley,
Worcestershire sauce, basil, paprika and sherry and
bring to simmer. Remove from heat, add breadcrumbs and toss lightly.

Preheat oven to 400°F. Heat remaining oil and butter
in saucepan and sauté mushroom caps over high heat
1 to 2 minutes.

Place caps rounded side down in individual au gratin
dishes. Divide crumb mixture among caps. Dust
with Parmesan, dot with butter and sprinkle with
pepper. Bake until heated through, about 15 to
20 minutes.

SPINACH ROLLS A LA SULLY

SULLY'S
KANKAKEE, ILLINOIS

Makes 18 rolls

3 10-ounce packages frozen spinach,
   cooked and very well drained
1 pound mozzarella cheese, grated
1 cup freshly grated Parmesan cheese
¼ cup (½ stick) cold butter, cut into bits
2 tablespoons cinnamon

6 sheets phyllo dough
½ cup (1 stick) butter, melted

Preheat oven to 400°F. Lightly grease 2 baking
sheets. Combine spinach, cheeses, ¼ cup butter and
cinnamon in large bowl.

Place damp towel on flat surface. Cover with waxed
paper. Stack 6 sheets of dough on top of waxed
paper. Fold entire assembly in half like a book. Start
opening book, page by page, brushing each with
melted butter. Continue to center of book. Do not
brush center section. Close book with buttered
leaves on bottom and repeat process, working from
back toward center section again. The book should
now be open to center fold. Discard waxed paper
and brush phyllo with butter.

Preheat oven to 400°F. Divide filling into 3 equal
parts. With phyllo book open and facing you, place
1 portion of filling on dough 1 inch from the edge
nearest you. Spread filling in strip 2 inches wide
across width of dough, leaving border of phyllo 1
inch wide, to within 1 inch of sides. Using only 2
sheets of phyllo, roll up, first folding in side edges,
then front edge. Use towel and waxed paper to
facilitate rolling.

Make 2 more rolls in same fashion, using remaining
filling and 2 sheets of phyllo for each. Cut each roll
into 6 equal pieces about 2 inches long. Place on
baking sheets. Brush with melted butter. Bake until
golden brown, about 20 to 25 minutes, brushing
with additional butter every 10 minutes. Serve hot.

BEVERAGES

According to the late H. L. Mencken, there are only two types of beverage: the kind with alcohol, and the kind where somebody forgot to put it in. Mencken obviously preferred the alcoholic variety, and that is what most restaurants tend to specialize in. Bartenders engage in heated if informal competition to see who can come up with the most original mixed drink recipe. Some of these have become famous, and will forever be associated with the restaurant where they originated. There is the Singapore Sling, from the Raffles Hotel in Singapore; Fish House Punch, which was invented at the Fish House Club in Schuylkill, Pennsylvania, way back in 1732; the powerful Zombie, so called at Don the Beach-comber because of its effect on the imbiber; and many others with intriguingly whimsical names and an endless variety of ingredients, as you will see on the following pages.

Some mixed drinks—both the alcoholic and nonalcoholic kinds —are served during or after the meal, but their most popular form is the preprandial cocktail. There are many stories about how the "cocktail" got its name, but the best was told by James Fenimore Cooper of *Leatherstocking* fame. It seems that Colonial and French officers of George Washington's army used to gather in Betsy's Tavern near Yorktown. A hated Royalist farmer nearby had a fine collection of plump chickens, and the officers used to tease the inn's proprietress, Betsy Flanagan, who refused to buy from the enemy. One night Betsy made her guests eat their words. She greeted each gallant with the usual libation, and topped each mug with a rooster's tail from the Tory farmer's coop! A French officer raised a toast of "*Vive le cocktail*," and the name has stuck.

So—assuming the story is true—the next time you order a restaurant's special mixed drink, you can congratulate yourself for being both adventurous *and* downright patriotic.

Left to right, Mai Tai (see page 25), Bahia (page 23) and
Scorpion (page 22) from Trader Vic's in San Francisco.

POOR RICHARD'S BLOODY MARY

POOR RICHARD'S BUTTERY RESTAURANT
PROVINCETOWN, MASSACHUSETTS

"The highlight of Poor Richard's Sunday brunch."
    —Helaine M. Levy, Dix Hills, New York

8 to 10 servings

    1 46-ounce can tomato juice
    ½ cup beef bouillon
    3 ounces (6 tablespoons) fresh lime juice
    ¼ cup Worcestershire sauce
    2 teaspoons coarse salt
    1 teaspoon coarsely ground pepper
    1 teaspoon celery salt
    1 teaspoon dill
    ½ to 1 teaspoon hot pepper sauce
    1 teaspoon creamy horseradish

       Ice cubes
    1 quart vodka
       Cucumber slices, celery stalks and
       lime wedges (garnish)

Combine first 10 ingredients in large shaker or jar with tight-fitting lid and shake well.

Fill 12-ounce glasses with ice cubes. Add 3 ounces vodka to each and spiced tomato juice to fill. Garnish as desired.

SANGAREE

CHOWNING'S TAVERN
WILLIAMSBURG, VIRGINIA

"A sangria-type drink but made with Madeira."
    —Stephen K. Craven, McLean, Virginia

For each serving:

    1 cup crushed ice
    4 ounces Madeira
    3 ounces orange juice
    1 ounce fresh lemon juice
       Orange slice (garnish)

Put ice in large highball glass. Pour in Madeira, orange juice and lemon juice. Stir well and garnish with orange slice.

RAZ-MA-TAZZ

POLARIS LOUNGE
ATLANTA, GEORGIA

4 servings

    2½ cups softened French vanilla ice cream
    2½ ounces raspberry liqueur
    1½ ounces brandy
        Fresh raspberries (garnish)

Blend ice cream, liqueur and brandy until creamy. Garnish with fresh raspberries.

SALTY PELICAN

SALTY PELICAN BAY GARDEN
MORRO BAY, CALIFORNIA

"Its taste is similar to that of a margarita, but without tequila."
    —Myrtle Disney, Hacienda Heights, California

6 servings

        Kosher (coarse) salt
    ¼ lemon or lime

    1 cup crushed ice
    12 ounces sake
    8 ounces muscatel
    6 ounces margarita mix
       Lemon or lime slices (garnish)

Pour salt into saucer. Rub rims of 6 stemmed wine glasses with lemon or lime and roll outside rims of glasses in salt.

Combine ice, sake, muscatel and margarita mix in 5-cup blender. Mix for 20 seconds at high speed. Pour into salt-rimmed glasses and garnish with lemon or lime slices.

YELLOWBIRD

BAHAMAS PRINCESS HOTEL
FREEPORT, BAHAMAS

6 to 8 servings

    16 ounces (2 cups) orange juice
    16 ounces (2 cups) pineapple juice
    12 ounces (1½ cups) light rum
    8 ounces (1 cup) Galliano
    2 ounces (¼ cup) crème de banane
       Ice
       Pineapple cubes, orange slices and
       maraschino cherries (garnish)

Combine liquids in shaker and mix well. Pour into tall ice-filled glasses; garnish with fruit.

SCORPION

TRADER VIC'S
SAN FRANCISCO, CALIFORNIA

For each serving:

    1 scoop shaved ice
    2 ounces (¼ cup) orange juice
    2 ounces (¼ cup) light Puerto Rican rum
    1½ ounces (3 tablespoons) lemon juice
    1 ounce (2 tablespoons) brandy
    ½ ounce (1 tablespoon) orgeat syrup
       Ice cubes
       Gardenia (optional garnish)

Combine first 6 ingredients in blender or electric drink mixer and whirl on high until well mixed. Pour over ice cubes and garnish with gardenia, if desired.

TRADER VIC'S—A SAN FRANCISCO TRADITION

Off the beaten paths of downtown San Francisco, behind an unadorned façade, is a restaurant that has become a gathering place for the city's most sophisticated citizens and visitors. Inside, the four dining rooms of Trader Vic's create a pleasant ambience. The decor for the Tiki Room and Garden Room is tropical, with thatched roofs and wicker furniture. Primitive artifacts adorn the Safari Room, whereas the much sought-after Captain's Cabin features hand-hewn wood fixtures and knotted ropes.

The owner-founder of this and 19 other far-flung restaurants with the same name is Victor J. Bergeron, known to everyone as Trader. As an ailing youngster, he spent long hours in the kitchen with his French mother. "I liked cooking even then," he recalls. "I'd enjoy experimenting with recipes."

In 1934 Trader borrowed $500 and opened a restaurant in Oakland. He introduced Polynesian specialties after a meeting with Don the Beachcomber and then opened the San Francisco restaurant in 1951. In the early days he did his own marketing, believing that "eighty percent of preparing a superb meal is selecting fresh ingredients and not ruining them. The other twenty percent involves knowing what tastes good and taking the time and trouble in preparation."

Nearly all dishes are prepared to order, but the atmosphere in the kitchen is unhurried. Two huge red Chinese smoke ovens impart character to such specialties as marinated rack of lamb and smoked shark.

The Trader took an interest in California wines when many restaurateurs shunned them as second-rate. He went to the wineries, tasting with the producers, and bought sometimes even before the wines were on the market. Today the distinguished wine cellar is justifiably one of Victor Bergeron's greatest sources of pride.

BAHIA

TRADER VIC'S
SAN FRANCISCO, CALIFORNIA

For each serving:

  2½ **ounces (5 tablespoons) unsweetened pineapple juice**
   1 **ounce (2 tablespoons) coconut cream**
   1 **ounce (2 tablespoons) light Jamaica rum**
   1 **ounce (2 tablespoons) light Puerto Rican rum**
     Ice cubes
     Cracked ice
     Fresh mint sprig
     Pineapple and maraschino cherry (optional garnish)

Combine first 5 ingredients in blender, electric drink mixer or cocktail shaker and mix well. Fill tall glass with cracked ice and pour drink over. Garnish with mint and, if desired, fruit laced on pick.

TRADER VIC RUM CUP

TRADER VIC'S
KANSAS CITY, MISSOURI

4 servings

  2 **scoops cracked ice**
  1 **lemon, quartered**
  1 **lime, quartered**
  1 **orange, quartered**
  3 **ounces (6 tablespoons) light Puerto Rican rum**
  2 **ounces (¼ cup) orange juice**
  1 **ounce (2 tablespoons) Siegert's Bouquet rum or dark rum**
    Dash Angostura bitters
  1 **ounce (2 tablespoons) lemon juice**
  1 **ounce (2 tablespoons) orgeat syrup**

Place ice in blender. Squeeze juice from lemon, lime and orange quarters over ice; reserve citrus shells. Add remaining ingredients and blend well. Pour into large chilled bowl. Garnish with citrus shells.

SCARLETT

PITTYPAT'S PORCH
ATLANTA, GEORGIA

"Before dinner we ordered a cocktail called a Scarlett. It was the most unusual drink I've ever tasted."
—Leah McArthur, Enterprise, Alabama

1 or 2 servings

    1½ ounces dark rum
    1½ ounces cherry brandy
     1 ounce cream of coconut
     1 teaspoon fresh lemon juice
     1 teaspoon grenadine
        Crushed ice

Put first 5 ingredients with scoop of crushed ice in blender. Mix until frothy. Pour into chilled glass(es).

FLAMINGO DRINK

SONESTA BEACH HOTEL
BERMUDA

6 to 8 servings

     3 cups (24 ounces) fresh orange juice
     2 cups (16 ounces) fresh lemon juice
    1½ cups (12 ounces) Barbados rum
     6 tablespoons (3 ounces) grenadine syrup
        Ice cubes

Combine all ingredients except ice in tall container and shake well. Pour over ice and serve.

BLACK POWER COCKTAIL

BAGATELLE GREAT HOUSE
ST. THOMAS, BARBADOS, WEST INDIES

"An amazing combination of rum, Benedictine, orange juice and lime juice. It would be an interesting addition to any cocktail repertoire."
—Anne Leventhal, Montpelier, Vermont

For each serving:

     2 ounces (¼ cup) white rum
    ½ ounce (1 tablespoon) simple syrup
        (equal parts sugar and water boiled
        5 minutes), chilled
    ½ ounce (1 tablespoon) fresh lime juice
    ½ ounce (1 tablespoon) orange juice
     5 drops Benedictine
     3 drops Angostura bitters
        Cracked ice

Combine all ingredients except ice and blend well. Serve over cracked ice.

DA LUCIANO'S BANANA DAIQUIRI

DA LUCIANO
CHRIST CHURCH PARISH, BARBADOS

6 servings

     4 ripe bananas, cut into pieces
     6 ounces (¾ cup) light rum
     4 ounces (½ cup) simple syrup
     3 ounces (6 tablespoons) fresh lime juice
    ½ cup crushed ice
        Maraschino cherries (garnish)

Combine bananas, rum, syrup, lime juice and ice in blender. Mix until frothy. Pour into champagne glasses; garnish with maraschino cherries.

BLUEBEARD'S GHOST

BLUEBEARD'S CASTLE HOTEL
ST. THOMAS, U.S. VIRGIN ISLANDS

Makes 4 servings

     6 ounces (¾ cup) light rum
     3 ounces orange liqueur
     3 ounces fresh lemon juice
     3 ounces simple syrup
    2¼ ounces dry red wine
        Ice

Combine liquids in shaker or blender and mix well. Pour into tall glasses filled with ice.

LOTTA COLADA

COCONUT WILLIE'S, FONTAINEBLEAU HILTON
MIAMI BEACH, FLORIDA

"An unusual mixed fruit drink served in a coconut shell rimmed with shredded coconut. They call it 'a pina colada and then some.'"
—David C. Pelton, Rochester, New York

6 to 8 servings

     7 cups crushed ice
     3 cups cubed fresh pineapple
    2¾ cups pineapple juice
     1 15-ounce can cream of coconut
    ¼ cup half and half
    1½ cups 151-proof rum
        Shredded coconut
     3 to 4 ounces rum

In batches, combine first 5 ingredients in blender and mix thoroughly, about 3 minutes. Add rum and blend 1 minute longer. Serve colada in chilled glasses rimmed with coconut. Top each with ½ ounce rum.

MAI TAI

TRADER VIC'S
SAN FRANCISCO, CALIFORNIA

For each serving:

  2 ounces (¼ cup) Mai Tai rum or 1 ounce
    (2 tablespoons) dark Jamaica rum and
    1 ounce (2 tablespoons) Martinique rum
½ ounce (1 tablespoon) Curaçao
¼ ounce (1½ teaspoons) sugar syrup
¼ ounce (1½ teaspoons) orgeat syrup
  1 lime, halved
    Shaved ice
    Fresh mint sprig
    Pineapple and maraschino cherry
    (optional garnish)

Combine first 4 ingredients in cocktail shaker and shake well. Squeeze lime juice over shaved ice in double old-fashioned or similar sized glass, reserving one of halves. Pour drink over ice and decorate with reserved ½ lime, mint and, if desired, fruit laced on a cocktail stick.

NAVY GROG

THE PLANTATION
MOLINE, ILLINOIS

6 servings

    Crushed ice
  8 ounces (1 cup) fresh lemon juice
  8 ounces (1 cup) simple syrup
  8 ounces (1 cup) 151-proof dark rum
  4 ounces (½ cup) fresh orange juice
  4 ounces (½ cup) fresh grapefruit juice
  4 ounces (½ cup) 80-proof white rum
  6 skewers threaded with fresh pineapple
    wedge, cherry and mint sprig (garnish)

Fill 6 13-ounce glasses with crushed ice. Combine lemon juice, syrup, dark rum, orange juice, grapefruit juice and white rum in tall container and shake well. Pour over ice and garnish each serving with skewer of fresh fruit.

PANINI

PLANTATION GARDENS
KAUAI, HAWAII

"Panini means prickly pear in Hawaiian."
    —Bettye Ann Ewing, Honolulu, Hawaii

Makes 8 12-ounce drinks

  5 ripe medium bananas
  4 ounces frozen orange juice concentrate,
    thawed

  1 ounce banana liqueur
  1 cup simple syrup
  8 cups crushed ice
  8 ounces dark rum

Combine first 4 ingredients in blender and mix until smooth. Pour into large glass measure. For each drink put 1 cup crushed ice in blender, add ½ cup banana mixture and 1 ounce rum. Blend until semi-frozen. Serve immediately in tall glasses.

PLANTER'S PUNCH

ADMIRAL'S INN
ANTIGUA, WEST INDIES

"I am a great fan of rum punches and think I may have found the best ever."
    —Mrs. F. Richardson, Hartsdale, New York

10 servings

  ¼ cup sugar
  ¼ cup lime juice
  2 cups (1 pint) dark rum
  2 cups (1 pint) light rum
  ¼ cup Cointreau
  ¼ cup sweet vermouth
  ¼ cup crème de cacao
  ¼ cup Dubonnet
2¼ cups orange juice
2¼ cups pineapple juice
1¼ cups water
    Few dashes Angostura bitters
    Orange slices and maraschino cherries
    (garnish)

Mix sugar and lime juice, then add rums. Add remaining liquors, fruit juices, water and bitters and mix until thoroughly blended. Just before serving add ice and garnish with fruit.

SHEPHERD'S FRESH FRUIT SMOOTHIE

SHEPHERD RESTAURANT
ENCINITAS, CALIFORNIA

Makes about 2½ cups

  1 peeled banana, frozen
  1 cup apple juice
½ cup chopped fresh fruit (do not use
    citrus fruit)
  1 tablespoon raisins or chopped nuts

Combine all ingredients in blender and mix well. Pour into glasses and serve.

HOT APPLE PIE

CHUCK'S STEAK HOUSE
SAN MATEO, CALIFORNIA

"A hot apple cider drink, topped with whipped cream and cinnamon. It tastes exactly like the dessert it's named after." —Faye C. Arasim, Herndon, Virginia

4 servings

> 1 quart apple cider
> 3 to 4 cloves
> 5 ounces Tuaca (1¼ ounces per serving)
> Freshly whipped cream
> Cinnamon or cinnamon sticks

Bring apple cider and cloves just to boil in medium saucepan. Pour Tuaca into stremmed 8-ounce glasses. Strain cider into glasses to within ½ inch of rim. Top with whipped cream. Sprinkle with cinnamon, or serve with cinnamon sticks.

MILK PUNCH

BRENNAN'S
NEW ORLEANS, LOUISIANA

For each serving:

> 3 ounces half and half
> 1 teaspoon powdered sugar
> 1¼ ounces bourbon
> Dash vanilla
> Nutmeg (garnish)

Heat half and half and sugar in small saucepan until almost boiling, stirring frequently. Combine with bourbon and vanilla in shaker and mix well. Pour into warmed cup and top with nutmeg.

BEAR FOX COCKTAIL

ARLINGTON INN
ARLINGTON, VERMONT

For each serving:

> 1¼ ounces (2½ tablespoons) light rum
> 1 ounce (2 tablespoons) coffee liqueur
> ½ ounce (1 tablespoon) Cognac
> ¾ cup hot coffee
> Whipped cream and shaved semisweet chocolate (garnish)
> ½ ounce (1 tablespoon) Grand Marnier

Combine first 3 ingredients in large wine glass. Stir in coffee. Top with cream and chocolate. Pour Grand Marnier over.

CAFE CAPPUCCINO A LA RAYMON

JACQUES', SHERATON BATON ROUGE HOTEL
BATON ROUGE, LOUISIANA

8 servings

> 7½ ounces dark crème de cacao
> 5 ounces Amaretto
> 2½ ounces white rum
> 1½ ounces white crème de menthe
> Fresh hot coffee
> Whipped cream and shaved chocolate (garnish)

Combine all liqueurs in pitcher. Divide among preheated mugs and fill each with coffee to within ½ inch of rim. Add dollop of whipped cream to each and top with chocolate. Serve with straw and spoon.

CAPPUCCINO

LA FAMIGLIA
BEVERLY HILLS, CALIFORNIA

"Cappuccino from La Famiglia is this side of heaven. I dream about it." —Linda Singer, Sherman Oaks, California

6 to 8 servings

> 3 cups coffee
> 3 cups half and half
> 4 ounces (½ cup) dark crème de cacao
> 2 ounces (¼ cup) rum
> 2 ounces (¼ cup) brandy

Combine all ingredients and steam or heat in saucepan. Serve immediately.

GOLDEN SPIKE

CHATTANOOGA CHOO-CHOO
CHATTANOOGA, TENNESSEE

For each serving:

> 1¼ ounces white rum
> 1½ ounces coconut cream
> 1½ ounces orange juice
> 1½ ounces pineapple juice
> 1 ounce sweet and sour mix
> ½ ounce whipping cream (optional)

Blend ingredients and pour over ice in 12-ounce collins glass.

MUCKAMUCK TEA

MUCKAMUCK RESTAURANT
VANCOUVER, BRITISH COLUMBIA, CANADA

"A soothing and seemingly simple combination of juniper, gin, honey and lemon."
—Anne Leventhal, Montpelier, Vermont

Makes 8 6-ounce servings

> 42 **ounces juniper tea,* freshly brewed**
> 6 **ounces dry gin**
> 2 **tablespoons honey**
> 1 **lemon, thinly sliced**

Fill heatproof pitcher with juniper tea. Stir in gin, honey and lemon slices. Pour into warmed teacups and serve immediately.

*Available in health food shops.

FRENCH MINT TEA

THE IRON GATE
DECATUR, ALABAMA

Makes 2 quarts

> 13 **tea bags**
> ¼ **cup fresh mint leaves, lightly packed**
> **Water**
> **Juice from 2 freshly squeezed lemons**
> 1 **6-ounce can frozen orange juice concentrate**

> 1 **cup sugar**
> **Mint sprigs (garnish)**

Combine tea, mint leaves and 1 quart water in large saucepan. Cover, bring to boil and immediately remove from heat. Let steep 30 minutes. Add lemon juice, orange juice concentrate, sugar and additional water to make 2 quarts liquid. Strain and chill. Serve over ice and garnish with mint.

HALF WAY HOUSE HOT SPICED WINE

HALF WAY HOUSE
RICHMOND, VIRGINIA

"My husband and I have tried many different wines in many different ways, but nothing rates as high as the Hot Spiced Wine served at the Half Way House."
—Linda Majer, Costa Mesa, California

10 servings

> 1 **quart dry red wine**
> 1 **cup water**
> 1 **cup sugar**
> 1 **teaspoon whole cloves**
> 1 **cinnamon stick**
> 1 **lemon, sliced**
> ½ **orange, sliced**

Combine all ingredients in large saucepan. Bring to boil over high heat, then simmer 15 minutes. Strain and serve hot.

FROM THE TUREEN

Webster's dictionary defines *soup* as "A liquid food . . . often containing pieces of solid food." This may serve to describe something that comes out of a can, but it hardly does justice to what is, after all, the most ancient and the most diverse area of culinary art.

Soups have been with us ever since man learned to boil water. Some soup recipes, especially those accurately but somewhat patronizingly called "peasant soups," have been passed down virtually unchanged for hundreds of generations. Others are quite recent, the inventions of restaurant chefs who want to offer their patrons something a little different from the classic onion soup or the always mysterious soup of the day.

Until about fifty years ago, soups were a major part of American home cooking. But with the increase in the use of convenience foods, and the gradual disappearance of the ever-simmering stock pot, really good and truly interesting soups became the almost exclusive province of restaurants—where they have thrived. Today there is virtually no restaurant of any stature that does not feature at least one soup specialty on its menu. The variety is seemingly endless: elegant French *potages*, both clear and thickened with sauce; smooth veloutés and bisques; hearty main course soups such as bouillabaisse, the invention of which is attributed to everyone from the goddess Venus to the abbess of a Marseilles convent; minestrones from Italy, egg soups from China, borschts from Eastern Europe, cold fruit soups from Scandinavia, and native American chowders and gumbos—even a partial list would fill a book. All are perfect as a first course or a light meal, and most are refreshingly easy to prepare. The only difficulty is making a choice—which may be why Webster's also defines soup as "An unfortunate predicament."

Black Bean Soup (see page 36) and Corn Sticks (page 174)
from The Coach House in New York.

BOUILLABAISSE WITH ROUILLE

OYSTER BAR & RESTAURANT
NEW YORK, NEW YORK

4 servings

¼ cup olive oil
1 cup julienned onion (about 1 large onion)
½ cup chopped green onion
2 medium leeks, chopped
3 celery stalks, chopped
1 quart Fish Stock*
1½ cups chopped peeled tomatoes (about 4 medium tomatoes)
1½ teaspoons salt or to taste
1½ teaspoons fennel seeds
1 teaspoon freshly ground white pepper
½ teaspoon saffron or to taste
1 bay leaf

4 live blue-claw crabs (if unavailable, use cooked)
8 littleneck clams, scrubbed and drained
16 large fresh mussels, scrubbed and debearded
1½ pounds firm white fish (cod, halibut, haddock), cut into 8 serving pieces
1 1½-pound lobster, cut into chunks and claws cracked
4 sea scallops or 12 bay scallops
Salt and freshly ground pepper

4 slices French bread, toasted dry Rouille**

Heat olive oil in large kettle and add onions, leeks and celery. Sauté until onions are just translucent. Add Fish Stock, tomatoes and all seasonings and bring to boil.

Add live crabs (if using cooked, reserve and add at last minute to heat through). Cover kettle and boil 5 minutes. Add clams and mussels. Boil just until shells open. Remove clams and mussels from broth and set aside. Reduce heat and add fish, lobster and scallops. Place clams and mussels on top of fish. Cover again and simmer over low heat until fish is opaque and flakes when tested with a fork, about 8 to 10 minutes. If using cooked crab, add just before fish is completely cooked. Season to taste.

Place toast in each of 4 heated bowls. Divide fish and shellfish equally among bowls, cutting crabs in half with a cleaver. Pour broth over seafood. Serve with Rouille on the side.

*Fish Stock

Makes 1 quart

2 pounds fish trimmings
6 cups water
2 cups dry white wine
Bouquet garni consisting of 1 bay leaf,
1 teaspoon thyme, 3 inches celery leaves, 2 parsley sprigs and 10 peppercorns

Combine all ingredients in large pan and boil about 30 minutes. Lower heat and simmer uncovered until stock is reduced to about 1 quart of liquid. Strain through cheesecloth.

**Rouille

Makes about 1 cup

2 garlic cloves, finely minced
3 tablespoons olive oil
¼ teaspoon saffron
1 tablespoon water
¼ cup fine dry breadcrumbs
1 cup broth from bouillabaisse

Place garlic and olive oil in a blender or food processor and whirl to a smooth paste. Add saffron dissolved in water and blend again. Add breadcrumbs, then broth, mixing thoroughly.

Serve from bowl, allowing guests to stir tablespoon or more into each portion of Bouillabaisse.

CAULIFLOWER-CLAM CHOWDER

THE BUTCHER BLOCK
PLATTSBURGH, NEW YORK

10 to 12 servings

2 tablespoons (¼ stick) butter
2 small carrots, diced
1 small onion, diced
1 celery stalk, diced
1 shallot, minced
1½ tablespoons flour
3 6½-ounce cans chopped clams, drained (reserve liquid)
2 cups water
1 8-ounce bottle clam juice
½ cup dry white wine
1 small head cauliflower, cut into florets

½ cup whipping cream
2 tablespoons sherry
1 teaspoon chopped fresh parsley
½ teaspoon dried thyme leaves
½ teaspoon dried tarragon leaves

Melt butter in medium saucepan over medium-high heat. Add carrots, onion, celery and shallot. Reduce heat and cook, stirring occasionally, until vegetables are soft but not brown. Blend in flour and continue cooking about 2 minutes, stirring constantly. Slowly stir in reserved clam juice, water, bottled clam juice and wine. Add cauliflower and bring to boil. Reduce heat, cover partially and simmer until cauliflower florets are tender, about 15 minutes.

Stir in clams, cream, sherry and herbs. Simmer 5 minutes. Ladle into soup bowls.

SPINACH AND CLAM SOUP

THE WINE CELLAR
FORT LAUDERDALE, FLORIDA

"The Wine Cellar prepares such good food, we think it deserves a weekly visit. The Spinach and Clam Soup is one of our favorites."
                    —*Debra Elenson, Fort Lauderdale, Florida*

6 to 8 servings

 ½ medium onion, diced
 4 strips bacon, diced
 4 anchovy fillets, minced
 1 garlic clove, minced

 ½ cup (1 stick) butter
 2 tablespoons flour
 1 quart (4 cups) chicken stock
    (homemade preferred)
 1 10½-ounce package frozen spinach,
    thawed and squeezed dry
 2 6½-ounce cans clams, drained
 ½ pint (1 cup) whipping cream
    Salt and freshly ground pepper
    Pernod (optional)

Heat skillet over medium-high heat. Add onion, bacon, anchovies and garlic; sauté lightly. Remove mixture from heat.

Melt butter in large saucepan over medium-high heat. Add flour and stir constantly 2 to 3 minutes. Slowly stir in stock and bring to boil. Add onion/bacon mixture, spinach and clams and bring back to boil, stirring occasionally. Pour in cream and bring soup to boil a third time. Add salt and pepper to taste. Divide among bowls and add dash of Pernod to each, if desired.

OYSTER SOUP

IL GIARDINO
VANCOUVER, BRITISH COLUMBIA, CANADA

8 to 10 generous servings

 4 cups whipping cream
 1 quart shucked oysters in their own liquid
 1 cup dry white wine
 3 medium tomatoes, diced
 2 to 3 medium lemons, diced
 2 medium onions, diced
 3 garlic cloves, minced
 1 teaspoon crushed basil
 ½ teaspoon crushed thyme

 2 tablespoons (¼ stick) butter
 2 tablespoons flour
 1 cup milk, scalded

 ½ teaspoon salt
 ⅛ teaspoon white pepper
 ½ teaspoon hot pepper sauce
 2 tablespoons Worcestershire sauce

 1 tablespoon melted butter, paprika,
    chopped parsley (garnish)

Combine cream, oysters and wine in 4- to 5-quart pot. Add tomatoes, lemons, onions, garlic and herbs and cook over high heat to just below boiling point. Reduce heat and simmer until soup is reduced by ⅓, about 30 to 40 minutes, stirring occasionally.

While soup is simmering, melt butter over medium heat in small heavy-bottomed saucepan. Add flour and cook 2 to 3 minutes, stirring constantly. Slowly add milk and cook, stirring constantly, until sauce is thick and smooth.

Combine white sauce with soup and cook 3 minutes, stirring occasionally to blend. Add salt, pepper, hot pepper sauce and Worcestershire sauce. Taste for seasoning (soup should be spicy).

Pour into heated bowls and garnish each with drop or two of melted butter, sprinkling of paprika and chopped parsley.

SEAFOOD CHOWDER BASQUAISE

THE HOUNDSTOOTH
BOSTON, MASSACHUSETTS

"A delightfully spiced seafood chowder that thrilled my daughter and me."
                    —*Bill Helton, Danvers, Massachusetts*

12 servings

 2 to 3 tablespoons olive oil
 3 to 4 garlic cloves, minced
 2 to 3 carrots, diced
 2 green peppers, seeded and diced
 1 red pepper, seeded and diced
 1 cup chopped celery
 1 large onion, diced
 3 to 4 tomatoes, peeled and chopped
 1 pound mushrooms, sliced
 1 cup diced zucchini
 1 cup diced eggplant
 8 ounces langostinos or baby lobster tails
 8 ounces shrimp, peeled and deveined
 8 ounces scallops, coarsely chopped
 8 ounces clams, minced
 8 ounces lump crabmeat
 8 ounces whitefish, cut into cubes
 1 cup dry vermouth
 1 teaspoon cayenne
    Salt and freshly ground pepper
    Toasted garlic bread (garnish)

Heat oil in Dutch oven over medium-high heat. Add garlic and sauté 1 to 2 minutes. Add next 5 ingredients and sauté until onion is translucent. Reduce heat to medium, add tomatoes and cook 10 to 20 minutes. Stir in mushrooms, zucchini and eggplant and cook just until vegetables are crisp-tender. Add fish in order given and pour vermouth over. Reduce heat and simmer 20 minutes longer. Stir in cayenne and salt and pepper to taste. Ladle into heated bowls and serve topped with slice of garlic bread.

CALDO XOCHITL

EL MIRADOR RESTAURANT
SAN ANTONIO, TEXAS

"A Mexican soup with a fragrant combination of chicken, garlic, herbs and spices. It is served in a bowl over rice." —Helen Manks, Austin, Texas

12 servings

    4 or 5 garlic cloves, minced
    1 tablespoon dried oregano
    ¼ teaspoon ground cloves
    2½ quarts water
    1 2½- to 3-pound frying chicken
    1 tablespoon chicken stock base
    1 tablespoon salt
    1 tablespoon ground cumin
    1 teaspoon freshly ground pepper
    3 bay leaves
    1 sprig fresh basil
    2 cups sliced zucchini
    1½ cups quartered and sliced carrots
    1½ cups diced green bell pepper
    1 medium onion, sliced
    1 17-ounce can garbanzo beans, drained

Garnish

    El Mirador Rice*
    1 bunch green onions, chopped
    ½ bunch fresh cilantro (leaves only), chopped
    1 or 2 fresh jalapeño chilies, chopped
    2 firm tomatoes, cubed
    1 avocado, seeded and cubed

Mix garlic, oregano and cloves to a paste. Bring water to boil in large pot. Add chicken, stock base, salt, cumin, pepper, bay leaves, basil and garlic paste. Return water to boil, skimming foam as it rises to top. Let chicken simmer until cooked, about 45 minutes to 1 hour. Remove chicken and set aside to cool. Add zucchini, carrots, bell pepper, onion and beans to pot and bring to boil. Reduce heat and simmer until tender, about 15 minutes.

Meanwhile, remove skin and bones from chicken; shred meat. When vegetables are tender, add meat to soup and heat through.

For each serving, place ¼ cup El Mirador Rice in soup bowl. Pour soup over and top with onion, cilantro, chilies, tomatoes and avocado.

*El Mirador Rice

12 servings

    ¾ cup long-grain rice
    Lemon juice

    2 tablespoons oil
    2 medium tomatoes, chopped
    2 medium green bell peppers, chopped
    1 garlic clove, minced
    1 tablespoon chicken stock base
    1 cup hot water
    1 teaspoon ground cumin
    ¼ teaspoon salt
    Freshly ground pepper

Cover rice with hot water. Add squeeze of lemon juice and let soak for 5 minutes. Drain thoroughly in colander.

Heat oil in large skillet. Add rice and sauté until golden. Drain off any excess fat. Stir in tomatoes, peppers and garlic and sauté 5 minutes. Add chicken base dissolved in water and seasonings. Reduce heat, cover and simmer 15 minutes; do not remove lid while rice is cooking. Fluff with fork.

CRAB AND CORN BISQUE

COMMANDER'S PALACE
NEW ORLEANS, LOUISIANA

8 servings

    ½ cup (1 stick) butter
    1½ cups chopped green onion tops
    2 tablespoons all purpose flour
    1¼ teaspoons Creole Seafood Seasoning (see page 88)
    1 teaspoon granulated garlic
    Pinch thyme
    1 quart (4 cups) Crab Stock*
    2 12-ounce cans whole kernel corn, drained
    1½ cups whipping cream
    1 pound lump crabmeat

Melt butter in 3-quart saucepan over medium heat. Add onion and sauté until wilted. Stir in flour, Creole Seafood Seasoning, garlic and thyme and continue cooking until flour begins to stick to pan. Blend in Crab Stock, reduce heat and simmer until stock thickens, about 15 minutes. Add corn and simmer an additional 15 minutes. Slowly stir in cream and blend well. Gently add crabmeat. Remove from heat and let stand 30 minutes. Reheat gently over very low heat, being careful crabmeat does not break up into flakes and cream does not curdle. Serve immediately.

Any remaining bisque should be reheated in a double boiler.

*Crab Stock

Makes 1 quart

    1½ quarts (6 cups) water
    6 hard-shelled medium crabs
    6 celery stalks
    2 medium onions, quartered
    1½ tablespoons liquid crab boil (optional)**

Combine all ingredients in large saucepan and bring to boil over high heat. Reduce heat and simmer 3 hours, adding more water as necessary to make 1 quart stock. Strain.

**Available in specialty food stores.

WEDDING SOUP

WINE MERCHANT
AKRON, OHIO

John Piscazzi, owner of the Wine Merchant, explains how Wedding Soup got its name: "My father said that when he was very young in Italy, poor people only saw meat and meat-flavored broth on their wedding day or when so ill as to be near death."

10 to 12 servings

Broth

  1 **5-pound stewing chicken, halved or cut into pieces**
  4 **quarts water**

  6 **plum tomatoes**
  4 **celery stalks**
  4 **sprigs parsley**
  2 **large carrots**
  1 **large onion**
  1 **slice fresh ginger**
  1 **teaspoon dill**
 ¼ **cup chicken soup base or concentrate**

Meatballs

 ½ **pound lean ground veal**
 ¼ **cup Italian breadcrumbs**
  1 **egg, lightly beaten**
  4 **teaspoons grated Parmesan cheese**
  1 **teaspoon minced parsley**
  1 **small garlic clove, minced**
 ¼ **teaspoon freshly ground pepper**
  3 **tablespoons olive oil**

 ½ **pound kale, spinach, escarole or curly endive, coarsely chopped**

For broth: Place chicken in 8-quart pot. Add water and bring to boil over high heat. Reduce heat to medium; skim.

Add next 7 ingredients. Return to boil, cover and simmer over low heat about 3 to 4 hours. About ½ hour before chicken is done, stir in soup base. Remove chicken and reserve for another use. Cool broth slightly and strain. Refrigerate broth several hours or overnight. Remove solidified fat.

For meatballs: Combine first 7 ingredients and form into ¾-inch balls. Heat olive oil in large skillet over medium heat. Add meatballs and sauté until browned on all sides. Drain on paper towels.

Bring broth to boil over high heat. Reduce heat to low, add meatballs and simmer uncovered about 10 minutes. Add greens and cook 5 minutes. Serve immediately.

CHICKEN BISQUE

THE PANTRY RESTAURANT
PORTLAND, OREGON

8 to 10 servings

  1 **3-pound fryer chicken**
  4 **celery stalks, chopped**

  4 **carrots, chopped**
  2 **onions, chopped**
  3 **tablespoons salt**

  2 **cups (4 sticks) butter**
 ¾ **cup flour**

 ½ **cup chopped pimientos**
 ½ **cup chopped blanched green pepper**
 ½ **teaspoon freshly ground pepper**

Place chicken in large pot and add water to cover (about 3 quarts). Add vegetables and salt and bring to boil. Reduce heat and simmer until chicken is tender and separates easily from bone. Remove chicken from stock and set aside. Reserve stock. Shred or chop chicken.

To make roux, melt butter in 3-quart saucepan over low heat. Stir in flour and cook for 1 or 2 minutes.

Bring 8 cups reserved chicken stock to slow boil and gradually stir into roux. Simmer until soup takes on a glaze, about 15 minutes.

Add pimientos, green pepper, ½ cup shredded or chopped chicken and ground pepper. Simmer for few minutes, stirring constantly. Serve in heated bowls. Use remaining chicken in salad or crepes.

GREEK LEMON CHICKEN SOUP

MICHAELS RESTAURANT
ROCHESTER, MINNESOTA

8 to 10 servings

  8 **cups chicken broth**
 ½ **cup plus 1 tablespoon fresh lemon juice**
 ½ **cup shredded carrot**
 ½ **cup chopped onion**
 ½ **cup chopped celery**
  6 **tablespoons concentrated chicken soup base**
    Freshly ground white pepper

 ¼ **cup (½ stick) butter, room temperature**
 ¼ **cup all purpose flour**

  8 **egg yolks, room temperature**
  1 **cup cooked long-grain rice**
  1 **cup diced cooked chicken**
  8 **to 10 lemon slices (garnish)**

Combine broth, lemon juice, carrot, onion, celery, soup base and pepper in Dutch oven and bring to boil over high heat. Reduce heat, cover partially and simmer until tender, about 20 minutes.

Blend butter and flour in shallow bowl until smooth. Using back of fork, scrape butter mixture into hot soup a little at a time, stirring well after each addition. Simmer 10 minutes, stirring frequently.

Meanwhile, beat yolks in large bowl of electric mixer on high speed until light and lemon colored. Reduce speed and gradually mix in some of hot soup. Return mixture to saucepan and cook until heated through. Stir in rice and chicken. Ladle soup into bowls. Garnish with lemon slices.

MULLIGATAWNY SOUP

TIDDY DOLS EATING HOUSE
LONDON, ENGLAND

John Campbell, Director of Tiddy Dols Eating House, tells us that mulligatawny was very popular with British officers serving in India during the British colonial period, because it was easy to carry along flasks of the hot soup on winter forays into the hills.

8 servings

   1 **large chicken, cut into pieces**
   ¼ **pound veal trimmings, cut up**
   6 **cups water**

   3 **tablespoons (⅜ stick) butter**
   4 **large onions, chopped**
   2 **garlic cloves, minced**

   2 **heaping teaspoons curry powder**
   5 **tablespoons cornstarch**

     Juice of 1 lemon
     Salt and pepper
   1 **cooking apple, peeled and sliced**

     Boiled rice

Simmer chicken and veal trimmings in 6 cups water for about 1 hour.

Melt butter in large skillet and sauté onions and garlic until translucent.

Mix curry powder and cornstarch with about ¼ cup chicken/veal stock to form paste. Add to soup and blend thoroughly. Stir in onions and garlic. Cook about 30 minutes. Chill.

Thirty minutes before serving, cut chicken into small pieces, discarding bones and skin. Return chicken to soup. Add lemon juice, salt and pepper to taste and reheat. About 20 minutes before serving add apple. Serve with boiled rice.

SOPA DE TORTILLA

SALMAGUNDI
SAN FRANCISCO, CALIFORNIA

6 to 8 servings

   3 **pounds chicken pieces**
   4 **quarts water**
   1 **teaspoon celery seeds**
   1 **teaspoon whole black peppercorns**
   2 **garlic cloves, peeled**

   1 **1-pound can whole peeled tomatoes, undrained**
   1 **onion, cut into 1-inch pieces**
   1 **green pepper, cut into 1-inch squares**
   3 **sprigs fresh cilantro**
   ½ **teaspoon ground cumin**
   ¼ **teaspoon cayenne pepper**
   ¼ **teaspoon freshly ground white pepper**

   1 **garlic clove, minced**
   1 **10-ounce package frozen corn**
   4 **green onions, coarsely chopped**
     Salt

   1 **cup cooked rice**
   2 **teaspoons minced fresh parsley**
     Tortilla chips and freshly grated cheddar cheese (garnish)

Combine chicken and water in stockpot. Add celery seeds, peppercorns and garlic tied in small cheesecloth square. Cover and bring to boil, then reduce heat and simmer until chicken is tender, about 45 minutes. Remove chicken from broth and let cool.

Strain broth and return to stockpot. Add next 8 ingredients, cover and simmer 30 minutes. Add corn and green onion and simmer 10 minutes more. Season with salt to taste.

Meanwhile, skin and bone chicken. Dice meat into 1-inch pieces. Add to broth with rice and parsley and heat through. Ladle into warm bowls and garnish with tortilla chips and cheddar cheese.

POTAGE ST. GERMAIN

MAGIC PAN

"I'm always on the lookout for good hearty soups—they're such great main courses for family meals and informal entertaining. At our local Magic Pan, I came across a fine one not long ago, called Potage St. Germain."   —Linda Lico, San Jose, California

Makes about 3½ quarts

   1 **1-pound ham bone**
   4½ **cups water**
   2 **cups chicken stock or 1 13¾-ounce can chicken broth**
   2 **cups split peas, rinsed**

   ⅔ **cup finely chopped leeks or green onions**
   ⅓ **cup finely chopped carrots**
   ⅓ **cup finely chopped celery**
   ½ **teaspoon sugar**
   ⅛ **teaspoon marjoram**
   ⅛ **teaspoon freshly ground pepper**
   2½ **cups milk**
   1 **cup whipping cream**
   ¾ **cup finely chopped cooked ham**
   ½ **cup finely chopped cooked chicken**

Place ham bone in large pot or Dutch oven. Add water, chicken stock and peas and bring to boil over medium heat. Skim. Reduce heat and simmer, stirring occasionally, 30 minutes.

Add vegetables and seasonings and continue to simmer gently, stirring occasionally, until peas are very soft and mixture is thick, about 30 to 40 minutes. Remove ham bone. Gradually stir in milk and cream. Add ham and chicken. Simmer, stirring occasionally, about 10 minutes. Adjust seasoning if necessary.

GOULASH SOUP

BEETHOVEN RESTAURANT
SAN FRANCISCO, CALIFORNIA

"Simply marvelous—a marriage of beef, paprika and caraway."
—*Lorraine A. Pajerek, Endicott, New York*

6 servings

- 6 **tablespoons vegetable shortening**
- 2 **medium onions, finely chopped**

- 1 **pound beef chuck, cut into ¾-inch cubes**

- 3 **tablespoons tomato paste**
- 3 **tablespoons paprika**
- 1 **tablespoon caraway seeds**
- 1 **garlic clove, crushed**
- 1½ **teaspoons dried marjoram**
- 1 **teaspoon finely grated lemon peel**
  Dash hot pepper sauce
  Pinch sugar
- 8 **cups water**
- 2 **small potatoes, peeled and cut into ¾-inch cubes**
  Salt and freshly ground pepper

Melt 3 tablespoons shortening in 8-quart stockpot over medium heat. Add onions and sauté until golden. Remove from heat.

Melt remaining shortening in large skillet over medium-high heat. Add meat in batches and brown well on all sides. Add to onion. Pour small amount of water into skillet and stir up any browned bits clinging to bottom. Blend into meat mixture.

Stir in tomato paste, paprika, caraway seeds, garlic, marjoram, lemon peel, hot pepper sauce and sugar. Add water and mix well. Place over high heat and bring to boil. Reduce heat, cover partially and simmer 1½ hours. Add potato and continue cooking until potatoes are tender, about 20 minutes. Skim off fat. Season soup to taste with salt and pepper. Ladle into bowls and serve.

SECOND CHANCE OXTAIL SOUP

SECOND CHANCE
ANN ARBOR, MICHIGAN

Chef Ollie Kiesel recommends that the soup be prepared a day in advance and chilled; reheat just before serving.

6 to 8 servings

- 3 **pounds oxtails, disjointed**

- 2 **cups water**
- ¼ **cup barley**

- 1 **medium onion, chopped**
- ½ **cup chopped celery**
- ½ **cup chopped carrot**
- ¼ **cup chopped rutabaga**

- 1 **medium tomato, peeled, seeded and chopped**

- ¼ **cup dry white wine**
- 1½ **teaspoons marjoram**
- 2 **teaspoons salt**
  Pinch garlic powder
  Pinch dill
  Pinch nutmeg or mace

Place oxtails in 6-quart pot. Add water to cover and bring to boil over high heat. Cover and simmer until meat is very tender and can be easily removed from bones, about 2½ to 3 hours. Cool, then cover and refrigerate overnight. Skim fat from surface of stock, reserving ¼ cup fat. Remove meat from bones, discarding fat that clings.

Bring 2 cups water to boil in medium saucepan. Add barley, cover and simmer until tender, about 35 to 40 minutes. Drain.

Heat oxtail fat in medium skillet. Sauté onion, celery, carrot and rutabaga about 3 to 4 minutes. Stir in meat.

Heat 6 cups oxtail broth in large pot. Stir in barley, vegetable-meat mixture, tomato and wine and bring slowly to boil. Stir in remaining ingredients and cook about 5 minutes over medium heat. Refrigerate several hours or overnight. Skim any fat from surface and reheat just before serving.

ROQUEFORT SOUP

CAN CAN PARISIEN BISTRO
SAN FRANCISCO, CALIFORNIA

"I approached the Roquefort Soup rather skeptically, never having heard of such a thing, but it was excellent."
—*Judith E. Garry, Daly City, California*

8 to 10 servings

- ½ **cup (1 stick) butter**
- 1 **large head white cabbage, chopped**

- 1 **medium head cauliflower, coarsely chopped**
- 6 to 7 **cups chicken broth**

- 1 **cup whipping cream**
- ¼ **cup Roquefort cheese**
  Salt and freshly ground pepper
  Buttered croutons

Melt butter in 4-quart saucepan. Add cabbage, stir to coat well, and cook covered over low heat until soft, about 15 minutes, stirring occasionally with wooden spoon.

Add cauliflower and chicken broth. Bring to boil over high heat. Reduce heat, cover and simmer until vegetables are tender, about 30 to 45 minutes.

In blender or food processor, mix cream and cheese. Stir into soup, season to taste with salt and pepper and garnish with croutons.

If desired, soup may be pureed. Cool slightly, place in blender or food processor and puree in batches. Reheat just before serving time.

TOWNHOUSE CHEESE SOUP

TOM BELL'S TOWNHOUSE
ALBERT LEA, MINNESOTA

6 servings

    4 small carrots, cut into 1-inch matchsticks
    3 celery stalks, cut into 1-inch matchsticks
 1½ cups chicken stock

    2 tablespoons (¼ stick) butter
    2 tablespoons finely chopped onion
    ¼ cup flour
    3 cups hot chicken stock
    1 cup shredded sharp cheddar cheese
    1 8¾-ounce can whole tomatoes,
       undrained, chopped
   10 drops hot pepper sauce
    ⅛ teaspoon nutmeg
       Salt to taste
    ¼ cup dry white wine (optional)
 1½ cups whipping cream, heated
       Popcorn or chopped parsley (garnish)

Add carrots and celery to 1½ cups chicken stock in 1- to 2-quart saucepan. Bring to boil, reduce heat and simmer until tender, about 15 minutes. Set saucepan aside.

Melt butter in 4- to 5-quart saucepan over medium heat. Add onion and sauté until translucent but not brown. Add flour, blend well and cook 5 to 7 minutes, stirring continuously; do not brown. Slowly stir 3 cups hot chicken stock into flour mixture and cook over low heat, whisking constantly, until sauce thickens. Blend in cheese and stir until cheese melts. Add tomatoes and undrained vegetables. Season with pepper sauce, nutmeg, salt and wine. Just before serving, stir in hot cream. Garnish with popcorn or chopped parsley.

BLACK BEAN SOUP

THE COACH HOUSE
NEW YORK, NEW YORK

Makes about 10 cups

 2½ cups dried black beans
   10 cups water

    2 tablespoons fat (reserved from
       Beef Stock*)
    1 cup chopped onion
    ½ cup chopped celery
    7 cups Beef Stock*
    2 cups water
    1 teaspoon chopped fresh garlic

    ¼ cup sherry or Madeira
    1 teaspoon salt
    ½ teaspoon freshly ground pepper
    2 hard-cooked eggs, finely chopped
    1 or 2 lemons, thinly sliced and dipped in
       minced fresh parsley (garnish)

Soak beans in 10 cups water for at least 12 hours in refrigerator. Drain well.

Heat fat in large Dutch oven over medium-high heat. Add onion and celery and sauté until tender. Add beans, stock, 2 cups water and garlic and simmer uncovered, stirring occasionally, until tender, about 2½ hours, adding water if needed to keep beans covered. Transfer to blender in batches (or work through coarse sieve or food mill) and mix until roughly pureed.

Turn into large saucepan and stir in sherry, salt and pepper. Place over medium heat and bring to serving temperature, stirring occasionally. Gently blend in chopped egg. Ladle into serving bowls and garnish with lemon.

*Beef Stock

Makes 8 cups

    3 pounds beef bones
    3 pounds ham shank (including bone and
       rind), meat cut up
    ¾ pound meaty beef shinbone
    ¾ teaspoon black peppercorns
    ¼ teaspoon celery seeds
    3 whole cloves
   15 cups water

Combine all ingredients in large pot and bring to boil. Reduce heat, cover partially and simmer 8 to 10 hours. Strain. Return to clean pan and simmer until reduced to about 8 cups. Let cool, then cover and refrigerate overnight. Remove layer of fat from top (reserve 2 tablespoons to use in soup).

AUSTRIAN CREAM CHEESE SOUP

SOUPOURRI
SEATTLE, WASHINGTON

"I am a devoted patron of soup and salad restaurants, and my frequent business trips allow me to try many of them across the country. One favorite is the Soupourri. Their Austrian Cream Cheese Soup is an absolute treasure."

—Paul Schofield, Hingham, Massachusetts

10 to 12 servings

    6 tablespoons (¾ stick) butter
    6 leeks, white part only, chopped
    4 celery stalks, chopped
    6 tablespoons all purpose flour
    5 cups chicken stock
    3 cups water
    1 teaspoon salt

    1 pound cream cheese (slightly warmed
       in double boiler or microwave)
 1½ to 2 cups plain yogurt, slightly warmed

4 egg yolks, beaten
Freshly ground white pepper
Chopped fresh chives or parsley
(garnish)

Melt butter in Dutch oven over medium-high heat. Add leeks and celery and sauté until leeks are transparent. Stir in flour and cook an additional 3 minutes. Add stock, water and salt and bring to a boil, stirring occasionally. Reduce heat and simmer, partially covered, for 15 minutes.

Whisk cream cheese, yogurt and egg yolks in medium bowl until smooth. Gradually add 2 cups soup mixture, blending thoroughly. Add to Dutch oven and stir over low heat until soup is heated through; do not boil. Season with white pepper and sprinkle with chives or parsley.

LENTIL SOUP

CHATEAU VEGAS
LAS VEGAS, NEVADA

6 servings

2 slices bacon, finely chopped
1 to 2 tablespoons vegetable oil (optional)
1 celery stalk, diced
1 carrot, diced
¼ medium onion, diced
1 garlic clove, minced
2 quarts (8 cups) water
1 pound lentils, soaked overnight, rinsed and drained
¼ cup diced canned tomatoes
1 bay leaf

6 frankfurters, thinly sliced
1 tablespoon steak sauce
½ teaspoon freshly ground pepper
½ teaspoon salt or to taste

Fry bacon in Dutch oven until almost crisp, adding oil if necessary. Add celery, carrot, onion and garlic and sauté until onion is translucent, about 3 to 4 minutes. Stir in water, lentils, tomatoes and bay leaf and bring to boil over high heat. Reduce heat and simmer until tender, about 1 hour.

Stir in remaining ingredients and continue cooking until frankfurter slices are heated, about 10 minutes.

RICE FLORENTINE SOUP

THE FARMER'S DAUGHTER RESTAURANT
ORLAND PARK, ILLINOIS

10 servings

2 cups chopped onion
1 cup chopped leeks
1 garlic clove, minced
3 tablespoons olive oil

5 cups chopped spinach
10 cups chicken stock
½ cup uncooked rice

1 tablespoon grated Parmesan cheese
⅓ cup unsweetened waffle batter (optional)
Salt, pepper and grated nutmeg to taste

In a 4-quart pot, sauté onion, leeks and garlic in olive oil until soft, but not brown.

Add chopped spinach and cook 10 minutes. Add stock and rice. Bring to boil and simmer until rice is cooked, about 20 minutes.

Mix Parmesan cheese with waffle batter, if desired, and force batter through colander into soup. If waffle batter is not being used, simply stir cheese into soup. Return soup to boil and remove from heat. Add seasonings and serve.

SOUTH COAST LIMA BEAN CHOWDER

SALMAGUNDI
SAN FRANCISCO, CALIFORNIA

6 to 8 servings

1 3-pound frying chicken, cut up
4 quarts water
Bouquet garni consisting of 4 bay leaves, 6 peppercorns and 1 teaspoon whole thyme
1 onion stuck with 4 cloves

3 tablespoons flour
5 tablespoons water

1 16-ounce can tomatoes
2 medium potatoes, peeled and diced
1 10-ounce package frozen corn
2 10-ounce packages frozen baby lima beans
1 teaspoon Worcestershire sauce
¼ teaspoon cayenne pepper

1 cup whipping cream
Salt
4 sprigs fresh parsley, minced (garnish)

Place chicken in 4 quarts water in large soup kettle with bouquet garni and onion. Bring to boil. Cover and simmer until chicken is tender, about 45 minutes. Remove chicken. Cool, bone and chop meat into 1-inch pieces and set aside. Strain broth, return to pot and bring to boil.

Mix together flour and 5 tablespoons water to form paste. Add to soup, stirring until thickened.

Add tomatoes and potatoes. Simmer, covered, about 20 minutes. Add corn, lima beans, Worcestershire sauce and cayenne pepper. Simmer 15 minutes more.

Add chicken and whipping cream. Season to taste with salt. Continue cooking about 1 minute longer, but do not boil. Garnish with parsley and serve.

CREAM OF ARTICHOKE SOUP

FOURNOU'S OVENS
SAN FRANCISCO, CALIFORNIA

"Whenever my friends and I want to splurge on a wonderful evening in San Francisco, we dine at Fournou's Ovens. Their exotic Cream of Artichoke Soup with hazelnuts is a favorite of mine."
—*Ann D. Sultan, Stanford, California*

10 servings

> 2 **large artichokes**
> 8 **cups chicken stock**
>
> ½ **cup hazelnuts**
>
> ¾ **cup rice flour**
> 1 **cup whipping cream**
>   **Salt and pepper**
> 2 **tablespoons sherry or to taste**

Remove all leaves, stem and choke from artichokes and discard, reserving bottoms only. Poach in water to cover 1 hour. Remove with slotted spoon and add to large saucepan with 6 cups chicken stock.

Preheat oven to 300°F. Spread nuts in small baking pan and toast about 10 minutes. Retain oven heat. Cool nuts slightly, then rub in towel to completely remove brown skins. Return nuts to oven and toast until golden brown, about 10 minutes longer, watching carefully. Remove from oven and crush to a fine consistency. Add to artichoke bottoms and stock and simmer 30 minutes. Puree in blender, processor or food mill and return to pan.

Gradually add rice flour to remaining 2 cups chicken stock and stir until smooth. Add to soup, place over high heat and whisk until it comes to a boil. Reduce heat and simmer 15 minutes, stirring frequently. Add cream and season with salt and pepper. Blend in sherry just before serving.

BORSCHT

THE RUSSIAN TEA ROOM
NEW YORK, NEW YORK

Makes about 8 cups

> ½ **cup finely chopped carrots**
> 1 **cup finely chopped onion**
> 1 **cup finely chopped beets**
> 1 **cup finely chopped celery**
> 1 **parsnip, finely chopped**
>
> 1 **tablespoon butter**
> 2 **cups beef stock**
> 1 **cup finely shredded cabbage**
> 1 **cup tomato pulp or strained stewed tomatoes**
>   **Salt and pepper**
>   **Sour cream, fresh dill (garnish)**

Barely cover carrots, onion, beets, celery and parsnip with boiling water in a 3-quart pot. Cover pot and allow vegetables to simmer for 20 minutes.

Add butter, stock, cabbage and tomatoes. Cook, covered, for 15 minutes. Season with salt and pepper. Pour soup into bowls. Garnish with teaspoonful of sour cream and sprinkling of fresh dill.

BROCCOLI, MUSHROOM AND LEEK CREAM SOUP

THE FIREPOND
BLUE HILL, MAINE

"The Firepond is a reconstructed smithy on Main Street in Blue Hill, Maine. They serve a soup made from a superb combination of broccoli, mushrooms and leeks."
—*Mrs. J. Wasilevitch, Huntington, New York*

Makes 2½ quarts

> 6 **tablespoons (¾ stick) butter**
> 2 **cups beef stock (homemade preferred)**
> 2 **cups chicken stock (homemade preferred)**
> 2 **pounds broccoli, coarsely chopped**
>
> ¾ **pound mushrooms, sliced**
> ½ **pound leeks, split and coarsely chopped**
>
> ⅓ **cup white wine**
> ½ **small shallot, minced**
> ⅛ **teaspoon dried basil**
> 1 **cup half and half**
> 1¼ **cups whipping cream**
>
>   **Salt and freshly ground pepper**

Combine 2 tablespoons each butter, beef stock and chicken stock in large skillet. Place over medium-high heat, add broccoli and cook until soft. Puree in blender or food processor in 3 batches adding at least ½ cup stock with each batch. Transfer to large saucepan or Dutch oven and add remaining stocks. Heat through, stirring occasionally. Cover and keep warm over low heat.

Heat remaining butter in skillet. Sauté mushrooms and leeks lightly. Add to soup.

Combine wine, shallot and basil in heavy-bottomed medium saucepan and reduce over medium heat until all liquid evaporates, watching carefully to avoid scorching. Meanwhile, heat half and half and 1 cup whipping cream in small saucepan just until hot. Whisking constantly, add cream in slow steady stream to shallot-basil mixture, and cook over medium heat until reduced by ⅓. Whisk cream mixture into warm soup. (At this point soup can be cooled and frozen for future use.)

When ready to serve, reheat soup just to simmering point. Fold in remaining whipping cream and salt and pepper to taste.

HUNGARIAN CREAM OF GREEN

LITTLE'S
PAONIA, COLORADO

3 to 4 servings

> 3 **cups good quality chicken stock**
> ½ **pound fresh green beans or 1 10½-ounce package frozen green beans, thawed**
> 2 **small potatoes, peeled and quartered**
> ½ **large onion, quartered**
> ¼ **cup (½ stick) butter**
> 2 **tablespoons snipped fresh dill**
> 2 **small garlic cloves, crushed**
>   **Salt and freshly ground pepper**
>
> ¼ **cup sour cream, room temperature**
>   **Juice of ½ lemon**

Combine stock, beans, potatoes, onion, butter, dill and garlic in large saucepan over high heat and bring to boil. Reduce heat, cover and simmer until vegetables are tender, about 20 to 25 minutes. Taste and add salt and freshly ground pepper.

Transfer soup to blender in batches and puree until smooth. Return to saucepan. Stir in sour cream and lemon juice. Cook on low until heated through.

CREAM OF BELL PEPPER SOUP

GREGORY'S RESTAURANT
ALBION, CALIFORNIA

8 servings

> 4 **green bell peppers, seeded and diced**
> 8 **ounces sorrel leaves, finely chopped***
>   **Juice of ½ lemon**
> 4 **cups (or more) chicken stock**
> 3 **shallots, finely chopped**
> 1 **teaspoon finely chopped chives**
> 1 **teaspoon salt**
> ¼ **teaspoon white pepper**

Roux

> 3 **tablespoons (⅜ stick) butter**
> 3 **tablespoons flour**
> ½ **to ⅔ cup half and half**

Combine peppers, sorrel and lemon juice in bowl; set aside. In medium saucepan, heat 4 cups stock until simmering. Add pepper-sorrel mixture, shallots, chives, salt and white pepper. Cover and simmer 30 minutes.

Transfer pepper-sorrel mixture to blender using slotted spoon and add enough of cooking liquid to cover; reserve remaining liquid. Puree until completely smooth.

For roux: Melt butter in medium saucepan. Stir in flour and cook until light golden. Add reserved liquid and puree. Return to boil, reduce heat and simmer 10 minutes, stirring constantly. Remove from heat and let cool slightly. Add half and half.

Strain through fine sieve; discard pulp. Thin with additional chicken stock if desired.

*Spinach sprinkled with juice of 1 lemon can be substituted for sorrel.

CARROT CREAM SOUP

MOUNT KENYA SAFARI CLUB
NANYUKI, KENYA

"I had heard that the carrot soup was excellent, and found that it was indeed one of the best soups I've tasted."
—Ruth Everingham, San Francisco, California

Makes 12 cups

> ¼ **cup (½ stick) butter**
> ½ **cup chopped onion**
> 3⅔ **cups minced carrots**
> 1 **cup flour**
> 8½ **cups chicken stock**
>
> ½ **cup whipping cream**
>   **Salt and pepper**

In 4-quart saucepan, melt butter over medium heat. Add onion and cook until soft. Add carrots and stir in flour, mixing well. Cook, stirring constantly, about 2 minutes. Still stirring, add chicken stock and bring to boil. Lower heat, cover and cook ½ hour, stirring occasionally.

Blend in cream, add salt and pepper to taste and serve immediately.

PEANUT CARROT COUNTRY SOUP

TRADER VIC'S
VICTORIA, BRITISH COLUMBIA, CANADA

8 servings

> ½ **cup (1 stick) butter**
> 2 **cups chopped carrots**
> ½ **cup chopped onion**
> ½ **cup chopped celery**
> 3 **tablespoons flour**
> 2 **quarts chicken stock**
> 1 **cup smooth peanut butter**
> 1 **cup whipping cream**
> 1 **teaspoon salt**
> ¼ **teaspoon celery salt**

Melt butter in large saucepan over medium heat. Add carrots, onion and celery and sauté until vegetables are translucent but not browned. Stir in flour, mixing thoroughly. Add chicken stock and stir until soup comes to a boil and thickens slightly. Reduce heat, cover partially and simmer 30 minutes. Pour through strainer, pressing down on vegetables before discarding pulp. Place peanut butter in large mixing bowl. Whisk in broth 1 cup at a time until smooth. Whisk in cream. Add salt and celery salt. Return to saucepan and heat through; do not boil.

CREAM OF EGGPLANT SOUP

COMMANDER'S PALACE
NEW ORLEANS, LOUISIANA

12 to 16 servings

  6 tablespoons (¾ stick) butter
  3 cups diced onion
  3 cups diced celery
  2 large eggplants, unpeeled and diced
  3 cups diced potatoes
  1 teaspoon curry powder
  ½ teaspoon thyme
  ½ teaspoon sweet basil
  8 cups chicken stock
  4 cups whipping cream

Melt butter in 6-quart pot. Sauté onion, celery, eggplant and potatoes. Add seasonings and cook, uncovered, over medium heat, stirring frequently, until potatoes are tender, about 10 to 15 minutes. Stir in stock and cook, uncovered, over medium heat until mixture begins to thicken, about 45 minutes. Remove from heat and add cream. Serve immediately.

SOPA DE AJO
(Garlic Soup)

HOTEL GRAN CAPITAN
CORDOBA, SPAIN

6 servings

  1½ quarts white stock (made by boiling
      beef knuckle in water)
  2 tablespoons olive oil
  12 garlic cloves
  6 thin slices bread, cut into small cubes
  ½ teaspoon red pepper
    Salt
  6 eggs

Prepare stock. Heat oil in large saucepan. Add garlic and sauté until golden. Quickly add bread cubes, pepper and stock and simmer 5 minutes. Add salt to taste. Lightly beat 1 egg in each bowl, add hot soup and stir gently. Serve immediately.

KALE SOUP

BRAX LANDING
HARWICH PORT, MASSACHUSETTS

According to Brax Landing, this hearty soup was once the staple food of Portuguese fishermen sailing the Atlantic—it provided all the meat and vegetables they would have during their lengthy voyages. The cook kept a pot constantly simmering in the galley, adding ingredients as needed. The flavor improves as it cooks down.

12 servings

  4 quarts beef stock
  2 cups chopped kale
  3 potatoes, peeled and diced
  1 1-pound can stewed tomatoes
  ½ pound linguini, cut into 2-inch pieces
  1 large Spanish onion, coarsely diced
  3 garlic cloves, minced
  1 teaspoon freshly ground pepper
  1 teaspoon thyme
    Salt
  1 cup cooked red kidney beans

In large pot, combine all ingredients except kidney beans. Simmer 3 hours. Add beans and simmer 15 minutes longer.

THE BAKERY'S CREAM OF CAULIFLOWER SOUP

THE BAKERY
CHICAGO, ILLINOIS

"When I stop in Chicago, The Bakery is always at the top of my list of places to visit. One of my all-time favorite dishes is the superb cauliflower soup they make there."
    —D. Barbara Moore, Topeka, Kansas

8 to 10 servings

  2 tablespoons vegetable oil or shortening
  ½ cup chopped onion
  1 small carrot, peeled and grated
  1 cup chopped celery
  1 head cauliflower (about 1 pound), cut
    into florets
  2 tablespoons chopped parsley

  8 cups chicken stock
    Bouquet garni (½ teaspoon peppercorns,
    1 teaspoon tarragon, ½ bay leaf)

  ¼ cup (½ stick) butter
  ¾ cup flour
  2 cups milk
  1 cup half and half
  1 tablespoon salt or to taste

  1 cup sour cream

Heat oil in 8- to 10-quart stockpot over medium heat. Add onion and sauté until translucent, stirring frequently. Add carrot and celery and cook 2 minutes, stirring frequently. Add cauliflower and 1 tablespoon parsley. Cover, reduce heat to low and cook 15 minutes, stirring occasionally to prevent mixture sticking.

Add chicken stock and bouquet garni and bring to boil over medium heat. Reduce heat and simmer about 5 minutes.

Melt butter in 2-quart saucepan. Stir in flour to make roux. Slowly add milk, whisking constantly to blend. Bring mixture to boil over medium heat, stirring frequently, until mixture is thick and smooth. Remove from heat and stir in half and half. Stir sauce into simmering soup. Season to taste with salt and simmer gently for about 15 to 20 minutes.

Just before serving, remove bouquet garni. Mix a few tablespoons of soup with sour cream. Stir sour cream mixture into soup along with remaining chopped parsley. Reheat and serve.

MARKET SOUP

DAPHNE AND VICTOR'S
OTTAWA, ONTARIO, CANADA

6 to 8 servings

    2 tablespoons (¼ stick) butter
    1 medium carrot, chopped
    1 stalk celery, chopped
    1 large parsnip, chopped
    ½ small onion, chopped
    ¼ small turnip, chopped
    1 garlic clove, minced

    1 cup water
    2 tablespoons dry barley
    2 tablespoons dry lentils

    3 medium tomatoes, peeled and chopped
    1 8¾-ounce can kidney beans, drained
    1 2-ounce jar beef base
  2½ teaspoons Worcestershire sauce
    ¼ cup fresh oregano or 2 tablespoons dried
    2 teaspoons parsley, minced
    1 teaspoon onion salt
    1 bay leaf
    ½ cup canned corn, drained
    3 cups homemade beef broth

Heat butter in a 1½- to 2-quart saucepan. Add next 6 ingredients and sauté approximately 3 minutes, stirring constantly.

Bring water to boil in large saucepan. Add barley and lentils, reduce heat and simmer until lentils are soft and water is absorbed, about 10 minutes.

Add remaining ingredients and bring soup to boil over medium heat, stirring frequently. Reduce heat, cover and simmer at least 30 minutes.

CREAM OF MUSHROOM SOUP

THE CAFE BUDAPEST
BOSTON, MASSACHUSETTS

12 servings

    ½ ounce imported dried mushrooms
    1 cup boiling water

    ½ cup (1 stick) butter
    ½ cup diced onion
  1½ pounds fresh mushrooms, thinly sliced
    3 tablespoons flour
    2 tablespoons chicken base concentrate
    7 cups cold water
    1 tablespoon lemon juice
    1 tablespoon salt
    ¼ teaspoon black pepper

    2 cups half and half or light cream
    1 cup sour cream
    3 tablespoons finely chopped parsley

       Croutons (garnish)
       Chopped parsley (garnish)

Wash dried mushrooms in cold water. Place in bowl and cover with boiling water. Soak 30 minutes.

Melt butter in 4-quart saucepan and add onion. Sauté until onion is translucent. Add half fresh mushrooms and sauté over low heat until liquid is evaporated. Add flour, stir with wire whisk, and cook for 3 to 5 minutes. Dissolve chicken base in cold water and add to saucepan, stirring with whisk until liquid is smooth. Add remaining fresh mushrooms, soaked dried mushrooms and their liquid, lemon juice, salt and pepper and bring to boil. Reduce heat and cook 10 to 15 minutes more.

Add half and half, sour cream and parsley, blending with wire whisk. Simmer again for 10 to 15 minutes. Adjust seasoning.

Garnish with croutons and parsley.

LA CUISINE SOUPE A L'OIGNON GRATINEE

LA CUISINE RESTAURANT
WINDSOR, ONTARIO, CANADA

8 servings

    ½ cup peanut oil
    6 large brown onions, coarsely chopped
    1 teaspoon thyme
    3 bay leaves
    1 bottle dry red wine
   10 cups beef consommé
    8 slices stale French bread
  1½ pounds Swiss cheese, grated

Heat oil in large pot. Add onions and sauté until cooked but not brown. Add thyme and bay leaves. Stir in wine. Bring to boil and let soup reduce for a few minutes. Add consommé and cook uncovered for 20 minutes.

Pour soup into 8 large ovenproof soup bowls. Top each with slice of French bread. Sprinkle with cheese. Broil quickly until bubbling and golden. Serve at once.

MINESTRONE SOUP

ADRIANO'S RISTORANTE
LOS ANGELES, CALIFORNIA

6 to 8 servings

    ¼ cup dried pinto beans

    1 slice bacon, diced
    1 cup diced zucchini
    ½ cup diced peeled eggplant
    ½ cup chopped leek
    ½ cup chopped fennel
    ¼ cup chopped onion
    ¼ cup diced celery
    2 tablespoons diced carrot
 1¾ quarts (7 cups) beef or chicken stock
    ½ cup dry white wine
    1 large tomato, peeled, seeded and chopped
    ½ cup diced peeled potato
    ½ teaspoon tomato paste
    ½ cup cooked pasta

    ¼ cup chopped fresh parsley
    ½ bunch fresh basil leaves
    2 garlic cloves
      Pinch dried oregano
      Salt and freshly ground pepper

Soak pinto beans in enough cold water to cover, at least 3 hours or overnight.

Drain beans well. Transfer to small saucepan. Cover with cold water. Bring to boil over medium-high heat. Reduce heat and simmer until tender. Drain and set aside.

Sauté bacon briefly in Dutch oven over medium-high heat. Add zucchini, eggplant, leek, fennel, onion, celery and carrot and sauté until vegetables are slightly softened. Stir in stock, wine, tomato, potato and tomato paste and bring to boil. Reduce heat and simmer 30 minutes. Add beans and pasta and cook until heated through.

Mash together parsley, basil, garlic and oregano in small bowl. Add to soup a little at a time, tasting after each addition. Season with salt and pepper to taste. Ladle soup into bowls and serve immediately.

MINESTRONE FREDDO

RISTORANTE DIANA
BOLOGNA, ITALY

4 servings

    1 cup finely chopped carrot
    1 cup finely chopped onion
    1 cup finely chopped celery
    ½ cup chopped ham or prosciutto
    2 tablespoons (about) olive oil
    2 to 3 potatoes, peeled and thinly sliced
    2 zucchini, thinly sliced
    1 cup thinly sliced green beans

    ½ head savoy cabbage, thinly sliced
    1 large tomato, peeled, seeded and chopped
    1 tablespoon tomato paste
    ½ teaspoon salt
    ¼ teaspoon freshly ground pepper

    ⅓ cup uncooked rice
    ¼ cup freshly grated Parmesan cheese
    1 teaspoon minced garlic
    1 teaspoon chopped fresh basil leaves
      (about 10 leaves)

Combine first 5 ingredients in Dutch oven or stockpot over low heat and cook, stirring frequently, until vegetables are pale golden, about 20 minutes. Add potatoes, zucchini and beans and continue cooking several minutes. Blend in cabbage and cook until softened. Stir in tomato, tomato paste, salt and pepper, blending well. Add enough water to almost cover (about 2 quarts). Bring to boil, cover partially, reduce heat and cook at slow boil 1 hour.

Stir in rice and continue cooking until rice is al dente, about 10 to 15 minutes; do not overcook. Blend in remaining ingredients, mixing well. Let cool to room temperature before serving.

DRIED BLACK MUSHROOM BARLEY SOUP

MICHAEL'S CANOGA INN
CANOGA PARK, CALIFORNIA

"The peasant-style black mushroom soup is robust and satisfying." —David J. Estrin, Tarzana, California

6 servings

    1 ounce dried mushrooms

    8 cups water
    ½ cup barley
    1 tablespoon beef soup base
    1 tablespoon chicken soup base

    1 to 2 tablespoons butter or margarine
    ¾ cup finely chopped carrot
    ½ cup finely chopped celery
    ½ cup finely chopped onion
    ⅓ cup finely chopped leek

    2 tablespoons flour
      Worcestershire sauce
      Hot pepper sauce
      Salt and freshly ground white pepper

Soak mushrooms in several changes of cold water until thoroughly clean. Drain. Cook in fresh water until tender, about 25 minutes. Strain and chop mushrooms finely.

Bring water to boil, add barley and cook until liquid is reduced to 6 cups, about 30 minutes. Reduce heat; stir in soup bases; cover and simmer.

Melt butter in large skillet over medium-high heat. Add chopped celery, carrot, onion and leek and sauté just until tender but not browned.

DINING AT RISTORANTE DIANA

The city of Bologna is the gastronomic heart of Northern Italy. So celebrated is the bounty of its cuisine that the city is nicknamed Bologna *la Grassa*—Bologna the Abundant.

Ristorante Diana is one of Bologna's most popular, a triumph in a city where people eat exceptionally well at home and demand the best when dining out. The restaurant flourishes under the direction of manager Athos degli Esposti. He seems to be everywhere at once: orchestrating the arrangement of tables outside on the veranda; and supervising displays of appetizers and cold entrées, amid the regional rustic décor characteristic of Bologna.

Diners come to Ristorante Diana from all over the world, drawn by the informality and unpretentiousness, but mostly by the regional specialties. Hearty minestrone Freddo is one of the most sought-after first courses or light luncheon dishes in the summer. Pasta comes in a variety of indigenous forms, but the undisputed trinity is tagliatelle, tortellini and lasagne. Among Ristorante Diana's most favored pastas is its Lasagne Verde with Ragù alla Bolognese. Ragù, a robust sauce of pancetta, beef, vegetables and tomatoes, is such an important part of the city's cuisine that frequently a dish described as *alla Bolognese* simply means sauced with ragù.

The restaurant's dessert menu offers a selection of final temptations that ranges from simple fruits in season to the Torte di Riso, a cakelike delicacy of rice and almonds lightly sprinkled with liqueur.

Remove ½ cup liquid from soup and blend with flour in small bowl until smooth. Stir into soup. Add mushrooms and sautéed vegetables, stirring constantly. Add seasoning to taste. Allow to simmer an additional 15 minutes, stirring frequently.

CHINESE-STYLE MUSHROOM EGG DROP SOUP

SALADALLEY
PHILADELPHIA, PENNSYLVANIA

"I love my new home in Florida, but I will certainly miss Philadelphia for the best soup I've ever tasted—chicken egg drop mushroom with bean sprouts and scallions."
—*Penny Kay, Fort Lauderdale, Florida*

8 to 10 servings

- 1½ **quarts chicken stock***
- 6 **ounces fresh mushrooms, sliced**
- 3 **ounces fresh spinach, coarsely shredded or chopped**
- 1 **to 2 slices fresh ginger, peeled and minced**
- 1 **to 2 garlic cloves, minced**
- 2 **tablespoons plus 2 teaspoons soy sauce**
- ½ **teaspoon sugar**
- ⅛ **teaspoon freshly ground pepper**
- ⅛ **teaspoon crushed red pepper**

- ¼ **cup dry sherry**
- 2 **tablespoons cornstarch**
- 2 **ounces vermicelli, cooked and drained**
- 1 **egg, lightly beaten**
- 1 **tablespoon sesame oil**
- ½ **pound fresh bean sprouts**
- ½ **bunch green onions, chopped**

Bring stock to boil in large pot over high heat. Reduce heat, add next 8 ingredients and simmer about 30 minutes.

Mix sherry and cornstarch in measuring cup to form a thin paste. Set aside.

Ten minutes before serving, bring soup to boil. Stir cornstarch mixture to remove any lumps. Blend into soup in slow steady stream. Cook soup, stirring constantly, until clear and slightly thickened. Stir in vermicelli. Remove from heat.

Pour in egg slowly, then stir gently with fork until egg forms light strands. Stir in sesame oil. Divide bean sprouts and green onion among soup bowls and ladle hot soup over.

*Saladalley uses mushroom stock for a vegetarian version of this soup.

CREME DE PETITS POIS

DOMAINE CHANDON
YOUNTVILLE, CALIFORNIA

10 to 12 servings

     3 to 4 cups chicken stock
     2 pounds unshelled fresh peas, well
       washed, strings removed, or 2½ to
       3 pounds frozen peas
       Small piece uncooked bacon or bacon
       rind (optional)
     2 cups whipping cream
     ¼ cup (½ stick) unsalted butter, cut
       into pieces
       Salt

Bring stock to boil in large saucepan over medium-high heat. Add unshelled or frozen peas and bacon and cook until very soft. Drain off most of liquid, reserving some for thinning soup, if necessary. Press mixture through fine sieve or food mill. Transfer puree to saucepan and cook gently until heated through. Remove from heat and add cream and butter, stirring until butter is melted. Taste and season with salt if desired. Serve immediately.

CREAM OF VEGETABLE SOUP

LE CELLIER
SANTA MONICA, CALIFORNIA

6 to 8 servings

     ¾ cup (1½ sticks) butter
     ¾ cup diced onion
    1½ cups diced potato
     ¾ cup peeled diced tomato
     ¾ cup diced carrot
     ¾ cup diced green beans
     ¾ cup coarsely chopped broccoli
     ¾ cup minced leek
     ¾ cup minced zucchini
     1 garlic clove, minced
    1½ teaspoons sugar or to taste
       Salt and freshly ground pepper to taste

    1½ quarts (6 cups) chicken stock

     ½ cup whipping cream
       Chopped parsley (garnish)

Melt butter in large stockpot over medium-high heat. Add onion and sauté 1 to 2 minutes. Reduce heat to low and add remaining ingredients except stock, cream and parsley. Cook until vegetables are soft but not browned, about 20 to 25 minutes.

Add stock and bring to boil over medium-high heat. Reduce heat; simmer about 10 minutes. Remove from heat and cool slightly.

Transfer to blender or processor in batches and puree until smooth. Taste and adjust seasoning. Return to stockpot, place over medium heat and gradually stir in cream. Heat through but do not boil. Garnish each serving with parsley.

SUMMER SQUASH SOUP

GREYLOGS
CAESAR'S HEAD, SOUTH CAROLINA

8 servings

     ¼ cup (½ stick) butter
     2 tablespoons vegetable oil
     1 large onion, minced
     2 garlic cloves, minced
     3 pounds crookneck squash, thinly sliced
    3½ to 4 cups chicken stock (homemade
       preferred)
     1 cup half and half
    1½ teaspoons salt
     ½ teaspoon freshly ground white pepper
     8 thin slices crookneck squash (garnish)
       Minced fresh parsley (garnish)

Heat butter and oil in large pan over medium-high heat. Add onion and garlic and sauté until translucent and soft. Add squash and chicken stock. Simmer until squash is tender. Transfer in batches to blender, adding a little half and half to each batch, and blend until smooth. Stir in salt and pepper, and more half and half if needed (soup should be fairly thick). Serve hot or chilled topped with squash slice and minced parsley garnish.

TOMATO BISQUE

WESTIN GALLERIA HOTEL
HOUSTON, TEXAS

"One of the most glorious soups I have ever tasted."
    —Mrs. Wallace D. Mackenzie, Glencoe, Illinois

8 to 10 servings

     ¼ pound bacon
     4 large garlic cloves, minced
    1½ onions, finely chopped
     6 celery stalks, finely chopped
     1 bay leaf
     1 teaspoon thyme
     1 28-ounce can tomatoes, diced
       (reserve juice)
     1 6-ounce can tomato paste

     2 tablespoons (¼ stick) butter
     3 tablespoons flour
     1 quart whipping cream, room
       temperature
     ½ onion, finely chopped
     1 small bay leaf
     2 whole cloves
       Salt and freshly ground pepper

Cook bacon in large skillet until fat is rendered; remove meat (use as desired). Add garlic to fat and sauté until lightly browned. Add 1½ chopped onions, celery, bay leaf and thyme and sauté until onion is translucent. Add tomatoes with juice and tomato paste and bring to boil, stirring occasionally. Reduce heat, cover and simmer 30 minutes.

Heat butter in large saucepan. Stir in flour and bring to boil, stirring constantly. Remove from heat and slowly add cream, then next 3 ingredients. Place over medium heat and cook, uncovered, 45 minutes, stirring occasionally. Strain through fine strainer into tomato mixture. Add salt and pepper to taste. Cover and simmer, stirring occasionally, about 15 minutes. Stir in a little milk if thinner consistency is preferred.

ORANGE AND TOMATO SOUP

DUNAIN PARK
INVERNESS, SCOTLAND

"We hesitated at first to try such an unusual sounding combination as Orange and Tomato Soup, but finally took the plunge—it was excellent."
  —Mrs. C. Guillon, Montreal, Quebec, Canada

6 servings

  4 medium onions, finely chopped
  1 medium potato, peeled and finely chopped
  4 garlic cloves, minced
  3 tablespoons (⅜ stick) butter
  1 16-ounce can tomatoes, chopped
  Juice and grated rind of 1 orange
  1 10-ounce can chicken broth

  ½ cup whipping cream
  Salt and pepper
  Sugar (optional)

In large saucepan, slowly sauté onions, chopped potato and garlic in butter. Add tomatoes, orange juice, orange rind and broth. Simmer 30 minutes.

Just before serving, add cream and season to taste with salt, pepper and a little sugar if desired.

SWISS CHARD SOUP

ANNE MENNA'S
FORT BRAGG, CALIFORNIA

"Last year my husband and I visited this quaint little place. . . . The cuisine was delightful, the hospitality and service, charming. The Swiss Chard Soup was out of this world."
  —Cheryl L. Kamins, Los Angeles, California

Makes about 2 quarts

  1 bunch Swiss chard, washed and dried
  ¼ cup (½ stick) butter
  3 celery stalks, thinly sliced
  1 large onion, thinly sliced
  1 large carrot, thinly sliced
  1 small leek, white part only, thinly sliced
  1 cup peeled and diced raw potato
  3 cups chicken stock

  1 cup half and half
  Salt
  White pepper
  Nutmeg
  Chervil
  Sour cream or crème fraîche (garnish)
  Chopped parsley (garnish)

Separate leaves from ribs of Swiss chard. Thinly slice ribs and set aside. Chop leaves and set aside. Heat butter in large saucepan over medium heat. Add celery, chard ribs, onion, carrot and leek and sauté until wilted. Add potato and stock, cover and simmer until vegetables are tender. Remove from heat and set aside to cool briefly.

Puree in small batches in blender, adding chopped chard leaves to last few batches. Return to pan and stir in half and half and seasonings to taste. Reheat but do not boil. To serve, pour into heated bowls and garnish with sour cream or crème fraîche and chopped parsley.

NORTHUMBERLAND BREAD SOUP

TEN DOWNING
SAN DIEGO, CALIFORNIA

8 servings

  1 1-pound loaf of bread (white or sourdough), broken into pieces
  2½ quarts chicken stock
  2 large carrots, coarsely chopped
  2 celery stalks, coarsely chopped
  1 large onion, coarsely chopped
  1 parsnip, coarsely chopped
  1 white turnip, coarsely chopped
  ¼ cup (½ stick) butter
  ½ cup all purpose flour
  Salt and freshly ground white pepper

  1 cup whipping cream
  1 cup milk

Soak bread in 2 quarts chicken stock in large stockpot until bread is soft. Add vegetables and bring to boil. Reduce heat and simmer until tender, stirring often to prevent sticking. Let cool.

Puree in batches in blender (soup can be refrigerated at this point until ready for use).

Melt butter in small saucepan over low heat. Add flour and cook 2 to 3 minutes without browning. Add salt and pepper. Return pureed mixture to stockpot with remaining 2 cups chicken stock and bring to boil. Add roux and cook until soup thickens and is creamy, stirring occasionally.

Just before serving, add cream and milk and heat through but do not let soup return to boil. Adjust seasoning if necessary.

WATERCRESS SOUP

THE HOLE IN THE WALL
BATH, ENGLAND

12 servings

    3 cups (4 bunches) washed and finely
        chopped watercress
    3 cups thinly sliced potatoes
 1¾ cups chopped onion
    1 teaspoon minced garlic cloves
    2 cups chicken stock

    2 cups milk
    1 cup heavy cream
    1 tablespoon salt
    1 teaspoon freshly ground pepper

In 4-quart saucepan, mix watercress, potatoes, onion and garlic with stock. Bring to boil, cover and simmer gently until vegetables are tender, about 30 minutes. Puree in blender and then press through medium sieve.

Return puree to pot. Add milk, cream, salt and pepper and reheat; do not boil. If soup is too thick, thin with more milk. Adjust seasonings if necessary.

BISQUE OF SQUASH-APPLE

ASA RANSOM HOUSE
CLARENCE, NEW YORK

"A most unusual soup . . . thick and very delicately flavored." —Adele R. Haas, Tonawanda, New York

6 to 8 servings

    4 cups chicken stock
    1 medium butternut squash, unpeeled,
        seeded and chopped
    2 large tart apples, peeled and chopped
    1 small onion, peeled and chopped
  ⅛ teaspoon rosemary

    6 tablespoons (¾ stick) butter
    6 tablespoons flour
  ¾ cup whipping cream or half and half
        Salt and pepper
        Diced apples (optional garnish)

Combine stock, squash, apples, onion and rosemary in 4-quart saucepan. Cover and simmer over low heat until squash is tender, about 10 to 15 minutes. Puree in blender or food processor; return to pan.

Melt butter in 1-quart saucepan. Stir in flour and cook 2 to 3 minutes over medium heat, stirring constantly. Stir into squash puree; simmer, uncovered, 15 minutes over low heat. Add cream and season with salt and pepper to taste. Pour into serving bowls and sprinkle with diced apple.

HOT APPLE SOUP

PETRI'S RESTAURANT
NAPA, CALIFORNIA

6 to 8 servings

    1 tablespoon butter
    1 large onion, chopped
    1 quart (4 cups) chicken stock
    2 large green apples, cored, peeled and
        chopped
  ¾ teaspoon curry powder or to taste
        Juice of ½ large lemon

    3 tablespoons (⅜ stick) butter
  ¼ cup all purpose flour

  ½ cup half and half

Melt 1 tablespoon butter in large saucepan over medium-high heat. Add onion and sauté until soft but not brown. Stir in stock, apples, curry powder and lemon juice and bring to boil. Reduce heat and simmer for about 10 minutes.

Melt remaining butter in another large saucepan over medium heat until foam subsides. Blend in flour and cook 1 to 2 minutes, stirring constantly. Gradually stir in soup until well blended. When mixture reaches boiling point, remove from heat.

Strain into first saucepan, pressing apple and onion with back of spoon. Stir in half and half. Cook just until heated through. Taste and adjust seasoning.

CHILLED CREAM OF ALMOND SOUP

THE BROWNSTONE
LOS ANGELES, CALIFORNIA

12 servings

    5 tablespoons (⅝ stick) butter
    2 teaspoons chopped shallots
    2 teaspoons salt
    2 teaspoons white pepper

    2 quarts chicken broth
  ¾ cup blanched almonds

    1 quart half and half
    1 quart whipping cream
  ½ cup white wine
    1 tablespoon almond extract
        Finely sliced almonds (garnish)

Melt butter in large pot and sauté shallots with salt and pepper until shallots are soft, 8 to 10 minutes.

Add chicken broth and almonds and bring to full rolling boil. Add half and half, cream, wine and almond extract and cook over medium heat for 15 minutes. Cool and strain. Serve chilled with sprinkling of finely sliced almonds.

COLD CUCUMBER AND SPINACH SOUP

AU RELAIS
SONOMA, CALIFORNIA

4 servings

    2 tablespoons (¼ stick) butter
    1 onion, coarsely chopped
    1 large potato, peeled and coarsely
       chopped
    1 leek with 2 inches of green, split,
       washed thoroughly and coarsely
       chopped
    3 cups chicken stock
    3 sprigs fresh parsley
       Salt and freshly ground pepper

    2 cucumbers, peeled, seeded and
       coarsely chopped
    ½ bunch (about 5 ounces) spinach,
       blanched and chopped
    ½ cup sour cream
    1 tablespoon mayonnaise
    1 teaspoon horseradish
       Juice of 2 lemons
       Dash hot pepper sauce
    1 avocado (garnish)

Melt butter in large saucepan over medium heat. Add onion, potato and leek. Reduce heat, cover and cook about 5 minutes. Add chicken stock, parsley, salt and pepper to taste and bring to boil. Reduce heat and simmer 20 minutes. Let cool, then puree in blender until smooth. Chill thoroughly.

Add remaining ingredients except avocado and puree until smooth. Chill. Taste and adjust seasoning. Just before serving, peel, seed and dice avocado and stir into soup.

BILI-BI FROID
(Cold Mussel Soup)

THE JOCKEY CLUB
WASHINGTON, D.C.

4 servings

    ½ cup (1 stick) butter
    ½ cup all purpose flour

    2 large shallots, finely chopped
    1 cup dry white wine
    ½ cup finely chopped parsley
    ⅛ teaspoon freshly ground white pepper
   38 small fresh mussels (about 2½ pounds),
       cleaned and debearded

    4 cups (1 quart) whipping cream
       Salt and freshly ground pepper

       Worcestershire sauce

Melt ¼ cup butter in small saucepan over low heat. Remove from heat and whisk in flour. Return to low heat and cook, stirring constantly, until roux is light brown, about 8 minutes. Set aside.

Combine shallots, wine, parsley, remaining butter and white pepper in 6-quart saucepan and bring to boil over medium-high heat. Add mussels, cover and cook, shaking pan occasionally until mussels open. (Discard any mussels that do not open.) Transfer mussels to bowl using slotted spoon. Cover and refrigerate.

Place cooking liquid over medium-high heat and reduce to 2 cups. Blend in 1 teaspoon roux (refrigerate remainder for future use). Reduce heat to medium-low, add cream and cook about 30 minutes (do not overcook or broth will become too dark). Add salt and pepper to taste. Strain soup into large bowl. Cover and refrigerate.

Just before serving, transfer mussels to bowls. Taste soup and adjust seasoning, adding Worcestershire sauce to taste. Ladle over mussels and serve.

CREAM OF APPLE AND TURNIP SOUP WITH SHERRY

THE RED LION INN
STOCKBRIDGE, MASSACHUSETTS

6 servings

    4 cups chicken stock or broth
    1 small butternut squash (about 1
       pound), peeled, seeded and coarsely
       chopped
    2 tart green apples, peeled and
       coarsely chopped
    1 medium onion, coarsely chopped
    1 small turnip, peeled and chopped
   1½ teaspoons salt
    ¼ teaspoon freshly ground pepper
       Pinch rosemary

    2 large egg yolks
    ¼ cup whipping cream
    2 tablespoons sherry

Combine stock, squash, apples, onion, turnip and seasonings in 4-quart saucepan and bring to boil over high heat. Cover and simmer until vegetables are soft, about 45 minutes. Transfer to large bowl and allow to cool slightly. Puree in batches, using food processor or blender; return to saucepan.

Beat yolks and cream with whisk in small bowl. Gradually add about 1 cup puree. Stir into remaining soup. Add sherry and reheat but do not boil. Pour into heated bowls and serve immediately.

GAZPACHO

EL FARO RESTAURANT
NEW YORK, NEW YORK

6 servings

- 2 large ripe tomatoes, peeled
- ½ medium red onion, peeled
- ¾ medium white Spanish onion, peeled
- ¾ medium cucumber, peeled
- 1 green pepper, seeded
- 1 clove garlic, mashed
- 1½ cups tomato juice
- 1 tablespoon paprika
- 1 teaspoon salt
- ¼ cup olive oil
- 4 cups cold water
- 1 cup breadcrumbs
- ½ cup each: chopped green onions, small cubes of green pepper and cucumber (garnish)

Cut first 5 ingredients into large chunks; place in blender or food processor with garlic and liquefy. Pour into large bowl. Add tomato juice, paprika, salt, olive oil, water and breadcrumbs. Stir to blend. Add chopped green onions and small chunks of cucumber and green pepper for garnish. Cover and chill well. Serve very cold.

PEACH SOUP

NINTH STREET HOUSE
PADUCAH, KENTUCKY

"Especially memorable was the Peach Soup, served plain as a first course, or spooned over pound cake and garnished with fresh blueberries and cream as a lovely dessert."

—Mrs. Alan K. Chester, Baldwin, New York

6 to 8 servings

- 1 cup water
- ¼ cup sugar
- 1 teaspoon whole cloves
- 1 cinnamon stick
- 1½ tablespoons arrowroot dissolved in 2 cups dry white wine
- 2½ pounds frozen peaches, defrosted, undrained and pureed

Combine first 4 ingredients in medium saucepan and bring to boil over medium-high heat. Reduce heat, cover and simmer 30 minutes. Strain and return to pan. Dissolve arrowroot in wine and blend thoroughly into syrup. Bring to boil, stirring occasionally. Let cool, then add pureed peaches. Chill well. Ladle into bowls and serve.

CANTALOUPE SOUP

THE CASTLE RESTAURANT
LEICESTER, MASSACHUSETTS

"A cold soup with orange juice, cantaloupe, honey and cinnamon. It is a very original combination."
—Nita B. Dowd, Worcester, Massachusetts

8 to 10 servings

- 4 ripe small cantaloupes, peeled, seeded and cut into 1-inch chunks
- 1 6-ounce can orange juice concentrate
- 1 cup honey*
- ½ to 1 teaspoon cinnamon
- ½ pint (1 cup) whipping cream
- ½ cup Calvados
  Mint sprigs (garnish)

Puree cantaloupe in blender or processor until smooth. Stir in remaining ingredients except mint and mix well. Chill thoroughly. Serve in chilled stemmed glasses or glass bowls and garnish with mint sprigs.

*Decrease honey if cantaloupes are very sweet.

ICED PARSLEY SOUP

BERNARD'S
BOYNTON BEACH, FLORIDA

8 servings

- 3 leeks, finely chopped
- 2 medium onions, finely chopped
- 2 tablespoons (¼ stick) butter

- ½ bay leaf
- 3 cups chicken broth
- 5 medium potatoes, peeled and sliced
- 1 tablespoon salt

- 3 cups heavy cream
- 1 tablespoon Worcestershire sauce
  Salt and pepper

- 2 cups chopped parsley
- 1 cup chicken broth

In 3- or 4-quart pan, sauté leeks and onions in butter until translucent. Add bay leaf, 3 cups chicken broth, potatoes and salt. Cover and simmer 35 to 40 minutes. Press through fine sieve or puree in batches in food processor or blender. Chill well.

When cold, stir in cream. Season with Worcestershire sauce and salt and pepper to taste.

Puree parsley with remaining 1 cup chicken broth in blender. Stir into soup. Chill until ready to serve.

RUM AND PLUM POT

SALISHAN LODGE
GLENEDEN BEACH, OREGON

6 to 8 servings

    1 quart (4 cups) water
    1 cup sugar
    ½ teaspoon vanilla
    ½ teaspoon cinnamon
    ½ teaspoon ground allspice
    1 pound fresh plums (about 6 small),
       halved and pitted

    2 cups Demerara rum or to taste
       Lemon wedges (garnish)

Combine water, sugar, vanilla, cinnamon and all-spice in 3-quart saucepan and bring to boil over high heat. Add plum halves, reduce heat and simmer until plums are tender, about 5 minutes. Let cool. Refrigerate until thoroughly chilled.

Transfer mixture to blender in batches and puree. Pour into serving bowl. Add rum to taste. Cover and chill at least 24 hours. Ladle into bowls and garnish with lemon wedges.

COLD APPLE SOUP

TWIGS, THE CAPITAL HILTON
WASHINGTON, D.C.

Makes about 3 quarts

    8 apples
    2 cups apple juice
       Juice of 2 lemons
    1 tablespoon sugar or to taste
    1 cinnamon stick
    ½ teaspoon vanilla

    2 cups orange juice
    2 cups whipping cream
    3 tablespoons Cointreau or Triple Sec

Peel, core and quarter 6 apples. Combine with apple juice, lemon juice, sugar, cinnamon stick and vanilla in large saucepan. Cover and cook over medium heat until apples are very soft, about 20 minutes. Let cool, then cover and refrigerate 24 hours.

Remove cinnamon stick. Add orange juice and whipping cream to apples and puree in batches in blender until smooth. Pour into chilled tureen. Shred remaining 2 apples (unpeeled) and stir into soup along with liqueur. Serve immediately.

STRAWBERRY SOUP

FOUR AMBASSADORS
MIAMI, FLORIDA

Makes 1½ quarts

    1½ cups water
    ¾   cup light-bodied red wine
    ½   cup sugar
    2   tablespoons fresh lemon juice
    1   stick cinnamon
    1   quart strawberries, stemmed and pureed

    ½   cup whipping cream
    ¼   cup sour cream

Combine water, wine, sugar, lemon juice and cinnamon in 3- to 4-quart saucepan and boil, uncovered, 15 minutes, stirring occasionally. Add strawberry puree and boil, stirring frequently, 10 minutes more. Discard cinnamon stick and cool.

Whip cream. Combine with sour cream and fold into strawberry mixture. Serve at cool room temperature.

COLD MELON SOUP

CHILLINGSWORTH
BREWSTER, MASSACHUSETTS

6 to 8 servings

    3 cups coarsely chopped ripe cantaloupe melon
    3 cups coarsely chopped ripe honeydew melon

    2 cups fresh orange juice
    ⅓ cup fresh lime juice
    3 tablespoons honey
    2 cups dry champagne

    1 cup whipping cream
       Fresh mint leaves (garnish)

Finely chop 1½ cups each of cantaloupe and honeydew melons. Set aside.

Place remaining coarsely chopped melons in blender with orange juice, lime juice and honey, and puree (this will take only a few seconds). Pour into large bowl. Stir in champagne and reserved melon. Cover and refrigerate until ready to serve.

Pour into iced bowls. Whip cream and use as garnish with fresh mint leaves.

SALAD BOWL

For years, salads were considered by many people to be nothing more than edible plate decoration—something to occupy the mind and fork during the long wait between the appetizer and the main course. But the recent trend toward lighter, fresher meals has given salads a new prominence in the gastronomic world. Today, the salad is not only an important part of most meals; it is often the *whole* meal. And in order to please an increasingly diet-conscious clientele, chefs are constantly coming up with new combinations of vegetables, fruits and other ingredients—fresh, cooked or marinated, simple or complex, plain or tossed with any one of a staggering array of dressings.

Whether you like yours before the meal, as a side dish or in lieu of dessert, it is the dressing that makes the salad. Originally, salads were simply raw leaf vegetables lightly sprinkled with salt (from the Latin word *sal*, or salt—hence the name). As French *haute cuisine* developed in the eighteenth and nineteenth centuries, hard-and-fast rules were laid down concerning salad dressings. Almost all cold salads were dressed with a vinaigrette, simply olive oil and wine vinegar with a few herbs and possibly a bit of shallot added. It never varied, and while in some cases a mayonnaise dressing or a plain mustard cream might be substituted, anything more exotic was frowned upon.

That has changed, and most would agree that the change is for the better. The influence of a wide range of ethnic cuisines, together with the ready availability of all sorts of herbs, spices, flavored vinegars and other ingredients, has led to constant experimentation with salad dressings. Today almost no two restaurants' house dressings are the same—certainly a plus for the adventurous diner.

Even if you do not follow Voltaire's advice to cultivate your own garden, the secret of any successful salad is to use only the best—and freshest—ingredients. Then all you need is a little imagination.

Spinach Salad Flambé from the Prince of Wales Grille at the Hotel del Coronado in San Diego (see page 56).

ALANI CHICKEN SALAD

LEHR'S GREENHOUSE RESTAURANT
SAN FRANCISCO, CALIFORNIA

8 servings

  3 cups diced cooked chicken
  ¾ cup mayonnaise
  1 cup finely diced celery
    Salt and white pepper
  8 medium tomatoes
    Crisp lettuce leaves
    Asparagus tips, carrot sticks, fresh
    pineapple slices, halved hard-cooked
    eggs and ripe olives (garnishes)

    Macadamia Rum Dressing*
  ¼ cup chopped macadamian nuts

Mix chicken with ¼ cup mayonnaise; chill about 2 hours. Toss chicken with remaining mayonnaise and celery. Season to taste with salt and pepper. Cut each tomato about ¾ through into 6 equal sections. Fill each with chicken salad. Place in lettuce cup and garnish with asparagus tips, carrot sticks, pineapple slices, eggs and olives.

Just before serving, pour Macadamia Rum Dressing over and top with macadamian nuts.

Macadamia Rum Dressing

Makes 1 cup

  ¼ cup pineapple juice
  ¾ cup mayonnaise
  1 teaspoon rum extract

Combine all dressing ingredients. Mix well and chill.

ORIENT EXPRESS CHICKEN SALAD

ORIENT EXPRESS
SAN FRANCISCO, CALIFORNIA

"When business travels take me to San Francisco, I try to find time for lunch at a lively Middle Eastern-style restaurant called the Orient Express. They prepare a creamy chicken salad that is very unusual."
—Jerold King, Tucson, Arizona

6 to 8 servings

  1 quart chicken stock
  3 whole chicken breasts, split

  ⅓ cup raisins
  ¾ cup mayonnaise
  ¾ cup sour cream
  2 apples, cored and diced
  1 cup diced celery heart
  1 cup slivered almonds, toasted
  1 bunch parsley, finely chopped
    Juice of 1 lemon
    Salt and freshly ground pepper

  1 head butter lettuce, separated into leaves
  1 tomato, thinly sliced
  ¼ cup (about) Vinaigrette (page 60)

Bring stock to boil. Add chicken breasts, reduce heat and poach until chicken is just cooked, about 10 minutes. Remove and let cool; reserve stock for another use. Discard bones and skin; cut meat into ½-inch pieces.

Plump raisins in warm water about 20 minutes. Combine chicken, mayonnaise, sour cream, apples, celery, almonds, raisins, parsley and lemon juice. Season with salt and pepper to taste. Cover and refrigerate until ready to serve.

Arrange lettuce and tomato on platter. Top with salad and sprinkle with Vinaigrette.

SALADE LANGOUSTINE

RESTAURANT BOCUSE
LYONS, FRANCE

4 servings

  8 cups (2 quarts) water
  1 sprig thyme
  1 sprig tarragon
    Pinch salt
  20 large langoustine or shrimp

Sauce

  ¾ cup whipping cream
  2 tablespoons Dijon mustard
  1 tablespoon catsup
  1 tablespoon minced fresh tarragon
  1 tablespoon minced fresh chives
  1½ teaspoons Worcestershire sauce
    Juice of ½ lemon
    Salt and freshly ground pepper

Vinaigrette

  3 tablespoons vinegar
  2 tablespoons Dijon mustard
    Salt and freshly ground pepper
  ½ cup plus 1 tablespoon olive oil or walnut oil

  4 artichoke bottoms, poached and quartered
  32 very thin green beans, blanched and halved
  8 large mushrooms (stems removed), cut julienne

  12 tender inner leaves of butter lettuce
  16 Belgian endive leaves
  16 snow peas, blanched
  12 avocado slices
  20 tomato slices
  16 red apple slices
  8 shrimp heads (optional garnish)

Combine water, thyme, tarragon and salt in large saucepan and bring to simmer over low heat. Add shrimp and cook until just pink, about 1 to 2 minutes. Drain shrimp immediately; let cool. Peel shrimp, leaving tails intact, devein and set aside.

For sauce: Combine all ingredients in large bowl. Blend in shrimp.

For vinaigrette: Combine vinegar, mustard, salt and pepper to taste in small bowl. Whisk in oil until well blended.

Combine artichoke pieces and ½ of vinaigrette in medium bowl and mix well. Combine green beans and mushrooms in another medium bowl and toss with remaining vinaigrette.

To assemble: For each serving, place 3 lettuce leaves in center of plate. Line 5 shrimp down center of leaves, overlapping slightly and with tails facing same direction. Arrange 4 endive leaves with yellow points outward at upper left of plate. Arrange 1 snow pea in center of each endive leaf. Place 3 overlapping slices of avocado at lower left of plate. Mound 4 artichoke wedges at top of plate. Arrange ¼ of green bean and mushroom mixture at upper right. Overlap 5 tomato slices at lower right. Place 4 apple slices, overlapping, at bottom of plate. Garnish each plate with 2 shrimp heads, if desired.

APPLE TREE MARINATED VEGETABLE SALAD

THE APPLE TREE
XENIA, OHIO

"I would love to use this recipe for buffets and dinner parties since it could be served as a salad or vegetable dish. A small portion in my refrigerator would also make a scrumptious and low calorie snack."
—Linda Stoner, Dayton, Ohio

8 servings

Dressing

    2 cups vegetable oil
    1 cup white vinegar
    ½ cup wine vinegar
    ½ cup lemon juice
    ¼ cup salt or to taste
    1 teaspoon oregano
    1 teaspoon dry mustard
    1 teaspoon dehydrated onion
    1 teaspoon granulated garlic
    ½ teaspoon anise seeds

Salad

    4 cups sliced zucchini (about 4 small zucchini)
    2 cups sliced yellow squash (about 2 small squash)
    2 cups broccoli florets and chopped stems (about ¼ bunch)
    1½ cups bite-sized cauliflower florets (about ¼ head)
    1 cup sliced carrots (about 2 small carrots)
    1 cup sliced red onion (about 1 medium onion)
    1 cup halved cherry tomatoes

For dressing: Combine ingredients in large jar and mix well.

For salad: Combine vegetables in large bowl. Pour approximately 2 cups dressing over vegetables and refrigerate several hours before serving, stirring occasionally.

Store remaining dressing in refrigerator.

CARROT JALAPENO MARINADE

THE ANNEX
SAN DIEGO, CALIFORNIA

Makes about 6 cups

    12 large carrots, peeled and sliced diagonally into ½-inch chunks
       Ice cubes
    1 12-ounce can whole jalapeño peppers, rinsed
    2 large onions, thinly sliced
    1 cup oil
    1 cup white distilled vinegar
    1 teaspoon salt

Place carrots in large bowl, cover with hot water (140°F to 160°F) and let stand about 30 minutes. Drain and plunge into cold water, add a few ice cubes and let stand 15 to 20 minutes.

Combine jalapeños with remaining ingredients. Drain carrots and add to mixture. Cover and refrigerate.

Marinade improves with age and will keep in refrigerator up to 4 months.

RAITA

INDIAN OVEN
NEW YORK, NEW YORK

6 to 8 servings

    1 cup plain yogurt
    ½ cup sour cream
    2 tomatoes, diced
    1 medium cucumber, diced
    ½ small onion, diced
    1 teaspoon cumin seeds
    1 garlic clove, minced
    ½ teaspoon salt
    ¼ teaspoon freshly ground pepper
    ⅛ to ¼ teaspoon red pepper
       Cilantro (garnish)

Mix yogurt and sour cream with fork in medium bowl until smooth. Add remaining ingredients except cilantro and blend well. Chill. Garnish with cilantro just before serving.

GREEK SALAD

TA-BOO RESTAURANT
PALM BEACH, FLORIDA

8 servings

 1 medium head iceberg lettuce
 1 large head romaine lettuce
 1 medium head escarole
 3 large ripe tomatoes, cut into wedges
 1 large Spanish onion, thinly sliced
 2 green peppers, thinly sliced
24 Greek olives (calamatas)
24 Greek peppers (peperoncini)
 ½ pound feta cheese, crumbled
16 anchovy fillets
 8 hard-cooked eggs, sliced
 8 small radishes (optional)
   Greek Salad Dressing*

Tear crisp, cold salad greens into bite-sized pieces. Place in large salad bowl and toss to combine. Add remaining ingredients and toss. Serve on chilled salad plates.

Greek Salad Dressing

Makes 2 cups

 ½ cup red wine vinegar
 1 teaspoon salt
 ¼ teaspoon freshly ground black pepper
 ½ teaspoon sugar
 1½ teaspoons dry mustard
 1½ teaspoons oregano leaves
 ½ minced garlic clove
 ½ teaspoon lemon juice
 1½ cups olive oil

Mix all ingredients except olive oil. Let stand 15 minutes to allow flavors to blend. Add oil gradually and mix well.

BLACKHAWK SALAD BOWL

BLACKHAWK RESTAURANT
CHICAGO, ILLINOIS

"It is served with all the dinner entrees, and the waiter spins the salad right at the table."
—Marilyn McClory, Westmont, Illinois

6 to 8 servings

 1 3-ounce package cream cheese, room temperature
 3 ounces bleu cheese, crumbled
 5 to 6 tablespoons water

 1 egg
 1 tablespoon plus 1½ teaspoons fresh lemon juice
 1 cup vegetable oil
 ¼ cup red wine vinegar
 2 tablespoons mayonnaise
 2 tablespoons chopped chives

 1 tablespoon sugar
 1½ teaspoons Worcestershire sauce
 ¾ teaspoon paprika
 ¾ teaspoon salt
 ½ garlic clove, crushed
 ¼ teaspoon prepared hot mustard
 ¼ teaspoon white pepper

 8 cups torn salad greens
 1 hard-cooked egg, chopped
   Seasoned salt
   Freshly ground pepper
 8 anchovy fillets (garnish)

Beat cheeses in small bowl until smooth. Beat in water 1 tablespoon at a time until mixture is pourable. Set aside.

Combine egg, lemon juice and ¼ cup oil in blender and mix on medium speed 15 seconds. Increase speed to high and add remaining oil in slow steady stream, stopping occasionally to scrape down sides of container. Add vinegar, mayonnaise, chives, sugar, Worcestershire sauce, paprika, salt, garlic, mustard and white pepper and blend until smooth.

Combine salad greens in large bowl with enough dressing to coat. Sprinkle with hard-cooked egg and seasoned salt and toss gently. Add 2 to 3 tablespoons cheese mixture and pepper to taste and toss again. Garnish with anchovies.

Remaining dressing and cheese mixture can be covered and refrigerated for up to 2 weeks.

SALADE CHAMPENOISE

DOMAINE CHANDON
YOUNTVILLE, CALIFORNIA

A simple, rustic dish that is a favorite in France's Champagne region and is one of the most popular salads served at Domaine Chandon.

8 servings

 2 pounds potatoes, freshly cooked, peeled and thinly sliced
 1½ pounds green beans, cooked crisp-tender, drained and cut into 3- to 4-inch slices
 1 small can anchovies, drained and cut into 1-inch slices
   Green and black olives
 4 eggs, hard-cooked and sliced
   Fresh lemon juice
 ½ bottle Vinaigrette Champagne*

Line bottom of large glass serving dish with ⅓ of potatoes. Top with ½ of beans, anchovies and olives. Repeat layering, ending with last ⅓ of potatoes. Garnish with sliced eggs and additional anchovies and olives, if desired. Sprinkle with lemon juice to taste. Pour wine over and serve immediately. Pass Vinaigrette separately.

*If possible, use Champagne vinegar and/or Champagne mustard to prepare vinaigrette.

CHAMPIGNONS A L'AIOLI

CAFE SHELBURNE
SHELBURNE, VERMONT

"For garlic fanciers everywhere."
— *Michele Wood, Woodbury, Connecticut*

6 to 8 servings

Marinade

- ½ **cup dry white wine**
- 1 **tablespoon fresh lemon juice**
- 1 **tablespoon olive oil**
- ½ **teaspoon Worcestershire sauce**
- 1 **bay leaf**
- ¼ **teaspoon salt**
- ¼ **teaspoon rosemary**
- ¼ **teaspoon sage**
- ¼ **teaspoon savory**
- ¼ **teaspoon thyme**
- ⅛ **teaspoon freshly ground pepper**

- 1½ **pounds fresh mushrooms, quartered**

Sauce Aïoli

- 6 to 8 **small garlic cloves**
- 3 **egg yolks**
- 1 **tablespoon Dijon mustard**
- 1 **tablespoon fresh lemon juice**
- ¼ **teaspoon salt**
- ⅛ **teaspoon freshly ground pepper**
- ½ **cup olive oil**

- **Butter lettuce leaves**
- **Chopped fresh parsley (garnish)**

For marinade: Whisk together ingredients in large bowl until thoroughly blended.

Stir in mushrooms, cover and marinate in refrigerator 24 hours, stirring occasionally.

For Sauce Aïoli: Place garlic in small heavy bowl or mortar and pound until mashed into very smooth paste. Stir in egg yolks, mustard, lemon juice, salt and pepper and blend well. Slowly add olive oil drop by drop, whisking constantly until sauce is consistency of heavy cream. Add remaining oil a little faster in a thin steady stream, whisking constantly until all oil is incorporated. Cover sauce and refrigerate until cold.

To serve, transfer mushrooms with slotted spoon to another large bowl and toss with cold aïoli. Spoon onto bed of chilled lettuce; garnish with parsley.

EDIBLE SALAD BOWL

THE CARSON CITY "NUGGET" STEAK HOUSE
CARSON CITY, NEVADA

Makes 24

- **Vegetable oil for deep frying**
- 24 **egg roll skins (about 6¾x6¾ inches)**

Pour oil into wok or deep fryer to depth of 3 inches and heat to 375°F. Lay 1 egg roll skin flat on surface of oil and press with ladle until completely submerged. Without removing ladle, fry skin until golden brown and crisp, about 1 to 2 minutes. Carefully remove from oil, slip ladle out and invert "bowl" onto paper towel to drain. Let cool completely. Repeat with remaining skins.

BERRY'S SALAD

BERRY'S
WINSTON-SALEM, NORTH CAROLINA

"I enjoyed a most unusual combination of fresh spinach and strawberries. This would be a cool spring luncheon surprise." — *Marsha Ball, Bowie, Maryland*

6 to 8 servings

- 2 **bunches fresh spinach, washed and dried**
- 1 **pint fresh strawberries, washed, hulled and halved**

- ½ **cup sugar**
- 2 **tablespoons sesame seeds**
- 1 **tablespoon poppy seeds**
- 1½ **teaspoons minced onion**
- ¼ **teaspoon Worcestershire sauce**
- ¼ **teaspoon paprika**
- ½ **cup vegetable oil**
- ¼ **cup cider vinegar**

Arrange spinach and strawberries attractively on individual serving plates.

Place next 6 ingredients in blender. With blender running, add oil and vinegar in slow steady stream until thoroughly mixed and thickened. Drizzle over strawberries and spinach and serve immediately.

SAUERKRAUT SALAD

THE CANTEEN RESTAURANT
CHITTENANGO, NEW YORK

"The Canteen Restaurant serves a variety of different relishes, but the one I especially liked was the Sauerkraut Salad. It would be terrific to take on a picnic or serve at a barbecue." — *Esther Kurak, Syracuse, New York*

6 to 8 servings

- 1 **cup sugar**
- ½ **cup vegetable oil**
- ¼ **cup white wine vinegar**
- 1 **cup chopped onion**
- 1 **cup chopped green pepper**
- 1 **cup chopped celery**
- ¼ **cup chopped pimiento**
- 2 **teaspoons caraway seeds**
- 5 **cups fresh sauerkraut, partially drained**

Combine sugar, oil and vinegar in deep bowl and stir until sugar dissolves. Blend in onion, pepper, celery, pimiento and caraway seeds. Add sauerkraut and toss to coat completely. Refrigerate overnight.

SPINACH SALAD FLAMBE

PRINCE OF WALES GRILLE, HOTEL DEL CORONADO
SAN DIEGO, CALIFORNIA

6 servings

  6 **12-ounce bunches of spinach, washed
     and dried thoroughly**
  6 **hard-cooked eggs, sliced**
  ¼ **teaspoon salt**
  ½ **teaspoon ground pepper**

12 **bacon strips, chopped and fried crisp**
  ¾ **cup bacon drippings**
  ½ **cup malt vinegar**
  ¼ **cup lemon juice**
  4 **teaspoons sugar**
  1 **teaspoon Worcestershire sauce**
1½ **ounces brandy (100 proof)**

Tear spinach into bite-sized pieces and place in large salad bowl. Add egg slices, salt and pepper.

Mix remaining ingredients except brandy in small saucepan and heat until very hot. Heat brandy briefly, add to saucepan and ignite. Pour flaming dressing over spinach and toss gently but thoroughly. Serve on warm salad plates.

SWEET AND SOUR SPINACH SALAD

D'AMICOS
MEDINA, OHIO

6 to 8 servings

  4 **egg yolks**
  1 **teaspoon dry mustard**
  1 **teaspoon salt**
  ¼ **teaspoon freshly ground white pepper**
  ½ **cup olive oil**
  ¼ **cup sugar**
  3 **tablespoons red wine vinegar
     Juice of ½ lemon**

  1 **large bunch spinach (stems discarded),
     torn into pieces**
12 **white mushrooms, thinly sliced**
  ¾ **cup cooked crumbled bacon (about
     ½ pound uncooked)**

Beat yolks in small bowl until light and lemon colored. Add mustard, salt and pepper and blend well. Whisking constantly, add oil drop by drop, then in slow steady stream, until thickened. Stir in sugar, vinegar and lemon juice and mix well.

Place spinach in large salad bowl. Add mushrooms, bacon and dressing and toss well.

SALADE PANACHEE WITH MUSTARD DRESSING

JARED'S
ASHEVILLE, NORTH CAROLINA

6 to 8 servings

  2 **heads salad bowl or other leafy lettuce,
     torn into pieces**
  ¼ **pound fresh mushrooms, sliced
     Mustard Dressing*
     Tomato slices, pitted black olives, cubed
     ham, chopped egg, capers (garnish)**

Toss lettuce, mushrooms and Mustard Dressing in large bowl until thoroughly mixed. Transfer to platter and top with garnishes.

Mustard Dressing

Makes about 2 cups

  3 **egg yolks**
2½ **tablespoons red wine vinegar**
  ¾ **teaspoon salt**
  ½ **teaspoon freshly ground white pepper**
  ½ **teaspoon garlic powder
     Pinch nutmeg**
1½ **cups olive or vegetable oil**
2½ **tablespoons hot Dijon mustard**
  1 **tablespoon finely chopped chives**
  1 **teaspoon bottled seasoning**

Rinse small bowl of electric mixer in hot water and dry thoroughly. Using medium speed, beat yolks, vinegar, salt, pepper, garlic powder and nutmeg. Increase speed to high and begin adding about ½ cup oil drop by drop, then add remainder in slow steady stream, beating until thickened. Stir in Dijon mustard, chopped chives and bottled seasoning. Taste and adjust seasoning.

ZUCCHINI SALAD

THE ELEGANT ATTIC
TAHOE CITY, CALIFORNIA

6 servings

  3 **medium zucchini, thinly sliced**
  ⅔ **cup cider vinegar**
  ½ **cup shredded green pepper**
  ½ **cup shredded celery**
  ½ **cup shredded yellow onion**
  ½ **cup sugar**
  ⅓ **cup oil**
  ¼ **cup Burgundy**
  2 **tablespoons red wine vinegar**
  1 **teaspoon salt**
  ½ **teaspoon freshly ground pepper**

Combine all ingredients in large bowl and mix thoroughly. Cover and refrigerate at least 6 hours before serving.

Salad will keep up to 2 weeks in refrigerator.

CAFE IN THE BARN RICE SALAD

CAFE IN THE BARN
SEEKONK, MASSACHUSETTS

4 to 6 servings

    4 cups cooked rice
    ½ cup diced green pepper
    2 tablespoons finely chopped green onion
    3 tablespoons finely chopped radishes
    ½ cup finely chopped celery
    ½ cup sweet pickle relish
    1 garlic clove, minced
    ¾ teaspoon nutmeg or to taste
    1 tablespoon curry or to taste
    ⅛ teaspoon cloves or to taste
    ¼ cup mayonnaise
      Salt

Combine all ingredients. Chill for 3 to 4 hours. Serve well chilled.

SUNOMONO

YAMATO
LOS ANGELES, CALIFORNIA

"Japanese food is a favorite of mine, and recently I was served a simple but delicious cucumber salad at Yamato. The dressing was light yet extremely flavorful."
    —Barbara Dixon, Marina del Rey, California

6 servings

    1 large cucumber, lightly peeled and
      thinly sliced
    ¾ teaspoon salt
    ¾ cup cider vinegar
    ½ cup sugar
      Lettuce leaves (optional)
      Tomato slices, crabmeat and tiny shrimp
      (garnish)

Sprinkle cucumber slices with salt. Allow to stand at room temperature 1 hour. Gently squeeze slices until soft and pliable.

Combine vinegar and sugar in small bowl, stirring until sugar dissolves. Add about half of vinegar mixture to cucumber and toss lightly; drain. Just before serving pour remaining vinegar mixture over cucumber. Divide among individual small bowls or, if desired, spoon onto lettuce leaves and garnish with sliced tomatoes, crab and shrimp.

JAPANESE NOODLE SALAD

WINDOWS ON THE WORLD
NEW YORK, NEW YORK

6 servings

    ½ ounce (about 6) dried Japanese
      mushrooms*
    8 ounces udon (Japanese noodles)*
    3 tablespoons sesame oil
    3 tablespoons Japanese soy sauce*
    1 tablespoon rice vinegar or to taste
    ¼ teaspoon crushed dried hot red
      pepper flakes
    2 tablespoons chopped green onion
    1 tablespoon chopped fresh cilantro
      (optional)

Soak mushrooms in warm water 1 hour. Squeeze to remove water; discard stems and thinly slice caps. Cook noodles in boiling salted water just until al dente. Drain and rinse with cold water. Combine mushrooms, oil, soy sauce, vinegar and peppers in same pan used for noodles and warm through over medium heat. Add noodles, toss to coat and cook just until heated. Garnish with green onion and cilantro, if desired.

*Available in oriental markets.

GERMAN SLAW

THE MEADOWS
MIDDLETOWN, OHIO

6 to 8 servings

    8 bacon slices, cut into small pieces

    3 tablespoons sugar
    1 teaspoon salt
    ½ teaspoon white pepper
    ⅛ teaspoon Beau Monde Seasoning
    ¼ cup wine vinegar
    ¾ cup water

    1 medium head cabbage, finely chopped
    ¼ cup minced onion (optional)
    ½ cup thinly sliced green or red bell pepper

Fry bacon slowly until crisp. Remove from drippings with slotted spoon and drain on paper towels.

Add sugar, salt, pepper and Beau Monde to bacon drippings and stir until dissolved. Add combined vinegar and water and cook slowly until dressing is slightly reduced, about 10 minutes.

Pour dressing over chopped cabbage and onion. Top with bacon and pepper strips.

FRESH FRUIT FANTASIA

NEIMAN-MARCUS

For each serving:

    1 large cup-shaped iceberg lettuce leaf

    2 sections grapefruit
    2 slices cantaloupe
    2 slices honeydew
    1 slice orange
    2 slices pineapple
    2 cubes watermelon or a few slices of
      plum, nectarine or peach
    3 fresh strawberries or cherries

      Poppy Seed Dressing*

Wash and dry lettuce leaf and tear in half lengthwise. Put halves inside each other to form cup.

Peel fruit. Place fruit into lettuce cup in order listed, starting with grapefruit and ending with 3 strawberries.

Top with Poppy Seed Dressing and garnish with additional strawberries if desired.

Note: Fresh Fruit Fantasia can be topped with raspberry ice or cottage cheese and served surrounded with banana bread sandwiches, grapes and parsley for garnish.

*Poppy Seed Dressing

Makes 4¼ cups

    1½ cups sugar
     2 teaspoons dry mustard
     2 teaspoons salt
     ⅔ cup vinegar
     3 tablespoons onion juice*
     2 cups salad oil
     3 tablespoons poppy seeds

Mix together sugar, mustard, salt and vinegar in blender. Add onion juice and blend thoroughly. With blender running, add oil slowly and continue blending until thick. Add poppy seeds and whirl for a few more seconds. Store covered in cool place or keep in refrigerator.

*To make onion juice, grate large white onion on fine side of grater, or chop it in blender, then strain.

AVOCADO SALAD DRESSING

J'S
SAN BERNARDINO, CALIFORNIA

Makes 6 cups

    2 avocados
      Juice of 2 lemons
    2 cups mayonnaise
    2 cups sour cream
    ½ onion, minced
    2 tablespoons honey
    2 tablespoons Worcestershire sauce
    1 garlic clove, minced
    ½ teaspoon salt

      Pinch cayenne pepper

Split avocados in half, remove seed, scoop out meat and mash with lemon juice. Add remaining ingredients and blend very well. Allow to mellow in refrigerator for at least one day.

CELERY SEED DRESSING

THE GOLDEN LAMB INN
LEBANON, OHIO

Makes about 2 cups

    ½ cup sugar
    1 tablespoon celery seeds
    1 teaspoon dry mustard
    1 teaspoon salt
    1 teaspoon grated onion
    1 cup salad oil
    ⅓ cup vinegar

Combine sugar, celery seeds, mustard, salt and onion in jar. Add small amount of oil and mix well. Then add vinegar and oil alternately, ending with oil. Shake well before serving.

CHEDDAR CHEESE DRESSING

THE PROUD POPOVER
BOSTON, MASSACHUSETTS

Makes 3 cups

    2 eggs
    2 teaspoons brown sugar
   1½ teaspoons salt
    1 teaspoon dry mustard
    1 teaspoon Worcestershire sauce
    1 teaspoon prepared horseradish
    2 cups salad oil
    ¼ cup vinegar
    ¼ cup fresh lemon juice

    ¼ pound cheddar cheese, grated
    3 green onions, finely chopped

Combine eggs, sugar, salt, mustard and Worcestershire sauce in mixing bowl and beat with electric mixer 2 to 3 minutes. Blend in horseradish. Very slowly pour in ½ cup oil, beating constantly. Mix in vinegar and lemon juice alternately with remaining oil and beat 2 to 3 minutes longer.

Transfer to blender and mix until creamy, 10 to 15 seconds. Do not allow to become as thick as mayonnaise.

Combine cheese and onion in medium bowl. Pour mixture over; blend well. Refrigerate before serving.

YELLOW BRICK BANK DRESSING

YELLOW BRICK BANK RESTAURANT
SHEPHERDSTOWN, WEST VIRGINIA

"House dressing is hardly a grand enough name for the tasty dilled salad dressing served at the Yellow Brick Bank." —Terri West, Beckley, West Virginia

Makes about 2½ cups

      2 cups olive oil
    ½ cup red wine vinegar
      1 egg
      2 garlic cloves, pressed
      2 teaspoons Dijon mustard
    ½ teaspoon dried oregano
    ½ teaspoon dried dill
        Salt and freshly ground pepper

Combine all ingredients in quart jar. Shake thoroughly. Chill 2 hours before serving.

KANPAI GINGER SALAD DRESSING

KANPAI JAPANESE RESTAURANT
PITTSBURGH, PENNSYLVANIA

Makes about 1½ cups

    ½ cup soy oil
    ¼ cup soy sauce
    ⅓ cup diced onion
    ¼ cup diced celery
      3 tablespoons plus 1 teaspoon rice vinegar
      2 tablespoons peeled, diced fresh ginger
      2 teaspoons sugar
  1½ teaspoons grated lemon rind
    ½ teaspoon catsup
    ¼ teaspoon black pepper

Place all ingredients into blender or food processor and blend until vegetables are pureed. Store in covered jar. Shake thoroughly before using.

GORGONZOLA DRESSING

CASTLE RESTAURANT
OLEAN, NEW YORK

Makes about 2 cups

      1 cup mayonnaise
    ½ cup tomato juice
      1 teaspoon Worcestershire sauce
      2 dashes hot pepper sauce
      1 small garlic clove, crushed
    ½ teaspoon salt
    ⅛ teaspoon pepper
    ¾ cup grated Gorgonzola cheese (for best results, freeze before grating)

Combine well all ingredients except cheese. Blend in cheese. Toss with salad greens just before serving.

LEMON MAPLE DRESSING

THE INN AT THE MOUNTAIN
STOWE, VERMONT

"Prize-winning chef Anton Flory created a delicious dip for fresh fruit—a combination of lemon or lime juice with honey or maple syrup." —Freda Earnest, Woodstown, New Jersey

Serve with fresh fruit or cottage cheese.

Makes 2 cups

      1 cup pure maple syrup or honey
    ½ cup fresh lemon or lime juice
    ½ teaspoon paprika
      1 cup whipping cream, whipped

Combine syrup, lemon juice and paprika in small bowl and blend well. Gently fold whipped cream into mixture. Cover and refrigerate before use.

MISO DRESSING

THE GARDEN NATURAL FOODS RESTAURANT
MIAMI SPRINGS, FLORIDA

"I love experimenting with new tastes in salads for meals at home. . . . The Garden Natural Foods Restaurant presents a most delicious house dressing." —Tona Mendoza, Miami, Florida

Makes 4 cups

      2 cups vegetable oil
      1 cup water
    ½ cup white miso paste*
    ¼ cup tamari* or soy sauce
    ¼ cup rice vinegar or cider vinegar
      3 green onions, finely chopped
      1 tablespoon honey

Combine ingredients in blender and mix well. Keeps 3 to 4 days in refrigerator.

*Available in natural food stores or oriental markets.

PUBLIC HOUSE SALAD DRESSING

THE PUBLIC HOUSE
ATLANTA, GEORGIA

Makes about 1 pint

    ¾ cup soy sauce
      3 tablespoons fresh lemon juice
      1 teaspoon sugar
      1 teaspoon toasted sesame seeds
      1 teaspoon chopped onion
  1¼ cups peanut oil

Combine all ingredients except oil in blender on low speed, or in food processor equipped with steel knife. Blend or process until onion is minced. With machine running, add oil in thin stream and blend or process until oil is thoroughly incorporated.

BON APPÉTIT SALAD DRESSING BASICS

VINAIGRETTE SAUCE

Makes about ½ cup

- **1 small to medium garlic clove, peeled**
- **1 teaspoon coarse salt**
- **½ teaspoon freshly ground pepper (white preferred) or to taste**
- **½ teaspoon dry mustard**
- **1 teaspoon Dijon or Düsseldorf mustard**
- **1 egg, beaten, or 2 tablespoons whipping cream (optional)**
- **2 tablespoons olive oil**
- **2 tablespoons tarragon vinegar or wine vinegar**
- **1 teaspoon fresh lemon juice**
- **¼ cup vegetable oil (peanut, corn, safflower, etc.)**

On cutting board, mash together garlic and salt until they almost form paste and transfer to mixing bowl. Add pepper, mustards, egg or cream, if desired (egg or cream smoothes dressing and keeps it from separating) and olive oil. Stir vigorously with whisk or wooden spoon. Slowly add vinegar and lemon juice, stirring constantly. Continuing to stir, add vegetable oil drop by drop until all has been absorbed.

Vinaigrette Marinade

Prepare Vinaigrette Sauce with equal parts vinegar and oil. Mix in 1 tablespoon sweet pickle relish. Pour over crisply cooked drained vegetables such as mushrooms, cauliflower, green beans or artichoke hearts, and marinate overnight.

HERB VINEGAR

Makes 1 quart

- **1 tablespoon chopped fresh mint**
- **1 tablespoon chopped fresh chives**
- **1 tablespoon chopped shallot**
- **1 tablespoon savory**
- **1 tablespoon brown sugar**
- **1 teaspoon salt**
- **3 bay leaves**
- **½ cinnamon stick**
- **¼ teaspoon nutmeg**
- **1 quart mild white distilled vinegar, heated to boiling**

Combine herbs and seasonings in large bottle or jar with tight-fitting lid. Pour vinegar over, cover and let stand 10 days, shaking once a day. Strain.

Variations: Each herb can be used alone. Garlic, tarragon, cloves, mace, allspice, basil, dill, thyme and rosemary are all excellent additives. For an unusual vinegar, use raspberries, strawberries, chili or horseradish.

MAYONNAISE

All ingredients should be at room temperature or slightly warm.

Makes about 1½ cups

- **2 egg yolks***
- **1 teaspoon Dijon mustard or more to taste**
- **1 tablespoon tarragon or wine vinegar or lemon juice**
- **⅓ cup olive oil**
- **⅔ cup peanut oil**
- **Salt and white pepper**

Mixer or Whisk Method: Place yolks, mustard and vinegar in large bowl and beat 1 minute. Add ½ oil very slowly, drop by drop, beating vigorously and constantly (if oil is added too rapidly, yolks will not completely absorb oil and mayonnaise will have a runny consistency). You may add remaining oil by teaspoonfuls, beating constantly. Add salt and white pepper to taste.

Blender or Food Processor Method: Place yolks, mustard, vinegar, salt and pepper in blender or food processor equipped with steel blade. Turn motor on and immediately begin adding oil in thin stream. When all oil has been added and mixture is thick, stop machine.

*If using food processor method, 2 whole eggs can be substituted for 2 egg yolks. This will produce a slightly less stiff mayonnaise.

To Stabilize:

If homemade mayonnaise is to be stored for more than a day or so, it must be stabilized to prevent separating. For each cup of completed mayonnaise, beat in 2 teaspoons boiling water or stock (chicken or beef).

To salvage separated mayonnaise:
a. Put 1 tablespoon mayonnaise into a warm, dry bowl with 1 teaspoon prepared mustard or 1 tablespoon boiling water. Whip until creamy. Add remaining mayonnaise a tablespoon at a time, beating vigorously after each addition, or
b. Place fresh egg yolk in bowl. Beat in separated mixture plus ½ cup oil to balance extra yolk.

TRAMP'S HONEY AND LEMON DRESSING

TRAMP'S
PITTSBURGH, PENNSYLVANIA

Makes 1 cup

- ½ cup fresh lemon juice
- ½ cup olive oil
- 1 tablespoon honey
- ¼ teaspoon cider vinegar
- 1 teaspoon salt
- ½ teaspoon freshly ground white pepper
  Pinch garlic powder
- ¼ cup chopped green onion
  Dash dry sherry

Combine lemon juice and oil in medium bowl and whisk briskly. Combine honey and vinegar in small bowl and stir until honey is dissolved. Add to lemon juice mixture. Blend in salt, pepper and garlic powder. Add onion and sherry and mix well. Transfer to airtight container and refrigerate overnight. Shake before using.

LEMON-MUSTARD DRESSING

McCABE'S
CHARLESTON, SOUTH CAROLINA

Makes about 1 quart

- ¾ cup dry white wine, preferably Chablis
- 2 tablespoons dry mustard
- 8 egg yolks
- 2 cups vegetable oil
- 3 tablespoons fresh lemon juice
- 1 tablespoon chopped fresh chives or parsley
- 1 teaspoon salt
- 1 teaspoon sugar

Combine wine with mustard in large mixing bowl and let stand ½ hour. Add egg yolks and mix well with whisk (do not use electric mixer). Add oil very slowly, beating constantly. When dressing is thick, blend in all remaining ingredients.

This dressing keeps well in refrigerator.

SOUR CREAM WITH VEGETABLES DRESSING

THE NATURAL KITCHEN
TAMPA, FLORIDA

Makes 2 cups

- 1 cup sour cream
- ¼ cup mayonnaise
- 3 tablespoons unprocessed honey
- 1 tablespoon fresh lemon juice
- ½ teaspoon dill
- ⅛ teaspoon vegetable seasoned salt
- ¼ cup minced red cabbage
- 2 tablespoons minced fresh celery leaves
- 1 tablespoon minced green onion
- 2 to 3 sprigs fresh parsley, minced

Combine first 6 ingredients in medium bowl and mix with wooden spoon. Add remaining ingredients and blend well. Refrigerate at least 1 hour for flavors to meld before serving as dip or over salad greens.

Will keep well in refrigerator for up to 1 week.

CREAMY PEPPER DRESSING

UNIVERSITY INN
PITTSBURGH, PENNSYLVANIA

Makes about 3 cups

- 2 cups mayonnaise
- ½ cup milk
- ¼ cup water
- 2 tablespoons freshly grated Parmesan cheese
- 1 tablespoon freshly ground pepper
- 1 tablespoon cider vinegar
- 1 teaspoon fresh lemon juice
- 1 teaspoon finely chopped onion
- 1 teaspoon garlic salt
  Dash red pepper sauce
  Dash Worcestershire sauce

Whisk all ingredients until well combined. Chill thoroughly before serving.

SAUCES AND CONDIMENTS

Often it is the little touches that turn a good meal into a fine one, or transform a fine meal into a truly memorable event. It may be something to do with the table setting: an elegant floral centerpiece, perhaps, or an especially attractive china service. In a restaurant, it might be a waiter who anticipates your every wish but is somehow never obtrusive. Or it may be an item on the menu, a small *lagniappe* that by itself might go unnoticed, but which helps to make the whole meal greater than the sum of its parts.

Principal among these "go-withs" are napping sauces, dipping sauces, special seasonings, flavored butters, and condiments such as relishes, chutneys and pickles. All are part of the good cook's repertoire, called upon when a dinner plan needs just that extra bit of imagination in order to be pronounced perfect.

The sauces and condiments in this chapter, which range from a curried mayonnaise for shrimp cocktail to a piquant peach chutney, are representative of the little "special effects" that restaurant chefs use to keep their customers coming back for more. They will all work just as well at home—any time you need a surprise.

Ingredients for Antipasto al Sole from Tambo de Oro
in San Diego (see page 67).

BEURRE AUX FINES HERBES

THE WOODBOX
NANTUCKET, MASSACHUSETTS

"I have been experimenting with herb butters for years and have never tasted any as delicious as this."
—Cherry Oman, Winchester, Massachusetts

Makes 14x1-inch roll

 1 cup (2 sticks) butter, room temperature
¼ cup Worcestershire sauce
¾ to 1 teaspoon anchovy paste
½ cup chopped fresh parsley
⅛ teaspoon paprika
⅛ teaspoon garlic powder
⅛ teaspoon freshly ground pepper

Combine butter, Worcestershire sauce and anchovy paste in blender or food processor and mix until smooth. Add remaining ingredients and process until evenly distributed through butter. Transfer to waxed paper or aluminum foil and shape into roll about 1 inch in diameter. Freeze until ready for use. Serve in ¼- to ½-inch slices.

CREAMY HERB SAUCE

BELVEDERE RESTAURANT & CABARET
SANTA ROSA, CALIFORNIA

This is an excellent sauce for grilled, poached or baked fish. Garnish with minced parsley and lemon wedges.

Makes about 2 cups

¼ cup (½ stick) butter
 1 cup finely minced mushrooms
¼ cup finely minced shallots or green onions
 1 teaspoon finely minced garlic

 2 tablespoons flour
¾ cup whipping cream
¼ cup dry vermouth
 2 teaspoons lemon juice
¼ teaspoon oregano
¼ teaspoon basil
Pinch thyme
Salt and pepper

 2 tablespoons finely minced parsley
 1 tablespoon capers, washed and drained

Melt butter in small saucepan; sauté mushrooms, shallots and garlic over medium heat until soft, about 2 to 3 minutes.

Blend in flour thoroughly. Add cream, vermouth, lemon juice, oregano, basil, thyme, salt and pepper. Cook, stirring constantly, until mixture thickens.

Add parsley and capers. Thin sauce, if desired, with more cream.

CURRY SAUCE A LA MONIQUE

THE WINE CELLAR RESTAURANT
NORTH REDINGTON BEACH, FLORIDA

This curry sauce is good with a variety of seafoods.

8 servings

 1 cup mayonnaise
 1 cup sour cream

 1 garlic clove, minced
 2 teaspoons curry powder
 3 tablespoons olive oil
 3 tablespoons sugar
Juice of 2 medium oranges
 2 tablespoons fresh lemon juice
 2 tablespoons chopped mango chutney
Salt and freshly ground pepper
 1 ounce Bombay gin

Combine mayonnaise and sour cream in medium mixing bowl.

In small saucepan or skillet over low heat, sauté garlic and curry powder in olive oil until well blended. Remove from heat and stir into mayonnaise-sour cream mixture. Add sugar, orange and lemon juices, chutney, salt and pepper to taste and blend until smooth. Chill. Just before serving, stir gin into sauce.

GINGER SAUCE

NEW OTANI HOTEL
TOKYO, JAPAN

6 to 8 servings

5½ ounces (½ cup plus 3 tablespoons) Japanese soy sauce
¼ cup peeled grated apple
¼ cup grated onion
2½ tablespoons sake*
 2 tablespoons mirin*
 4 teaspoons sesame seeds, toasted
 1 tablespoon grated fresh ginger
Pinch aji-no-moto* or monosodium glutamate (optional)

Combine ingredients in pint jar with tight-fitting lid. Shake well to blend.

*Available in oriental markets.

PEACH CHUTNEY

HILLTOP HERB FARM
CLEVELAND, TEXAS

Makes about 6 pints

 1 medium onion
 1 small garlic clove
 1 cup seedless raisins

    8 cups peeled, sliced peaches
    1 tablespoon chili powder
    1 cup chopped crystallized ginger
    2 tablespoons mustard seeds
    1 tablespoon salt
    1 quart cider vinegar
 2¼ cups light brown sugar, firmly packed

Finely chop onion, garlic and raisins.

In large kettle, combine onion mixture with remaining ingredients and mix well. Bring to boiling point, stirring constantly until sugar is dissolved. Reduce heat. Simmer, uncovered, stirring occasionally, until quite thick and deep brown in color, about 45 to 60 minutes. Remove from heat.

Ladle chutney into hot, sterilized pint jars. Seal immediately according to manufacturer's directions.

SHALLOT SAUCE

OYSTER BAR & RESTAURANT
NEW YORK, NEW YORK

"The Oyster Bar & Restaurant is one of the finest seafood restaurants in New York City. The shallot sauce served with oysters and clams on the half shell is absolutely the best my husband and I have ever tasted."
—Ann Linn, Eastchester, New York

Makes 1 cup

  ½ cup tarragon vinegar
  ½ cup red wine vinegar
   2 medium shallots, minced
   2 teaspoons freshly ground pepper

Combine vinegars in glass container with tight-fitting lid. Add shallots and pepper and shake well. Chill before serving.

Sauce can be refrigerated indefinitely.

SOUR CREAM DILL SAUCE

HOST INTERNATIONAL RESTAURANT
LOS ANGELES INTERNATIONAL AIRPORT
CALIFORNIA

Makes about 4 cups

 2½ cups mayonnaise
   1 cup sour cream
   3 tablespoons freshly grated Parmesan cheese
   3 tablespoons chopped fresh dill or 1 teaspoon dried dill
   3 tablespoons finely chopped onion
   1 tablespoon plus 1 teaspoon cider vinegar
   1 tablespoon freshly ground pepper
   2 teaspoons fresh lemon juice
   2 teaspoons Worcestershire sauce
   2 garlic cloves, crushed

Combine ingredients in processor or blender and mix well. Chill before serving.

PFLAUMENMUSS

HORST MAGER'S DER RHEINLANDER
PORTLAND, OREGON

Makes 2 cups

  ½ pound pitted dried prunes
   1 cup water
   1 cup sugar
  ½ teaspoon ground cinnamon
  ¼ teaspoon ground cloves
  ¼ teaspoon ground ginger
     Pinch nutmeg

   1 teaspoon cornstarch
 1½ teaspoons cold water

Put prunes through fine blade of meat grinder or finely chop with knife. Bring water to boil in heavy medium saucepan. Stir in sugar, spices and prunes. Return to boil, stirring constantly. Reduce heat and simmer gently 10 minutes.

Dissolve cornstarch in cold water and stir into prunes. Remove from heat. Spoon into containers. Let cool and refrigerate.

KOSHER PICKLES

RONNIE'S
ORLANDO, FLORIDA

"It isn't the ample portions, the nominal prices, or the quick, courteous service at Ronnie's that make me homesick. It's the memory of bowls of freshly cured kosher pickles—placed on every table and accompanied by freshly pickled beets and tomatoes, sauerkraut and coleslaw." —Peter Burrows, St. Louis, Missouri

Makes 1 gallon

   4 pounds pickling cucumbers, thoroughly washed
  ¼ cup salt
   2 quarts (8 cups) water
   5 garlic cloves, coarsely chopped
   2 tablespoons mixed pickling spices
   1 bunch fresh dill
   1 slice day-old Jewish-style rye bread

Arrange cucumbers in 1-gallon glass jar or stoneware crock. Stir salt into water and pour into jar. Add garlic and pickling spices. Lay dill over top. Add rye bread. Cover with plastic wrap and weight with small heavy object to keep cucumbers submerged. Let stand at room temperature 3 days, then refrigerate 5 days before serving.

CLASSIC SAUCE RECIPES FROM THE BON APPÉTIT KITCHENS

HOLLANDAISE SAUCE

Makes about 1¾ cups

- ¼ **cup water***
- 1½ **tablespoons fresh lemon juice**
- ¼ **teaspoon salt**
  Pinch freshly ground white pepper

- 3 **egg yolks**
- 1 **cup (2 sticks) unsalted butter, melted**

Mix water, lemon juice, salt and pepper in small saucepan. Bring to boil, reduce heat and simmer until liquid is reduced to 2 tablespoons. Set pan in larger pan of cold water to cool.

Beat yolks in heavy, nonaluminum, 1-quart saucepan until thick and creamy. Slowly beat in lemon reduction. Whisk over very low heat (or beat with electric mixer set on medium speed) until thickened, about 3 to 4 minutes. Do not allow eggs to become too thick or dry. Remove from heat and begin slowly drizzling warm, not hot, melted butter into yolks, beating constantly until all butter has been added and sauce is just pourable. If it is too thick to pour, thin with a little hot water.

*If serving sauce with fish, substitute white wine, dry vermouth or clam juice for water.

BECHAMEL SAUCE

Makes 1½ cups (medium consistency)

- 3 **tablespoons (⅜ stick) butter**
- ¼ **cup finely chopped onion**
- 3 **tablespoons all purpose flour**
- 2 **cups scalded milk, half and half or whipping cream**
- ¼ **teaspoon salt**
- 3 **white peppercorns**
- 1 **sprig parsley**
- ¼ **stalk celery, thinly sliced**
  Pinch nutmeg

In heavy, nonaluminum 2-quart saucepan, melt butter over low heat. Add onion and cook until soft but not browned. Whisk in flour to make roux. Cook, whisking constantly, until roux is frothy and free of lumps, about 2 to 3 minutes. Remove saucepan from heat and slowly add ½ hot liquid, whisking constantly. Add remaining liquid and continue whisking until sauce is smooth, about 3 to 5 minutes. Return sauce to medium-low heat and add remaining ingredients. Simmer uncovered, stirring frequently with wooden spoon, until sauce is reduced by about ¼, about 20 to 30 minutes. Remove from heat and strain.

VELOUTE SAUCE

Follow directions for making Béchamel Sauce, replacing milk or cream with chicken, fish or veal stock, depending on food sauce is to be served with.

MORNAY SAUCE

Makes about 2 cups

- 1½ **cups medium Béchamel or Velouté Sauce**
- ¼ to ½ **cup grated Gruyère, Swiss or sharp cheddar cheese**
- ¼ **cup grated Parmesan cheese**
- 1½ **teaspoons Dijon mustard**
- ¾ **teaspoon dry mustard**
- 2 **egg yolks, beaten**

Place Béchamel or Velouté Sauce in small heavy-bottomed saucepan over low heat. Stir in cheeses and mustards. Add small amount of hot sauce to egg yolks, beating constantly. Return yolk mixture to sauce and blend thoroughly with whisk. Over low heat, bring sauce just to boiling point.

MARINARA SAUCE

Makes 3 cups

- 2 **tablespoons olive oil**
- 2 **garlic cloves, minced**
- 1 **28-ounce can tomato puree**
- 1 **tablespoon sugar**
- 1 **tablespoon minced fresh parsley**
- 1 **teaspoon oregano**
- 1 **teaspoon basil**
- 1 **teaspoon salt**
- ¼ **teaspoon pepper**

In 3-quart saucepan, heat olive oil and saute garlic until golden brown. Add remaining ingredients and simmer for 15 minutes, partially covered to prevent splattering.

May be refrigerated 2 weeks or frozen up to 6 months.

ANTIPASTO AL SOLE

TAMBO DE ORO
SAN DIEGO, CALIFORNIA

Makes 3 quarts

1¼ cups olive oil
 2 garlic cloves, minced
 ½ cup finely chopped parsley
 3 9¾-ounce jars Italian marinated vegetables, drained
 1 28-ounce can tomato puree
 2 16-ounce cans button mushrooms, drained
 2 16-ounce cans quartered artichoke hearts, drained
 1 16-ounce can pitted black olives, drained
 1 5-ounce jar pearl onions, drained
 1 3-ounce jar mixed stuffed green olives, drained
   Salt and freshly ground pepper
 1 7-ounce can Italian tuna in olive oil, undrained
 1 4⅜-ounce tin sardines in tomato sauce, undrained

Sterilize enough glass jars of assorted sizes to hold 3 quarts of antipasto.

Heat ¼ cup olive oil in large skillet. Add garlic and parsley and sauté until garlic is golden. Add marinated vegetables, tomato puree, mushrooms, artichoke hearts, black olives, onions and green olives. Simmer until cauliflower (in Italian vegetables) is tender, about 20 minutes. Season with salt and pepper to taste.

Remove from heat and gently fold in tuna, sardines and remaining oil. Cool to room temperature. Fill glass jars and tighten lids securely.

Antipasto al Sole improves with age and may be refrigerated for up to 4 months.

FROM THE SEA

Try to calculate the myriad kinds of fish and shellfish that find their way from ocean, lake and stream to the dining table. Multiply that number by just the *standard* methods of preparation— poaching, grilling, frying, baking; whole, stuffed, filleted; in stews, gumbos, salads; *en croute, en papillote, en laitue*; drawn, marinated, even, as *sashimi* or *ceviche*, uncooked—and the resulting figure would be astronomical. The *Larousse Gastronomique* lists 150 ways of preparing sole alone, and that only covers the classics. There are, to repeat the old cliche, plenty of fish in the sea, and that is a great boon for both sportsmen and cooks.

Until fairly recently, the type of fish and shellfish offered on the menu depended on the restaurant's location; if you lived in the Midwest and wanted *moules mariniere*, you were just about out of luck. But jet travel, modern refrigeration techniques and the increased sophistication of diners have changed all that, and now you are likely to find sea bass in Illinois, scallops in Colorado and pompano in Oregon. It is still true that the best fish is the one just caught, but much the same could be said about truffles—and no one complains when they are brought to the table.

Classically, fish was almost always a separate course, providing among other things an excuse to sample a good white wine. And shellfish were usually relegated to the appetizer tray. But with today's emphasis on lighter meals, the low-calorie, high-protein characteristics of fish and shellfish make them ever more popular as main courses, and almost no two dishes are alike.

To the ancient Greeks, the fish was a symbol of infinity. The recipes in this chapter are a sampling of the nearly infinite ways chefs have invented for preparing the fisherman's catch.

Seafood Gumbo from Commander's Palace in New Orleans (see page 88).

BLANQUETTE DE LOUP DE MER AUX POIREAUX
(Sea Bass in White Wine with Leeks)

LE FRANÇAIS
WHEELING, ILLINOIS

4 servings

- **2 to 3 tablespoons (¼ to ⅜ stick) unsalted butter, softened**
- **3 tablespoons finely minced shallot**
- **1 5- to 6-pound sea bass fillet (skin on), cut into 1½-inch slices or 1 3-pound sea bass fillet or halibut steak, cut into slices ¾- to 1-inch thick**
  Salt and freshly ground pepper
- **3 leeks, white part only, cut julienne and blanched**
- **1½ cups dry white wine (preferably Chablis)**
- **1½ cups fish fumet**

- **1 cup whipping cream**
- **2 egg yolks**
  Juice of ½ lemon
- **4 tablespoons (½ stick) unsalted butter, cut into 4 pieces**

- **1 tablespoon olive oil**
- **2 tomatoes, peeled, seeded and chopped**

Preheat oven to 450°F. Select shallow, heatproof baking dish just large enough to accommodate fish. Cut waxed or parchment paper size of dish. Grease paper and dish with 2 to 3 tablespoons softened butter. Sprinkle dish with shallot. Season fish lightly with salt and pepper and arrange over shallot. Distribute leeks over and around fish. Add wine and fumet to baking dish.

Place paper buttered side down over fish. Bring liquid to simmer over direct heat. Transfer dish to oven and bake until fish is slightly springy to the touch and still underdone (it will continue to cook after being removed from oven), about 20 minutes.

Remove from oven and drain liquid into non-aluminum saucepan. Keep fish warm, covered with buttered paper and with lid. Reduce liquid over high heat to about 1 cup. Remove from heat.

Beat cream with yolks and lemon juice. Gradually whisk in ½ cup reduced liquid 1 tablespoon at a time, beating well after each addition. Whisk back into remaining liquid, place over very low heat and continue whisking until thickened. Remove from heat and whisk in 4 tablespoons butter 1 piece at a time, beating in completely after each addition. Cover and keep warm in bain-marie.

Heat oil in small skillet over medium-high heat. Add tomato and sauté briefly until just heated through. Pour sauce over fish and garnish each serving with spoonful of tomato. Serve immediately.

LOUP EN CROUTE WITH SAUCE CHORON
(Sea Bass in Puff Pastry)

RESTAURANT BOCUSE
LYONS, FRANCE

6 servings

Fish

- **1 3-pound whole fresh sea bass, striped bass or salmon (unscaled)**
  Salt and freshly ground pepper
- **3 large sprigs tarragon**
- **4 sprigs thyme**
- **2 tablespoons finely chopped fresh chives**
  Olive oil

- **1⅔ pounds puff pastry**
- **1 egg yolk, lightly beaten**

Sauce Choron

- **6 large shallots, minced**
- **¾ cup red wine vinegar**

- **6 egg yolks**
- **¼ cup water**
- **2¼ cups (4½ sticks) butter, melted and clarified**
- **1 tablespoon chopped fresh chives**
- **2 teaspoons tomato paste**
- **2 teaspoons chopped fresh tarragon**
  Pinch salt and freshly ground pepper

For fish: Cut top and bottom fins off fish with scissors. Using sharp knife, cut slit along backbone from head to tail. With boning knife behind gill on one side of fish, cut between skin and flesh, gently pulling with fingers to remove skin along entire length. (Leave head and tail intact.) Repeat on other side. Remove bone from underside and backbone with fingers. Generously sprinkle inside and out with salt and pepper. Arrange tarragon in slits. Place thyme in gills. Sprinkle inside and out with chives. Brush fish with olive oil. Transfer to platter, cover and chill 12 hours or overnight.

Preheat oven to 350°F. Generously oil large baking sheet. Divide pastry in half. Roll each half on lightly floured surface into rectangle ⅛ inch thick, 8 inches wide and 2 inches longer than fish. Place half of dough diagonally on baking sheet. Arrange fish on dough; brush beaten egg on dough around fish. Cover with second half of pastry. Press dough around fish to form outline, sealing with side of hand and trimming almost all excess. Using small knife, trim excess to resemble lower fin. Brush pastry generously with yolk. Roll out excess pastry. Cut out leaf shape to resemble top fin. Roll small ball of dough for eye. Form rope 7 inches long to outline head. Arrange on pastry. Use top of sharp knife to score fins, tail and gills and to draw in mouth. Form scales by pressing plain pastry tip into dough at an angle. Brush again with yolk. Bake until pastry is golden brown, about 1½ hours.

For sauce: Meanwhile, bring shallots and vinegar to boil in small saucepan over high heat and let boil until vinegar is evaporated and shallots are dry.

Whisk 6 egg yolks and water in top of double boiler set over simmering water until yolks are light and lemon colored. Stir in 2 tablespoons shallots. Add butter in slow steady stream, whisking constantly until completely incorporated. Stir in chives, tomato paste, tarragon, salt and pepper. Taste and add more shallots and chives if desired. (Can be prepared up to 2 hours ahead.)

Just before serving, heat sauce in medium saucepan over barely simmering water. If sauce separates, place 1 to 2 tablespoons ice water in small bowl. Add sauce and whisk until blended and smooth.

Transfer fish to platter and serve immediately with Sauce Choron.

STRIPED BASS ADRIATIC

THE COACH HOUSE
NEW YORK, NEW YORK

6 servings

    2 carrots, thinly sliced lengthwise
1½ tomatoes, chopped
    1 small onion or 4 green onions, finely chopped
  12 black peppercorns, crushed
    1 bay leaf
 ½ teaspoon dried oregano
 ½ teaspoon dried basil
    1 cup dry white wine
 ½ cup clam juice or water
 ½ cup olive oil
      Juice of 2 lemons
 ½ cup chopped fresh parsley
      Salt

    1 4-pound striped bass or whitefish (including head), cleaned

  12 mussels, scrubbed and well washed
    8 clams, scrubbed and well washed
    8 large uncooked shrimp, unshelled but slit and deveined

      Lemon slices (garnish)

Combine first 11 ingredients with ¼ cup parsley and salt to taste in bowl.

Preheat oven to 375°F. Slit fish lengthwise along backbone and place in heavy baking pan just large enough to accommodate. Spoon vegetable mixture over fish. Set over high heat and cook rapidly about 15 minutes to reduce liquid, frequently shaking pan and stirring carefully.

Arrange mussels, clams and shrimp around fish. Bake until mussel and clam shells open, about 30 minutes. If all do not open, cover pan with foil and continue baking a few minutes longer; discard any that still have not opened.

Spoon off as much liquid as possible into saucepan (tent fish with foil and keep warm) and simmer until reduced by about ½. Arrange lemon slices over fish and pour reduced liquid over top. Sprinkle with remaining ¼ cup parsley and serve immediately.

SEA BASS WITH GINGER, PEPPERCORNS AND BEANS

LES FRERES TROISGROS
ROANNE, FRANCE

4 servings

 ¼ cup dry white wine
    1 1½x1-inch piece fresh ginger, peeled and cut into fine julienne

3½ cups Fish Fumet (see page 87)
 ¼ cup dry vermouth
    2 shallots, minced
1¾ cups whipping cream

    2 tablespoons (¼ stick) butter
    4 ½-pound sea bass steaks or fillets, cut 1 inch thick
    2 teaspoons black peppercorns, coarsely crushed
      Salt

    2 tablespoons (¼ stick) butter, cut into 6 pieces
    8 french-cut green beans, cooked until crisp-tender (garnish)

Combine wine and ginger in small cup. Marinate overnight in refrigerator.

Strain marinade into heavy saucepan, reserving ginger. Add Fish Fumet, vermouth and shallots to marinade and boil over medium-high heat until reduced to thick syrup, about 20 minutes. Add cream and continue boiling until thickened, about 10 minutes. Strain sauce, set aside and keep warm.

Preheat oven to 400°F. Melt 2 tablespoons butter in baking dish. Add fillets, turning in butter to coat. Sprinkle with pepper and salt to taste. Cover with foil and bake until fish loses its translucency, about 10 minutes.

Just before serving, return sauce to pan and add reserved ginger. Bring to boil and cook 1 minute. Season with salt and pepper to taste. Reduce heat to low and whisk in butter 1 piece at a time, making sure each piece is thoroughly incorporated before adding next. Divide sauce among 4 heated serving plates. Drain fillets carefully and place 1 in center of each plate. Garnish with beans and serve.

STRIPED BASS LIVORNESE

BLU ADRIATICO
FLUSHING, NEW YORK

6 to 8 servings

  2 **pounds striped bass or other firm white fish (steaks or thick fillets)**
 ¼ **cup all purpose flour**
 ½ **cup olive oil**
  1 **small onion, sliced**
 ¼ **cup sliced pitted olives (both green and black)**
 ¼ **cup chopped oil-packed anchovy fillets**
  2 **tablespoons capers, rinsed and drained**
  1 **cup tomato sauce**
     Minced fresh parsley (garnish)

Dredge fish lightly in flour. Heat most of olive oil in large skillet over medium heat. Add fish and sauté lightly on both sides. Remove fish and pour off oil. Wipe pan. Return fish to skillet and add remaining oil, onion, olives, anchovies and capers. Cover and simmer about 20 minutes. Add tomato sauce and cook until heated through and fish is opaque. Garnish with parsley.

SELLE DE LOTTE
(Monkfish with Spinach and Béarnaise Sauce)

RESTAURANT BOCUSE
LYONS, FRANCE

4 to 6 servings

  1 **2-pound whole fresh monkfish or sole, skinned (dark meat discarded) and sliced into 4 to 6 fillets ½ inch thick**
  2 **teaspoons chopped fresh tarragon or 1 teaspoon dried**
 ¼ **teaspoon dried thyme**
     Salt and freshly ground pepper
     Olive oil
  8 **garlic cloves, unpeeled and flattened**
  1 **teaspoon dried chervil**

  2 **bunches fresh spinach, stemmed**

 ¼ **cup (½ stick) butter**
  2 **to 3 garlic cloves, peeled and crushed**

Béarnaise Sauce

 ¾ **cup white wine vinegar**
  5 **tablespoons finely chopped shallots**
     Freshly ground pepper
  4 **egg yolks, beaten**
  1 **cup (2 sticks) butter, melted and clarified**
  1 **teaspoon dried tarragon**
  1 **teaspoon dried chervil**
  1 **teaspoon minced fresh parsley**
 ¼ **teaspoon dried thyme**
     Salt

     Olive oil
 ¼ **cup (½ stick) butter**

Arrange fillets on platter. Sprinkle with tarragon, thyme, salt and pepper to taste. Drizzle oil over top; sprinkle with unpeeled garlic and chervil. Cover fillets with plastic and chill overnight.

Add ½ spinach to large saucepan boiling salted water. When water returns to boil, immediately remove spinach with slotted spoon and transfer to large bowl ice water. Drain, squeeze dry and spread out on work surface. Repeat with remaining spinach. Sprinkle with salt and pepper.

Melt butter in large skillet over medium heat. Blend in peeled garlic and cook slowly until butter is light brown. Remove skillet from heat. Add spinach and toss. Keep warm.

For sauce: Combine vinegar, shallots and pepper in small saucepan over medium-high heat and bring to boil. Let boil until vinegar evaporates and shallots are dry. Transfer 1 tablespoon shallots to metal bowl. Add yolks. Set over hot water over low heat and beat until consistency of mayonnaise. Remove from heat. Add butter teaspoon at a time, beating constantly. Mix in tarragon, chervil, parsley, thyme, salt and pepper. Taste and adjust seasoning. Cover and keep warm.

Remove garlic from fish and reserve. Coat bottom of heavy large skillet with olive oil. Place over medium-high heat. Add ¼ cup butter and reserved garlic and sauté until mixture is light brown. Remove garlic from skillet. Add fish fillets and sauté on both sides until lightly browned, about 3 to 4 minutes. Transfer fish to serving platter. Top with sauce and surround with spinach. Serve immediately.

BAKED BONED FLOUNDER RICOTTA

FISHER'S OF BUCKS
CORNWELLS HEIGHTS, PENNSYLVANIA

4 servings

  2 **tablespoons (¼ stick) butter**
  1 **garlic clove, crushed**
  1 **large green onion, finely chopped**
     Pinch ground thyme
     Salt and freshly ground pepper

  6 **ounces ricotta cheese**
1½ **tablespoons lightly beaten egg**
1½ **teaspoons finely chopped fresh parsley**

  1 **pound flounder or sole fillets, cut into 8 pieces**

  8 **¼-inch-thick tomato slices**
  2 **tablespoons (¼ stick) butter, melted**
     Juice of ¼ lemon
12 **ounces (¾ pound) mozzarella cheese, shredded**
     Paprika

Melt 2 tablespoons butter in small skillet over medium heat. Add garlic and onion and sauté until softened, about 2 to 3 minutes. Season to taste with thyme, salt and pepper.

Combine ricotta, egg, parsley and onion-garlic mixture in small bowl and mix until smooth. Cover and refrigerate 1 hour.

Preheat oven to 350°F. Lightly butter shallow baking dish. Arrange ½ of fillets in single layer in dish. Divide ricotta mixture among fillets, spreading evenly. Top with remaining fillets, pressing to enclose filling.

Top each portion with 2 tomato slices, then brush lightly with melted butter. Sprinkle with salt and pepper. Squeeze lemon juice over top. Add small amount of water to pan to prevent sticking. Bake until fish is almost cooked through, about 15 to 20 minutes. Top fillets with cheese. Dust with paprika. Continue baking until cheese melts and fish flakes easily, about 5 minutes.

BAKED PIKE WITH GARLIC IN A SPRINGTIME SAUCE

LES FRERES TROISGROS
ROANNE, FRANCE

4 servings

Sauce

 1 **medium tomato, peeled, seeded, juiced and diced**
 ¼ **teaspoon coriander seeds, crushed**
  Juice of 1 lemon
 ½ **cup olive oil**
  Salt and freshly ground pepper
 1 **tablespoon minced fresh parsley**
 1 **tablespoon minced fresh chervil**
 1 **tablespoon minced fresh tarragon**
 1 **tablespoon minced fresh basil**

 1 **3- to 4-pound fresh pike, red snapper or other white fish**
 3 **garlic cloves, halved lengthwise**
  Salt and freshly ground pepper
  Flour

 3 **tablespoons (⅜ stick) butter**

For sauce: Combine tomato, coriander and lemon juice in blender. With machine running, add olive oil a drop at a time, mixing constantly until thickened. Season to taste and whisk in herbs.

Preheat oven to 400°F. Make 6 slits along backbone of fish and place half garlic clove in each slit. Pat fish dry with paper towels. Sprinkle with salt and pepper and dip lightly in flour.

Melt butter in large skillet over medium-high heat until hazelnut colored. Add fish and brown on each side. Transfer to baking dish and bake 10 minutes for each inch of thickness, basting frequently. Fillet fish and divide among 4 heated serving plates. Discard garlic.

Pour sauce into baking dish and cook gently over direct heat, scraping up any bits clinging to bottom of pan. Spoon some of sauce over fish and pass remainder separately. Serve immediately.

Any other fresh herbs such as dill, chives or mint can also be used in sauce.

SALMON WESTPORT

MIRABEAU RESTAURANT
SEATTLE, WASHINGTON

"My husband and I recently spent a lovely vacation in Seattle, where we had a delicious dinner at the Mirabeau Restaurant—salmon poached in white wine."
   —Mrs. Al Clerx, Culver City, California

6 servings

 1 **8-ounce can stewed tomatoes, drained and chopped**
 ¼ **cup chopped onion**

 6 **8-ounce salmon fillets**
 6 **cups dry white wine**

 3 **tablespoons (⅜ stick) butter**
 1 **tablespoon cornstarch**

 ½ **pound mushrooms, chopped**
 1 **small shallot, minced**

 1½ **cups whipping cream, whipped**
  Salt and freshly ground pepper

Combine tomatoes and onion in small saucepan. Cover and simmer 30 minutes. Remove from heat and set aside.

Poach salmon in wine until fish flakes with fork and has lost its translucency, about 10 minutes. Transfer to heatproof serving dish and keep warm. Increase heat to high and cook wine until reduced to about 1 cup. Transfer to small saucepan.

Combine 1 tablespoon butter and cornstarch to form paste. Place wine over medium heat and gradually whisk in paste. Cook briefly, whisking constantly until mixture thickens. Cool slightly.

Preheat broiler on high setting. Melt remaining butter in medium skillet. Add mushrooms and shallot and sauté about 3 minutes. Stir in tomato mixture. Spoon over salmon.

Fold whipped cream into wine mixture. Season to taste with salt and pepper. Gently spread over fish. Broil until golden brown, about 1 to 2 minutes.

SALMON EN CROUTE

CHEZ PAUL
CHICAGO, ILLINOIS

6 to 8 servings

      2 salmon fillets, 1½ to 2 pounds each
      1 cup fresh sorrel or spinach, stems
        removed
      5 hard-cooked eggs, chopped
      ¼ cup chopped fresh parsley
      ¼ cup chopped onion
        Salt and freshly ground pepper

      1 pound puff pastry dough
      1 egg, lightly beaten

        Sorrel Sauce*

Lay 1 fillet on waxed paper. Finely chop sorrel or
spinach by hand or in food processor. Spread over
fillet. Mix together eggs, parsley and onion. Spread
evenly over sorrel or spinach. Season with salt and
pepper to taste. Cover with other fillet.

Preheat oven to 425°F. Roll out puff pastry dough
on pastry cloth to thickness of about ¼ inch,
making one long piece large enough to wrap fish. Cut
off ends and save for decorations. Wrap fish in
pastry very carefully. Seal seam and ends with beaten
egg. Cut small leaves, flowers, diamonds and other
patterns from leftover puff pastry.

Carefully place salmon on ungreased cooking sheet,
seamside down. Cut diagonal slits about 2 inches
apart down center. Decorate with cut-outs, using
beaten egg as "glue."

Bake for 30 minutes. Lower oven temperature to
375°F and bake for 15 minutes more. Allow to stand
few minutes before slicing. To serve, cut into slices
1½ inches thick. Serve with warm Sorrel Sauce.

*Sorrel Sauce

6 to 8 servings

      3 shallots, chopped
      ¼ cup fish stock
      1½ cups dry vermouth
      1 cup white wine

      2 cups cream
        Salt and white pepper
      3 cups finely chopped fresh sorrel or
        spinach

      3 egg yolks
        Lemon juice

Combine shallots, fish stock, vermouth and wine in
2-quart saucepan. Cook over medium-high heat
until reduced to about ½ cup, about 45 minutes.

Add cream and salt and white pepper to taste. Cook
over medium heat, stirring frequently, for 10 minutes. Add sorrel or spinach and heat 3 to 4 minutes.

Beat egg yolks. Remove sauce from heat and stir a
little of it into yolks. Then slowly stir yolk mixture
back into sauce. Return to heat and cook 3 to 4
minutes. Season with lemon juice to taste. Keep
sauce hot; do not boil.

FILET DE SAUMON EN LAITUE
(Braised Salmon in Lettuce)

RESTAURANT BOCUSE
LYONS, FRANCE

4 servings

      2 tablespoons dry white wine

      8 large shallots, minced
      ¾ cup white wine vinegar
      ¾ cup dry white wine
        Freshly ground pepper

      4 large butter lettuce leaves

      1 pound fresh salmon tail, skinned, boned
        and cut into four 4-ounce fillets
        Salt
      4 teaspoons butter, room temperature
      1 tablespoon chopped fresh chives
        Softened butter

      3 tablespoons whipping cream
      1 tablespoon water
      1½ cups (3 sticks) butter, cut into pieces
        Juice of 1 lime
        Fresh chives, chopped

      4 baby carrots, cut julienne, blanched until
        crisp, drained and sautéed in butter
        (garnish)

Generously butter baking sheet and sprinkle with
2 tablespoons white wine. Set baking sheet aside.

Combine shallots, vinegar, ¾ cup wine and pinch
pepper in medium saucepan and bring to boil over
high heat. Continue cooking until liquid evaporates.
Transfer shallots to small plate and set aside.

Cut tough ribs from lettuce leaves. Blanch leaves in
large saucepan of boiling salted water about 40
seconds. Plunge into cold water to stop cooking
process. Drain; dry with paper towels.

Sprinkle fillets on each side with salt and pepper. Set
each on lettuce leaf. Dot each with 1 teaspoon butter
and sprinkle with chopped chives. Fold leaf over,
enclosing fillet completely. Arrange chive side up on
prepared sheet. Brush tops with softened butter to
prevent drying. Cover with parchment paper and set
aside. (Fillets can be prepared ahead to this point.
Cover with damp towel instead of paper.

Preheat oven to 375°F. Combine 2 to 3 tablespoons
reserved cooked shallots with cream, water and salt
in medium saucepan over medium heat and bring to
boil slowly. Gradually whisk in 1½ cups butter. Add
additional shallots, if desired. Stir in lime juice and
chives to taste.

Bake salmon until just cooked through, about 3 to 4
minutes. Transfer to platter. Top with sauce, garnish
with baby carrots and serve.

SUPREME OF RED SNAPPER DUGLERE

THE JOCKEY CLUB
WASHINGTON, D.C.

*A delicate white wine sauce tops the flaky red snapper.
Serve with puff pastry crescents and boiled potatoes.*

8 servings

    1½ cups finely chopped shallots
    ½ cup sliced mushrooms (optional)
    8 6-ounce fillets of red snapper (about
       3 pounds)
       Salt and freshly ground white pepper

    1 tablespoon butter
    6 tomatoes, peeled, cored, seeded and
       coarsely chopped
    2 bay leaves
    ½ teaspoon dried thyme

    4 cups (1 quart) plus additional
       Fish Fumet*
    1 cup dry white wine
    4 cups (1 quart) whipping cream

       Chopped fresh parsley (garnish)

Generously butter 2 large skillets. Sprinkle each
with ¾ cup shallots and sliced mushrooms if desired.
Arrange snapper in single layer in bottom of each
skillet and season with salt and pepper. Set aside.

Melt butter in large saucepan over medium-low
heat. Add tomatoes, remaining shallots, bay leaves,
thyme, salt and pepper to taste and sauté until liquid
has evaporated, about 20 to 30 minutes. Remove
from heat and set aside.

Reduce 4 cups Fish Fumet in medium saucepan over
high heat until syrupy and coats bottom of pan.
Meanwhile, pour wine into small saucepan and cook
over medium-high heat until reduced to ⅓ cup.
Cook whipping cream in large saucepan over
medium-high heat until cream coats back of spoon.
Blend Fumet and wine into cream. Set sauce aside;
keep warm.

Preheat oven to 375°F. Add enough Fumet to
snapper to cover. Cover skillets with parchment
paper. Place over medium heat and bring to simmer.
Transfer to oven and bake until fish is firm to touch,
about 12 to 15 minutes. Drain well and arrange on
individual plates. Blend white wine sauce into
tomato mixture and spoon over fish, coating evenly.
Garnish with parsley.

*Fish Fumet

Makes about 1 quart

    1 pound (about) fish trimmings
       (do not use salmon)
    4 cups (1 quart) cold water
    2 tablespoons tarragon vinegar
    1 celery stalk with leaves, cut into
       2-inch pieces

    1 carrot, cut into 2-inch pieces
    1 leek (white part only), split
    ¼ medium head lettuce
    5 white peppercorns
    3 fresh dill sprigs
    1 bay leaf
    ½ teaspoon dried thyme
    ½ teaspoon salt

Combine all ingredients in 4- to 5-quart saucepan
and bring to boil over medium-high heat. Reduce
heat and simmer, uncovered, about 45 minutes.
Strain through colander or cheesecloth-lined
strainer before using.

PLANTATION GARDENS OPAKAPAKA

PLANTATION GARDENS
KAUAI, HAWAII

*"This fish is out of the world! It's presented on a bed of
watercress with a fresh ginger sauce."*
                  —*Margaret Lundberg, Seattle, Washington*

6 servings

    ½ cup dry white wine
    ½ onion, thinly sliced
    1 bay leaf
       Pinch dried thyme
    ½ cup whipping cream
    ½ cup (1 stick) butter, cut into pieces
    ½ garlic clove, crushed
    1 small slice fresh ginger, peeled and
       minced
    2 sprigs fresh parsley, finely chopped
    ½ teaspoon soy sauce
       Salt and freshly ground pepper

    1 tablespoon butter
    6 3½- to 4-ounce red snapper fillets

       Watercress sprigs
       Lemon wedges and chopped fresh
       parsley (garnish)

Combine wine, onion, bay leaf and thyme in
medium saucepan and bring to boil over medium-
high heat. Continue cooking until liquid is almost
evaporated. Reduce heat, add cream and simmer
until mixture coats spoon, about 2 minutes. Press
through strainer and return to saucepan. Stir in ½
cup butter, blending thoroughly. Add garlic, ginger,
parsley and soy sauce. Season sauce mixture to taste
with salt and pepper.

Melt remaining butter in heavy skillet over medium
heat. Sprinkle fillets with salt and pepper. Add to
skillet and fry on both sides until lightly browned
and cooked through. Transfer to heated plate.

Arrange watercress on serving platter. Reheat sauce
gently, adding any juices accumulated around fish.
Cook until slightly thickened. Arrange fillets on
watercress and top with sauce. Garnish with lemon
wedges and chopped parsley. Serve immediately.

RED SNAPPER CASSEROLE

HARPOON HENRY'S RESTAURANT
SAN DIEGO, CALIFORNIA

"On our way to Mexico we stopped at Harpoon Henry's in San Diego for dinner. It turned out to be one of the highlights of our trip. The favorite dish of our group was the red snapper topped with chili sauce and melted cheese. Absolutely delicious."
—Ruth Pilley, Grass Valley, California

6 servings

- 1½ **pounds (6 4-ounce fillets) red snapper or other firm-fleshed fish**
- ½ **to 1 cup flour**
  Salt and freshly ground pepper
- 3 **to 4 tablespoons (⅜ to ½ stick) butter**
- 6 **ounces green chili sauce**
- 12 **ounces Monterey Jack cheese, grated**
- 6 **ounces cheddar cheese, grated**
- 2 **tablespoons minced fresh parsley (garnish)**

Preheat oven to 350°F. Coat fillets with flour seasoned with salt and pepper to taste. Heat butter in medium skillet and lightly sauté fillets on both sides, 2 at a time, adding more butter as needed. Transfer fillets to individual casserole dishes. Divide sauce and then cheeses among them. Bake about 12 minutes. Sprinkle with parsley.

BANANA SHERRIED SOLE PORTOFINO AMANDINE

GEPETTO'S TALE OF THE WHALE
HOLLYWOOD, FLORIDA

4 to 6 servings

- 3 **cups all purpose flour**
- ½ **cup beer**
- ½ **cup milk**
- ½ **cup club soda**
- ⅛ **teaspoon salt**
- ⅛ **teaspoon white pepper**
  Dash hot pepper sauce

- ¾ **cup (1½ sticks) butter**
- 4 **ounces slivered almonds**
- 2 **tablespoons banana liqueur**

- ⅔ **cup sugar**
- ¾ **cup cream sherry**
- 1 **medium lemon**

  Oil for deep frying
- 4 **medium bananas, peeled and halved crosswise**
- 1 **pound fresh sole (lemon, gray or petrale), cut into serving portions**

Combine 2 cups flour and next 6 ingredients in large bowl and mix well. Set aside.

Melt ¼ cup butter in small skillet over medium-high heat. Add almonds and sauté until golden. Immediately stir in liqueur. Remove from heat.

Melt remaining butter in another small saucepan over medium heat. Stir in sugar, sherry and sautéed almonds. Squeeze lemon directly into pan. Cook 2 to 3 minutes, stirring constantly. Keep warm.

Heat oil in deep fryer or large pan to 375°F. Roll bananas, then fish, in remaining flour. Drop bananas into batter. Remove one at a time with fork and shake off excess batter. Deep fry in batches (make sure bananas do not touch), turning frequently until golden brown, 4 to 5 minutes. Remove with slotted spoon and drain on paper towels. Keep warm. Dip fish in remaining batter and cook following same procedure as for bananas. Arrange bananas and fish alternately on heated platter. Serve with almond-sherry sauce.

BIRD & BOTTLE FILLET OF SOLE

THE BIRD & BOTTLE INN
GARRISON, NEW YORK

6 servings

Sauce

- 2 **egg yolks**
- ½ **cup (1 stick) butter, melted**
- ¼ **cup (½ stick) butter**
- 2 **tablespoons flour**
- 1 **cup milk, scalded**
- ¼ **teaspoon white pepper**
  Dash nutmeg

- ¾ **cup dry white wine**
- ¼ **cup finely chopped shallots**

- 6 **5- to 6-ounce fillets of sole**
- 2 **large tomatoes, peeled, seeded and minced**
- 1 **cup sliced fresh mushrooms**
- 1½ **cups fish stock**

- 1 **cup whipping cream, whipped**

For sauce: Place yolks in medium mixing bowl and beat thoroughly with whisk until thickened. Gradually beat in melted butter. Melt remaining butter in small saucepan. Stir in flour to make roux. Add milk and cook over medium heat, stirring constantly, until thickened, about 4 to 5 minutes. Let cool. Stir in yolk mixture and add pepper and nutmeg to taste.

Place wine and shallots in large ovenproof sauté pan. Reduce wine over low heat to about 1 tablespoon.

Preheat oven to 350°F. Arrange fish over shallots. Add tomatoes and mushrooms. Pour fish stock over. Cover and bake just until fish flakes, 15 to 20 minutes. Remove from oven and drain off stock.

Preheat broiler. Fold whipped cream into sauce and spoon over fish. Run under broiler to brown, watching closely.

MERRY OLD SOLE

THE CHOWDERHEAD
GOLD BEACH, OREGON

"Gold Beach is a place of nostalgia to me. On my visits I always try to include a special sole dinner at The Chowderhead."
—Lewis Mayhew, Seattle, Washington

1 to 2 servings

  2 small fillets of sole
  5 to 6 medium scallops
 ¼ cup Dungeness crab
 ¼ cup small salad shrimp
 ¼ cup shredded mozzarella or Monterey Jack cheese
 ¾ cup hollandaise sauce
    Paprika and minced parsley (garnish)

Preheat oven to 450°F. Lightly butter individual casserole. Place one sole fillet on bottom and layer with scallops, crab, shrimp and cheese. Top with second fillet and cover with hollandaise. Bake until fish flakes and sauce is bubbly, 10 to 15 minutes. Sprinkle with paprika and parsley.

PETRALE SOLE STUFFED WITH SHRIMP

DEBAUCHERY
MISSION BEACH, CALIFORNIA

8 servings

Stuffing

 1½ cups finely chopped celery
  ½ cup finely chopped onion
  3 cups small precooked shrimp (about 1 pound)
  2 cups water

  1 cup mayonnaise
  1 cup finely crushed plain potato chips
    Pinch cayenne pepper

 16 fillets of fresh petrale sole, 6 to 7 ounces each

  1 pound (4 sticks) sweet butter, melted
    Pinch paprika

Combine celery, onion and shrimp in saucepan with 2 cups water. Bring to boil, reduce heat and simmer 1 minute. Drain.

Put shrimp mixture into bowl and combine with mayonnaise, potato chips and cayenne pepper.

Preheat oven to 350°F. Place an equal amount of stuffing on 8 fillets. Cover each with second fillet.

Coat each of 8 individual baking dishes with a little melted butter. Place stuffed fillet in each dish. Pour remaining melted butter over fish. Sprinkle lightly with paprika. Bake until fish flakes with a fork, about 20 to 25 minutes. Do not overcook.

FILLET OF DOVER SOLE ARCHIDUC

THE JOCKEY CLUB
WASHINGTON, D.C.

6 to 8 servings

  6 shallots, finely chopped
 12 1-pound fillets of sole
    Salt and freshly ground white pepper
  1 cup dry white wine
  4 cups (1 quart) Fish Fumet (see page 75)

  5 cups whipping cream

  ½ cup finely diced carrot
  ½ cup finely diced celery
  ½ cup finely diced leek
  2 tablespoons brandy
  2 tablespoons Madeira
  2 tablespoons port

Preheat oven to 450°F. Generously butter 9x13-inch nonaluminum flame-proof baking dish and sprinkle bottom with shallots. Fold fillets in half with white side out. Arrange in single layer in dish and season with salt and pepper to taste. Add wine and enough Fumet to almost cover fish. Bring mixture to boil over medium-high heat. Cover with parchment paper and bake just until translucent, about 5 minutes. Transfer fish to platter using slotted spoon; set aside and keep warm.

Place baking dish over high heat and reduce liquid to syrup, about 10 to 12 minutes. Reduce heat to medium-high, add cream and cook until sauce coats back of spoon. Season with salt and white pepper to taste. Keep warm.

Combine carrot, celery, leek, brandy, Madeira and port in medium saucepan and cook over medium-high heat until liquid is evaporated. Blend vegetables into sauce, pour over fish and serve.

SWORDFISH STEAK WITH LEMON AND CAPERS

LE ST. GERMAIN
LOS ANGELES, CALIFORNIA

6 servings

  3 to 4 lemons

  6 slices swordfish (about 8 ounces each)
    Salt and freshly ground white pepper
    Milk
    All purpose flour

 12 tablespoons peanut oil
  1 teaspoon butter

  5 tablespoons (⅝ stick) unsalted butter
 ¼ cup drained capers
  2 tablespoons chopped fresh parsley
    (garnish)

Carefully peel lemons, discarding all of white pith. Cut white membrane from lemon sections. Remove segments, then dice and set aside.

Generously season swordfish with salt and white pepper to taste. Dip each slice in milk. Coat with flour, shaking off excess.

Heat 6 tablespoons oil in large skillet over medium-high heat. Stir in ½ teaspoon butter. Add 3 slices of fish and sauté until lightly browned on both sides. Reduce heat and continue cooking until fish is opaque and feels firm to touch. Transfer to heated serving platter and keep warm. Repeat with remaining oil, ½ teaspoon butter and fish.

Wipe out skillet. Add remaining butter and cook over medium heat until lightly browned. Stir in reserved lemon and capers. Pour over fish, garnish with chopped parsley and serve immediately.

GUEST TROUT

LAKE YELLOWSTONE HOTEL
YELLOWSTONE NATIONAL PARK, WYOMING

"Guests of the hotel can catch their own freshwater trout for dinner. And the way the chef prepares them is delicious!" —Richard Warnick, Bethesda, Maryland

6 servings

 24 seedless grapes
    Dry white wine

  6 fresh trout, cleaned

    Juice of 1 lemon (about 3 tablespoons)
 ½ cup (1 stick) butter, room temperature

    Lemon wedges (garnish)

Combine grapes in medium saucepan with enough wine to cover. Place over low heat and bring to simmer. Cook 10 minutes; do not boil. Drain well and set aside.

Preheat oven to 500°F. Wrap each trout tightly in foil and arrange on baking sheet. Bake until fish is just cooked through, about 8 to 10 minutes.

Meanwhile, place 8-inch skillet over low heat. Add lemon juice and cook 2 minutes. Add butter and cook, stirring constantly, until butter is melted and sauce is heated, about 15 minutes. Stir in grapes.

Remove fish from foil and arrange on serving platter. Top with butter sauce and garnish with lemon wedges.

TROUT WINSLOW

WINSLOW'S DINING AT MINNIE COLE'S
CASHIERS, NORTH CAROLINA

6 servings

Béarnaise Sauce

  5 cups tarragon vinegar
 1½ medium onions, chopped
 ¼ cup chopped fresh parsley
  5 teaspoons coarsely ground black pepper
 1½ pounds (6 sticks) butter
 12 egg yolks

  6 8- to 10-ounce rainbow trout, boned
    Whole wheat flour
    Peanut oil
 ½ cup dry white wine

  1 pound jumbo lump crabmeat
 ½ cup (1 stick) butter, melted
    Chopped parsley, paprika and lemon
    wedges (garnish)

For sauce: Combine vinegar, onions, parsley and pepper in 3-quart saucepan. Cook over medium heat until liquid is almost evaporated and onions are translucent. Place in blender, or food processor with steel knife, and puree. Melt butter in same saucepan and add pureed mixture. Place egg yolks in top of double boiler over low heat and slowly blend in melted butter mixture until sauce has thickened slightly. Remove from heat and allow to stand at room temperature.

Preheat oven to 375°F. Oil 9x5-inch baking dish and preheat. Roll trout in flour. In 10- to 12-inch skillet, lightly coated with peanut oil, brown fish on 1 side only, 2 or 3 at a time. Transfer trout, browned side up, to preheated baking dish and bake until fish flakes with fork, about 8 minutes. Remove from oven and immediately sprinkle with wine. Remove fish to warm platter.

While trout is baking, sauté crab in melted butter. Place crab in trout cavities. Cover with Béarnaise Sauce and garnish with parsley, paprika and lemon.

LES PROVINCES FROG LEGS

LES PROVINCES
REDWOOD CITY, CALIFORNIA

The restaurant recommends boiled potatoes as an accompaniment.

4 to 6 servings

18 pairs small frog legs, unthawed if frozen, separated
   Milk

   Flour
   Salt and freshly ground pepper
1 cup (2 sticks) unsalted butter
¼ cup dry white wine
2 tablespoons veal stock
2 garlic cloves, minced
1 teaspoon minced shallot
1 generous tablespoon chopped parsley (garnish)

Soak unthawed frog legs overnight in refrigerator in milk to cover (this removes any fishy taste they may have). Drain well.

Roll or shake frog legs in flour seasoned with salt and pepper. Heat about ½ butter in large heavy frying pan over medium heat. Add frog legs and sauté until golden brown. Transfer to heated platter and keep warm. Wipe out pan drippings. Return pan to medium-high heat, add remaining butter and heat until foamy. Add wine, stock, garlic and shallot and stir well. Pour over frog legs, sprinkle with parsley and serve immediately.

COSMO'S STEAMED CLAMS

COSMO'S UNDERGROUND
LAS VEGAS, NEVADA

6 servings

2 tablespoons olive oil
2 teaspoons minced garlic
72 littleneck clams
5¾ cups (46 ounces) clam juice
3 cups water
1 16-ounce can whole ground tomatoes
1 cup dry white wine
½ cup (1 stick) butter
2 teaspoons salt
2 teaspoons crushed red pepper
2 teaspoons dried oregano leaves
2 teaspoons dried basil leaves
2 teaspoons chopped fresh parsley

In stockpot or Dutch oven, heat olive oil over medium heat until haze forms. Add garlic and sauté until golden. Remove from heat and add remaining ingredients. Cover and bring to boil, stirring occasionally. When clams open remove from heat and let stand 5 minutes. Serve in soup plates.

CLAMS CASINO

BROOKSIDE COUNTRY CLUB
MACUNGIE, PENNSYLVANIA

6 servings

2 cups rock salt
36 medium cherrystone clams on half shell
   Hot pepper sauce

2 large green peppers, minced
2 medium Bermuda onions, minced
½ pound bacon, diced
   Salt and freshly ground pepper

¼ to ½ cup fresh breadcrumbs
¼ to ½ cup (½ to 1 stick) butter, melted

Cover large shallow baking sheet or jelly roll pan evenly with rock salt. Arrange clams over top. Shake 1 or 2 drops hot sauce on each shell beneath clam. Set aside.

Sauté peppers and onions with bacon in large skillet until vegetables begin to soften. Remove from heat and season to taste.

Preheat broiler. Spoon mixture on top of each clam and sprinkle evenly with breadcrumbs. Moisten with melted butter. Run under broiler briefly until bubbly and lightly browned; do not overcook. Transfer to plates and serve immediately.

WANCHESE CRAB CAKES

THE SEA RANCH
KILL DEVIL HILLS, NORTH CAROLINA

"While visiting the fascinating Outer Banks of North Carolina, we dined at The Sea Ranch, where we had the most wonderful crab cakes—hot and spicy and deep fried."
   —Jayne H. Willows, Medford Lakes, New Jersey

Makes 6 cakes

1 pound crabmeat, flaked
¾ cup cracker crumbs
1 large egg, lightly beaten
2 tablespoons minced onion
2 tablespoons mayonnaise
1 tablespoon Worcestershire sauce
1 tablespoon prepared mustard
¾ to 1½ teaspoons hot pepper sauce
1 teaspoon salt
½ teaspoon freshly ground pepper
   Cracker crumbs

   Oil for deep frying

With fork, mix together first 10 ingredients in medium bowl. Form into 3-inch patties and roll in additional cracker crumbs.

Heat oil in skillet or deep-fat fryer to 375°F. Fry patties until golden brown, about 3 minutes per side. Drain on paper towels and serve immediately.

BAKED CRAB JOCKEY

THE JOCKEY CLUB
WASHINGTON, D.C.

4 to 6 servings

    2 tablespoons (¼ stick) butter
    3 large shallots, finely chopped
    2 teaspoons curry powder
   10 ounces fresh crabmeat
       Dash Worcestershire sauce
       Salt and freshly ground pepper
    ¾ cup Velouté de Poisson*
    ¼ cup Hollandaise Sauce**
    ¼ cup whipping cream, whipped

Preheat broiler. Melt butter in medium skillet over medium-high heat until light brown. Stir in shallots and curry powder. Increase heat to high, add crabmeat and sauté about 1 minute. Blend in Worcestershire sauce, salt and pepper to taste. Gently stir in Velouté, Hollandaise and whipped cream, being careful not to break up crabmeat. Transfer mixture to individual scallop shells or small broilerproof dishes. Broil until top is golden and serve.

Velouté de Poisson

Makes 1½ cups

    3 tablespoons (⅜ stick) butter
    ¼ cup finely chopped onion
    3 tablespoons all purpose flour
    2 cups hot Fish Fumet (see page 75)
    3 white peppercorns
    1 parsley sprig
    ¼ celery stalk, thinly sliced
    ¼ teaspoon salt
       Pinch freshly grated nutmeg

Melt butter in nonaluminum medium saucepan over low heat. Add onion and cook until soft but not browned. Remove from heat and whisk in flour. Cook, whisking constantly, until roux is frothy and free of lumps, about 2 to 3 minutes. Remove saucepan from heat and slowly add ½ of hot Fish Fumet, whisking constantly. Add remaining Fish Fumet and continue whisking until sauce is smooth, about 3 to 5 minutes. Place over medium-low heat and add remaining ingredients. Simmer, uncovered, stirring frequently with wooden spoon, until sauce is reduced by about ¼, about 20 to 30 minutes. Strain before using.

**Hollandaise Sauce*

Makes about 1 cup

    ⅓ cup water
    1 teaspoon fresh lemon juice
    ¼ teaspoon salt
    ¼ teaspoon freshly ground white pepper

    3 egg yolks, beaten
   1¾ cups (3½ sticks) unsalted butter, melted
       Pinch ground red pepper (optional)
   1½ tablespoons whipping cream

Combine water, lemon juice, salt and pepper in small saucepan and cook over high heat until reduced to 2 tablespoons. Let cool.

Place over low heat, add egg yolks and whisk constantly until mixture is thick and lemon colored; do not overcook or yolks will curdle. Reduce heat to lowest setting and add butter 2 tablespoons at a time, thoroughly incorporating after each addition. Blend in red pepper if desired. Stir in cream to thin to desired consistency.

IMPERIAL CRAB

NEW WILLIAMSBURG INN
WHITE MARSH, MARYLAND

8 servings

    ½ medium green pepper, diced
    2 teaspoons diced pimiento
    2 tablespoons (¼ stick) butter

    ⅔ cup plus 2 tablespoons mayonnaise
    3 egg yolks
   2½ teaspoons seafood seasoning
       Dash hot pepper sauce
    ½ teaspoon onion salt
    2 teaspoons Worcestershire sauce
    1 teaspoon dry mustard
    2 pounds fresh jumbo lump crabmeat

    3 egg whites
       Lemon juice to taste

Sauté green pepper and pimiento in butter. Do not overcook. Set aside to cool.

Place ⅔ cup mayonnaise, egg yolks, 2 teaspoons seafood seasoning and other seasonings in mixing bowl. Add sautéed pepper and pimiento and mix thoroughly. Gently stir in crabmeat. Refrigerate for 30 minutes.

Preheat oven to 450°F. Spoon crabmeat mixture into 8 shell ramekins. Bake mixture for 10 minutes.

While crab is baking, beat egg whites until stiff. Mix with remaining mayonnaise, lemon juice and remaining seafood seasoning.

Remove ramekins from oven. Spread egg white topping over crabmeat mixture. Place under broiler for few minutes until golden brown on top. Serve immediately.

CRAB IN BLACK BEAN SAUCE

LUNG KEE RESTAURANT
VANCOUVER, BRITISH COLUMBIA, CANADA

"On a vacation stop in Vancouver last year, friends and I came upon a terrific Chinese dish—crab in a black bean sauce. For anyone who has enjoyed both Chinese fare and seafood, this would be especially treasured."
—Joan Strausman, Long Beach, California

6 servings

  2 **large green peppers, sliced lengthwise into ¼-inch strips**
  2 **medium onions, sliced**
  1 **tablespoon minced garlic**
  1 **tablespoon fermented black beans,* rinsed and dried**
  1 **tablespoon sugar**
  1 **tablespoon soy sauce**
  1 **tablespoon oyster sauce**
  1 **tablespoon Chinese wine* (sake or pale dry sherry may be substituted)**
 1½ **teaspoons salt**
   Freshly ground white pepper

   Oil for deep frying
  3 **large crabs, boiled, cracked into pieces and well dried**
  ½ **cup cornstarch**

Combine first 4 ingredients in bowl. In separate bowl blend sugar, soy sauce, oyster sauce, wine, salt and pepper to taste.

Heat oil in wok to 375°F for deep frying. Meanwhile, lightly coat crab pieces with cornstarch. Deep fry a few pieces at a time, cooking each batch about 1 minute. Drain well on paper towels. Remove all but 1 or 2 tablespoons of oil from wok.

To stir-fry: Set wok over high heat 30 seconds, swirling to coat sides and bottom with oil. When light haze forms add pepper mixture and stir-fry 1 to 2 minutes. Immediately add crab and soy sauce mixture. Stir-fry 2 minutes. Serve on heated platter.

*Available in oriental markets.

CAPTAIN BUDDY'S DEVILED CRAB

BUDDY'S SEAFOOD RESTAURANT
CHARLESTON, SOUTH CAROLINA

For a traditional South Carolina low country feast, serve with Hush Puppies and crisp, creamy coleslaw.

8 to 10 servings

  ½ **cup (1 stick) butter or margarine**
  1 **cup finely chopped celery**
  1 **cup finely chopped green pepper**
  ½ **cup finely chopped onion**
  2 **pounds crabmeat, flaked**
  4 **hard-cooked eggs, finely chopped**
  1 **cup mayonnaise**
  ¾ **cup crushed soda crackers**
  2 **tablespoons minced fresh parsley or parsley flakes**
   Salt and freshly ground pepper
   Hot pepper sauce
  3 **to 4 tablespoons milk (optional)**

Preheat oven to 350°F. Melt butter in large skillet over medium heat. Add celery, green pepper and onion and cook, stirring constantly, until vegetables are soft, about 5 minutes. Add crabmeat, chopped eggs, mayonnaise, cracker crumbs and parsley and toss lightly. Season with salt, pepper and hot pepper sauce to taste. (If mixture seems too thick, stir in milk 1 tablespoon at a time.)

Butter scallop or blue-crab shells. Fill evenly with crab mixture. Bake until tops are golden brown, about 30 to 35 minutes. Serve immediately.

DOCKSIDE MURPHY'S MARYLAND CRAB STEW

DOCKSIDE MURPHY'S
SALISBURY, MARYLAND

Makes about 1 gallon

  3 **slices bacon, cut into ½-inch pieces**
 2½ **pounds onions, chopped**
  1 **pound carrots, peeled and chopped**
  1 **pound celery, chopped**
  3 **medium green peppers, seeded and diced**
 1½ **pounds tomatoes, diced and crushed**
   Pinch granulated garlic
   Pinch salt and freshly ground pepper
 1½ **gallons (6 quarts) hot water**
  ¼ **cup chicken stock base**
  1 **10-ounce can whole clams, undrained**

  3 **medium potatoes, peeled and diced**
  ½ **cup plus 2 tablespoons Worcestershire sauce**
  2 **tablespoons fresh lemon juice**
   Pinch Old Bay Seasoning*
 1½ **pounds crabmeat, cooked**

Sauté bacon in large saucepan or Dutch oven until crisp. Add onions, carrots, celery and green peppers and sauté until lightly golden, about 10 to 15 minutes. Gradually stir in hot water, chicken stock base and clams until well combined. Simmer 3 to 4 hours, uncovered, stirring occasionally.

Add potatoes, Worcestershire sauce, lemon juice and seasoning and simmer ½ hour longer. Add crabmeat and heat through. Serve hot.

*Available in specialty food stores.

PAPILLOTE OF LOBSTER, BRAINS AND SCALLOPS

RESTAURANT ANDRE DAGUIN, HOTEL DE FRANCE
AUCH, FRANCE

In Auch this dish is prepared by arranging slices of duck foie gras, lobster and black truffles in a butterfly design inside a foil package. The lobster sauce is dolloped onto the foil first, and the slices are then arranged to create a multicolored pattern of butterfly wings. Chives, tarragon, coriander and parsley are sprinkled on top. As soon as the papillotes (foil packages) puff in the oven, they are placed on hot wrought-iron paddles and rushed to the diners. In this adaptation (prepared at the Chaîne dinner in New York), calf's brains were substituted for the foie gras because their texture is similar, and scallops were added to make the dish more substantial. The lobster sauce is rich, delicious and worth the expense. Leftover lobster sauce can be frozen.

8 servings

 2 **sets calf's brains**
   Salted ice water

Court Bouillon

 4 **cups water**
 ½ **cup dry white wine**
 1 **large carrot, peeled and coarsely chopped**
 1 **celery stalk, coarsely chopped**
 6 **black peppercorns**
 2 **whole cloves**

Lobster Sauce

16 **cups (4 quarts) water**
 1 **3½-pound live lobster**

 2 **small carrots, peeled and chopped**
 2 **small celery stalks, chopped**
 2 **shallots, minced**
 1 **small onion, peeled and quartered**
 1 **small turnip, peeled and quartered**
 ¼ **teaspoon dried thyme**
 ¼ **teaspoon dried tarragon**
 5 **or 6 fresh parsley sprigs**
 1 **bottle (25.4 ounces) dry vermouth**
 4 **cups fish fumet, strained***

 6 **cups whipping cream**

16 **bay scallops (about 1 pound)**
   Salt and freshly ground pepper
 1 **tablespoon minced fresh chives**
 1 **tablespoon minced fresh parsley**
1½ **teaspoons minced fresh tarragon (optional)**

Soak brains several hours in refrigerator in enough salted ice water to cover.

For Court Bouillon: Combine all ingredients in large deep saucepan. Bring to boil, reduce heat and simmer 1 hour. Remove from heat and let cool. Cover and chill.

Remove brains from water with slotted spoon. Discard membranes, vessels and threads. Place in chilled Court Bouillon and bring to simmer over very low heat. Remove from heat and let cool. Cover and refrigerate until ready to use.

For Lobster Sauce: Bring water to boil in large stockpot, lobster steamer or couscousière. If using stockpot, place large colander over top to fit tightly. Press lobster tail underneath close to body and hold claws together. Place in colander, cover tightly and steam 15 minutes. Using tongs, transfer lobster to wooden surface and let cool.

Sever tail from head. Remove and discard tough sac (near eyes). Remove coral (eggs, if there are any) and tomalley (liver) and set aside. Cut off and crack claws. Remove meat in two large pieces and reserve. Using cleaver, chop claw shells, head and small legs. Remove tail shell, leaving meat in one piece. Discard intestinal vein. Cut tail meat into 12 even medallions. Cover all lobster meat with plastic wrap and refrigerate until ready to be used.

Chop tail shell into small pieces. Combine chopped claw and tail shells, head and small legs in large skillet with carrots, celery, shallots, onion, turnip and herbs. Cover and cook over low heat 5 minutes. Add vermouth and continue cooking uncovered, stirring frequently, until liquid is reduced to 1 cup. Add fish fumet. Increase heat to medium-low and stir frequently until liquid is reduced to 1 cup. Total reducing time is about 1½ hours.

Increase heat to high and add cream. Continue cooking over high heat, stirring frequently, until liquid is reduced to 2 cups. Strain liquid into another saucepan, discarding shells and vegetables. Using whisk, stir in reserved coral and tomalley and cook gently over low heat 5 minutes, stirring constantly. Strain into third saucepan, taste and adjust seasoning if desired. Cool.

Place 2 baking sheets in oven and preheat to highest setting. Cut 8 sheets of heavy duty aluminum foil, each about 12x16 inches, for papillotes.

To assemble: Drain brains and pat dry with paper towels. Cut each half into 4 even slices. Season lobster, scallops and brains with salt and pepper. Spread out sheets of foil. Distribute lobster, scallops and brains equally in center of top half of each sheet. Cover with 2 to 3 tablespoons sauce. Combine chives, parsley and tarragon and sprinkle evenly over sauce. Fold foil, securing ends tightly to avoid leakage. (Papillotes may be prepared in advance to this point and refrigerated.) Place papillotes side by side on hot baking sheets and bake until well puffed, about 4 minutes. Transfer to plates and serve immediately.

*Fish fumet is a highly concentrated essence of fish, prepared by stewing the bones, skin and heads in wine or stock until liquid is greatly reduced.

LOBSTER FRICASSEE PRIMAVERA WITH BEURRE BLANC

RESTAURANT BOYER
REIMS, FRANCE

12 servings

- 2 quarts water
- 1 tablespoon salt
- 1 medium celery root (8 ounces)
- ½ pound green beans, cut julienne into 2-inch lengths
- 6 large carrots (tips trimmed), cut into 1¾-inch lengths and turned* (24 turned carrots)
- 2 large turnips, cut into 1¾-inch lengths ½ inch wide and turned* (24 turned turnips)

Beurre Blanc

- ¼ cup white wine vinegar
- ¼ cup fish stock or clam juice
- 2 large shallots (2 ounces), minced
- 1 cup (2 sticks), unsalted butter, chilled and cut into tablespoon-size pieces
  Pinch ground red pepper
  Salt and freshly ground pepper

- 4 tablespoons (½ stick) unsalted butter
- 4 1½-pound lobsters, cooked, shelled and cut into 2-inch chunks (about 1½ pounds meat)

  Parsley sprigs (garnish)

Bring water to boil with salt in 4-quart saucepan over high heat. Peel celery root; cut julienne into 2-inch lengths. Immediately add to pan and return water to boil. Let boil 30 seconds. Remove with slotted spoon (maintain water at boil) and transfer to large bowl of ice water. Add beans to pan and boil 30 seconds. Remove with slotted spoon (maintain water at boil) and transfer to bowl of ice water. Add carrots to pan and boil 4 minutes. Remove with slotted spoon (maintain water at boil) and add to ice water. Add turnips to pan and boil 2 minutes. Transfer to ice water using slotted spoon. When completely cool, drain well and set aside.

For Beurre Blanc: Combine vinegar, stock and shallots in small saucepan and cook over medium heat until liquid is reduced to 3 tablespoons. Whisk in butter 1 piece at a time, making sure each piece is completely incorporated before adding the next; do not boil. Remove from heat and season to taste with red pepper, salt and pepper. Keep warm.

To assemble: Melt 2 tablespoons butter in each of 2 8-inch skillets over medium-high heat. Add vegetables to 1 skillet and lobster to the other. Cook both until heated through. Season vegetables and lobster with salt and pepper.

Place lobster in center of serving platter or individual plates. Arrange vegetables over top. Spoon some of Beurre Blanc over vegetables and garnish with parsley. Pass remaining Beurre Blanc.

If Beurre Blanc needs reheating, warm gently (do not boil), whisking constantly.

*"Turning" refers to carving vegetables uniformly into oval pieces, usually 1½ to 1¾ inches in length. The trimmings can be used in soups and stocks.

HAITIAN LOBSTER

L'AUBERGE
STRAFFORD, PENNSYLVANIA

4 servings

Sauce Caribe

- ¼ pound fresh spinach, chopped
- 1¼ cups mayonnaise
- 3 anchovy fillets, finely chopped
- 2 small garlic cloves, minced
- 1½ teaspoons finely chopped chives
- 1 teaspoon finely chopped parsley
- 1 teaspoon capers
  Juice of ¼ lemon
  Salt and freshly ground pepper

Lobster

  Oil
- 1 cup breadcrumbs
- ¼ cup ground almonds
- 1½ tablespoons chopped chives
- 8 4-ounce lobster tails, shells discarded
- 1 cup mayonnaise

For sauce: Combine all ingredients in small bowl and blend well. Cover and refrigerate overnight. (Remove from refrigerator and let stand at room temperature about 1 hour before serving.)

For lobster: Heat oil in deep fryer to 350°F. Combine crumbs, almonds and chives in shallow bowl and mix well. Coat lobster with mayonnaise, wiping off excess. Roll lobster in crumb mixture, coating completely. Fry until golden brown on all sides, about 5 minutes. Drain well. Arrange on platter. Serve with Sauce Caribe.

MOULES MARINIERE

LA MASCOTTE
COMMACK, NEW YORK

"On several occasions I have sampled the mussels in white wine sauce from La Mascotte. No matter how often I try them, they are always better than I remember."
—*Judy Loveless, St. James, New York*

6 servings

> 5 pounds mussels, thoroughly cleaned and rinsed
> 1 cup chopped fresh parsley, lightly packed
> ¾ cup dry white wine
> 6 tablespoons (¾ stick) unsalted butter
> 3 tablespoons minced shallot
> 1½ teaspoons salt
> 1½ teaspoons freshly ground pepper
>
> ½ cup fish velouté
> 6 tablespoons whipping cream
>   Chopped fresh parsley (garnish)

Combine first 7 ingredients in 5- to 6-quart Dutch oven. Cover and bring to boil, then simmer until mussels open, about 5 to 10 minutes, turning occasionally. Transfer with slotted spoon to serving platter and cool slightly. Discard top half of each shell. Cover mussels with foil and keep warm.

Cook pan juices over high heat until reduced by ¾. Lower heat and, stirring constantly, add velouté and cream. When heated through pour over mussels. Garnish lightly with parsley and serve.

IPSWICH AND CHERRYSTONE CLAM PAN ROAST

OYSTER BAR & RESTAURANT
NEW YORK, NEW YORK

For each serving:

> 8 freshly opened Ipswich and cherrystone clams (juice reserved)
>
> 2 tablespoons (¼ stick) butter
> 1 tablespoon chili sauce
> 1 teaspoon Worcestershire sauce
> ¾ teaspoon paprika
>   Pinch celery salt
> ½ cup whipping cream
>
> 1 slice day-old white bread, toasted

Cut off tough necks of clams and remove black bands. Rinse clams in their own juice until free of sand. Set aside. Strain juice through muslin cloth and reserve ¼ cup.

Place clams, 1 tablespoon butter and remaining ingredients except clam juice, cream and toast in top of double boiler over boiling water (water should not touch upper pan). Stir 1 minute. Add cream and reserved clam juice; stir constantly until edges of clams begin to curl, about 4 minutes.

Pour immediately over toast slice placed in warmed soup bowl. Top with remaining butter and serve.

Note: A combination pan roast may be made by substituting the following for 6 of the clams: 2 freshly opened oysters, 2 scallops and 2 raw shrimp, shelled and deveined.

BROUET DE COQUILLES ST. JACQUES

THE CHURCH RESTAURANT
STRATFORD, ONTARIO, CANADA

"One of the highlights of our visit last summer to the Stratford Shakespeare Festival was The Church Restaurant's superb coquilles, served in a delicate cream base with fresh vegetables. We were certainly surprised when the waiter informed us that this rich-tasting dish was actually cuisine minceur."
—*Larry Wine, Evanston, Illinois*

6 servings

> 4 tablespoons (½ stick) butter
> 3 carrots, sliced
> 1 small celery heart, sliced
> 1 European cucumber (also known as hothouse cucumber) cut into ½-inch cubes
> 24 small mushrooms, sliced
>
> ¾ cup white wine
> 2 pounds scallops, washed thoroughly
> 2 cups Crème Fraîche*
>   Salt and pepper
>   Coarsely chopped fresh chervil and/or parsley (garnish)

Melt 2 tablespoons butter in 1-quart saucepan over medium heat and sauté carrots 5 minutes. Reduce heat, add celery and cook 5 minutes. Add cucumber and mushrooms, cover and cook 5 minutes more.

In separate pan, reduce wine by ½. In large skillet, melt remaining butter over medium heat and sauté scallops 30 seconds; do not brown. Add vegetables with their pan juices, reduced wine and Crème Fraîche. Cook 3 minutes and season to taste with salt and pepper (scallops should not be overcooked). If slightly thicker sauce is desired, remove scallops and vegetables from pan and reduce sauce slightly over medium-high heat; return scallops and vegetables to sauce and serve. Garnish with chervil and/or parsley.

Crème Fraîche

> 2 cups whipping cream
> 1 tablespoon buttermilk

Mix cream and buttermilk in covered jar and shake 2 minutes. Let stand at room temperature until thick, about 8 hours. Place in refrigerator.

BAKED BAY SCALLOPS

KINGSTON HARBOUR YACHT CLUB
MT. PROSPECT, ILLINOIS

"Garlic, garlic, garlic describes the scallops served at the Kingston Harbour Yacht Club. My wife and I enjoyed these crisp, buttery morsels at a marvelous dinner there."
—Lawerence T. McCarthy, Lombard, Illinois

4 servings

    1 **cup (2 sticks) butter, room temperature**
    1 **cup fresh breadcrumbs**
    6 **garlic cloves, crushed**
    2 **tablespoons finely minced onion**
  ½ **cup chopped fresh parsley**
    2 **ounces (¼ cup) white wine or sherry**
      Juice of ½ lemon
      Salt and freshly ground pepper

    2 **tablespoons vegetable oil**
    2 **tablespoons diced onion**
 1½ **pounds fresh bay scallops**
  ½ **pound mushrooms, sliced**

Mix together butter, breadcrumbs, garlic, minced onion, parsley, wine, lemon juice and salt and pepper to taste. Form into roll and wrap with waxed paper. Chill garlic butter until firm, at least 1 hour.

Preheat oven to 450°F. Grease shallow baking dish or au gratin pan. Heat oil in large skillet over medium heat until haze forms. Add diced onion and sauté until soft but not browned. Add scallops and mushrooms and salt and pepper to taste and sauté briefly. Drain off liquid. Arrange scallop mixture in prepared dish. Slice garlic butter and arrange evenly over scallops. Bake until butter is hot and bubbly, about 5 to 10 minutes. Serve immediately.

Scallops can also be broiled. Place about 3 inches from heat and broil until bubbly, 3 to 5 minutes.

COQUILLES ST. JACQUES

CAFE AT THE MEWS
PROVINCETOWN, MASSACHUSETTS

6 to 8 servings

    7 **tablespoons (⅞ stick) butter**
    3 **tablespoons flour**
  ½ **cup bottled clam juice**
  ½ **cup white wine**
      Pinch tarragon
      Pinch thyme

    2 **egg yolks, beaten**
  ½ **cup light cream**
      Salt and white pepper

    2 **pounds sea scallops**
      Flour
    1 **teaspoon olive oil**

    2 **garlic cloves, minced**
  ½ **cup minced shallots**

  ½ **cup grated Swiss cheese**

Melt 3 tablespoons butter in medium skillet. Remove from heat and stir in flour. Return skillet to heat and add clam juice and wine. Stir in tarragon and thyme. Cook until sauce becomes smooth and thick, about 2 to 3 minutes.

Combine egg yolks with light cream in saucepan. Slowly beat hot sauce into egg-cream mixture. Season with salt and white pepper to taste and cook slowly for a few minutes, stirring occasionally.

Prepare scallops by removing all shell chips, grit and sand. Cut scallops into bite-sized pieces. Dust with flour, shaking off excess. Heat 3 tablespoons butter with olive oil in skillet. Sauté scallops until lightly browned. Set aside. Add remaining butter to same skillet and sauté garlic and shallots.

Combine sauce, scallops and shallot-garlic mixture. Refrigerate until ready to use.

Spoon mixture into shell-shaped ramekins and sprinkle with Swiss cheese. Brown under broiler, turning ramekins for even browning. Serve at once.

COQUILLES ST. JACQUES EN SAUCE CHAMPAGNE AU KIWI
(Braised Scallops in Champagne Sauce with Sliced Kiwi)

ERNIE'S
SAN FRANCISCO, CALIFORNIA

4 servings

    2 **tablespoons (¼ stick) unsalted butter**
    1 **large shallot, chopped**
    1 **cup brut Champagne or dry white wine**
      Salt and freshly ground white pepper
 1½ **pounds fresh scallops**

    3 **cups whipping cream**
  ¼ **cup (½ stick) unsalted butter, cut into pieces**
    2 **kiwi fruit, peeled, sliced ⅛ inch thick (garnish)**

Heat 2 tablespoons butter in large skillet over medium heat. Add shallot and sauté lightly. Add Champagne or wine and simmer until reduced by half. Season to taste with salt and white pepper. Add scallops, top with piece of buttered parchment or waxed paper and simmer gently until just cooked through, about 2 to 3 minutes. Remove scallops with slotted spoon and keep warm.

Increase heat and reduce juices to glaze. Blend in cream and simmer until thickened and mixture lightly coats spoon, about 20 minutes. Whisk in remaining butter. Taste and adjust seasoning. Divide sauce among warmed dinner plates. Arrange scallops over sauce and top each with slice of kiwi.

SCALLOPS LANDAISE

TALK OF THE TOWN
HILLSDALE, NEW JERSEY

4 servings

>   2 cups beer
>   1 teaspoon salt
>   1 to 1½ teaspoons freshly ground pepper
>   40 scallops
>
>   Flour
>   2 tablespoons olive oil
>   2 tablespoons white vinegar
>
>   ¼ cup (½ stick) sweet butter
>   ¼ cup (½ stick) salted butter
>   1 cup chopped walnuts

Combine beer, salt and pepper in medium bowl; add scallops and marinate 15 minutes at room temperature.

Drain scallops; coat with flour. Heat oil in large skillet and sauté scallops until golden brown. Heat vinegar in small saucepan or ladle. Add to scallops and blend thoroughly. Keep warm.

Melt sweet and salted butter in medium skillet over medium-low heat. Add walnuts and sauté 3 to 4 minutes. Add to scallops and serve immediately.

COQUILLES ST. JACQUES AU GINGEMBRE
(Scallops with Ginger)

SPAGO
LOS ANGELES, CALIFORNIA

2 servings

>   6 ounces puff pastry
>   1 egg, lightly beaten
>
>   ½ cup Sauternes
>   1 shallot, minced
>   1½ teaspoons minced fresh ginger
>   10 ounces bay scallops (or sea scallops, halved horizontally)
>   3 tablespoons whipping cream
>   ¾ cup (1½ sticks) chilled unsalted butter, cut into small pieces
>   Salt and freshly ground pepper
>   2 teaspoons fresh lemon juice or to taste
>
>   2 green onions or 1 small leek, cut into ¼-inch-thick slices

Preheat oven to 450°F. Roll out puff pastry into 10-inch circle ¼ inch thick. Place on baking sheet and cut out 8-inch circle from center, discarding excess pastry. Brush with egg. Cut concentric circle 1 inch in from edge and halfway through pastry. Chill pastry 10 minutes. Bake 15 minutes, reduce heat to 350°F and continue to bake until pastry is golden brown, about 15 to 20 minutes. Return oven temperature to 450°F. Carefully lift off pastry cover formed by concentric circle and gently remove moist dough inside shell.

Combine wine, shallot and ginger in medium saucepan and bring to boil over medium heat. Add scallops and cream and cook 1 to 2 minutes. Remove scallops using slotted spoon. Increase heat to medium-high and cook liquid until reduced to 2 tablespoons, adding any juices drained from scallops. Whisk in all but 1 teaspoon butter 1 piece at a time. Season with salt and pepper. Add lemon juice. Set sauce aside.

Melt remaining 1 teaspoon butter in small skillet over high heat. Add green onion and cook 30 seconds. Set aside.

Stir scallops into sauce and heat through. Reheat pastry shell and lid in oven for 2 minutes.

To serve, place pastry shell on heated platter and fill with scallop mixture. Sprinkle with green onion and top with pastry lid.

SCALLOPS PROVENÇALE

MAGIC FLUTE RESTAURANT
SAN FRANCISCO, CALIFORNIA

4 to 6 servings

>   1 basket cherry tomatoes
>
>   2 tablespoons finely chopped shallots
>   4 teaspoons chopped fresh thyme or 1 teaspoon dried thyme
>   4 teaspoons fresh whole basil or 1 teaspoon dried basil
>   1 garlic clove, minced
>   2 tablespoons olive oil
>
>   1½ pounds scallops
>   ½ cup dry white wine

Slice tomatoes in half. Seed with melon baller and place seeds and juice in small ramekin. Strain juice and reserve.

In large heavy pot, sauté shallots, 2 tablespoons each thyme and basil, and garlic in olive oil for 2 to 3 minutes. Add tomato juice and cook over medium-high heat until mixture is reduced to gravylike thickness. Add tomatoes and cook 10 minutes. Let set about 30 minutes.

In large covered frying pan, poach scallops in wine mixed with remaining thyme and basil until tender, about 10 to 15 minutes. Remove scallops with slotted spoon and set aside. Add tomato mixture to wine and cook over medium-high heat until again reduced to gravylike consistency. Add scallops and heat through.

CREAM OF COQUILLES ST. JACQUES WITH LEEKS

LES FRERES TROISGROS
ROANNE, FRANCE

4 servings

    2 large leeks (white part only), cut into fine 1½-inch julienne
    2 tablespoons (¼ stick) butter

    1 cup Fish Fumet*
    ¼ cup cream sherry
    1½ pounds large fresh scallops, quartered
    1 cup whipping cream
      Salt and freshly ground pepper

Wash leeks thoroughly, but do not dry. Melt butter in heavy large skillet over low heat. Add leeks, cover and let sweat until tender and translucent, stirring occasionally, about 10 to 15 minutes. Remove from heat and set aside.

Add Fish Fumet and sherry to skillet and heat just until liquid trembles. Add scallops and poach 2 minutes. Remove scallops using slotted spoon and keep warm. Increase heat and boil liquid until reduced by ½, scraping up any bits clinging to bottom of pan. Add cream and continue boiling until thickened. Return leeks to skillet and heat through. Season to taste with salt and pepper. Divide leeks and sauce among 4 heated serving plates and arrange scallops on top. Serve immediately.

*Fish Fumet

Makes about 6 cups

    2 pounds (about) fish trimmings (do not use salmon)
    2 quarts (8 cups) cold water
    ¼ cup tarragon vinegar
    2 celery stalks with leaves, cut into 2-inch pieces
    2 carrots, cut into 2-inch pieces
    2 leeks, white part only, split
    ½ medium head of lettuce
   10 white peppercorns
    5 sprigs fresh dill

    3 sprigs parsley
    2 bay leaves
    1 teaspoon dried thyme
    1 teaspoon salt

Combine all ingredients in 4- to 5-quart saucepan and bring to boil. Reduce heat and simmer uncovered 45 minutes. Strain through colander or cheesecloth-lined strainer before using.

CASSOLETTES DE SCAMPI ET PETONCLES
(Ramekins of Shrimp and Scallops)

LE FRANÇAIS
WHEELING, ILLINOIS

Wild rice is a good accompaniment.

6 to 8 servings

    2 pounds fresh spinach, trimmed

    ¾ pound scallops
    1 pound uncooked medium shrimp, shelled
    6 tablespoons (¾ stick) butter, clarified
      Salt and freshly ground pepper
      Sauce Béarnaise*
      Peeled, seeded and coarsely chopped tomato sautéed in olive oil (garnish)

Blanch spinach in boiling salted water until barely tender. Drain well. Divide among individual shells or ramekins.

Sauté scallops and shrimp in butter over medium-high heat until scallops are opaque and shrimp are pink, about 4 minutes. Remove from heat and season lightly with salt and pepper. Divide over spinach and top with Béarnaise Sauce. Run under preheated broiler briefly until top is golden, watching carefully to prevent burning. Garnish with chopped tomato and serve immediately.

*Sauce Béarnaise

Makes 1½ to 2 cups

    ½ cup red wine vinegar
    3 tablespoons finely chopped shallots
    1 tablespoon minced fresh tarragon or ½ teaspoon dried
    2 teaspoons minced fresh chervil or ⅜ teaspoon dried
    ½ teaspoon salt
    ¼ teaspoon freshly ground pepper

    4 egg yolks
    1 cup (2 sticks) unsalted butter, cut into pieces (softened)

    ¼ cup whipping cream

Combine first 6 ingredients in heavy saucepan and bring to boil over high heat. Reduce heat and simmer until liquid is reduced to about 2 tablespoons, about 5 minutes. Let cool.

Lightly whisk yolks. Add to vinegar-shallot mixture, blending well. Place pan over low heat and whisk until mixture thickens and becomes creamy, removing pan from heat occasionally as you whisk to prevent yolks from curdling. Whisk in butter 1 piece at a time, blending completely before adding more. Continue whisking until consistency of light mayonnaise. Cover and keep warm in bain-marie.

Just before serving, whip cream until stiff and fold into yolk mixture.

SEAFOOD GUMBO

COMMANDER'S PALACE
NEW ORLEANS, LOUISIANA

Although this gumbo does not have a traditional roux base, the seasoning puts it in the Creole category. The absence of a roux affords a unique light texture.

8 main course servings or 16 appetizer servings

  2 **quarts (8 cups) Seafood Stock***
16 **crab claws**
  3 **cups diced onion**
  2 **cups diced green pepper**
  1 **16-ounce can whole tomatoes, undrained**
  1 **cup tomato puree**
  3 **tablespoons gumbo filé****
  2 **10-ounce packages frozen cut okra, unthawed**
  ¼ **cup Creole Seafood Seasoning*** or to taste**
 1½ **tablespoons granulated garlic**
 1½ **teaspoons thyme**
 1¼ **teaspoons saffron**
  4 **bay leaves**
  ½ **teaspoon salt**
60 **large raw shrimp, peeled and deveined**
24 **fresh oysters**
  1 **pound lump crabmeat**

Combine Seafood Stock, crab claws, onion, green pepper, tomatoes and tomato puree in 8-quart saucepan or Dutch oven. Place over medium heat and bring to boil. Reduce heat and simmer 10 minutes. Add all remaining ingredients except seafood and return to simmer for an additional 10 minutes. Add seafood and continue cooking 10 minutes, adding more Seafood Seasoning to taste if desired (gumbo should be spicy but full bodied).

*Seafood Stock

The highest quality Creole cookery utilizes stocks or reduction of stocks. Naturally, fresh ingredients are preferred, but frozen may be substituted if necessary.

Makes 2 quarts

  2 **quarts water**
  6 **celery stalks, cut into 2-inch pieces**
  2 **medium onions, peeled and quartered**
  2 **garlic cloves**
  ½ **lemon**
      Fresh shrimp heads and/or shells, lobster heads and/or shells, fresh fish bones (use these ingredients singly or in combination)

Combine all ingredients in large saucepan or stockpot and bring to rapid boil. Reduce heat to low and simmer slowly 2 to 8 hours, depending on strength of flavor desired. Strain before using.

Reduction is a technique best achieved after stock is strained, and reduced stock is normally used when a recipe calls for a small amount of liquid or stock with a more intense flavor. Return the desired amount of strained stock to saucepan or skillet and bring to boil over high heat. Reduce heat to low and simmer uncovered until evaporation reduces stock to quantity required.

**Available in specialty food stores.

***Creole Seafood Seasoning

Makes 2 cups

  ⅓ **cup plus 1 tablespoon salt**
  ⅓ **cup plus 1 tablespoon paprika**
  ⅓ **cup cayenne pepper**
  ¼ **cup black pepper**
  ¼ **cup granulated garlic**
  3 **tablespoons granulated onion**
  3 **tablespoons thyme**

Thoroughly combine all ingredients in small bowl.

Can be stored indefinitely in tightly lidded glass jar.

GAMBERETTI DI MARE

THE BUTTERY
KEY WEST, FLORIDA

2 servings

  ½ **cup (1 stick) butter**
  1 **garlic clove, crushed**
  1 **tablespoon plus 1 teaspoon chopped fresh parsley**
  1 **tablespoon plus 1 teaspoon chopped fresh chives or green onion tops**
  2 **teaspoons brandy**
      Dash ground cloves
      Dash freshly grated nutmeg
20 **uncooked medium shrimp, peeled and deveined**
  8 **medium mushroom caps**
  2 **medium tomatoes, cut into 8 wedges**
  1 **medium green pepper, cut into ¼-inch strips**
  1 **teaspoon flour**
  1 **tablespoon plus 1 teaspoon dry vermouth**
      Freshly cooked rice or linguine

Melt butter in large skillet over medium-high heat. Stir in garlic, parsley, chives, brandy, cloves and nutmeg. When butter is hot and bubbly, add shrimp, mushrooms, tomatoes and pepper and sauté until shrimp are just cooked through. Transfer to heated platter using slotted spoon. Keep warm.

Add flour to skillet and stir constantly until well blended, scraping up any browned bits clinging to bottom. Stir in vermouth to deglaze pan. Reduce heat and simmer until sauce thickens, about 2 to 3 minutes. Pour over shrimp and vegetables. Serve immediately with rice or linguine.

THE COACH HOUSE—THE QUINTESSENTIAL NEW YORK RESTAURANT

There are few restaurants whose phenomenal success and popularity virtually defy criticism. But even the most prestigious writers and critics in the food world say only good things about The Coach House, which has been going strong in Greenwich Village for over thirty years. It is the pride and joy of its owner, Leon Lianides, and a gastronomic haven for all who measure the quality of life in terms of what they eat.

The restaurant is a visual reflection of its owner's taste: brick walls, red banquettes, rainbows of fresh flowers, a highly personal collection of English and American paintings and displays of both food and the noble French and American wines so loved by Lianides.

Part of the restaurant's originality stems from the fact that the menu is a gastronomic melting pot of no particular ethnic persuasion. There are French escargots de Bourgogne and striped bass poached in court bouillon but also good old American chicken pie and prime ribs of beef, and lobster prepared with tangy Greek feta cheese. Piping hot corn sticks are served to every diner.

Lianides sums up the food at The Coach House in four words: "Simplicity, quality, timing and continuity." Dishes are served with few frills, on the theory that "beautiful foods are simple foods." He speaks nightly with his seafood dealers and personally selects his meat from two purveyors ("just to keep them both on their toes"). Someone on his staff makes the trip to Hunts Point to choose fresh fruits and vegetables; fresh eggs are brought to the restaurant twice a week by a friend on Long Island; bread is delivered daily by a local Italian baker. Dedication is no doubt the secret behind the restaurant's remarkable continuity.

GRILLED SHRIMP WITH MUSTARD SAUCE

THE COACH HOUSE
NEW YORK, NEW YORK

2 servings

- **10 to 12 large uncooked shrimp, unshelled but slit and deveined**
- **1½ cups dry white wine**
  Juice of 1 lemon
- **10 black peppercorns, crushed**
- **3 shallots, chopped**
- **2 garlic cloves, crushed**
- **1½ tablespoons olive oil**

- **8 to 10 lemon slices (garnish)**
  Mustard Sauce*
- **2 tablespoons chopped fresh parsley (garnish)**

Combine first 7 ingredients in medium bowl and stir to coat shrimp thoroughly. Let marinate at room temperature for 2 to 3 hours.

Remove shrimp, reserving marinade, and transfer to small broiler pan. Broil shrimp just until they turn pink, about 8 to 10 minutes. Arrange on heated plates. Insert lemon slice between each. Spoon Mustard Sauce over and sprinkle with parsley.

*Mustard Sauce

2 servings

- **12 ounces light-bodied red wine**
- **1 large onion, sliced**
  Reserved marinade from shrimp
- **5 to 6 teaspoons Dijon mustard or to taste**
- **2 to 3 teaspoons Meat Glaze (optional) (see page 116)**

Combine wine, onion and marinade in 2-quart saucepan. Bring to boil and cook until liquid is reduced by ½. Strain. Return to saucepan over low heat and whisk in mustard and Meat Glaze, if desired. Continue cooking, whisking constantly, until sauce is slightly thickened and coats whisk. Adjust seasoning.

GARIDES TOURKOLIMANO
(Greek Shrimp)

MICHAELS RESTAURANT
ROCHESTER, MINNESOTA

"While visiting Rochester, I dined at Michaels Restaurant, which had been recommended to me by friends. The Pappas family has owned Michaels for three generations. I had a most marvelous Greek shrimp dish—Garides Tourkolimano."

— *Margaret Higgins, Del Mar, California*

6 servings

    3 pounds raw large shrimp, peeled
       and deveined
    ½ cup lemon juice

    ½ cup (1 stick) butter, whipped
    1 garlic clove, minced
    1 cup chopped green onion tops
    3 large tomatoes, peeled and cut into
       wedges
    1 teaspoon oregano
      Salt and pepper
    1 pound feta cheese, crumbled
    ¾ cup cream sherry

Sprinkle shrimp with lemon juice and set aside.

Melt butter in large skillet. Sauté garlic, green onion tops and tomato wedges. Add shrimp and season with oregano, salt and pepper to taste. Turn shrimp frequently and sauté until pink. Add feta cheese and cream sherry. Bring to boil and cook 3 to 4 minutes. Remove shrimp carefully to casserole. Spoon cheese-sherry mixture over shrimp.

GAMBERI ALLA LIVORNESE

BLUE FOX
SAN FRANCISCO, CALIFORNIA

"I have had the opportunity to do some fairly extensive traveling to various parts of the world and have eaten in many fine restaurants. Probably the best meal I have ever eaten was at the Blue Fox. Their version of scampi without garlic was absolutely delicious."

— *Charles E. Kohlerman, Baltimore, Maryland*

The Blue Fox serves Gamberi Alla Livornese with small French rolls, split and spread with butter and Parmesan cheese, then toasted under a broiler. They are perfect for dipping in the wine-butter sauce.

4 servings

    16 large prawns, peeled, deveined and
        butterflied
     2 cups milk
       Flour
       Salt and pepper
       Oil

    1½ cups dry white wine
     3 tablespoons lemon juice
       Salt
       Hot pepper sauce
     1 teaspoon arrowroot
     2 tablespoons dry white wine
     6 tablespoons (¾ stick) butter, softened,
        cut into small pieces
        Chopped parsley (garnish)

Place prawns in medium bowl. Add milk and soak about 15 minutes. Combine flour with salt and pepper to taste. Drain prawns and dredge in flour mixture. In deep skillet, heat 1 inch oil to 375°F. Fry prawns until very lightly browned, about 2 minutes. Remove and drain on paper towels; keep prawns warm.

In medium saucepan, combine 1½ cups wine and lemon juice; season with salt and hot pepper sauce to taste. Bring to boil over medium heat. Dilute arrowroot in 2 tablespoons wine and pour into hot wine mixture. Cook about 10 to 15 seconds. Remove from heat and add butter, beating with whisk until smooth. Add prawns, coating thoroughly with sauce. Heat briefly, about 1 minute. Garnish with parsley and serve.

RASA SAYANG HOTEL LAMBOK

RASA SAYANG HOTEL, BATU FERINGGI BEACH
PENANG, MALAYSIA

"The entire Malaysian menu was a rare and delicious treat, but we became especially fond of a breakfast dish called Lambok."

— *Mrs. Thomas R. Murray, Seoul, Korea*

6 servings

    1¼ cups uncooked rice
     3 cups chicken broth

     3 tablespoons (⅜ stick) butter
     3 garlic cloves, minced
     3 jumbo shrimp, peeled, deveined and
        chopped
     1 large chicken breast, split, skinned,
        boned and chopped
     6 ounces red snapper, chopped
     6 ounces lean lamb, chopped
     ⅓ cup soy sauce
        Salt and pepper
     1 small piece fresh ginger, shredded; 3
        chopped red chilies; ¼ cup chopped
        green onion (garnish)

Cook rice in chicken broth. Set aside.

Melt butter in large skillet. Add garlic and cook about 1 minute. Add shrimp, chicken, red snapper and lamb. Cook about 5 minutes. Add rice to meat mixture in skillet. Add soy sauce and salt and pepper to taste. Cook for 2 to 3 minutes. Garnish with ginger, red chilies and green onion.

PRAWNS AMARETTO

LONGHI'S CAFE
LAHAINA, MAUI, HAWAII

6 servings

 24 large unshelled prawns, slit from inner
    curve to butterfly
    Flour
  6 tablespoons (¾ stick) butter

 4½ ounces brandy
 4½ ounces Amaretto
  3 ounces dry white wine
  3 oranges, halved
  6 tablespoons whipping cream
  1 tablespoon orange zest (peel)

Dredge prawns lightly in flour. Melt butter in large skillet over medium-high heat until bubbly. Add prawns shell side down and sauté about 4 minutes on each side. Transfer to heated platter; keep warm.

Increase heat and add brandy, Amaretto and wine. Squeeze juice from orange halves directly into skillet, stirring constantly. Add cream and zest and continue stirring until well blended. Return prawns to pan and heat through, between 2 and 3 minutes.

SAUTEED SHRIMP WITH FRESH VEGETABLES AND HERBS

THE JANE DOONER RESTAURANT
ENGLEWOOD, NEW JERSEY

Chef Ray Kaminski suggests preparing the vegetable-shrimp portion of this recipe in two batches to ensure proper crispness of vegetables.

4 servings

 ½ cup (1 stick) butter
  1 pound raw shrimp, shelled and deveined
 1½ cups coarsely chopped onion
 1½ cups cauliflower florets
 1½ cups broccoli florets
 ½ cup thinly sliced small carrots
 ½ cup coarsely chopped green pepper

  2 medium tomatoes, peeled and quartered
  1 cup chicken broth
 ¼ cup sherry
 ¾ teaspoon basil
 1½ tablespoons cornstarch or arrowroot
 ¼ cup cold water
    Salt and freshly ground pepper
  3 cups cooked rice

Heat ¼ cup butter in wok or large skillet over medium-high heat. Add ½ shrimp and sauté until just barely pink; do not allow butter to brown. Immediately add ½ each: onion, cauliflower, broccoli, carrot and green pepper and stir-fry 3 minutes. Transfer to bowl. Repeat with remaining butter, shrimp and vegetables.

Return all shrimp and vegetables to wok. Add tomatoes, broth, sherry and basil and bring to boil. Immediately add cornstarch dissolved in water, gently pouring down side of wok so thickening heats before coating shrimp and vegetables. Simmer 30 seconds, stirring constantly. Season to taste with salt and pepper. Serve immediately over rice.

SHRIMP ALMENDRINA

PEPIN
ST. PETERSBURG, FLORIDA

6 to 8 servings

  2 eggs
  2 cups milk
  2 cups flour
    Salt and freshly ground pepper

 2½ pounds jumbo shrimp, peeled and
    deveined, tails left intact
  4 cups sliced almonds

    Oil for deep frying
    Orange Mustard Sauce*

Beat eggs until light and fluffy in medium bowl; stir in milk. Gradually mix in flour, blending well. Add salt and pepper to taste.

Holding shrimp by tail, dip into batter, allowing excess to drip back into bowl; do not cover tails with batter. Sprinkle all sides of batter-coated shrimp with almonds. Place on cookie sheet and refrigerate at least 2 hours before frying.

Heat oil to 375°F. Deep fry shrimp a few at a time, just until they turn pink, about 2 minutes; do not overcook. Drain on paper towels and keep warm until all shrimp have been cooked. Serve immediately with Orange Mustard Sauce.

Orange Mustard Sauce

Makes about 1 cup

 ¾ cup sweet orange marmalade
 ¼ cup chicken or beef stock
  2 tablespoons fresh lemon juice
  1 teaspoon dry mustard
    Few drops hot pepper sauce

Thoroughly combine all ingredients.

SHRIMP REMOULADE

COMMANDER'S PALACE
NEW ORLEANS, LOUISIANA

6 servings

   ½ cup Creole mustard*
   ½ cup prepared mustard
   ½ cup catsup
   ¼ cup white vinegar
   ¼ cup horseradish
   ¼ cup Worcestershire sauce
   3 tablespoons paprika
   2 cups finely minced celery
1½ cups minced green onion
   ⅓ cup oil or olive oil
   5 eggs, lightly beaten
   1 bunch parsley, minced
   4 bay leaves
   1 lemon, seeded and diced
   2 tablespoons garlic powder
   1 tablespoon salt
   1 teaspoon hot pepper sauce
     Juice of 1 lemon

     Boiled Shrimp,** well chilled
     Shredded lettuce

Combine first 7 ingredients in blender, or food processor fitted with steel knife, and mix well. Add remaining ingredients except shrimp and lettuce and blend thoroughly. Cover and chill several hours or overnight.

About 2 hours before serving, peel shrimp and place in shallow dish. Cover generously with some of sauce and marinate until serving time. Line individual serving plates with small amount of shredded lettuce. Top with shrimp and a little extra sauce and serve immediately.

Leftover sauce can be stored in sealed jar in refrigerator up to 3 weeks.

**Boiled Shrimp

6 servings

   1 gallon (16 cups) Seafood Stock
     (see page 88) or water
   6 ounces liquid crab boil*
   2 lemons, halved
   1 large onion, halved
   3 bay leaves
   1 tablespoon cayenne pepper
 36 large unpeeled raw shrimp, deveined

   1 gallon (16 cups) cold water
   ¾ cup salt
   1 quart ice

Combine stock, crab boil, lemons, onion, bay leaves and cayenne in 8-quart stockpot and bring to boil over medium-high heat. Boil rapidly 15 minutes.

Add shrimp, cover and return to boil, cooking until shrimp are pink, about 1 to 2 minutes.

Meanwhile, combine cold water and salt and stir until salt is dissolved. Drain shrimp and drop into cold salted water. Add ice and let stand until shrimp are well chilled, about 10 minutes. Drain completely and refrigerate, covered, until ready to use.

*Creole mustard and liquid crab boil are available in specialty food stores.

SHRIMP BENIHANA

BENIHANA
NEW YORK, NEW YORK

"We have frequently enjoyed the meals served at the Benihana restaurants. Especially intriguing are the piquant sauces they serve with shrimp and chicken."
     —Axel and Janet Camp, Commack, New York

For each serving:

   4 to 5 large shrimp, peeled, deveined
     and flattened
     Salt

   1 teaspoon butter
   1 teaspoon whipping cream
   2 tablespoons soybean oil
   1 tablespoon chopped fresh parsley
     Juice of ½ lemon
     Benihana of Tokyo Ginger Sauce*
     Benihana of Tokyo Magic Mustard
     Sauce**

Sprinkle shrimp with salt; set aside.

Combine butter and cream. Place griddle or large skillet over medium heat until hot. Oil griddle and add shrimp. Sauté until opaque, about 3 minutes on each side. Remove shrimp and dot with butter-cream mixture. Sprinkle with parsley and return to griddle. Cook 1 to 2 minutes longer. Squeeze lemon juice over shrimp and remove from griddle. Serve with ginger or mustard sauce.

Variation: One boned ½ chicken breast cut into small pieces may be substituted for shrimp. Eliminate butter-cream mixture and parsley; add 1 tablespoon toasted sesame seeds with the lemon juice.

*Benihana of Tokyo Ginger Sauce

Makes about 1 cup

   1 small onion, sliced
   ½ cup soy sauce
   ¼ cup vinegar
   1 small piece fresh ginger root or
   ⅛ teaspoon ground ginger

Place all ingredients in blender and mix at high speed until ginger root and onion are finely chopped, about 2 minutes.

**Benihana of Tokyo Magic Mustard Sauce*

Makes about 1¼ cups

   3 tablespoons dry mustard
   2 tablespoons hot water
   1 tablespoon sesame seeds, toasted
  ¾ cup soy sauce
  ¼ garlic clove, crushed
   3 tablespoons whipping cream, whipped

In small mixing bowl, combine mustard and water to form paste. Place in blender with remaining ingredients except cream and blend at high speed about 1 minute. Remove and stir in whipped cream.

SHRIMP IN BEER

PUMP HOUSE INN
CANADENSIS, PENNSYLVANIA

6 servings

  32 medium raw shrimp
  2½ cups flour

   ¾ cup light domestic beer
  1½ teaspoons salt
  1½ teaspoons paprika

     Oil for deep frying
     Chinese Mustard*

Peel and devein shrimp, leaving tails intact. Dredge shrimp in 2 cups flour.

Pour beer into bowl. Sift remaining flour, salt and paprika into beer. Mix thoroughly with wire whisk until batter is light and frothy.

Heat oil in deep-fat fryer until it reaches 375°F. Dip floured shrimp into batter and fry in oil a few at a time, about 4 minutes. They should be crisp and puffy. Keep warm until ready to serve. Serve with Chinese mustard.

*Available in oriental markets.

SHRIMP ROSEMARY

LAURITA'S
GEORGETOWN, COLORADO

3 to 4 servings

     Olive oil
   2 tablespoons (¼ stick) butter, clarified

   ⅓ cup minced onion
   2 garlic cloves, minced
   ½ teaspoon dried sweet basil
   ½ teaspoon coarsely ground black pepper
  20 large shrimp, shelled, deveined and
      butterflied
   ½ cup cream sherry
   ½ cup minced fresh tomatoes
   2 tablespoons minced parsley
      Garlic salt

Into 12-inch skillet, pour olive oil to depth of approximately ⅛ inch. Add butter and melt over medium heat. Add onion and garlic and sauté until transparent. Add basil, black pepper and shrimp. Increase heat to high and sauté 1 minute. Add cream sherry, tomatoes, parsley and garlic salt to taste. Swirl skillet until shrimp curl.

SHRIMP FIJI

THE BACK PORCH CAFE
REHOBOTH BEACH, DELAWARE

6 to 8 servings

   1 cup fresh orange juice
   1 cup dry white wine
   ½ cup honey
  1½ teaspoons grated fresh ginger

   6 tablespoons (¾ stick) butter, clarified
  12 garlic cloves, crushed
  36 uncooked medium shrimp
   1 tablespoon grated fresh ginger
   1 cup slivered almonds
      Freshly cooked rice

Combine orange juice, wine, honey and 1½ teaspoons ginger in small bowl. Set aside.

Heat butter with garlic in wok or large skillet until butter is bubbly. Add shrimp and 1 tablespoon ginger and sauté briefly. Stir in almonds and continue cooking until almonds are golden and shrimp are cooked through. With slotted spoon, remove shrimp, garlic and almonds to heated platter. Pour off excess butter from skillet. Return skillet to burner and heat briefly. Add orange juice mixture and bring to boil. Reduce heat and simmer 1 minute. Return shrimp mixture to skillet and heat through. Serve immediately over rice.

POULTRY

To borrow a phrase from Brillat-Savarin, poultry is to the cook what canvas is to the painter: the raw material which, in skillful hands, becomes a work of art. And if you extend the analogy a little, it is easy to see that the gastronomy of poultry from Taillevent to Bocuse is as rich and varied as the history of painting from Michelangelo to Wyeth. The enormous range of poultry recipes available today—using duck, squab, turkey, goose, Rock Cornish hens and the many varieties of chicken—is a never-ending boon to the cook looking for something "just a little different."

In the world of poultry, chicken is the unquestioned king. And in the 4,000 years since some unknown genius first figured out how to domesticate wild jungle fowl, chicken has found its way to the table in every imaginable guise. The recipes in this chapter attest to chicken's worldwide popularity; they include the distinctive flavors and styles of preparation of France, England, Italy, the Middle East, Greece, Morocco, China, Mexico and, of course, the United States, where every region has its own heritage of chicken dishes. Statistics show that chicken is the most popular main-course dish in the country. Not surprising, since it is economical, highly nutritious, easy to prepare and the ultimate in culinary adaptability.

Duck and squab are also well represented here. Both were once-in-a-blue-moon luxuries not too long ago, but their popularity has mushroomed because of greatly increased availability—not to mention the fact that *nouvelle cuisine* chefs find them marvelous mates for the new, lighter fruit-based sauces invented in recent years. A relative newcomer to the poultry scene is the hybrid Rock Cornish hen—small, delicate roasters, each one a perfect portion.

The late Michael Field once estimated that a collection of all known poultry recipes would fill a fair-sized public library. Here is a sampling of the best.

Caneton de Challans au Citron from Taillevent in Paris (see page 110).

BLANC DE VOLAILLE
(Stuffed Chicken Breasts with Vegetable Sauce)

RESTAURANT BOCUSE
LYONS, FRANCE

4 servings

  2 3- to 3½-pound roasting chickens
     Salt and pepper

Stock

  1 carrot, cut into chunks
  1 medium onion, quartered
  1 celery stalk (with leaves)
  1 medium leek (with 2 inches of green), quartered and washed
  1 tomato, peeled (optional)

  1 sprig tarragon
  1 sprig thyme

Sauce

  2 cups plus 2 tablespoons crème fraîche

  1 carrot, cut into very fine julienne
  1 leek, trimmed and cut into very fine julienne
  1 celery stalk, cut into very fine julienne
  8 fresh morels* (or 4 large mushrooms, sliced horizontally into sixths)
  2 tablespoons (¼ stick) butter
  2 snow peas, blanched and cut into fourths
     Salt and freshly ground pepper

Stuffing

  ½ cup fine julienne of celery
  ½ cup fine julienne of leek
  ½ cup fine julienne of carrot
  2 teaspoons chopped fresh chives
  8 fresh morels*
  4 teaspoons butter

Slit chickens along breastbone and peel off skin. Remove wishbone and cut off ½ breast for each serving. Form arc-shaped pocket in each chicken breast by slitting horizontally, leaving ½ inch at each end. Sprinkle all surfaces with salt and pepper. Set aside. Cut off legs (reserve for another use). Remove wings, crack and chop. Trim off excess fat. Crack carcasses with heavy knife.

For stock: Combine carcasses, wings, carrot, onion, celery, leek, tomato, tarragon and thyme in large saucepan and cover with water. Cover and boil gently over medium heat for 30 minutes to 1 hour.

For sauce: Strain 3 cups stock into large saucepan, reserving remainder. Place over medium-high heat and bring to boil. Reduce heat and simmer until stock is reduced to 1½ cups. Add Crème Fraîche and cook until mixture is again reduced to 1½ cups.

Meanwhile, combine julienne of carrot, leek and celery stalk in strainer set in pan of boiling water over medium-high heat. Blanch vegetables until crisp-tender, about 5 to 10 seconds. Plunge into ice water to stop cooking process. Drain and pat dry and add to sauce. Sauté morels in 2 tablespoons butter and add to sauce with snow peas. Season with salt and pepper. Remove from heat; keep warm.

For stuffing: Combine ½ cup each celery, leek and carrot in strainer set in pan of boiling water over medium-high heat. Blanch until crisp-tender, about 5 to 10 seconds. Plunge into ice water to stop cooking process. Drain and pat dry. Transfer to medium bowl. Add chives and toss. Arrange 6 tablespoons vegetable mixture inside each chicken breast. Top each with 2 morels. Carefully close pocket and press edges to seal. Top each with 1 teaspoon butter. Wrap tightly in 10-inch piece of plastic wrap, twisting ends to seal. Transfer to shallow large saucepan. Strain enough reserved stock into saucepan to cover chicken. Bring to boil over medium-high heat. Reduce heat to medium and poach chicken about 8 to 10 minutes, turning carefully once or twice. Remove chicken from pan using slotted spoon and let drain.

Divide sauce evenly among plates. Unwrap 1 breast, slice diagonally into fourths and arrange on plate in pinwheel pattern. Repeat with remaining breasts. Serve immediately.

*Dried morels can be substituted for fresh. Combine in bowl with enough boiling water to cover. Let stand until softened. Drain well and pat dry with paper towels.

BUTTERMILK PECAN CHICKEN

PATCHWORK QUILT COUNTRY INN
MIDDLEBURY, INDIANA

8 servings

  ¾ cup (1½ sticks) butter

  1 cup buttermilk
  1 egg, lightly beaten
  1 cup flour
  1 cup ground pecans
  ¼ cup sesame seeds
  1 tablespoon paprika
  1 tablespoon salt
  ⅛ teaspoon pepper

  2 3½-pound broiler-fryers, cut up
  ½ cup pecan halves

Preheat oven to 350°F. Place butter in large shallow roasting pan and melt in oven. Remove and set aside.

Mix buttermilk and egg in shallow dish. Combine flour, ground pecans, sesame seeds, paprika, salt and pepper in medium bowl.

Coat chicken in buttermilk mixture, then in flour mixture. Place in roasting pan, turning to coat all sides with butter, finishing with skin side up. Scatter pecan halves over chicken and bake until chicken is deep golden brown, about 1½ to 1¾ hours.

BONELESS CHICKEN MICHELE

MILOS COUNTRY HOUSE
POTTSTOWN, PENNSYLVANIA

"Since we live only 15 miles from Pottstown, my husband and I have visited Milos frequently. We have ordered many different items from the menu, and, to my amazement, we have always been pleased. I am still dreaming about one specialty of the house—a boneless breast of chicken stuffed with crab and wild rice."
—Rosemary Lorine, Lafayette Hill, Pennsylvania

6 servings

- 3 2½ to 3-pound frying chickens

- ½ cup wild rice

- 8 tablespoons (1 stick) butter
- ⅓ cup finely chopped shallots
- ⅓ cup finely chopped carrots
- ¼ cup plus ⅓ cup finely chopped celery
  Salt and pepper
- ½ pound Alaskan king crabmeat
- ½ cup Sauce Velouté*

- ½ cup finely chopped onion
- ¼ cup chopped parsley
- ⅛ teaspoon thyme
- ⅛ teaspoon sage
- 1 small garlic clove, crushed
- 1 bay leaf, crushed
  Salt and pepper
- 4 cups ½-inch fresh bread cubes
- 1 cup chicken stock

- 2 onions, thinly sliced

  Salt and pepper

- ¼ cup (½ stick) butter, melted
  Celery salt
  Pepper
  Paprika

Split chickens (or have butcher do it) and remove all bones except wing bone and drumstick bone.

Rinse wild rice in cold water. Cook according to package directions.

In 10-inch skillet, melt 2 tablespoons butter and sauté shallots, carrots and ¼ cup celery until soft. Add salt and pepper to taste. Combine rice and vegetables and mix thoroughly. Cool. When completely cool, add crabmeat and Sauce Velouté. Chill until ready to use.

In 12-inch skillet, melt ¼ cup butter and sauté chopped onion and remaining celery until tender. Blend in seasonings and mix well. Add bread cubes and toss. Stir in ¼ cup chicken stock.

In 10-inch skillet, melt 2 tablespoons butter and sauté sliced onions until soft. Place in roasting pan.

Preheat oven to 350°F. Place chicken halves on work surface, skin side down. Season lightly with salt and pepper. With sharp knife, cut pocket in breast and stuff with ⅙ of wild rice stuffing. Cut pocket in thigh and leg and place ⅙ of bread stuffing into pocket. Continue with 5 remaining chicken halves.

Place chicken skin side up on bed of onions in roasting pan. Brush skin with melted butter and season with celery salt, pepper and paprika. Add remaining ¾ cup chicken stock to roasting pan. Place in oven and roast until cooked and lightly brown, about 45 minutes, basting often.

Remove chicken to serving platter. Pour pan juices on top before serving.

*Sauce Velouté

Makes ¾ cup

- 2 teaspoons butter
- 1 tablespoon flour
- ½ cup chicken stock
- ¼ cup whipping cream
  Salt and white pepper

Melt butter in small saucepan. Stir in flour to make roux. Add chicken stock, cream, salt and pepper to taste and stir over medium heat until Velouté Sauce thickens. Keep warm.

POLLO AL JEREZ

EL TIO PEPE
WASHINGTON, D.C.

6 servings

- 3 1½-to 2-pound chickens, quartered
  Salt and pepper to taste
  Paprika
- ½ cup flour

- 1 cup olive oil
- 10 garlic cloves, finely minced (use blender or food processor)
- 1 pound fresh mushrooms, thinly sliced
- ½ cup dry sherry
- 3 cups reduced chicken stock (preferably homemade)
- 2 tablespoons chopped parsley (garnish)
  Cooked white rice

Remove small bones and scraps from chicken breasts and thighs (use for stock, if desired). Season with salt, pepper and paprika. Coat with flour.

Heat oil in 10- to 12-inch skillet. Brown chicken on all sides and transfer to 6-quart pot. Add garlic and mushrooms to remaining oil and sauté quickly. Stir in sherry, scraping cooked bits from bottom of pan. Add stock and bring to boil. Pour over chicken. Return to heat and cook uncovered 15 to 20 minutes. Skim fat. Garnish with parsley; serve with rice.

B'STILLA

DAR MAGHREB
LOS ANGELES, CALIFORNIA

12 servings

- 1 cup (2 sticks) butter
- 2 3-pound chickens, quartered

- 2 cups chopped onion
- ½ cup chopped parsley
- ½ cup finely chopped cilantro
- 2 teaspoons paprika
- 1 teaspoon ground ginger
- ¼ teaspoon turmeric
- 1 teaspoon salt
- ⅛ teaspoon pepper
- 1 cup water

- 12 eggs
  Salt

- ½ cup peanut oil
- 10 ounces blanched almonds
- ¾ cup granulated sugar
- ½ teaspoon cinnamon

- 1 tablespoon clarified butter
- 1 1-pound package phyllo dough

  Powdered sugar, cinnamon (garnish)

In large skillet, melt 1 stick butter until foamy. Sauté chicken quarters until browned on both sides. As they brown, transfer to platter.

Pour all but thin film of butter from skillet. Sauté onion, stirring frequently, until soft and translucent. Stir in parsley, cilantro, paprika, ginger, turmeric, salt, pepper and water. Mix thoroughly and bring to boil. Add chicken and any liquid that has accumulated on platter. Reduce heat and simmer until chicken is tender, about 30 minutes. Remove chicken and cool. Reserve broth. Bone chicken, but leave skin on. Separate meat with skin into bite-sized pieces and set aside.

Measure 1½ cups reserved broth into saucepan. Bring to boil and add ½ stick butter. Beat eggs, pour into broth and whip over moderate heat until eggs are soft creamy curds. Salt to taste; set aside.

Heat peanut oil in skillet. Fry almonds until deep golden color. Cool. Grind nuts and mix with granulated sugar and cinnamon.

Coat bottom of 14-inch skillet with clarified butter. Lay 2 sheets of phyllo dough across bottom of skillet, letting it overhang 6 to 8 inches all around. Spread ¾ eggs on dough. Next spread on ½ ground almonds and ½ chicken. Follow with layers of remaining eggs, chicken and almonds.

Preheat oven to 450°F. Melt remaining ½ stick butter. Fold filo across top of chicken-egg mixture. If sheets don't cover top, use additional sheet to completely cover. Brush dough with melted butter.

Bake until top is golden brown, about 30 to 35 minutes. Remove from oven. Invert B'stilla onto large heated serving plate. Sprinkle powdered sugar over top to thickness of ¼ inch. Decorate with crisscross of cinnamon.

CHICKEN ENCHILADAS WITH GREEN SAUCE

DON HERNANDO'S
BEVERLY HILLS, CALIFORNIA

The secret to the wonderful flavor of this sauce is the tomatillo, a fruit generally known as the Mexican green tomato; available canned in this country under the names tomatillos enteros, tomatitos verdes, or peeled green tomatoes. The mature fruit is yellow, but it is usually used green, and gives a lovely color to sauces. There is no substitute for the tomatillo, since ordinary unripe tomatoes do not have the same characteristics.

8 servings

- 2 to 2¼ pounds chicken pieces
- 2 to 3 celery stalks, cut into 1-inch chunks
- 1 onion, cut into large chunks
  Salt and pepper

Green Sauce

- 1 quart chicken stock
- 2 pounds tomatillos, peeled
- 5 fresh serrano chilies, seeds and pith removed, minced
- 2 garlic cloves, minced
- 1 onion, diced
- ½ bunch cilantro, minced
- ¼ teaspoon oregano
- ¼ teaspoon freshly ground black pepper
  Pinch sugar
  Pinch salt

- 1 tablespoon butter
- 1 tablespoon flour

Filling

- 2 green bell peppers, diced
- 2 onions, diced
- 2 large tomatoes, peeled and diced
- 3 canned whole green peeled chilies, seeded and diced
  Chicken stock (optional)

  Oil
- 16 corn or flour tortillas
- 16 thin slices Monterey Jack cheese
  Sour cream, black olives (garnish)

Place chicken pieces in large pot and cover with water. Add celery, onion chunks, salt and pepper to taste and cook until chicken is tender, about 40 minutes. Remove chicken from broth and set aside to cool. Strain broth and reserve for sauce.

For sauce: Combine all ingredients except butter and flour in large saucepan. Bring to boil over medium heat, stirring occasionally and skimming off foam as it rises to surface. Reduce heat and simmer, stirring occasionally, until sauce is consistency of puree, about 1 hour, gently piercing tomatillos with fork as they become soft. Strain sauce and return to pan.

Combine butter and flour to form paste. Add to sauce; cook over medium heat until sauce returns to boil and thickens slightly. Set aside; keep hot.

For filling: Combine peppers, onions, tomatoes and chilies in large skillet. Place over medium heat and cook until soft, stirring constantly and moistening with chicken stock if necessary.

Remove meat from cooled chicken and shred. Add chicken to filling and cook few minutes more. Season with salt and pepper to taste.

To assemble: Preheat oven to 250°F. Lightly oil skillet and fry tortillas until soft, about 10 to 20 seconds on each side. Roll each tortilla gently in paper towel to remove excess oil and keep pliable. Place about ¼ cup filling in each tortilla, roll up and place seam side down in lightly greased 9x13-inch baking dish. Top each with thin slice cheese. Bake until heated through and cheese melts, about 20 minutes. Cover with hot green sauce and top each enchilada with sour cream and an olive.

CHICKEN FIORENTINA

LA DOLCE VITA
BEVERLY HILLS, CALIFORNIA

6 servings

> **6 small whole chicken breasts, skinned, boned and halved**
> **½ cup (8 tablespoons) freshly grated Romano cheese**
> **½ cup cooked spinach, well drained**
> **2 egg yolks**
> **⅛ to ¼ teaspoon nutmeg**
> **½ teaspoon salt**
> **¼ teaspoon freshly ground pepper**
> **3 tablespoons (⅜ stick) unsalted butter**
> **6 slices prosciutto**
> **6 slices Jarlsberg cheese**
> **3 slices mortadella sausage, cut in half**
> **2 tablespoons pine nuts**
>
> **Flour**
> **3 eggs, lightly beaten**
> **Finely crushed breadcrumbs**
> **¾ cup vegetable oil**
>
> **6 tablespoons (¾ stick) butter**
> **10 large white mushrooms, sliced**
> **½ cup Marsala**

Remove mignon (small strip of meat extending lengthwise under fillet) from each chicken breast. Place both fillet and mignon between 2 pieces of waxed paper and pound gently until meat is about ¼ inch thick. Set the flattened mignons aside.

Preheat oven to 400°F. Lay all 12 fillets on working surface and sprinkle liberally with Romano cheese, reserving 2 tablespoons cheese. Combine spinach, egg yolks, remaining Romano, nutmeg, salt and pepper in blender and puree. Spoon mixture on each of 6 fillets. Top each with 1½ teaspoons butter, 1 slice each prosciutto, cheese and mortadella, and 1 teaspoon nuts.

Using 2 mignons per fillet, arrange over both ends so filling is covered as much as possible. Lay remaining 6 fillets lengthwise over mignons. Gently pinch edges closed, forming oval shape.

Dust chicken with flour, dip into beaten egg and lightly roll in breadcrumbs. Pour oil into baking pan, add chicken and turn to coat with oil. Bake 45 minutes, turning as needed for even browning. Carefully transfer to serving platter and keep warm.

Drain oil from pan, leaving browned bits. Place pan over medium heat, add 6 tablespoons butter and let melt. Add mushrooms and Marsala and heat through, stirring constantly. Spoon over chicken and serve immediately.

CHICKEN BREASTS WITH HERB MOUSSELINE SAUCE

WALDORF-ASTORIA
NEW YORK, NEW YORK

4 servings

> **2 large whole chicken breasts, halved, boned and skinned**
> **¼ cup dry white wine**
> **¼ cup water**
> **Salt and freshly ground pepper**
>
> **2 egg yolks**
> **¼ cup whipping cream**
> **2 tablespoons chopped mixed fresh herbs (tarragon, basil, savory, chervil and/or parsley)**
> **Fresh lemon juice**

Place chicken in small saucepan to fit snugly. Add wine and water and season lightly with salt and pepper. Cover and bring to boil; reduce heat and simmer about 10 minutes. Set aside; keep warm.

In nonaluminum double boiler, combine yolks with cream and ¼ cup cooking liquid from chicken. Place over simmering water and stir vigorously with whisk until sauce is thick and creamy. Add herbs and lemon juice, salt and pepper to taste. Drain chicken, transfer to heated platter and cover with sauce.

CHICKEN GLORIA

DANA PLACE INN
JACKSON, NEW HAMPSHIRE

"The Dana Place Inn serves many impressive dishes, our favorite being Chicken Gloria. Unfortunately, we are able to make the visit only once a year. . . ."
—Mrs. Bernard Stone, Worcester, Massachusetts

6 servings

    1 cup orange marmalade
  ¾ cup Burgundy
  ¾ cup water
  ½ cup orange juice
    1 8-ounce can apricots, drained and pureed
    2 tablespoons red currant jelly
    2 tablespoons brown sugar
    2 tablespoons cornstarch
  ¼ cup cold water

    6 8-ounce chicken breast halves, skinned, boned and lightly pounded
      Flour
      Salt and pepper
      Oil
  ¼ cup sherry
  ¼ cup brandy
      Halved apricots and chopped fresh parsley (garnish)

Combine first 7 ingredients in saucepan and simmer gently over low heat, stirring frequently until well blended. Slowly add cornstarch dissolved in water, stirring constantly. Simmer sauce until thickened, about 5 minutes.

Meanwhile, dredge chicken breasts lightly in flour seasoned with salt and pepper. Heat oil in large skillet, add chicken and sauté until golden brown on both sides; do not overcook. Drain on paper towels. Pour off oil and wipe out skillet. Return chicken to pan, add sherry and brandy and simmer 2 minutes. Stir in apricot sauce, spooning over chicken to coat lightly. Transfer to heated platter and garnish with apricot halves and chopped parsley. Serve with remaining sauce.

CHICKEN MARENGO

CAFE JOHNELL
FT. WAYNE, INDIANA

6 servings

    6 medium chicken breasts, skinned and boned
  ¼ cup (½ stick) butter
    1 green pepper, julienned
    1 small onion, julienned
    1 cup sliced fresh mushrooms
  ½ cup black olives
    2 small fresh tomatoes, cut into small pieces

    2 cups whole canned tomatoes
  ½ cup olive oil
      Garlic
      Salt and pepper

Cut chicken breasts into fillets and flatten. Sauté lightly in butter until golden brown. Pour off excess butter; add green pepper, onion, mushrooms, olives and fresh tomatoes to chicken.

In blender, mix canned tomatoes, olive oil, garlic and salt and pepper to taste. Pour over chicken. Simmer until vegetables and chicken are tender.

CHICKEN PILLOWS

CLASSIC RESTAURANT
PROVIDENCE, RHODE ISLAND

2 servings

    1 whole chicken breast, halved, skinned, boned and pounded slightly
    1 garlic clove, halved
    1 ounce prosciutto
    1 ounce mozzarella cheese, thinly sliced
    2 tablespoons seasoned breadcrumbs

    2 tablespoons medium dry sherry
    2 tablespoons (¼ stick) butter, clarified
      Salt and freshly ground pepper
    1 tablespoon chopped parsley (broadleaf, if available)

Preheat oven to 350°F. Lightly grease small shallow baking dish.

Rub chicken breasts with cut garlic clove. Place prosciutto and cheese over chicken. Sprinkle with breadcrumbs. Roll up, starting at broader end, and secure with toothpicks. Place in baking dish.

Combine sherry and butter and heat briefly. Pour over chicken. Season with salt and pepper to taste. Bake until chicken is done, about 20 to 25 minutes. Sprinkle with parsley.

CHICKEN QUEEN ELIZABETH

LA DONA LUZ
TAOS, NEW MEXICO

"A visit to La Dona Luz was a pleasurable intermission from our holiday ski trip. We were intrigued by a dish called Chicken Queen Elizabeth."
—Mrs. Randley A. Smith, El Paso, Texas

6 servings

    6 chicken breast halves, boned, skinned and pounded thin
      Seasoned salt
      Freshly ground pepper
    6 teaspoons finely chopped fresh parsley
    6 thin slices Swiss cheese
    6 thin slices ham
  ¼ cup (½ stick) butter, melted
    1 cup fresh breadcrumbs

Sauce

1½ cups canned whole tomatoes,
    partially drained
¾ cup whipping cream
1 tablespoon dry white wine
1 teaspoon salt
1 teaspoon sugar
    Pinch garlic powder
    Pinch freshly ground white pepper

    Freshly cooked rice
    Apricot halves (garnish)

Preheat oven to 325°F. Season chicken breasts with salt and pepper to taste. Top each with 1 teaspoon parsley, 1 slice cheese and 1 slice ham. Roll tightly. Brush with some of butter and sprinkle with ½ of breadcrumbs.

Arrange compactly crumbed side down in 6-inch square baking dish. Pour remaining butter over top and sprinkle with remaining crumbs. Cover and bake 45 minutes. Remove cover and continue baking until top is golden brown, about 30 minutes. Set aside and keep warm while preparing sauce.

For sauce: Combine all ingredients in medium saucepan over medium-high heat and bring to boil. Reduce heat and simmer sauce for 3 to 5 minutes.

Spoon rice onto serving platter. Arrange chicken over top. Cover with sauce and garnish with apricots.

CHICKEN WING KAI

SIAMESE PRINCESS
LOS ANGELES, CALIFORNIA

4 to 6 servings

1 pound extra lean ground pork
3 tablespoons chopped cilantro
3 tablespoons anchovy sauce
    (3 tablespoons butter mixed with
    1 teaspoon anchovy paste)
1 tablespoon freshly ground white pepper
1 tablespoon minced garlic
1 tablespoon sugar

12 chicken wings

    Oil for deep frying
    Cucumber Relish Sauce*

Combine pork, cilantro, anchovy sauce, pepper, garlic and sugar and let stand 1 hour at room temperature.

Bone chicken wings (this procedure is easier if chicken is slightly frozen). Using very sharp small knife, start at large end of wing and carefully push meat down bone, making sure skin remains attached to meat. At joint, use point of knife to work meat away from bone and tendons. Continue along entire length of wing, working slowly so meat does not tear. Discard bones.

Divide pork mixture evenly among wings, packing firmly and folding skin over to secure.

Heat oil to 375°F. Add wings few at a time and deep fry until golden brown, about 7 to 10 minutes. Drain on paper towels and keep warm. Serve chicken wings with Cucumber Relish Sauce.

Cucumber Relish Sauce

4 to 6 servings

⅓ cup rice vinegar
1 tablespoon firmly packed brown sugar
1 medium cucumber, thinly sliced

Combine vinegar and brown sugar. Stir in cucumber and mix well.

CHICKEN WITH WALNUTS IN PLUM SAUCE

MING GATE
HAMPTON, VIRGINIA

"Whenever friends and I want to go to a Chinese restaurant, we invariably choose the Ming Gate. My favorite dish is a fragrant combination of juicy chicken pieces, walnuts and a sweet sauce with ginger."
    —Mrs. Ken Murov, *Newport News, Virginia*

1 cup walnut halves

1 tablespoon beaten egg
1 tablespoon oil
1 teaspoon cornstarch
6 chicken thighs (about 1½ pounds),
    boned, skinned and cut into ½-inch
    pieces

½ cup oil

2 tablespoons plum or hoisin sauce
1 1-inch piece ginger, peeled and
    finely chopped
1 teaspoon sugar
1 teaspoon soy sauce
¼ teaspoon sesame oil
2 green onions, finely chopped (garnish)

Pour boiling water over walnuts and let stand 5 minutes. Drain and pat dry.

Combine egg with 1 tablespoon oil and cornstarch in small bowl. Add chicken pieces and toss gently to coat them evenly.

Heat ½ cup oil in wok over medium-high heat until haze forms. Add walnuts and fry until golden, about 45 seconds. Remove with slotted spoon and drain on paper towels. Add chicken to wok and cook until golden, about 3 minutes. Drain well.

Pour off all but thin film of oil. Return pan to heat, add plum or hoisin sauce, ginger, sugar, soy sauce and sesame oil and stir until combined. Reduce heat and simmer, stirring constantly, until sauce begins to glisten, about 1 to 2 minutes. Add chicken and walnuts and mix thoroughly with sauce. Transfer to heated serving platter and garnish with chopped green onions.

LUCIA'S FLAUTAS

ZAPATA'S MEXICAN RESTAURANT
PORTLAND, OREGON

Makes 20 to 24

  2 cups chicken stock or broth
  3 chicken breast halves

  1 tablespoon oil
  1 cup finely chopped peeled tomatoes
  ½ cup finely chopped onion
  2½ tablespoons cumin
  1 tablespoon minced garlic
    Salt and pepper

    Oil for deep fat frying
 20 to 24 tortillas

  1 to 1½ cups guacamole

In medium saucepan, bring stock to boil over high heat. Reduce heat to low, add chicken breasts, cover and cook 15 to 20 minutes. Drain, reserving 1 cup stock. Cool chicken slightly, then chop finely.

Heat 1 tablespoon oil in medium skillet. Add tomatoes and onion and sauté over medium heat 5 minutes. Add chicken, stock, cumin, garlic, salt and pepper to taste. Simmer, uncovered, over low heat 25 minutes. Drain and let cool.

Heat oil to 375°F for deep fat frying. Dip tortillas into hot oil one at a time to soften, about 10 seconds. Remove and drain on paper towel. Immediately place 1 tablespoon chicken mixture on tortilla and roll up tightly. It is important to fill and roll each tortilla immediately after softening to prevent the flautas from cracking.

When all tortillas are filled, fry at 375°F until crisp. Drain on paper towels. Serve warm on large platter surrounding a bowl of guacamole.

Flautas may also be cut in ½ and served with guacamole as hors d'oeuvres.

GUMBO YA YA
(Chicken and Andouille Sausage Gumbo)

COMMANDER'S PALACE
NEW ORLEANS, LOUISIANA

8 servings

  1 5-pound chicken, cut into 10 pieces
    Salt
    Cayenne pepper
    Garlic powder
  2½ cups all purpose flour

  1 cup oil
  2 cups chopped onion
  2 cups chopped green pepper
  1½ cups chopped celery
  6 cups chicken stock

  1 pound andouille sausage or
    kielbasa, diced
  1½ teaspoons minced fresh garlic

    Salt and freshly ground pepper
    Steamed white rice

Arrange chicken on baking sheet and season evenly with salt, cayenne and garlic powder. Let stand 30 minutes at room temperature. Combine chicken pieces and flour in large paper bag and shake until chicken is well coated.

Heat oil in large skillet over medium-high heat. Add chicken (reserve remaining flour) and brown on all sides. Remove with slotted spoon and set aside. Loosen any browned bits on bottom of skillet. Using whisk, add 1 cup reserved flour and stir constantly until roux is very dark brown. Remove from heat and add onion, green pepper and celery, stirring to blend thoroughly and prevent burning. Transfer to large saucepan. Stir in stock and bring to boil over medium-high heat. Reduce heat, add sausage and garlic, and simmer 45 minutes, stirring occasionally.

Remove chicken from bones and cut meat into ¼-inch pieces. Return to saucepan and heat through. Season with salt and pepper to taste and serve immediately over rice in individual soup bowls.

For variation, add stock to roux-vegetable mixture, bring to boil, reduce heat, add garlic and simmer 35 minutes. Strain out vegetable mixture and discard. Combine thickened stock with sausage and bring to boil. Reduce heat and simmer an additional 20 minutes. Add boned chicken pieces and season with salt and pepper. Heat through and serve immediately over steamed rice in individual soup bowls.

POULET A LA CREME DE POIRES ET ENDIVES
(Chicken with Pears and Endive)

ERNIE'S
SAN FRANCISCO, CALIFORNIA

2 servings

  2 cups chicken broth
  2 ripe pears
  4 chicken thighs or 2 chicken breast
    halves, skinned
    Salt and freshly ground white pepper

  1 cup whipping cream

  1 head Belgian endive, coarsely diced

Bring chicken broth to simmer in medium saucepan. Peel and core pears; reserve peel. Cut pears in uniform pieces and add to broth. Poach, uncovered, until tender. Drain, reserving broth. Transfer pears to processor or blender and puree until smooth. Combine broth and pear peelings in saucepan and bring to simmer. Season chicken with salt and

CREATIVE NEW DISHES FROM ERNIE'S

Victor and Roland Gotti were born into the restaurant business. In 1934 their father, Ambrogio, and Ernie Carlesso bought a small hotel and restaurant on the rowdy Barbary Coast. They closed the hotel, remodeled the restaurant and named it Ernie's Il Travatore, later shortened to Ernie's. In 1948 Roland and Victor took charge of the modest restaurant, tossed out the checkered tablecloths and created within the three dining rooms a Victorian opulence cherished by San Franciscans.

While keeping the best of the old, they continue to experiment. Nowhere is this philosophy more evident than on the menu, which features exciting innovative dishes. Ernie's talented young chef, Jacky Robert, born in Normandy and trained in Paris at Maxim's and Prunier, has been instrumental in making some of these changes.

In his version of the seventeenth-century dish, Le Pigeonneau en Chartreuse, individual portions are molded in soufflé dishes with a mosaic of colorful vegetables surrounding layers of squab and cooked cabbage. Color plays an important part in many dishes. Gourmandise de Légumes is a rainbow of layered and molded vegetable purees that are baked, unmolded and served with hollandaise. A glistening jewellike leek pâté, sparked with a bright red Coulis de Tomate, is a sophisticated overture to any meal.

Desserts at Ernie's reflect a satisfying mixture of both classics and new recipes. Just before sending La Tarte Tatin from the kitchen, Jacky caramelizes the top with a hot iron, giving it a burnished sugary finish. But for all the excitement in the kitchen, Ernie's remains an elegant institution, an oasis for romantics.

pepper to taste. Add to broth, cover and poach until just tender. Keep chicken warm in broth.

Boil cream in saucepan until reduced to ½ cup. Add pear puree and heat through. Strain through sieve. (Consistency should be like medium white sauce; if it seems too thick, stir in small amount of poaching liquid to thin.)

Make bed of endive on each plate. Top with chicken and cover with sauce.

SESAME CHICKEN IN CUMBERLAND SAUCE

MARTHA'S RESTAURANT
EDGARTOWN, MASSACHUSETTS

"I am planning a special dinner party for the near future and would love to prepare a chicken dish I tasted at Martha's Restaurant. I thought it was outstanding!"
—*Jane B. Weintraub, Scituate, Massachusetts*

12 servings

  2 cups breadcrumbs
  ¾ cup sesame seeds
  ½ cup freshly grated Parmesan cheese
  ¼ cup chopped fresh parsley
  1 teaspoon freshly ground white pepper
  6 chicken breasts, skinned, split, boned and pounded to ¼-inch thickness
  2 tablespoons (¼ stick) butter, melted

Cumberland Sauce

  3 large oranges
  3 large lemons
  1 cup red currant jelly
  2 tablespoons port
  2 teaspoons Dijon mustard
  ¼ teaspoon ground ginger
  Dash red pepper

Preheat oven to 425°F. Combine first 5 ingredients in medium bowl and blend well. Dip chicken breasts in butter and then coat with sesame breading. Place on baking sheet and bake 20 minutes. Serve immediately with warm Cumberland Sauce.

For sauce: Finely grate peel and squeeze juice from oranges and lemons. Place peel in large saucepan, cover with cold water and bring to boil. Drain. Repeat twice, then set aside. Combine juice and remaining ingredients in small saucepan and heat through. Stir in grated peel to taste.

CHICKEN WITH RASPBERRY VINEGAR SAUCE

LES PASTOUREAUX
PARIS, FRANCE

"During our recent wedding trip to Paris, we had the opportunity to eat at a beautiful little restaurant. Our entrée was a most unusual chicken."
—*Gail Scott, Boca Raton, Florida*

3 to 4 servings

    3 tablespoons (⅜ stick) butter
    1 tablespoon oil
    1 2½- to 3-pound fryer, cut into serving pieces
    ¾ teaspoon salt

    ¾ cup raspberry vinegar
    1¼ cups good quality chicken stock

    1¼ cups whipping cream
    Raspberry vinegar
    Salt and freshly ground pepper

Heat butter and oil in large skillet. Add chicken and sauté on all sides until golden brown. Remove from skillet using tongs and sprinkle with salt; set aside.

Drain off excess fat and return skillet to heat. Deglaze pan by adding ¾ cup raspberry vinegar. Return chicken to pan, add stock and simmer covered until chicken is tender and juices run clear. Transfer chicken to serving platter and keep warm.

Bring liquid in pan to boil, then reduce heat and cook until sauce is consistency of light cream. Add cream and reduce sauce again. Add additional vinegar, salt and pepper to taste. Stir in juices that have accumulated on platter. Pour sauce over chicken and serve.

EMPRESS FRESH PINEAPPLE AND LICHEE CHICKEN

EMPRESS OF CHINA
SAN FRANCISCO, CALIFORNIA

4 servings

    1 fresh pineapple
    1½ to 2 pounds skinned and boned chicken breasts, cubed
    ¼ cup chestnut flour*
    2 cups oil

    ½ cup white vinegar
    ½ cup pineapple juice
    ½ cup orange juice
    ½ cup tomato juice
    ½ cup sugar
    1½ teaspoons salt
    ½ fresh lemon

    1 tablespoon cornstarch
    2 tablespoons water

    1 8-ounce can lichees

Cut pineapple in ½, leaving leaves intact. Remove fruit from shell; dice fruit and set aside. Place shells on serving platter.

Dip chicken in flour. Deep fry in very hot oil (375° to 400°F) until golden brown, about 5 minutes; drain on paper towels.

Combine vinegar and juices, sugar and salt in saucepan. Squeeze lemon juice into sauce and place lemon half in pan. Bring to boil. Remove lemon shell. Stir in cornstarch dissolved in water. Return to boil and cook, stirring until thick and clear, about 1 to 2 minutes. Blend in chicken, pineapple and lichees and heat through. Spoon into pineapple shells and serve immediately.

*Available in oriental markets and specialty food stores.

HOT AND SPICY CHICKEN

MAX'S SON
DALY CITY, CALIFORNIA

"During a recent convention trip to San Francisco, my niece and her husband introduced us to a unique restaurant in Daly City. It was truly the food lovers' serendipity."
—*Linda Pistachio, Simi Valley, California*

6 to 8 servings

    3 cups water
    3½ cups all purpose flour
    ⅞ cup cornstarch
    3 ounces baking powder
    1 egg white

    Oil for deep frying
    2 pounds chicken (white meat only), cut into 1-inch cubes
    Chopped green onions (garnish)

    1 quart rice vinegar or other mild vinegar
    1½ pounds sugar
    2 tablespoons minced garlic
    2 tablespoons minced green onion
    2 teaspoons crushed red pepper flakes

Combine first 5 ingredients in large bowl and let rest in warm place until bubbles appear, 15 to 20 minutes. (Batter may be refrigerated until ready to use.)

Heat oil in deep fryer or wok to 375°F. Coat chicken with batter and fry in batches until golden brown. Drain well on paper towels. Transfer to warm serving plate and garnish with green onions.

Combine remaining ingredients in heavy saucepan. Stir over medium heat until vinegar flavor almost disappears and sauce thickens. Pass separately.

ORANGE-FLAVORED CHICKEN, CHINESE STYLE

LE DELICE
WHIPPANY, NEW JERSEY

"We enjoy eating at an elegant and charming restaurant called Le Délice. A specialty of the house is an orange-flavored chicken with snow peas."
—*Charlotte S. Tanenbaum, Short Hills, New Jersey*

3 to 4 servings

Marinade

 1 tablespoon soy sauce
 1 tablespoon rice wine
 2 teaspoons cornstarch
 1½ teaspoons minced fresh ginger
 1 teaspoon sesame oil
 1 pound chicken, boned, skinned and cut into ½-inch cubes

 2 teaspoons minced fresh orange peel

 2 tablespoons chicken stock
 1½ tablespoons soy sauce
 1 tablespoon rice wine
 2 teaspoons cornstarch
 1 teaspoon sesame oil
   Pinch freshly ground white pepper
 ¼ cup plus 2 tablespoons peanut oil (or more)

 6 to 8 snow peas
   Cooked rice

For marinade: Combine first 5 ingredients in small bowl. Add chicken and toss to coat well. Cover and marinate at room temperature at least 30 minutes, stirring occasionally.

Soak orange peel in enough water to cover, about 5 minutes. Drain and set aside.

Combine stock, soy sauce, rice wine, cornstarch, sesame oil and pepper in another small bowl and mix well. Set aside.

Heat ¼ cup peanut oil in wok. Drain chicken. Add to wok in small batches and stir-fry until cooked through, about 2 minutes, adding more oil if necessary. Remove with slotted spoon and set aside.

Wipe out wok. Heat 2 tablespoons peanut oil with orange peel and stir-fry 1 minute. Return chicken to wok with snow peas and soy mixture and stir-fry 3 minutes. Serve immediately over rice.

LEMON CHICKEN

JOY GARDEN
NEW YORK, NEW YORK

"I used to travel to New York City often and always made it a point to visit the Joy Garden in Chinatown for Lemon Chicken."   —*Linda Bruni, Laredo, Texas*

4 servings

Marinade

 1 tablespoon vegetable oil
 2 teaspoons soy sauce
 ½ teaspoon sherry
   Dash freshly ground pepper
 4 chicken breast halves, boned and flattened to ½-inch thickness
   Cornstarch

Lemon Sauce

 ¾ cup water
 3 heaping tablespoons sugar
 2 tablespoons catsup
   Juice of 1 large lemon
 1 teaspoon vegetable oil
   Dash salt
 1 teaspoon cornstarch dissolved in small amount of water

   Vegetable oil

 ⅔ cup bean sprouts
 ⅔ cup thinly sliced snow peas
 ⅔ cup thinly sliced bamboo shoots
 ½ cup thinly sliced water chestnuts
   Tomato wedges, lemon slices, green onion slices and crushed almonds (garnish)

For marinade: Combine first 4 ingredients in small bowl. Rub over chicken, allowing excess to drain off. Coat lightly with cornstarch. Refrigerate at least 30 minutes.

For Lemon Sauce: Combine first 6 ingredients in small saucepan. Bring to boil over medium-high heat, stirring occasionally. Add dissolved cornstarch and stir until slightly thickened. Keep warm.

Heat ½ inch vegetable oil in large skillet over medium-high heat until light haze forms. Fry chicken until golden brown on each side. Drain; cut into strips ¾ inch wide. Set aside; keep warm.

Wipe out skillet, add small amount vegetable oil and heat over medium-high until light haze forms. Add bean sprouts, snow peas, bamboo shoots and water chestnuts and stir-fry until crisp-tender. Transfer to heated platter. Top with chicken and spoon lemon sauce over. Garnish with tomato wedges, lemon slices, green onions and almonds.

POLLO AGRO DOLCE

SNOBS
ENDINBURGH, SCOTLAND

"While on a trip to Scotland last year, I dined with friends at a small restaurant in Edinburgh called Snobs. We had been referred there by another restaurant which was all booked up. Given directions, we set out on foot, only to find ourselves hopelessly lost. To our surprise, we were met by a young man who had been sent by Snobs to guide us the remaining blocks. We found this special kind of service was the norm at Snobs, and the food was superb too—especially the chicken breasts with sweet and sour sauce." —Lucille Graham, Modesto, California

8 servings

    6 tablespoons sugar
    ½ cup (1 stick) butter

    2 cups white wine vinegar
    1¾ cups finely chopped onion
    ½ cup dry white wine
    1 tablespoon Worcestershire sauce
      Salt and pepper

    8 chicken breast halves, skinned and boned
    ½ cup flour

    ½ pound Gruyère or Emmental cheese, sliced

Place sugar in heavy-bottomed 2-quart saucepan. Place over low heat and cook without stirring until sugar melts and caramelizes to golden brown. Remove from heat. Add ¼ cup (½ stick) butter and stir until melted.

Add vinegar and mix well. Return to heat and bring to boil, stirring constantly. Add onion and simmer until completely cooked, about 30 minutes, stirring occasionally.

Add wine, Worcestershire sauce, salt and pepper to taste. Simmer 3 minutes. Strain and cool.

Preheat oven to 250°F. Coat chicken with flour, shaking off excess. Melt remaining butter in large skillet. Sauté chicken breast halves over medium-high heat until golden, about 10 minutes on each side. Remove to platter.

Cut breasts almost in ½ horizontally and stuff with cheese. Place in baking pan just large enough to hold chicken breasts. Cover generously with sweet-sour sauce. Place in oven until cheese is melted. Serve hot.

POULET DIJONNAISE IN PHYLLO

COMPLETE CUISINE, LTD.
ANN ARBOR, MICHIGAN

"A day in Ann Arbor visiting our alma mater, the University of Michigan, was made memorable by a stop for lunch at a tiny restaurant called Complete Cuisine, Ltd. The chef prepared a mustard chicken in phyllo."
    —Dr. and Mrs. James Lesser,
        West Bloomfield, Michigan

6 to 8 servings

    ¼ cup (½ stick) unsalted butter
    3 whole large chicken breasts, skinned, boned and cut into strips 1 inch wide
      Salt and freshly ground white pepper
    ½ cup sharp Dijon mustard
    2 cups whipping cream
    5 phyllo pastry sheets (about 16x13 inches)
    ¾ cup (1½ sticks) unsalted butter, melted
    ¼ cup toasted fresh breadcrumbs

    1 egg
    1 teaspoon water

Melt ¼ cup butter in large skillet over medium heat. Sprinkle chicken with salt and pepper to taste. Add to pan and sauté until strips are no longer pink, about 5 minutes; do not overcook. Transfer to platter; keep warm.

Add mustard to skillet, scraping up any browned bits clinging to bottom of pan. Whisk in cream, blending thoroughly. Reduce heat to low and simmer until sauce is slightly thickened and reduced by ¼. Stir in any juices from chicken and cook until slightly reduced. Strain sauce over chicken pieces, tossing to coat completely.

Preheat oven to 450°F. Lay 1 sheet of phyllo on dry dish towel. Brush liberally with some of melted butter, then sprinkle with 1 tablespoon crumbs. Repeat 3 times. Top with last sheet of phyllo pastry, brushing only border with melted butter.

Arrange chicken over bottom third of long side of dough, leaving 2-inch border on all sides. Turn up bottom edge, then fold in sides, partially enclosing chicken. Roll up jelly roll fashion. Carefully place seam side down on ungreased baking sheet.

Beat egg with water in small bowl and use to glaze dough. Bake until phyllo is crisp and golden brown, about 12 to 15 minutes. Cut into 2-inch slices. Serve immediately.

TANGIERS TAGINE

AHMED'S/HENRI IV
CAMBRIDGE, MASSACHUSETTS

8 servings

    3 tablespoons vegetable oil
    8 chicken legs
    2 cups water
    2 garlic cloves, crushed
    ¼ teaspoon cinnamon
    ¼ teaspoon freshly grated nutmeg
      Salt and freshly ground pepper

1 cup pitted prunes
½ cup slivered almonds

   Freshly steamed couscous
¼ cup slivered almonds, toasted (garnish)

Preheat oven to 350°F. Heat oil in heavy large skillet over medium-high heat. Add chicken and brown well on all sides. Transfer to casserole or Dutch oven. Pour off excess oil from skillet. Add 1 cup water and stir, scraping up any browned bits clinging to bottom of pan. Pour over chicken. Stir in garlic, cinnamon, nutmeg and salt and pepper to taste. Add remaining water and blend well.

Cover and bake until chicken is almost tender, about 15 minutes. Add prunes and ½ cup almonds and continue baking until chicken is cooked through, about 15 minutes.

Spread couscous on large platter. Top with chicken and sauce. Sprinkle with remaining almonds.

SUPREMA DI POLLO

PORTHOLE EATING-HOUSE
BOWNESS-ON-WINDERMERE, ENGLAND

"On a trip to the Lake District of England last summer, we discovered the very interesting Porthole Eating-House on a little side street in Bowness-on-Windermere. I would love to impress some of my friends in Texas with the fabulous entrée I had there."
   —*Mrs. Donald L. Luffel, Houston, Texas*

6 servings

   3 whole chicken breasts, skinned, boned and halved

   6 ounces chicken liver pâté (homemade preferred)
   1 teaspoon ground fennel seeds
      Salt and freshly ground pepper
      Flour

   ¼ cup (½ stick) butter
   ½ cup dry white wine
   1 cup whipping cream
   1 cup Chicken Velouté*
   2 tablespoons brandy

Remove mignon (small strip of meat extending lengthwise under fillet) from each chicken breast. Place mignons between 2 pieces of waxed paper and pound gently until meat is about ¼ inch thick.

With very sharp knife, slit each fillet starting at thickest part of breast to form deep pocket that runs about ⅔ length of breast. Stuff each fillet with 2 tablespoons pâté. Cover each opening with flattened mignon. Season with fennel and salt and pepper to taste. Flour lightly.

Heat butter in large skillet over medium-high heat. Add breasts and sauté 4 minutes on each side. Pour off excess fat, add wine and reduce slightly. Add cream and reduce mixture by ½. Add Chicken Velouté and simmer 4 minutes. Stir in brandy and serve at once.

*Chicken Velouté

Makes about 1 cup

   2 tablespoons (¼ stick) butter
   2 tablespoons flour
   1 cup chicken broth
      Salt and freshly ground pepper

Melt butter in small saucepan over medium heat. Stir in flour and mix well. Slowly add broth and simmer, stirring constantly, until thickened. Season with salt and pepper to taste.

SUPREMES DE VOLAILLE FLAMBES AU SCOTCH

THE COMMON MAN
WARREN, VERMONT

"Recently we dined at The Common Man to celebrate my son's college graduation. We found the Suprêmes de Volaille Flambés au Scotch to be most elegant."
   —*Lorraine D. Viglione, Stroudsburg, Pennsylvania*

4 servings

   1 cup raisins
   ¾ cup plus 2 tablespoons Scotch whisky

   1 pound chicken breasts, skinned and boned
   3 tablespoons flour
      Salt
   4 tablespoons (½ stick) butter

   ½ medium onion, sliced

   ¼ cup whipping cream
   ¼ cup chicken broth

Marinate raisins in ¾ cup Scotch at least 24 hours.

Cut chicken into bite-sized pieces. Lightly flour and season with salt to taste. Sauté in 2 tablespoons butter until golden brown. Set aside and keep warm.

In large skillet, melt remaining 2 tablespoons butter. Add onion and marinated raisins, including marinade. Cook over medium heat 3 to 4 minutes.

Warm 1 tablespoon Scotch and flambé onion and raisins. Lower heat and add cream and broth. Simmer about 3 minutes.

Add chicken to sauce and simmer again for 3 minutes. Warm remaining Scotch; flambé chicken.

POULET A LA CREME
(Chicken with Mushroom-Cream Sauce)

RESTAURANT BOCUSE
LYONS, FRANCE

4 servings

    1 3- to 3½-pound roasting chicken
    1 cup dry white wine
    2 small leeks with 2 inches of green,
       quartered and washed
    1 carrot, cut into chunks
    1 onion, cut into chunks
    1 celery stalk with leaves
    5 to 6 sprigs tarragon
    2 sprigs parsley
    1 sprig thyme
       Salt and freshly ground pepper

    ½ cup plus 3 tablespoons (1⅜ sticks) butter
    5 garlic cloves, unpeeled and crushed

    1 pound small mushrooms, caps cut into
       4 to 6 pieces (stems reserved)
    ½ cup water
       Pinch coarse salt
    2 cups crème fraîche
       Beurre Manié* (optional)

    12 fresh morels** or medium mushrooms

       Juice of ⅓ lemon

Remove legs and thighs from chicken and set aside. Remove breast meat and cut in ½. Slice each in ½ diagonally and set aside. Break chicken carcass in ½ and transfer to stockpot. Add wine and enough water to cover. Add leeks, carrot, onion, celery, 3 sprigs tarragon, parsley, thyme, salt and pepper to taste. Bring to boil over high heat. Reduce heat to medium-high and cook 30 minutes.

Sprinkle reserved chicken pieces generously with salt and pepper. Melt ½ cup butter in large skillet over medium-high heat. Add garlic and sauté 2 to 3 minutes. Add chicken skin side up (in batches if necessary; do not crowd) and sauté until lightly browned on all sides. Remove chicken and garlic from pan using slotted spoon and drain on paper towels. Wipe fat from skillet. Return garlic to skillet. Add chicken skin side down. Stir in remaining tarragon sprigs and enough stock (with vegetables) to cover chicken completely. Taste and adjust seasoning. Bring to boil over medium-high heat. Reduce heat, cover and simmer until chicken is just tender (meat should offer no resistance when pierced with fork or knife), about 15 to 20 minutes. Remove from heat. Transfer chicken to bowl using slotted spoon. Skim fat from stock and discard. Set stock aside.

Meanwhile, combine mushroom caps, water, 1 tablespoon butter and pinch coarse salt in 8-inch skillet or sauté pan and bring to boil over high heat, stirring occasionally. Remove from heat and drain mushrooms well, discarding liquid. Add mushrooms and reserved stems to stock. Place over medium-high heat and cook until stock is reduced by ½. (Measure amount in skillet; if less than 2 cups add more stock, including vegetables, from stockpot.) Stir in crème fraîche and bring to boil. Continue cooking until reduced and thickened, gradually adding Beurre Manié if sauce does not thicken. Strain sauce into large saucepan, pressing vegetables with back of wooden spoon to extract as much liquid as possible.

Melt 2 tablespoons butter in small saucepan over medium-high heat. Add morels and sauté until liquid evaporates. Add to sauce. Add chicken and heat through; do not boil. Taste and adjust seasoning. (Can be prepared up to 2 hours ahead to this point and refrigerated. Heat slowly before serving.)

Just before serving, add lemon juice and bring barely to boil. Transfer chicken to platter, top with sauce and serve immediately.

Beurre Manié

    2 tablespoons (¼ stick) unsalted butter,
       room temperature
    2 tablespoons sifted all purpose flour

Combine butter and flour in small bowl and blend with fork until mixture resembles small peas.

**Dried morels can be substituted for fresh. Combine in bowl with enough water to cover. Let stand until softened. Drain well; pat dry with paper towels.

POULARDE A LA DARBY

PIGALL'S FRENCH RESTAURANT
CINCINNATI, OHIO

6 to 10 servings

    1 pound cooked white rice
    1 ounce truffles, chopped
    3 3- to 3½-pound chickens
       Softened butter

    2 celery stalks, chopped
    1 large onion, chopped
    1 tablespoon flour
    2 cups port wine
    1 cup water
    3 bay leaves
       Salt and pepper

    6 slices foie gras (optional)
    6 slices toast (optional)

Preheat oven to 425°F. Mix together rice and truffles and stuff chickens with mixture. Rub chickens with softened butter. Place chickens on their sides in large roasting pan. Place in oven for 10 minutes. Turn chickens on other side and roast 10 minutes.

Reduce oven temperature to 350°F. Place chickens breast side up and continue roasting until done, about 1 hour, basting every 15 minutes. When chickens are cooked, remove to large platter and keep warm.

Place roasting pan over medium heat and stir to loosen meat juices. Add chopped celery and onion to juices and cook for 2 minutes. Add flour and mix well. Add wine, water, bay leaves, salt and pepper to taste and simmer for 30 minutes. Strain and pour over roast chicken.

If desired, arrange foie gras on toast triangles and place around chicken.

POULETTES A LA BIERE

LE PETIT CAFE
BLOOMINGTON, INDIANA

8 servings

- ¼ cup (½ stick) unsalted butter
- ¼ cup vegetable oil
- 4 Rock Cornish hens, split in half

- 8 large shallots, minced
- 3 ounces (6 tablespoons) gin

- 2 tablespoons flour
- 1 quart beer
- 1 teaspoon crushed dried herbs (bay leaf, rosemary, tarragon and thyme) or bouquet garni

- 1 pound mushrooms, sliced
- 1 cup sour cream, room temperature
  Freshly cooked brown or wild rice

In large skillet or sauté pan, melt butter with oil over medium-high heat. Add hens and sauté until thoroughly browned. Remove and keep warm. Add shallots and sauté until lightly golden. Drain off all but 1 tablespoon fat. Return hens to skillet and flame with gin. Remove hens.

Dissolve flour in ½ cup beer. Slowly add to skillet, stirring until well blended. Add remaining beer and herbs and bring to simmer. Return hens and coat with sauce. Cover and simmer until meat is tender, about 45 minutes. Remove and keep warm.

Increase heat to high and cook until sauce is reduced by ½, stirring occasionally. Reduce heat, add mushrooms and let simmer 10 minutes. Remove from

heat and stir in sour cream. Return hens to pan and coat with sauce. Serve over brown or wild rice.

CANETON A L'ORANGE

THREE DOLPHIN INN
TOPANGA, CALIFORNIA

4 servings

- 2 4- to 5-pound ducklings
  Salt and freshly ground pepper
- 1 pound pitted prunes
- ¼ cup pureed garlic

Corn Bread Dressing

- 1 tablespoon margarine
- 1 cup finely chopped celery
- 6 ounces corn bread (or 2 large corn muffins), broken into pieces
- 4 ounces (4 regular slices) white bread, broken into pieces
- 1 cup chicken stock
- ¾ cup raisins (seedless white preferred)
- ½ cup flaked coconut
- 2 large eggs, beaten
- ¼ cup (½ stick) margarine, melted
- 1 teaspoon salt
- ¾ teaspoon sage
- ¾ teaspoon thyme
- ½ teaspoon tarragon
- ⅛ teaspoon freshly ground pepper
- ⅛ teaspoon nutmeg

- 2 ounces (¼ cup) orange liqueur

Preheat oven to 400°F. Season duckling cavities generously with salt and pepper and stuff with prunes. Prick entire surface of skin lightly with fork. Rub with pureed garlic. Place on rack in shallow roasting pan and bake until skin is crisp and juices run clear, about 1¾ to 2 hours. Remove from oven and cool slightly. Retain oven temperature.

Split ducklings in ½ using poultry shears. Remove prunes, chop coarsely and set aside. Using fingers, carefully remove and discard breast bone, rib bone and back bone from each duckling. Set birds aside.

For dressing: Melt 1 tablespoon margarine in medium skillet. Add celery and sauté briefly. Combine remaining ingredients except liqueur in large bowl. Add celery and reserved prunes.

Divide stuffing equally among duckling pieces, packing lightly. Place stuffing-side down in shallow baking pan. Bake, uncovered, 20 minutes. Transfer to heated serving platter. Warm liqueur in small saucepan. Pour over ducklings, ignite and serve immediately.

DUCK IN COINTREAU SAUCE

LE CLUB
SAN FRANCISCO, CALIFORNIA

"My daughter dined at Le Club and has raved ever since about the Duck in Cointreau Sauce. Since I'm the family gourmet cook, she has asked me to prepare this duck for her next birthday."
—*Mrs. R. C. Winthrop, Diablo, California*

8 servings

    3 4-pound ducks
    3 celery stalks, chopped
    1 large onion, chopped
    2 carrots, chopped
       Salt and pepper

    ½ cup dry sherry
    ¾ cup white wine
    1 cup hot water

    ¾ cup sugar
    2 tablespoons white vinegar
       Juice of 1 lemon
       Juice of 3 oranges
       Grated rind of 2 oranges
    2 teaspoons cornstarch
    ¼ cup Cointreau

Preheat oven to 375°F. Stuff duck cavity with celery, onion, carrots and salt and pepper to taste. Roast 1 hour and 20 minutes (20 minutes per pound). If ducks are very fat, turn 3 or 4 times during roasting. Drain fat.

Deglaze roasting pan with sherry, white wine and hot water. Boil 15 minutes. Drain off fat again.

In 1-quart saucepan, cook sugar until carmelized, stirring often to avoid burning. Add vinegar, lemon and orange juice and orange rind. Bring to boil and add to sauce in deglazed pan. Cook at slow boil for 10 minutes, stirring occasionally. Dissolve cornstarch in Cointreau and add to sauce. Add salt and pepper if needed.

Bone duck breasts and arrange breasts, legs and thighs on serving platter. Glaze duck with sauce.

CANETON DE CHALLANS AU CITRON
(Duckling with Lemon)

TAILLEVENT
PARIS, FRANCE

10 to 12 servings

Bigarade

    ½ cup sugar
    ⅓ cup plus 1 tablespoon red wine vinegar

Sauce

    2 to 3 tablespoons (¼ to ⅜ stick) butter
       Neck, wing tips and gizzards of 3 ducklings, chopped into small pieces
    2 carrots, cut into medium dice
    1 onion, cut into medium dice
 6½   cups Duck Stock*
 1½   cups dry white wine
    4 lemons, quartered

    3 ducklings (about 4 pounds each), trussed

Glazed Lemon Peel

    1 cup water
    ½ cup sugar
       Peel of 2 large lemons, cut into fine julienne

       Lemon segments
       Halved lemon slices (garnish)
    1 lemon, halved with fluted edge and sprinkled lightly with parsley (garnish)

For bigarade: Melt sugar in small heavy saucepan over low heat. Increase to medium-high heat and cook until light golden. Remove from heat and stir in vinegar to deglaze (sugar may tighten up like taffy, but will dissolve later). Set aside until ready to use.

For sauce: Melt butter in large heavy saucepan over medium-high heat. Add necks, wing tips and gizzards and cook, stirring occasionally, until well browned. Add carrot and onion and cook 5 minutes, stirring frequently. Discard fat from pan. Stir in bigarade, duck stock, wine and quartered lemons and bring to boil slowly, stirring frequently. When mixture boils, discard lemons. Reduce heat to medium-low and cook gently until liquid is reduced to about 3 cups, about 1½ hours. Strain through cheesecloth or very fine sieve. (Can be made 1 day ahead.)

For ducklings: Position rack in center of oven and preheat to 500°F. Prick skins of ducklings well all over. Arrange breast side down on rack in large roasting pan. Roast 20 minutes. Turn ducklings breast side up, discard trussing string and rearrange on rack. Reduce oven temperature to 400°F. Continue roasting, brushing with sauce several times, until breast meat is cooked through but still slightly pink, about 20 more minutes.

For glazed lemon peel: Meanwhile combine water and sugar in small saucepan and bring to boil over medium-high heat. Boil 1 minute. Add lemon peel, reduce heat to medium and simmer until limp. Remove with slotted spoon; drain on paper towels.

Transfer ducklings to platter. Nap with sauce. Arrange lemon segments in row down breasts. Mound glazed lemon peel on duckling at neck end. Garnish platter with lemon slices and fluted lemon halves. Serve immediately.

Duck Stock

This is made from the leftover bones and carcass of either cooked or uncooked duck. Do not use stuffed or smoked ducks, since they are too highly seasoned. Save the leftover bones and freeze until ready to use.

Makes about 8 to 9 cups

- 2 or more duck carcasses (cooked or uncooked) coarsely chopped
  Miscellaneous duck bones and giblets (do not use liver)
- 1 pound veal bones, preferably half marrow bones
- 2 tablespoons all purpose flour
- 2 large onions, chopped
- 2 large carrots, chopped

- 10 cups (or more) chicken broth, veal stock, water or combination
- 2 large garlic cloves
- 1 bay leaf
- 2 teaspoons dried thyme
- 1 teaspoon freshly ground pepper

Preheat oven to 450°F. Combine duck carcasses, bones, giblets and veal bones in shallow pan. Roast until dark brown, at least 1 hour, turning often to promote even browning. Sprinkle with flour. Add onions and carrots and roast another 15 minutes, stirring occasionally.

Transfer mixture to deep pot and add enough broth, stock or water to cover. Add garlic, bay leaf, thyme and pepper and simmer gently at least 4 hours, skimming foam as it accumulates on surface (particularly at beginning of cooking). When stock is brown and richly flavored, pour through fine strainer set over large bowl. Cover and refrigerate overnight. Remove all fat from surface before using.

BREAST OF DUCK WITH LINGONBERRY SAUCE AND ONION MARMALADE

DEJA-VU
PHILADELPHIA, PENNSYLVANIA

Shredded red cabbage in butter with salt and pepper can be substituted for onion marmalade.

2 servings

Glace de Canard

- 1 5- to 5¼-pound duck
- 2 to 3 tablespoons oil
- 1 cup water
- 1 tablespoon juniper berries
- 1 tablespoon whole black peppercorns

- 2 tablespoons (¼ stick) clarified butter

Lingonberry Sauce

- 1½ tablespoons raspberry vinegar
- 3 tablespoons honey-sweetened wild lingonberry conserve*
- 2 teaspoons whipping cream
- 1½ teaspoons glace de canard
  Freshly ground pepper
  Dash salt

Onion Marmalade

- 2 medium white onions, thinly sliced
- 1 cup Gamay wine
- ½ cup strawberry vinegar**
- 1 tablespoon unrefined honey
- 1 tablespoon rose hips
  Freshly ground pepper

For glace de canard: Remove breast meat from duck in 2 segments. Cover and refrigerate. Cut remaining duck into large pieces. Heat oil in large skillet over medium-high heat. Add duck pieces and brown well on all sides. Transfer to large stockpot using slotted spoon. Drain fat from skillet. Deglaze skillet with water, scraping up any browned bits, and add to stockpot. Add juniper berries, peppercorns and enough water to cover duck. Place over medium-high heat and bring to boil. Reduce heat to low and simmer until liquid is reduced to 1 cup, about 6 hours. Strain well; transfer liquid to small saucepan and cook over medium-high heat until reduced to 1 to 1½ tablespoons. Pour into small bowl.

Heat butter in large skillet over medium-high heat. Add duck breasts and sauté until golden but still rare, about 5 to 6 minutes. Transfer to platter; discard skin. Return breasts to skillet skinned side down and cook 1 to 2 minutes. Transfer to oven-proof platter and keep warm in 200°F oven.

For sauce: Discard butter from skillet. Add vinegar and deglaze. Add all remaining ingredients for sauce and cook over medium heat until reduced by ½. Set sauce aside.

For marmalade: Combine all ingredients in medium saucepan over medium-high heat and cook, stirring frequently, until liquid is absorbed, about 1 hour. Transfer to processor and mix using on/off turns until consistency of marmalade, about 10 seconds.

To assemble: Spoon marmalade into center of serving platter. Thinly slice duck breasts and arrange over marmalade. Top with sauce and serve.

*Available at natural food stores.
**For strawberry vinegar, combine 2 cups hulled strawberries and 1½ cups champagne vinegar in medium bowl and refrigerate for 2 days. Transfer to medium saucepan and bring to boil over medium-high heat. Strain into jar.

SALMIS OF DUCK LEGS AND THIGHS

RESTAURANT ANDRE DAGUIN, HOTEL DE FRANCE
AUCH, FRANCE

4 servings

> 4 **duck legs with thighs, skinned and trimmed of excess fat***
> **Dry Marinade (see page 15)**
>
> 2 **teaspoons rendered duck fat or clarified butter**
> 1½ **tablespoons minced shallots**
> ½ **cup Madiran or dry red wine**
> 2 **cups degreased full-flavored chicken stock**
> ⅔ **cup whipping cream**
> **Salt and freshly ground pepper**

Roll duck in marinade and place on wide shallow platter. Cover with plastic wrap and marinate 1 to 2 days, turning pieces every 12 hours to season.

Wipe meat to remove excess seasoning and any moisture that may have collected. Discard marinade. Melt fat in heavy skillet (large enough to hold legs and thighs in single layer) over medium heat. Add duck and shallots and sauté on all sides, turning with tongs until evenly browned, about 2 minutes. Add wine and continue cooking until reduced to glaze. Reduce heat to medium-low and add 1 cup chicken stock. Continue cooking 20 minutes to reduce liquid and intensify flavor of sauce. Add remaining 1 cup stock and continue cooking, covered, until legs and thighs are tender. Stir in cream, increase heat and bring to boil. Continue boiling 5 minutes, turning duck frequently. Using slotted spoon, transfer duck to heated serving dish. Continue cooking sauce over high heat, stirring constantly, until it becomes chestnut brown in color. Taste and season with salt and pepper. Pour sauce over duck.

*Reserve skin and excess fat for other uses.

PRESSED DUCK WITH SWEET AND SOUR PLUM SAUCE

TRADER VIC'S
SAN FRANCISCO, CALIFORNIA

2 to 3 main course servings; 8 to 10 appetizer servings

> 1 **4- to 5-pound Long Island or other domestic duckling, thawed if frozen**
> 1 **tablespoon five-spice powder**
> 1 **teaspoon salt**
>
> 1 **cup water chestnut powder***
>
> **Sweet and Sour Plum Sauce****
>
> **Oil for deep frying**
> **Crushed toasted almonds or macadamia nuts (garnish)**

Place duck in large kettle or Dutch oven with enough boiling water to cover. Add spices and salt and simmer, covered, until tender, about 1 to 1¼ hours. Remove duck from liquid and let cool.

Remove meat from bones and discard skin. Pour chestnut powder into small baking pan (an 8-inch aluminum pan works well; powder should be ½ to ¾ inch deep). Press meat into powder. Cover and steam until powder has gelatinized into thick, heavy crust, about 30 minutes. Remove from steamer and let cool. Cover and chill until ready to complete.

About 30 minutes before serving time, prepare Sweet and Sour Plum Sauce; set aside and keep warm. Warm serving platter in low oven.

Preheat oil in deep fryer to 375°F. Slice duck into bite-sized chunks and fry quickly in batches until crisp and browned. Remove with slotted spoon and drain on paper towels. Repeat until cooking is completed. Serve immediately with Sweet and Sour Plum Sauce topped with nuts.

*Water chestnut powder is available in oriental markets and in some larger grocery stores. Do not substitute.

***Sweet and Sour Plum Sauce*

Makes about 1½ cups

> 1 **cup plum preserves or jam**
> ½ **cup water**
> 2 **tablespoons catsup**
> 2 **tablespoons cider vinegar**
> 1 **teaspoon cornstarch dissolved in small amount cold water**

Combine first 4 ingredients in small saucepan and bring to boil. If sauce seems too thin, add cornstarch and water, stirring constantly until thickened. Reduce heat and keep warm until needed. Serve hot.

PIGEONNEAUX A SAUCE L'AIL
(Boned Squab with Garlic Sauce)

LE FRANÇAIS
WHEELING, ILLINOIS

6 servings

> 6 **14-ounce squab, dressed (livers reserved)**
> **Salt and freshly ground pepper**
>
> 7 **tablespoons (⅞ stick) unsalted butter**
> 36 **garlic cloves, unpeeled**
>
> ½ **cup dry white wine (preferably Chablis)**
>
> ½ **cup chicken stock (preferably homemade)**
> 3 **tablespoons brandy**
>
> 24 **medium mushrooms, trimmed**
> **Chicken Quenelles***

Have butcher bone squab without cutting them open (this is called "glove boning"), or do it yourself using following directions. Flash freeze squab until some ice crystals have formed. Clean out cavity. Rinse bird under cool water and pat dry with paper towels. Trim wings at joint, discarding tips. Stand bird upright. Using sharp knife, cut through wings where they join body. Loosen meat from breast bones by inserting your fingers between meat and carcass along keel bone and pushing against bone toward bottom. (You may want to scrape with knife from time to time instead of just using fingers.)

Turn bird over onto breast and carefully loosen meat from back by pushing with fingers or scraping with knife. Gradually turn skin "inside out" as you work. Cut thigh bones from joints using scissors and discard carcass. Turn bird skin side out, feeling for any small bones you may have missed. Return any small bits of meat to cavity. Season squab lightly with salt and pepper.

Preheat oven to 450°F. Melt 4 tablespoons butter in large ovenproof skillet over medium-high heat. Add squab and sauté until browned on all sides. Add garlic and brown quickly. Transfer to oven and roast, basting occasionally, until squab is done, 20 to 25 minutes.

Transfer squab and garlic to serving platter and keep warm. Deglaze skillet with wine. Peel 12 cloves of garlic and crush with flat of knife. Add to skillet.

Melt 1 tablespoon butter in small skillet over medium-high heat. Add reserved livers and sauté until evenly browned but still pink inside. Transfer to processor or blender and puree to paste. Add bit of wine mixture and blend well. Stir livers back into remaining wine mixture. Add stock and brandy, place pan over low heat and simmer until sauce is heated through.

Meanwhile, melt remaining 2 tablespoons butter in large skillet over medium heat. Add mushrooms and sauté until golden. Pour sauce over squab and garnish platter with mushrooms, remaining garlic cloves and Chicken Quenelles. Serve immediately.

*Chicken Quenelles

Makes about 6 dozen small quenelles

- 1 **pound chicken breast, boned and skinned**
- 1 **teaspoon salt**
- ½ **teaspoon freshly ground pepper**
- ¼ **teaspoon freshly grated nutmeg**
- 2 **egg whites, lightly beaten**
- 2 **cups whipping cream**

  Hot salted water or chicken stock

Grind chicken finely in processor or with meat grinder. Add salt, pepper and nutmeg and blend well. Gradually add egg whites, mixing vigorously after each addition. Gradually add cream and mix until mixture is firm enough to hold its shape. (If mixing by hand, when adding cream set bowl into larger bowl filled with cracked ice. Beat in cream by tablespoons.)

Generously butter large skillet. Dip 2 teaspoons into boiling water. Heap some of chicken mixture on 1 spoon and round it off with second spoon. Dip second spoon into hot water again, slip it under oval and slide quenelle into buttered skillet. Repeat until quenelles line skillet in single layer (do not crowd). Slowly add enough hot salted water or stock to skillet to float quenelles. Bring liquid to simmer over low heat and poach quenelles until firm, about 5 to 10 minutes (do not boil). Remove with slotted spoon and drain well on paper towels.

MINCED SQUAB

THE MANDARIN
SAN FRANCISCO, CALIFORNIA

4 to 6 servings

> **Oil for deep frying**
- ¼ **pound rice stick noodles (mai fun)***
- 1 **head iceberg lettuce, washed, trimmed and cut in half**
- ¼ **cup peanut oil**
- 2 **small squab, boned and finely chopped or 1 7- to 8-ounce chicken thigh, skinned, boned and finely chopped**
- 2 **green onions, white part only, minced**
- 12 **rehydrated black Chinese mushrooms, minced**
- 1 **cup water chestnuts, minced**
- 2 **to 3 tablespoons minced prosciutto or other ham**
  Small piece ginger root, peeled and crushed
- 1 **tablespoon cornstarch**
- 2 **tablespoons water**
- 1 **tablespoon sherry**
- 1 **tablespoon oyster sauce**
- 1 **tablespoon soy sauce**
- ½ **teaspoon sesame oil**
- ½ **teaspoon sugar**
  Pinch white pepper

Heat oil in deep fryer to about 375°F, until test noodle puffs without turning brown. (If noodle turns brown oil is too hot.) While oil is heating, pull noodles apart. Add few at a time and fry until puffed, about 1 to 2 seconds. Remove with slotted spoon and drain on paper towels. Crush slightly and arrange on platter.

Remove outer cup-shaped leaves from lettuce one by one and set on separate platter.

Heat peanut oil in wok or large skillet. Add squab and green onions and stir-fry briefly. Add next 4 ingredients and continue stir-frying 2 to 3 minutes. Dissolve cornstarch in water and add with remaining ingredients and stir-fry 1 minute. Spoon over noodles; serve immediately with lettuce wrappers.

*Available in oriental markets.

MEATS

The French word for meat, *viande*, derives from an older word that meant, literally, "life sustaining." While we know today that meat is not strictly necessary for sustaining life, it is nevertheless true that meat dishes of all kinds remain the most popular entrees in the Western world, and they form the largest part of most restaurant menus.

For much of our history, meat—whether pork, lamb, mutton, beef or veal—was simply roasted or boiled, usually in the form of a joint or chop. Embellishments were few, so the fourteen cooks in Henry VIII's employ must have had considerably less to do than his six butchers. It was not until the rise of restaurants in the late eighteenth century that some imagination was given to the preparation of meats. Gradually, a battery of sauces, stuffings and different methods of cooking was developed, and today there are as many kinds of meat dishes as there are diners to enjoy them.

The type of meat offered, and the way it is presented, varies with the background of the individual restaurant. A Greek or Indian establishment is apt to specialize in lamb. Italian chefs are particularly fond of veal. In Germany, pork is king, and Britain and America are the bastions of beef. French cuisine encompasses all types of meat, but there the sauce and presentation are as important as the cut.

The recipes that follow are a representative collection of international styles, and include everything from an elegant navarin of lamb to very down-home barbecued spareribs. Each is a centerpiece that will not only sustain life, but also make it much more flavorful.

*Saucisson en Croûte aux Deux Sauces from Le Français
in Wheeling, Illinois (see page 131).*

STEAK AU POIVRE

THE COACH HOUSE
NEW YORK, NEW YORK

4 servings

    2 18-ounce boneless prime strip sirloin
       steaks cut 2 inches thick
   ¼ cup coarsely cracked pepper

   ¾ cup dry red wine
   ½ cup Cognac
   ½ cup Meat Glaze*

Trim excess fat from steaks and render in heavy skillet over high heat. Press pepper onto both sides of meat. Remove unrendered fat from skillet, add steaks and sear 1 minute on each side. Reduce heat and continue cooking, allowing 6 minutes on each side for rare and 10 minutes per side for medium. Transfer meat to heated serving plates and keep warm while preparing sauce.

Pour off excess fat in skillet. Deglaze pan by adding wine and Cognac. Blend in Meat Glaze and cook over high heat until sauce thickens. Slice steaks, pour sauce over and serve immediately.

*Meat Glaze

    5 pounds veal bones, cracked
    2 pounds chicken necks and backs
    3 carrots
    2 large onions, unpeeled and cut
       into quarters
    2 celery stalks including leaves, cut coarsely
    3 garlic cloves, unpeeled and crushed
    2 bay leaves, crushed
    2 teaspoons salt
    1 teaspoon black peppercorns, crushed
       Pinch dried thyme

   ¾ cup all purpose flour

    2 cups dry red wine
    3 quarts canned beef broth
    2 cups tomato puree
    2 leeks including green part, cut coarsely
    3 sprigs Italian parsley

Preheat oven to 475°F. Combine bones, chicken parts, carrots, onions, celery, garlic, bay leaves, salt, peppercorns and thyme in large shallow roasting pan and roast uncovered for 50 minutes.

Remove pan from oven. Sprinkle flour over bones and stir to mix evenly. Return to oven and continue roasting 15 to 20 minutes. Transfer to stockpot.

Set roasting pan over medium heat. Add wine and cook, scraping bottom and sides of pan to loosen browned particles. Add to stockpot along with remaining ingredients. Bring to boil, skimming off foam as it accumulates, then reduce heat and simmer 3 to 4 hours, adding more broth or water if necessary. Skim off all fat. Remove bones; carefully strain stock into another large pot. Sauce should be consistency of whipping cream; continue simmering until further reduced, if necessary. Store in refrigerator or freezer.

BIFE A SOLAR

RESTAURANTE SOLAR DO LORETO
LISBON, PORTUGAL

"The decor and aroma of salt cod created an aura long to be remembered. The Bife á Solar was so good that we would like the recipe for our collection."
                    —Joe Glotfelty, Silver Spring, Maryland

6 servings

    2 1½-pound sirloin tip steaks, each cut into
       3 serving pieces
       Salt
    4 small garlic cloves, minced
    3 bay leaves, crushed
    3 tablespoons (⅜ stick) butter or margarine

   ½ cup corn oil
    6 firm bread slices (sourdough is good)

    6 eggs, beaten

   ½ cup milk
    1 tablespoon Worcestershire sauce

Sprinkle both sides of meat with salt, garlic and bay leaves. Place butter in 10-inch skillet over medium-high heat until sizzling. Brown meat on both sides, about 4 minutes per side. Remove from pan and keep warm. Reserve pan drippings.

Heat oil in another skillet until very hot. Add bread and fry quickly, about 10 to 15 seconds to a side. Drain on paper towels and keep warm.

Scramble eggs with oil left in second skillet; cover and keep warm.

Add milk and Worcestershire sauce to pan drippings. Cook over low heat for few minutes, stirring to loosen browned bits from bottom of pan.

Arrange fried bread slices on individual serving plates. Top with steak, scrambled eggs and sauce.

TERIYAKI STEAK

BEAMREACH RESTAURANT
KAUAI, HAWAII

4 servings

    4 small ¾-inch-thick New York strip steaks
       or 2- to 3-pound flank steak, trimmed
       and scored
   1¼ cups firmly packed light brown sugar

1   **cup soy sauce**
1   **½-inch piece fresh ginger, peeled and grated**
½   **garlic clove, crushed**
⅛   **teaspoon sesame oil**

Arrange steak in shallow dish. Combine remaining ingredients and blend well. Pour over steak. Cover and marinate in refrigerator at least 3 hours or overnight, turning occasionally. Broil or barbecue to desired doneness. (If using flank steak, slice diagonally across grain before serving.)

COTE DE BOEUF GRILLEE AUX TROIS SAUCES
(Grilled Rib Steak with Three Sauces)

TAILLEVENT
PARIS, FRANCE

6 servings

Sauce Béarnaise

2   **teaspoons fresh tarragon or 1 teaspoon dried**
2   **teaspoons fresh chervil or 1 teaspoon dried**

½   **cup tarragon vinegar or white wine vinegar**
½   **cup dry white wine or dry vermouth**
2   **tablespoons minced shallot or minced green onion (white part only)**
2   **tablespoons fresh tarragon or 1 tablespoon dried**
2   **tablespoons fresh chervil or 1 tablespoon dried**
2   **pinches salt**
2   **pinches freshly ground pepper**

8   **egg yolks, beaten until creamy**
2   **tablespoons water**
1½ **cups (3 sticks) unsalted butter, melted and warm (not hot)**
2   **teaspoons fresh lemon juice**
2   **pinches ground red pepper**

Sauce Bordelaise

¾   **cup dry red wine**
1   **medium shallot, minced**
1   **thyme sprig or 1 teaspoon dried**
1   **cup brown sauce**

Shallot Sauce

3   **tablespoons (⅜ stick) butter**
⅓   **cup minced shallot**
1   **cup demi-glace**
    Salt and freshly ground pepper

    Beef bones to yield 5 inches of marrow, soaked in ice water overnight

6   **1-pound beef rib steaks**

For béarnaise: Tie tarragon and chervil in double thickness of cheesecloth. Dip quickly into boiling water, then cold water; squeeze dry. Discard cheesecloth. Set herbs aside.

Mix vinegar, wine or vermouth, 2 tablespoons minced shallot, tarragon, chervil and salt and pepper in small saucepan and bring to boil. Reduce heat and simmer until mixture is reduced to about 2 tablespoons. Remove from heat and cool slightly. Strain into heavy-bottomed 1-quart nonaluminum saucepan,* pressing herbs with back of spoon to extract as much liquid as possible; discard herbs.

Add egg yolks and water to vinegar mixture and blend thoroughly. Whisk (or beat with electric mixer set on medium speed) over low heat until thickened, about 3 to 4 minutes; do not allow eggs to become too thick or dry. Remove from heat and slowly begin drizzling warm melted butter into yolks, beating constantly until all butter has been added and sauce is thick and creamy. (If sauce is too thick to pour, thin with small amount of hot water.) Stir in reserved herbs, lemon juice and ground red pepper. Set aside and keep saucepan in bath of warm water until ready to use.

For bordelaise: Combine red wine, shallot and thyme in small saucepan and boil until reduced to 2 tablespoons. Strain; return to saucepan. Add brown sauce and simmer 5 minutes, stirring occasionally. Set aside and keep warm until ready to use.

For shallot sauce: Melt butter in heavy medium saucepan over medium-low heat. Add shallot and cook, stirring constantly, until very tender, about 10 minutes. Add demi-glace and whisk until warmed through. Taste and season with salt and pepper. Set aside and keep warm until ready to use.

Drain marrow bones. Remove marrow and cut into ¼-inch slices. Transfer to small saucepan. Add enough cold salted water just to cover. Place over low heat and bring just to simmer. Drain marrow well; pat dry. Reserve 6 slices for garnish (if desired); stir remainder into sauce bordelaise.

Barbecue or broil steaks to desired doneness. Transfer to individual plates, top with reserved marrow and serve. Pass sauces separately.

*If heavy pan is not available, protect sauce from burning over direct heat by using heat diffuser or preparing sauce in top of double boiler set over 2 inches of very hot, but not simmering, water. Eggs will require about 10 minutes of beating in double boiler to reach proper consistency.

ROLLATINE DI MANZO AL FORNO

CHANGING SCENE LTD.
WALNUTPORT, PENNSYLVANIA

6 generous servings

  ¾ cup raisins
 12 thin slices top round steak (about
     5x3x¼ inches)
 12 wafer-thin slices cooked ham

  9 ounces sliced salami
  4 hard-cooked eggs
  ½ cup freshly grated Parmesan cheese
  ½ cup chopped fresh parsley
  3 garlic cloves, minced
  ½ teaspoon freshly grated nutmeg
  ½ teaspoon oregano
  ½ teaspoon salt
     Freshly ground pepper

 1¼ cups beef stock
 1¼ cups dry white wine
  4 bay leaves
  6 whole cloves
  2 tablespoons Marsala

     Cooked rice or noodles

Butter 9x13-inch baking dish. Sprinkle raisins with water and let stand about 15 minutes.

Flatten beef slices with mallet or heavy plate; do not use tenderizing mallet. Cover each piece of steak with slice of ham.

Using meat grinder, hand chopper or food processor fitted with steel knife, mince salami, raisins and eggs. Combine with cheese, parsley, garlic, nutmeg, oregano, salt and pepper. Spread mixture over beef and ham slices. Preheat oven to 375°F.

Fold over short sides of beef slices to keep stuffing in place and roll up. Tie each roll with 12-inch length of twine and arrange rolls in baking dish. Pour stock and white wine over, cover with foil and bake 30 minutes. Remove from oven. Add bay leaves, cloves and Marsala. Bake, uncovered, additional 30 minutes, basting several times.

Remove bay leaves and cloves. Clip and discard twine. Arrange rolls on bed of rice or noodles on warm platter. Pour pan juices over and serve.

MEDALLIONS OF BEEF TENDERLOIN CHASSEUR

YACHT HARBOR RESTAURANT
HONOLULU, HAWAII

6 servings

  2 pounds beef tenderloin, cut into
     2-ounce medallions

     Salt and pepper
     Flour
     Butter and oil

  1 teaspoon chopped garlic
  1 teaspoon chopped shallots
  1 pound fresh mushrooms, sliced
  1 pound fresh tomatoes, peeled, seeded
     and chopped
  1 teaspoon tarragon
  ½ cup Burgundy
  2 tablespoons chopped parsley

  1 quart Madeira Sauce*

Season medallions with salt and pepper to taste. Dredge in flour. Shake off excess. In large heated skillet, sauté medallions in equal amounts of butter and oil until medium rare, about 2 to 3 minutes per side. Transfer to large heated platter.

In same skillet, lightly sauté garlic and shallots. Add mushrooms, tomatoes and tarragon and sauté until mushrooms are tender. Add more butter and oil if necessary. Add wine and parsley and cook 2 to 3 minutes more.

Add Madeira Sauce and heat thoroughly. Pour over meat and serve.

Madeira Sauce

Makes 1 quart

  3 tablespoons (⅜ stick) butter, clarified
 1½ teaspoons minced garlic
  ½ teaspoon minced shallots
  ½ teaspoon cracked pepper

  ½ cup Madeira
  ¼ cup Burgundy

  4 cups brown sauce or beef gravy
  ¼ cup tomato puree
  2 tablespoons Worcestershire sauce
     Salt

In medium saucepan, combine butter, garlic, shallots and pepper and cook until shallots and garlic are lightly browned.

Add wines and cook over medium-high heat, stirring frequently, until sauce is reduced by ⅓.

Add brown sauce, tomato puree and Worcestershire sauce. Cook over medium heat for ½ hour, stirring occasionally. Season with salt to taste. Strain.

LONDON BROIL

BIG DADDY'S DEN
SALINE, MICHIGAN

8 servings

  1 cup Russian salad dressing
  1 cup dark French dressing
  1 medium onion, diced
  1 garlic clove, crushed
  ¼ cup mixed pickling spices

3 pounds flank steak, trimmed and sliced across grain into ¼-inch strips
½ cup red wine vinegar

8 slices provolone cheese

Pour salad dressings into large mixing bowl. Add onion, garlic and pickling spices and stir to blend. Add meat strips to salad dressing mixture and marinate at room temperature for 30 minutes. Add vinegar and stir thoroughly. Cover and refrigerate 30 minutes longer.

Preheat oven to 500°F. Divide meat evenly among 8 individual casseroles, or use 1 large shallow casserole, and cover with sauce. Bake 25 minutes (meat will be quite brown on top).

Remove from oven and preheat broiler. Place one slice provolone cheese on each casserole (or 8 slices over 1 large casserole) and place under broiler until cheese is bubbling. Serve at once.

BISTECCA PIZZAIOLA

JULIE'S RISTORANTE
OQUNQUIT, MAINE

"Julie's Ristorante features authentic family recipes from Naples, Italy. We enjoyed the Bistecca Pizzaiola because the tender beef strips in a tomato sauce were a nice change from the numerous seafood specialties of this popular resort area."
—*Dianne A. Tuttle, Troy, New York*

3 to 4 servings

½ cup olive oil
¼ cup (½ stick) butter
1½ pounds top round, trimmed and cut crosswise into very thin strips (about 3x1½ inches)*
½ pound mushrooms, sliced
½ large onion, thinly sliced
2 garlic cloves, thinly sliced
5 plum tomatoes, chopped, or 5 ounces canned Italian tomatoes
½ cup parsley leaves (preferably Italian)
½ teaspoon oregano
Salt and freshly ground pepper
1 cup dry red wine
½ cup freshly grated Parmesan cheese

Heat oil and butter in heavy large skillet over medium-high heat. Add meat and brown quickly on all sides. Transfer to large platter. Add mushrooms to skillet and sauté until edges are browned, about 3 to 5 minutes. Remove with slotted spoon and place over meat. Add onion and garlic to skillet and sauté until onion is lightly browned, about 3 to 5 minutes. Add tomatoes and mash slightly with fork. Stir in parsley and oregano. Season to taste with salt and pepper. Reduce heat and simmer 30 minutes. Stir in wine and cheese and simmer 15 minutes. Return meat and mushrooms to skillet, cover and simmer 1 hour. Stir occasionally; add more wine or water as necessary if mixture is too dry.

*Wrap meat securely and flash-freeze for 30 minutes to facilitate slicing.

LOWELL INN FONDUE BOURGUIGNONNE

LOWELL INN
STILLWATER, MINNESOTA

6 servings

Béarnaise Sauce

1 egg yolk
3 tablespoons (⅜ stick) butter, room temperature

⅓ cup tarragon vinegar
2 tablespoons fresh tarragon or 2 teaspoons dried
4 teaspoons finely chopped shallot
2 teaspoons dry white wine
½ teaspoon seasoned salt
½ teaspoon salt

1 cup mayonnaise

Spanish Sauce

3 tablespoons finely chopped watermelon pickle
2 tablespoons chili sauce
2 tablespoons pickle relish
1 tablespoon finely chopped banana pepper
4 teaspoons finely chopped carrot
4 teaspoons finely chopped green pepper
4 teaspoons finely chopped celery
2 teaspoons Worcestershire sauce
1 teaspoon prepared horseradish
6 drops hot pepper sauce
Salt and freshly ground pepper to taste

Fondue

3 pounds beef tenderloin
Corn oil

For Béarnaise: Whisk egg yolk in medium bowl until light and foamy. Beat in butter.

Combine vinegar and tarragon in small saucepan and bring to simmer over low heat. Cook 10 minutes. Remove from heat and stir in shallot, wine and salts. Cool.

Gradually add mayonnaise to egg yolk mixture. Slowly stir in cooled vinegar mixture. Transfer to serving dish. Cover sauce with plastic wrap and refrigerate overnight.

For Spanish sauce: Combine all ingredients in small bowl. Transfer to serving dish. Cover with plastic wrap and refrigerate overnight.

For fondue: Cut tenderloin into 1½-inch cubes. Cover with waxed paper and refrigerate 1 hour. Let stand at room temperature 1 hour. Half fill fondue pot with corn oil. Set over fondue burner and heat. Spear meat with fondue forks and cook 2 at a time in hot oil. Serve with sauces.

BOEUF A LA FICELLE

DOMAINE CHANDON
YOUNTVILLE, CALIFORNIA

Serve the beef stock base as a first course or side dish with homemade croutons, or pass Rémoulade Sauce or Dijon mustard on the side to accompany both meat and vegetables.

6 servings

    12 small new potatoes
    ½ pound carrots, julienned
    ½ pound turnips, cut into matchsticks
     6 leeks, white part only, quartered
     2 celery hearts
        Rich well-seasoned beef stock
        Butter

     1 4-pound beef fillet, trimmed and tied,
        room temperature
     1 sprig fresh parsley
     1 sprig fresh chervil
     1 sprig fresh tarragon
     2 tablespoons coarse salt
     1 teaspoon black peppercorns

        Croutons* or Rémoulade Sauce**

Peel strip ¾ inch wide around center of each potato. Place carrots, turnips, leeks, potatoes and celery hearts in separate saucepans with enough stock to cover and simmer gently over medium-low heat until just tender. Approximate cooking time for each vegetable: carrots, 5 to 6 minutes; turnips, 4 to 5 minutes; leeks, 4 to 5 minutes; potatoes, 8 to 10 minutes; celery hearts, 8 minutes. Drain stock into Dutch oven or small stockpot; dot vegetables with butter and keep warm in pans.

Place beef in stockpot or Dutch oven and cover with additional stock, then remove beef. Bring stock to boil over medium-high heat. Reduce heat and add beef, parsley, chervil, tarragon, salt and peppercorns. Cover and simmer gently until meat thermometer registers 145°F, about 1 hour.

To serve, place meat on heated platter and surround with individual mounds of vegetables. Serve stock separately with Croutons, as a sauce on the side, or pass Rémoulade Sauce as an accompaniment.

Any remaining broth can be strained and frozen.

*Croutons

6 servings

     6 large thick slices sourdough bread,
        crusts trimmed
        Butter
        Freshly grated Parmesan cheese

Preheat oven to 350°F. Lightly butter both sides of bread slices and sprinkle with cheese. Cut into ½-inch cubes. Place in single layer on baking sheet and toast about 20 minutes, stirring occasionally to brown evenly.

**Rémoulade Sauce

Makes about 4 cups

     4 cups (1 quart) mayonnaise
     6 cornichons, minced
     2 tablespoons capers, rinsed and drained
     1 teaspoon anchovy puree or to taste
        (optional)
        Minced fresh parsley, chervil, tarragon
        and chives to taste

Combine all ingredients and stir them together gently but thoroughly.

SAUERBRATEN WITH SWEET GRAVY

CAFE GEIGER
NEW YORK, NEW YORK

6 to 8 servings

     3 pounds beef bottom round or rump,
        cut thick
     1 teaspoon salt
    ½ teaspoon freshly ground pepper
     4 bay leaves
     8 cloves
    ½ teaspoon whole peppercorns
     2 medium onions, sliced
     1 green pepper, seeded and chopped
     1 celery stalk, chopped
     1 small carrot, minced
    2½ cups water
    1½ cups red wine vinegar

    ¼ cup (½ stick) butter
        Sauerbraten Gravy*

Rub meat well with salt and pepper. Combine with spices and vegetables in deep earthenware crock or ovenware glass dish. Heat water and vinegar to boiling point in medium saucepan. Pour over meat. Let cool, then cover tightly and refrigerate at least 48 hours, turning meat twice a day.

When ready to cook, remove meat and dry with paper towels; reserve marinade. Melt butter in Dutch oven over medium-high heat and brown meat on all sides. Meanwhile strain marinade. Pour over meat, cover tightly and let simmer slowly until meat is fork-tender, about 2 to 3 hours. Transfer meat to warmed serving platter, slice and keep warm while preparing Sauerbraten Gravy.

*Sauerbraten Gravy

6 to 8 servings

     4 teaspoons sugar
     3 cups cooking liquid
     1 cup water
     6 gingersnaps, crushed
     8 dried pitted prunes
        Salt and freshly ground pepper
    ½ cup sour cream (optional)

DOMAINE CHANDON—DINING IN THE NAPA VALLEY FOOTHILLS

In 1974 the French firm of Moët et Chandon, makers of Dom Pérignon Champagne for the last 250 years, dispatched Edmond Maudière, their "grand palate" of wine, to California's Napa Valley to establish the first French-owned winery in the United States, Domaine Chandon. The new vines produced their first grapes on schedule three years later.

Along a sloping hillside overlooking the vineyard's 1,500 acres, past big pots of roses and red camellias, is Domaine Chandon's restaurant. Inside, a vaulted ceiling of natural fir lends a feeling of unlimited spaciousness. With personal attention to every plate, Chef Philippe Jeanty, a native of Champagne, cooks from scratch for 200 people at lunch and 70 at dinner, five days a week.

"Everything here is prepared at the last minute," Jeanty says. "It is the only way to achieve the fresh, natural flavor of fish or vegetables. If you put green beans into the vinaigrette even an hour ahead, they are no longer green beans when you serve them."

His hardest job was training his American-born help to develop the French palate. Jeanty himself had to learn to adapt to American ingredients. "For example, American sparkling wine has a higher acidity than the French Champagne, so in a Champagne sauce I compensate by adding more butter and cream and then reducing more to make it taste French."

A perfectionist, Jeanty tastes and retastes, adding a touch more tarragon to a parsley-tarragon-sorrel mayonnaise. His eye is always open for the simple, elegant effect, as he arranges a perfect puff pastry to garnish a glazed, stuffed trout with Champagne sauce.

Melt sugar in 3- to 4-quart saucepan over low heat, stirring constantly until golden brown. Gradually stir in hot marinade, then add water. Add remaining ingredients except sour cream and cook until thickened, stirring constantly. Stir in sour cream, if desired. Ladle part of gravy over meat and pass remainder in gravy boat.

STEAK TIPS WITH MUSHROOMS AND ONIONS

J. P.'S PORTERHOUSE TOO
LATHAM, NEW YORK

3 to 4 servings

Garlic Butter

- 1 **pound (4 sticks) butter, room temperature**
- ½ **head garlic, peeled and minced**
- ¼ **cup dry white wine**
- 1 **tablespoon chopped fresh parsley**
- ¼ **teaspoon freshly ground pepper**

- 1 **large onion, sliced**
- ½ **pound mushrooms, sliced**

- 1 **pound beef tenderloin tips**
  Salt, freshly ground pepper and garlic powder
  Dash sherry

For garlic butter: Combine first 5 ingredients in bowl and mix on low speed of electric mixer until thoroughly blended.

Melt 2 tablespoons garlic butter in large skillet over medium-high heat. Add onion and sauté until golden. Add mushrooms and cook lightly. Transfer to plate and keep warm. Drain and wipe pan.

Season meat with salt, pepper and garlic powder to taste. Melt 1 tablespoon garlic butter in same skillet over medium-high heat. Add meat and sauté to desired doneness. Return onion and mushrooms to pan and stir to blend. Add sherry and serve immediately topped with additional garlic butter.

Remaining garlic butter may be frozen.

BOEUF AU FROMAGE

ONCE UPON A STOVE
NEW YORK, NEW YORK

"For several years I was fortunate enough to live practically next door to the charming Once Upon a Stove. I ate there regularly and never was served anything but a delicious meal! One of the house specialities was Boeuf au Fromage. . . ."
—*Mrs. Lucile Penington Ure, Nairobi, Kenya*

2 servings

    1 **pound sirloin or filet mignon, sliced in ¼-inch strips**
    ½ **cup flour**
    ½ **teaspoon salt**
    ¼ **teaspoon pepper**

    2 **tablespoons peanut oil**
    2 **tablespoons (¼ stick) butter**

    1 **cup beef stock**
    1 **tablespoon sour cream**

    2 **tablespoons Roquefort dressing**
    2 **tablespoons grated Parmesan cheese**

Coat beef strips with flour seasoned with salt and pepper; remove excess flour.

Heat peanut oil and butter in skillet. Sauté strips of beef few at a time on both sides. Remove beef strips from pan.

Pour beef stock and sour cream into skillet and mix well over low heat. Return beef to skillet and stir carefully. Remove from heat.

Preheat broiler. Place beef and sauce into greased casserole, top with Roquefort dressing and Parmesan cheese. Broil until slightly brown.

CHILI CON CARNE

CASA JUANITA
CLEARWATER, FLORIDA

"There is an exceptional Mexican restaurant in Clearwater, Florida, called Casa Juanita. They have several types of chili, but we like the one with shredded beef."
—*Patricia R. Jordan, Pinellas Park, Florida*

6 to 8 servings

    2 **pounds lean beef stew meat, cut into 1½- to 2-inch pieces**
    3 **medium tomatoes, diced**
 1½ **cups water**
    1 **cup chopped onion**
    2 **small garlic cloves, crushed**
    1 **teaspoon salt**

 1½ **cups tomato sauce**
    1 **4-ounce can chopped green chilies**
    1 **tablespoon chili powder**
    1 **tablespoon ground cumin**

Combine meat, tomatoes, water, onion, garlic and salt in 6-quart saucepan or Dutch oven and bring to boil over high heat. Reduce heat, cover and simmer, adding water as necessary so meat is always partially covered, until beef is tender enough to shred, about 2 hours. Remove meat and shred by pressing with back of spoon.

Return meat to saucepan. Add remaining ingredients, cover and simmer 30 minutes, stirring every 5 minutes. Serve hot.

MOUSSAKA

SUN LINE CRUISES
STELLA SOLARIS

"I have just returned from my second cruise on the Sun Line ship Stella Solaris. The dining room served the best moussaka I've ever tasted."
—*Teola Simpson, Hamlin, Texas*

8 servings

    1 **tablespoon butter**
    1 **cup finely chopped onion**
    2 **pounds lean ground beef**
 1½ **pounds tomatoes, peeled and sliced**
    ¼ **cup chopped fresh parsley**
    1 **6-ounce can tomato paste**
        Salt and pepper

        Vegetable oil
        Flour
    2 **large eggplants, peeled and sliced**
    2 **potatoes, peeled and sliced**

    1 **cup (2 sticks) butter**
    1 **cup flour**
    4 **cups hot milk**
    4 **slightly beaten eggs**
    1 **cup grated Parmesan cheese**
        Dash nutmeg
        Salt and pepper

Melt 1 tablespoon butter in large skillet. Sauté onion until soft. Add beef ½ pound at a time and cook in batches until brown. Add tomatoes, parsley and tomato paste. Cook 10 to 15 minutes. Season with salt and pepper to taste. Set aside.

Heat oil in large frying pan. Flour eggplant lightly. Sauté eggplant on both sides in hot oil until golden. Fry potatoes in same skillet, using additional oil if needed. Set aside.

Melt 1 cup butter in medium saucepan. Add 1 cup flour slowly, stirring to form smooth paste. Gradually add hot milk, stirring over low heat until thick and smooth. Mix in eggs and cheese; cook 1 minute. Season with nutmeg, salt and pepper to taste.

Preheat oven to 350°F. In 2-quart baking dish, arrange in alternating layers: potatoes, ½ meat sauce, ½ eggplant, ½ meat sauce, remaining eggplant. Pour cheese sauce over top. Bake until golden, about 50 to 60 minutes.

"BALTIMORE AND OHIO" BARBECUED BEEF RIBS

TWIN BRIDGE JUNCTION
FERNDALE, NEW YORK

6 servings

    4 cups chili sauce
  ½ cup fresh lemon juice
  ½ cup firmly packed dark brown sugar
    3 tablespoons Worcestershire sauce
    1 tablespoon hot pepper sauce
    1 tablespoon paprika
    1 teaspoon salt
    1 teaspoon freshly ground pepper

  18 roasted beef ribs or braised short ribs (or combination)

Combine all ingredients except ribs in large saucepan and bring to boil. Reduce heat and simmer 15 to 20 minutes, stirring occasionally.

Preheat oven to 350°F. Arrange ribs in single layer in large shallow roasting pan. Cover each rib with ¼ cup sauce. Bake until crisp, about 25 minutes.

BOLLITO MISTO (Mixed Boiled Meats)

RISTORANTE DIANA
BOLOGNA, ITALY

This dish is served at the Diana Restaurant accompanied by potato puree and hot peperonata.

8 to 10 servings

  1 3½- to 4-pound beef brisket
  1 3- to 3½-pound beef tongue
  1 celery stalk, cut into chunks
  1 carrot, cut into chunks
  1 onion, coarsely chopped
  2 large whole chicken breasts, skinned and boned

  1 large cotechino sausage* (thawed if frozen), soaked overnight in cold water
  1 large zampone* (pork sausage from Modena), if available, soaked overnight in cold water
    Salsa Verde**

Combine brisket, tongue and vegetables in large stockpot. Add water to cover. Bring to boil, reduce heat and simmer slowly 2½ hours, skimming foam as it accumulates on surface. Add chicken breasts and continue simmering until meat is tender and chicken is cooked through, about 1 hour.

Meanwhile, cook sausage(s) in another pot of barely simmering water to cover until cooked through, about 3½ hours.

Slice meats, poultry and sausage(s) and arrange on platter. Top with some of Salsa Verde and pass remainder separately.

Strained stock from cooking meat and poultry can be refrigerated or frozen and is ideal for cooking tortellini or other pasta.

*Available at Italian groceries and specialty stores.

**Salsa Verde*

Makes about ⅔ cup

  3 tablespoons minced fresh parsley
  2 tablespoons fresh lemon juice
  1 tablespoon capers, rinsed, drained and chopped
  1 teaspoon moutarde de meaux
  ⅛ teaspoon salt
  ½ cup olive oil

Combine all ingredients except oil in small bowl and blend well. Slowly add oil, whisking until well blended (mixture will not be like mayonnaise).

LAMB CURRY KHORMA

INDIA HOUSE
SAN FRANCISCO, CALIFORNIA

8 servings

    4 pounds boned lamb shoulder, very carefully trimmed of fat, cut into 1-inch cubes
 1½ tablespoons turmeric

   ⅓ cup oil
    6 medium onions, chopped
    3 garlic cloves, minced
 1½ cups water
    6 bay leaves
    6 whole cardamom seeds
    6 whole cloves
    1 cinnamon stick

    2 tablespoons cumin
 1½ teaspoons dill
    1 teaspoon ground coriander
   ¼ teaspoon each: mace, nutmeg, cayenne and ginger
    2 teaspoons salt

Roll lamb cubes in turmeric; set aside.

Heat oil in 12- to 14-inch skillet over medium heat. Add onions and garlic and sauté until deep golden brown, about 15 minutes. In small saucepan, combine water, bay leaves, cardamom seeds, cloves and cinnamon stick and bring to boil. Cover and continue boiling slowly 10 minutes.

Meanwhile, combine remaining seasonings except salt. Add to skillet, reduce heat to low and cook, uncovered, 10 minutes. Add lamb and salt and stir to blend thoroughly.

Strain liquid from boiled spices and stir into meat mixture. Cover and simmer until meat is tender, about 2½ to 3 hours. Cool and refrigerate several hours or overnight. Skim off solidified fat. Reheat before serving.

RACK OF LAMB

THE COACH HOUSE
NEW YORK, NEW YORK

For each serving

  1 **small rack of lamb (7 ribs)**

  1 **garlic clove, crushed**
  1 **teaspoon fresh lemon juice**
  1 **teaspoon vegetable oil**
     Salt and freshly ground pepper
  2 **teaspoons minced fresh parsley**
  ¼ **lemon**

Have butcher crack chine bone, remove all fat from meat, and French bones (cut about 1 inch of meat from end of ribs).

Preheat oven to 475°F. Rub garlic over bone side of meat; discard garlic. Rub meat with lemon juice, then with oil. Heat skillet over high heat until extremely hot. Sear lamb on all sides. Transfer to rack in roasting pan and sprinkle with salt and pepper to taste. Rub in parsley. Roast meat side up 10 minutes; turn meat over and continue roasting until lamb is well browned on outside but still pink inside, about 10 minutes longer. Place on heated plate, squeeze lemon over meat and serve.

RACK OF LAMB WITH VEGETABLES

THE ABBEY
ATLANTA, GEORGIA

"Not only were we impressed with the atmosphere (it's an old church that has been converted into a restaurant), but we very much enjoyed our meal—a rack of lamb with vegetables. We've had rack of lamb at many restaurants in this country and abroad, but the Abbey's tops them all."

—John T. McConnell, Peoria, Illinois

Serve surrounded with grilled vegetables such as tomatoes, zucchini, yellow squash and green beans.

6 to 8 servings

  2 **2½- to 3-pound racks of lamb, ribs partially split**
  2 **to 3 garlic cloves, minced**
     Salt and freshly ground pepper
  2 **medium carrots, diced**
  2 **medium onions, diced**
  2 **celery stalks, diced**

  ½ **cup dry breadcrumbs**
  ¼ **cup (½ stick) melted butter**
  4 **cups beef stock**
  1 **tablespoon tomato paste**
  2 **bay leaves**
  1 **garlic clove, minced**
  1 **teaspoon rosemary**

  1 **teaspoon cornstarch**
  ¼ **cup water**

Preheat oven to 350°F. Rub lamb with garlic and salt and pepper to taste. Cover rib bones individually with aluminum foil to keep them from burning. Place racks in large roasting pan, fat side up. Distribute carrots, onions and celery around meat. Roast, uncovered, until meat reaches desired degree of doneness on thermometer, about 25 to 30 minutes for medium.

Preheat broiler. Combine breadcrumbs with butter and spread over meat. Place under broiler about 1 to 2 minutes to brown. Remove meat from roasting pan and keep warm. Place pan on burners, cover and simmer 10 minutes. Stir in stock, tomato paste, bay leaves, garlic and rosemary. Bring to boil, cover and simmer 10 more minutes.

Dissolve cornstarch in water. Carefully stir into stock mixture, blending until smooth. Bring to boil, stirring constantly, over high heat; reduce heat to low and cook, uncovered, 5 minutes.

Place racks on serving platter. Strain sauce into sauceboat and serve separately.

INDONESIAN LAMB WITH COLD PEANUT SAUCE

TRADER VIC'S
SAN FRANCISCO, CALIFORNIA

4 servings

  ¾ **cup oil**
  ⅓ **cup diced celery**
  ⅓ **cup diced onion**
  1 **garlic clove, minced**
  ½ **cup prepared mustard**
  ¼ **cup cider vinegar**
  3 **tablespoons curry powder**
  3 **tablespoons honey**
  2 **bay leaves**
  2 **teaspoons A-1 sauce**
  1 **teaspoon oregano**
  2 **dashes hot pepper sauce**
     Juice and peel of 1 large lemon

  2 **racks of lamb, fat trimmed**

     Cold Peanut Sauce*

Heat oil in medium skillet over medium heat. Add celery, onion and garlic and sauté until onion is translucent. Reduce heat, stir in all remaining ingredients except lamb and peanut sauce and simmer briefly until heated through. Pour into bowl and cool slightly. Cover and refrigerate 2 hours to allow flavors to blend.

Transfer marinade to large shallow baking dish or pan. Add lamb, turning several times to coat. Cover and marinate in refrigerator 3 to 4 hours.

Place rack in center of oven and preheat to 550°F. Grease shallow baking pan. Drain marinade from meat and set aside. Wrap lamb in foil, leaving meaty portions exposed. Place in pan and brush with some of reserved marinade. For medium rare, bake 15 minutes total, turning once and basting frequently with remaining marinade. (Exact cooking time will depend on thickness of meat and desired doneness.) Serve immediately with Cold Peanut Sauce.

*Cold Peanut Sauce

Makes about 1 cup

- ½ **cup creamy style peanut butter, room temperature**
- ½ **cup coconut cream**
- 2 **tablespoons soy sauce**
- 1½ **teaspoons Worcestershire sauce**
- ¼ **teaspoon salt**
  Dash hot pepper sauce
  Juice of ¼ large lemon

Combine all ingredients in small mixing bowl and blend thoroughly. Cover and chill. Serve cold.

MUSTARD-GINGER LAMB CHOPS

DEJA-VU
PHILADELPHIA, PENNSYLVANIA

4 servings

- 4 **garlic cloves, crushed**
- 1 **2-inch piece ginger, peeled and coarsely chopped**
- 2 **teaspoons dry vermouth**
- 2 **teaspoons fresh lime juice**
- 2 **teaspoons white wine thyme vinegar***
- ¼ **teaspoon crushed red peppercorns**
- ¼ **teaspoon crushed green peppercorns**
  Pinch salt
- 1 **cup (scant) extra-strong Dijon mustard**
- 1 **teaspoon unrefined orange blossom honey**

  Salt and freshly ground pepper
- 16 **New Zealand lamb chops or 8 small American chops (trimmed of all fat and gristle), frenched**
- 6 **to 8 slices whole wheat bread, toasted, mixed in blender and sieved**
- 8 **tablespoons (1 stick) butter, melted and clarified**
- ⅓ **cup chopped fresh parsley**
- ⅓ **cup chopped shallot**

Combine garlic, ginger, vermouth, lime juice, thyme vinegar, peppercorns and salt in small saucepan and cook over medium-high heat until reduced by ½. Add mustard and honey and bring to boil, stirring constantly, until slightly reduced, about 5 to 8

minutes (mixture will be sticky). Strain through cheesecloth into jar with tight-fitting lid and seal tightly. Refrigerate until ready to use. (Can be prepared up to 6 weeks ahead.)

Lightly sprinkle salt and pepper over both sides of lamb chops. Spread 1½ to 2 teaspoons mustard mixture over all sides of each chop (if using American lamb, increase mustard to 2 to 3 teaspoons per chop). Dip all sides into breadcrumbs, covering completely and patting gently so breadcrumbs adhere. Heat 4 tablespoons butter in large skillet over medium-high heat until foam subsides. Add ½ of chops and brown on both sides (be careful not to burn; chops should be medium rare). Transfer to platter and keep warm. Repeat with remaining chops. Blend parsley and shallot, sprinkle lightly over top of each lamb chop and serve.

*For white wine thyme vinegar, combine ¼ cup white vinegar and 1 teaspoon dried thyme in small saucepan and bring to simmer over medium heat. Let simmer 5 minutes. Strain well before using.

LAMB WITH ARTICHOKES AND LEMON

GREEN LAKE GRILL
SEATTLE, WASHINGTON

"This dish was so good, it made a lamb fan out of my husband." —Pat Putman, Richland, Washington

6 servings

- 2½ **pounds boned leg of lamb (about 5 pounds with bone), cut into 1½-inch cubes**
  Salt and freshly ground pepper
  Ground oregano
- 3 **tablespoons olive oil (or more)**
- 6 **garlic cloves, minced**
- 2 **tablespoons fresh lemon juice**
- ½ **cup lamb or beef stock**
- 18 **artichoke hearts, halved**
- 8 **tablespoons (1 stick) unsalted butter**
  Chopped fresh parsley (garnish)

Sprinkle lamb generously with salt, pepper and oregano. Heat oil in large skillet over medium-high heat until haze forms. Add lamb in batches and brown well on all sides, adding more oil as necessary. Transfer lamb to platter and keep warm. Add garlic to pan and sauté briefly. Pour off all but thin film of oil. Add lemon juice to skillet and boil briskly over high heat, scraping up any browned bits clinging to bottom of pan. Stir in stock and artichokes. Continue cooking until sauce is reduced to glaze. Return lamb to skillet, tossing gently to coat with sauce. Stir in butter 1 tablespoon at a time until sauce is desired consistency. Sprinkle mixture with parsley and toss gently. Transfer to heated platter and serve immediately.

FILET D'AGNEAU EN FEUILLETE

BEAVER CLUB, THE QUEEN ELIZABETH HOTEL
MONTREAL, QUEBEC, CANADA

2 servings

- 1 10-inch loin or rack of lamb (2½ to 3 pounds)
- 2 tablespoons oil
- 1 teaspoon fresh thyme leaves or ½ teaspoon dried
- ½ teaspoon savory leaves

Sauce

- Bones and trimmings of loin or rack of lamb
- 1 small carrot, chopped
- ½ stalk celery, chopped
- ½ clove garlic, minced
- ½ onion, chopped
- ¼ teaspoon thyme
- ¼ teaspoon rosemary
- ½ bay leaf
- 1 tablespoon tomato paste
- ¼ cup dry white wine
- 2 cups water
- Salt and pepper

- ½ teaspoon salt
- Pinch pepper

Spinach

- ½ tablespoon salt
- 6 ounces fresh spinach leaves, washed, stems removed

- 1 tablespoon butter
- ½ garlic clove, minced
- 1 teaspoon chopped shallots or green onions
- Salt and pepper

- 6 ounces puff paste (use favorite recipe)
- 4 large thin slices prosciutto
- 1 egg, lightly beaten

Bone lamb, removing all fat (or have your butcher bone it), leaving approximately 7 to 10 ounces of meat. Reserve bones and trimmings for sauce. Rub lamb with 1 tablespoon oil, thyme and savory. Cover and marinate in refrigerator at least 2 hours, preferably overnight.

For sauce: Preheat oven to 400°F. Place bones and trimmings in small roasting pan and roast until golden brown, about 30 minutes. Add chopped vegetables, herbs and tomato paste. Stir well. Return to oven and continue roasting until vegetables are well browned, another 30 minutes. Remove from oven. Skim off fat and add wine. Reduce over high heat until all liquid has disappeared. Add water, stir well, and bring to boil. Transfer from roasting pan to medium saucepan and simmer 1½ hours. Strain, and reduce to about ¾ cup. Season to taste with salt and pepper if needed.

Season lamb with salt and pepper. In heavy skillet, heat remaining oil until it almost reaches smoking point. Sear lamb 10 seconds on each side. Remove from skillet and cool completely.

For spinach: In 2-quart pan, bring 1 quart water to boil. Add salt and spinach. Return to rapid boil, then place immediately under cold running water until spinach is cool. Drain well. Press spinach in cloth to squeeze completely dry.

In same skillet in which meat was served, melt butter. Add garlic and shallots and sauté until translucent. Add blanched spinach leaves. Toss lightly with fork and season to taste with salt and pepper. Chill.

Roll out puff paste into rectangle 8x12 inches or to size that easily covers meat. Place 2 slices prosciutto side by side across the middle. Place cold, seared lamb on the prosciutto. Spread cold spinach evenly over meat. Cover spinach with remaining prosciutto slices. Brush edges of dough with beaten egg. Fold long edges of dough over meat and press to seal. Place seam side down on baking sheet. Press down ends and cut off protruding dough about 1 inch from each end. Brush entire surface with egg and let dry 2 to 3 minutes. With fork, make crisscross pattern on top of pastry, being careful not to break through pastry. Refrigerate until ready to bake.

Preheat oven to 400°F. Place lamb in oven 12 to 15 minutes (a 7-ounce loin will be medium at 12 minutes, well done at 15; a 10-ounce loin will be medium at 15 minutes, well done at 17). Serve immediately. Pass sauce separately.

LAMB MOROCCAN

DEACON BRODIE'S TAVERN
DUBLIN, NEW HAMPSHIRE

6 servings

- 3 tablespoons olive oil
- 2 pounds lean lamb, cut into 1-inch pieces
- ½ pound mushrooms, sliced
- 1 medium onion, chopped
- 1 garlic clove, finely minced
- 1 pound tomatoes, peeled and quartered
- ½ cup raisins
- ½ cup toasted slivered almonds
- 2 tablespoons sugar
- 1 teaspoon cinnamon
- 1 teaspoon salt
- 1 teaspoon allspice
- ¼ cup chicken broth

Heat oil in large skillet until haze forms. Add lamb and sauté until browned on all sides. Add mushrooms, onion and garlic and sauté for 2 minutes. Add remaining ingredients except broth and simmer, adding broth as needed, until lamb is tender, about 30 to 45 minutes.

ROSETTE OF LAMB

SAN FRANCISCO
SYDNEY, AUSTRALIA

"One of the highlights of our recent visit to Australia was dinner at San Francisco, in the Hilton International Sydney. They served fillet of lamb wrapped in phyllo pastry, with a sauce of garlic and herbs."
—Jayne C. DeFiore, Knoxville, Tennessee

6 servings

  6 tablespoons (¾ stick) butter
  6 5- to 6-ounce lamb fillets (cut from rack or loin)

  6 phyllo sheets (17x13 inches)
    Melted butter
    Breadcrumbs
18 large spinach leaves (6 ounces), blanched, thoroughly drained and patted dry
    Salt and freshly ground pepper
  3 medium carrots, cut julienne, blanched and patted dry

Sauce

  6 tablespoons finely chopped onion
  1 garlic clove, crushed
    Pinch dried rosemary
  2 tablespoons fresh lemon juice
  3 cups beef stock
  2 tablespoons (¼ stick) butter, room temperature

Melt butter in medium skillet over medium-high heat until foam subsides. Add fillets few at a time and sauté quickly on all sides until browned. Remove lamb fillets to platter and let cool slightly. Set skillet aside.

Preheat oven to 400°F. For each fillet, place sheet of phyllo on work surface (keep remainder covered with damp towel to prevent drying). Brush with melted butter. Fold in ½ crosswise and brush again with butter. Sprinkle with breadcrumbs. Lay 3 spinach leaves at 1 end of dough. Pat fillet dry with paper towel (reserve juices on platter for use in sauce). Sprinkle meat with salt and pepper and set on spinach leaves. Top with carrots. Fold in sides of phyllo, then roll up and place seam side down on oiled baking sheet. Brush with butter and bake until lightly browned, about 15 minutes.

For sauce: Return skillet to medium-high heat. Add onion and sauté briefly. Stir in garlic and rosemary. Deglaze pan by adding lemon juice, meat juices and stock. Season to taste with salt and pepper. Boil until reduced by ⅓. Remove from heat and stir in butter. Serve lamb on heated plates; pass sauce separately.

NAVARIN D'AGNEAU
(Savory Ragout of Lamb)

RESTAURANT BOCUSE
LYONS, FRANCE

4 to 6 servings

  3 pounds lamb shoulder (trimmed of all fat), cut into 1½- to 2-inch cubes
    Salt and freshly ground pepper
  3 to 4 tablespoons vegetable oil
  3 tablespoons chopped garlic

  2 to 3 extra large carrots, cut into 2-inch lengths
 ½ large onion
  4 to 5 large sprigs tarragon
  2 sprigs thyme
  2 leeks, well trimmed
  2 bay leaves
  1 celery stalk (with leaves)
  1 large sprig basil
  3 tablespoons all purpose flour
  7 baby carrots
  5 medium tomatoes, cored, seeded, juiced and chopped
  1 cup dry white wine
  2 tablespoons tomato paste
    Coarse salt

  1 pound potatoes, peeled and quartered

 ½ pound small peas (petits pois)
  2 sprigs basil, chopped

Sprinkle lamb generously with salt and pepper. Heat oil in large skillet over high heat. Stir in garlic. Add lamb in batches (do not crowd) and brown well. Transfer to large saucepan. Pour in just enough warm water to cover.

Add sliced carrots and onion to skillet and brown well over medium-high heat. Discard any accumulated fat. Add carrots and onion to lamb with tarragon, thyme, leeks, bay leaves, celery and basil. Stir in flour, blending well. Add baby carrots, tomatoes, wine, tomato paste and salt. Cover and cook over high heat until lamb is tender, skimming off foam as necessary, about 45 minutes to 1 hour.

Meanwhile, cook potatoes in boiling salted water until just tender. Drain well. Transfer potatoes to bowl and cover with cold water. (Potatoes may be carved into decorative ovals if desired.)

Transfer meat and carrots to platter using slotted spoon. Strain sauce into medium bowl, pressing vegetables with back of spoon to extract as much liquid as possible. Return sauce to pan and cook over medium-low heat until slightly thickened. Add lamb, all carrots, drained potatoes, peas and chopped basil and heat through. Transfer to large dish and serve.

MONGOLIAN LAMB

THE MANDARIN
SAN FRANCISCO, CALIFORNIA

8 servings

    3 tablespoons oil
 1½ pounds boned leg of lamb, cut into
       thin strips
    2 bunches green onions, cut into
       2-inch pieces
    2 tablespoons soy sauce
    1 teaspoon sesame oil

    1 tablespoon cornstarch
    1 tablespoon water
       Buns* (optional)

Heat oil in wok over high heat. Stir-fry lamb 3 to 5 minutes. Add green onions, soy sauce and sesame oil. Toss ingredients well.

Combine cornstarch and water. Add to lamb and stir quickly until sauce begins to bubble. Serve as is or with buns.

Buns

8 servings

    8 cups all purpose flour
    1 teaspoon dry yeast
 1¼ cups lukewarm water
  ¼ cups hot water
       Oil

Place 4 cups flour in large bowl. Combine yeast and lukewarm water. Pour slowly into flour; mix with hands. If dough is too stiff add little more lukewarm water until pliable. Knead for several minutes. Cover with towel to keep moist. Allow dough to rest about 20 minutes.

Combine remaining flour and hot water with hands. Mix and knead until pliable. Then knead 2 doughs together. Cover with towel and allow dough to rest about 10 minutes.

Preheat oven to 475°F. Roll dough with balls of hands into long roll (about 18 to 20 inches long). Flatten with rolling pin. Spoon little oil over flattened dough and spread oil to edges of dough. Fold sides over lengthwise to meet in center. Slice dough into 2-inch strips. With seam side down, roll each strip flat and place on ungreased baking sheets. Bake 6 minutes and turn; bake 2 to 3 minutes more. To serve, split rolls open and fill with Mongolian Lamb.

SHISH KEBOB

THE VINTAGE PRESS, INC.
VISALIA, CALIFORNIA

6 to 8 servings

    2 pounds boned leg of lamb, cut into
       1½-inch cubes

  ½ medium onion, thinly sliced
  ½ cup chopped fresh parsley
  ¼ cup dry sherry
    2 garlic cloves, minced
    1 teaspoon salt
  ½ teaspoon freshly ground pepper
  ¼ teaspoon thyme
  ¼ teaspoon oregano
  ¼ cup olive oil

    1 box cherry tomatoes
  ¼ pound small white onions, parboiled
  ¼ pound mushrooms
    1 green pepper, seeded and cut into
       1½-inch squares
       Clarified butter

Combine first 9 ingredients in large bowl and let stand 10 minutes. Add olive oil and toss lightly. Cover; marinate in refrigerator 24 to 36 hours.

Prepare barbecue or preheat broiler. Skewer lamb alternately with tomato, onion, mushroom and green pepper square. Brush lightly with clarified butter and broil, turning frequently, until meat is cooked as desired.

CARNE DE PORCO A'ALENTEJANA

POUSADA DE SANTA MARIA
MARVAO, PORTUGAL

6 to 8 servings

    3 to 4 pounds lean pork, cut into
       ¾-inch cubes
    3 small heads garlic, unpeeled and crushed
    3 to 4 tablespoons paprika
    1 tablespoon salt
    2 cups dry white wine

    1 bunch fresh cilantro
    3 garlic cloves, peeled and crushed
    1 tablespoon olive oil
  ¼ teaspoon salt

    3 tablespoons oil
    2 cups dry white wine
 1½ pounds littleneck quahog clams

Combine pork, unpeeled garlic, paprika and salt in crock or glass bowl. Add 2 cups dry white wine. Cover and marinate in refrigerator at least 2 days, stirring several times.

Combine next 4 ingredients to form paste; set aside. Place meat with marinade in large skillet and bring to boil over high heat. Reduce heat slightly and cook, stirring occasionally, until liquid is evaporated, about 25 minutes. Remove meat from skillet. Wash skillet and return to heat.

Heat oil, add meat and fry, stirring continuously, until browned. Add remaining wine, cover and cook until meat is almost fork tender. Remove lid and continue cooking until almost all of liquid is evaporated. Stir in cilantro paste until well combined. Add clams hinge side up and simmer just until shells open. Discard any unopened clams. Serve at once.

GERMAN-STYLE SCHNITZEL

VINTAGE 1847 RESTAURANT, STONE HILL WINERY
HERMANN, MISSOURI

6 servings

  6 **boneless pork loin cutlets (about 2 pounds total), trimmed**

  ½ **cup all purpose flour**
  2 **teaspoons seasoned salt**
  ½ **teaspoon freshly ground pepper**
  2 **eggs**
  ¼ **cup milk**
1½ **cups fresh breadcrumbs**
  2 **teaspoons paprika**

  6 **tablespoons solid vegetable shortening**

  2 **tablespoons all purpose flour**
  ½ **teaspoon dried dill**
1½ **cups chicken broth**
  1 **cup sour cream, room temperature**

Place cutlets between 2 sheets of waxed paper and flatten to ¼- to ½-inch thickness. Cut small slits around edges of pork to prevent curling. Set aside.

Combine ½ cup flour, salt and pepper in shallow bowl or on sheet of waxed paper. Beat eggs with milk in another shallow bowl. Mix crumbs and paprika in small bowl or on another sheet of waxed paper.

Melt 3 tablespoons shortening in large skillet over medium heat. Dip cutlets in flour, then into egg mixture. Coat with crumbs, covering completely. Add 3 cutlets to skillet and sauté on both sides until coating is golden brown and meat is no longer pink, about 3 to 5 minutes per side. Transfer to platter and keep warm. Repeat procedure with remaining shortening and cutlets.

Combine remaining flour with dill. Add to skillet, scraping up any browned bits clinging to bottom of pan. Add broth, stirring constantly until well blended. Stir in sour cream and cook until heated through. Spoon over cutlets or pass separately.

MU SHU PORK

YANG TZE
HONOLULU, HAWAII

About 6 servings

  ⅓ **cup dry lily flower***
  ½ **cup tree ears***

  2 **tablespoons peanut oil (or more)**
  ½ **cup shredded uncooked pork**

  2 **eggs, well beaten**

  2 **cups shredded Chinese cabbage**
  ⅓ **cup chopped water chestnuts**
  1 **teaspoon chopped fresh garlic**
  2 **teaspoons soy sauce**
  ¼ **teaspoon salt**
  ¼ **teaspoon freshly ground pepper**
  2 **green onions cut into 1-inch pieces**
    Pao Bin**

Rinse dry lily flower and tree ears in cold water. Soak in cold water to cover 1 hour, until soft. Drain and finely chop.

Heat wok. When very hot, add peanut oil, turning wok to coat sides. Add shredded pork and stir-fry 2 minutes. Transfer to small bowl.

Add eggs to wok and stir-fry until cooked. Add to bowl and mix with pork.

Heat more oil if necessary. Quickly add shredded cabbage, chopped lily flower and tree ears, water chestnuts and garlic and stir-fry about 2 minutes. Thoroughly blend in pork and eggs. Season with soy, salt and pepper. Add green onions and cook about 1 minute. Taste for seasoning.

Place 2 to 3 tablespoons of Mu Shu Pork on each Pao Bin, roll up and serve.

*Available in oriental markets.

Pao Bin (thin pancakes)

Makes about 40

  2 **cups flour**
  ¾ **to 1 cup boiling water**

    Additional flour

  2 **tablespoons sesame oil**

If using food processor, place flour in work bowl. With motor running, add boiling water until dough forms ball. Transfer to small bowl, cover with damp towel and let stand 15 minutes.

If not using food processor, add boiling water gradually to flour, stirring with wooden spoon. When mixture forms mass (it will be lumpy) transfer to floured board and knead until dough forms soft, smooth ball. Place in small bowl, cover with damp towel and let stand 15 minutes.

Cut dough in ½. Place on lightly floured surface and roll each about ¼ inch thick. Cut into 2- to 2½-inch circles. Knead scraps together, roll out and repeat to cut more circles.

Brush ½ circles with sesame oil. Place each unoiled circle on 1 oiled circle. With rolling pin, roll each pair of circles into larger circle about 6 inches in diameter, keeping as round as possible.

Place ungreased 8-inch skillet over high heat to warm. Reduce heat to moderate. Place 1 pancake in skillet and cook until it puffs and blisters, about 30 seconds. Turn and cook second side. Flip onto towel and carefully separate into 2 pancakes. Stack on platter or on foil. When all are cooked, wrap in foil and place in warm oven until ready to serve.

SWEET & PUNGENT PORK

MANDARIN INN
NEW YORK, NEW YORK

2 servings

   2 large eggs, lightly beaten
   ¼ cup flour
   2 tablespoons cornstarch
   2 tablespoons dry sherry
   ¼ teaspoon salt
   ½ pound lean pork, cut into ¾-inch cubes

Sweet and Sour Sauce

   6 tablespoons sugar
   6 tablespoons vinegar
   2 teaspoons soy sauce
   ¼ cup tomato paste
   1 teaspoon cornstarch
   ½ teaspoon hot pepper sauce
   ¼ cup broth or water

   4 cups (1 quart) oil
   1 medium carrot, diced
   6 dried black mushrooms (soaked ½ hour
       in hot water, patted dry)
   1 cup cut-up broccoli florets

   2 teaspoons minced fresh ginger

Combine eggs, flour, 2 tablespoons cornstarch, sherry and salt in small bowl. Add pork and coat thoroughly. Refrigerate about 30 minutes.

For sauce: Mix sugar, vinegar, soy sauce, tomato paste, 1 teaspoon cornstarch, hot pepper sauce and broth in small bowl. Set aside.

Heat oil in wok over high heat to between 350°F and 375°F. Add pork and cook until golden brown, about 4 to 5 minutes. Remove with slotted spoon and drain on paper towels. Add carrot, mushrooms and broccoli; stir-fry 25 to 30 seconds. Remove vegetables and drain.

Pour off all but 2 tablespoons oil (reserve in refrigerator for future deep-fat frying). Add ginger and stir-fry about 5 seconds. Return pork and vegetables to wok. Mix in sauce. Stir-fry over medium-high heat until hot and well mixed. Serve immediately.

TENDERLOIN OF PORK

BLUE STRAWBERY RESTAURANT
PORTSMOUTH, NEW HAMPSHIRE

"Elegantly prepared pork in a sour cream sauce."
       —Ms. Cheryl Lynch, Deep River, Connecticut

10 to 12 servings

   1 8-pound pork tenderloin roast
   1 teaspoon salt
   ½ teaspoon pepper
   1 teaspoon marjoram
   2 bay leaves

Sauce

   ¼ cup (½ stick) butter
   6 shallots, thinly sliced
   ½ cup flour
   2 cups dry white wine
   1 pound fresh mushrooms, sliced
   2 Spanish onions, peeled and sliced
   1 cup sauerkraut and juice
   2 cups sour cream
   3 to 4 beef bouillon cubes
       Salt and pepper
   1 tablespoon chives

Preheat oven to 500°F. Rub pork roast with 1 teaspoon salt, ½ teaspoon pepper and ½ teaspoon marjoram. Place in roasting pan with bay leaves. Roast, uncovered, for 20 to 30 minutes. Remove from oven and drain off fat. Reduce heat to 350°F.

For sauce: In 4-quart saucepan, melt butter until it sizzles. Brown shallots lightly. Stir in flour and cook 2 minutes. Add wine and mix thoroughly. Add mushrooms, onions, sauerkraut and juice, sour cream, bouillon cubes, salt and pepper to taste, chives and remaining marjoram. Blend well.

Pour sauce over meat, cover and return to oven. Roast until juices run clear when pierced with fork, about 2½ to 3 hours (137°F. on meat thermometer). Slice and serve immediately.

BARBECUED BABY SPARERIBS

BOGART'S
PHILADELPHIA, PENNSYLVANIA

6 servings

   3 to 4 baby racks or 2 full-size racks
       pork spareribs

Barbecue Sauce

   ¼ cup oil
   2 medium onions, diced
   1 teaspoon minced garlic
   2 6-ounce cans tomato paste
   ¼ cup white vinegar
   ½ cup Worcestershire sauce
   ¼ cup honey
   2 teaspoons dry mustard
   2 teaspoons dried basil
   2 teaspoons salt

Preheat broiler. Place ribs on rack and broil about 6 inches from heat source 5 minutes on each side. Turn oven to 350°F. Cover ribs with foil and bake 30 minutes.

For sauce: Place oil in large skillet over medium-high heat until light haze forms. Add onion and garlic and sauté 2 minutes, stirring frequently; do not brown. Combine tomato paste and vinegar in small bowl and stir into onion and garlic. Add remaining ingredients and blend thoroughly. Simmer 10 minutes, stirring occasionally.

Discard foil. Coat ribs evenly with sauce. Return to oven and continue baking, uncovered, 30 minutes, basting several times with remaining sauce.

SAUCISSON EN CROUTE AUX DEUX SAUCES
(Sausage Baked in Pastry with Two Sauces)

LE FRANÇAIS
WHEELING, ILLINOIS

6 servings

  1 **pound boneless lean pork butt**
  ⅓ **pound fresh pork fatback or leaf lard**
  2 **teaspoons salt**
  ¼ **teaspoon freshly ground pepper**
  1 **small truffle, chopped, or 1 large dried shiitake mushroom, rehydrated, chopped**
  ½ **cup roasted shelled large pistachio nuts**
  ¼ **cup Napoleon brandy**
  ¼ **cup Madeira**

  1 **pound pâte feuilletée (puff pastry)**

  1 **egg yolk**
  1 **teaspoon water**

   Madeira Sauce*
   Beurre Blanc Sauce**

Combine pork and pork fat in processor and grind coarsely (or use meat grinder). Transfer to bowl. Add salt and pepper and blend thoroughly. Mix in truffle or mushroom. Add nuts, brandy and Madeira; blend well. Cover and chill several hours.

Divide puff pastry into 2 portions, with one just slightly larger than the other. On lightly floured surface, roll smaller portion into rectangle ¼ inch thick. Roll meat mixture into 12-inch cylinder 2 inches thick and place lengthwise on center of rectangle. Roll remaining pastry ¼ inch thick. Lay over meat. Cut away excess pastry, leaving just enough to enclose meat (reserve scraps). Pinch seams together. Using sharp knife, make slashes around sides of pastry.

Preheat oven to 450°F. Form excess pastry scraps into ball and roll out on lightly floured surface to thickness of ¼ inch. Cut small crescents from dough. Beat egg yolk with water and use to paint pastry cylinder. Arrange crescents over top for decoration and paint again with egg mixture.

Bake until pastry is golden brown and puffed along seam, about 25 to 35 minutes. Let stand 5 to 10 minutes before slicing. To serve, cut into slices about 1 inch thick. Arrange 2 slices on each heated serving plate. Pour about 1 tablespoon Madeira Sauce on 1 slice and about 1 tablespoon Beurre Blanc Sauce on the other.

*Madeira Sauce

Chef Jean Banchet enhances this sauce by adding about 1 tablespoon chopped truffle.

Makes about 1 cup

  6 **tablespoons oil**
  8 **to 10 pounds meaty beef and veal bones, cut into 3- to 4-inch pieces**
  4 **cups diced onion**
  2 **cups diced carrot**
  2 **cups diced celery**
 12 **whole black peppercorns**
  4 **sprigs fresh thyme or 1 teaspoon dried**
  3 **garlic cloves, unpeeled and crushed**
  2 **leeks including 1 inch green part, thinly sliced**
  2 **bay leaves**

  2 **gallons (8 quarts) water**
  3 **to 4 cups chopped tomatoes**
  1 **cup parsley leaves**

  ¼ **cup Madeira**
  1 **tablespoon chopped truffle (optional)**
  2 **to 2½ tablespoons (¼ stick or more) unsalted butter, cut into pieces**

Preheat oven to 425°F. Film bottom of large shallow roasting pan with 6 tablespoons oil. Add bones, turning to coat with oil. Roast about 2 hours, stirring and turning bones every 30 minutes. Add next 8 ingredients and roast another 30 minutes.

Transfer bones and vegetables to 12- to 16-quart stockpot. Stir 2 cups water into roasting pan, scraping up any browned bits that cling to bottom. Add to stockpot along with remaining water. Add tomatoes and parsley and bring to boil. Reduce heat and simmer very slowly 12 to 16 hours, skimming off any foam that accumulates on surface during first 2 to 3 hours of cooking.

Strain stock, reserving 2 cups and refrigerating or freezing remainder for later use. Pour 2 cups stock into small saucepan and boil over high heat until reduced to 1½ cups. Add Madeira and continue boiling until sauce is reduced to 1 cup. If desired, stir in chopped truffle. Turn heat to low and whisk in butter 1 piece at a time, beating well after each addition. Serve immediately.

**Beurre Blanc Sauce

Makes about 1½ cups

  ½ **cup dry white wine (preferably Chablis)**
  2 **tablespoons finely minced shallot**
  1 **cup (2 sticks) unsalted butter (well chilled), each stick cut into 8 slices**
  ½ **cup whipping cream**
  1 **tablespoon Dijon mustard**
  ¼ **teaspoon salt**
  ⅛ **teaspoon freshly ground pepper**

Combine wine and shallot in small saucepan. Cook over medium heat until wine is reduced to about 2 tablespoons. Remove from heat and whisk in butter 1 piece at a time, incorporating completely before adding another piece. After adding 2 or 3 pieces, return pan to very low heat and whisk in remaining butter in same manner (sauce will be consistency of light mayonnaise). Beat in cream, mustard, salt and pepper and blend well.

THE ROOF'S FILET DE VEAU BRILLAT-SAVARIN

THE ROOF
SALT LAKE CITY, UTAH

4 servings

   6 to 8 tablespoons (¾ to 1 stick) butter
   8 3-ounce veal fillets (preferably milk-fed veal, cut from loin)
    Salt and freshly ground pepper

  18 mushroom caps, thinly sliced
   3 to 4 tablespoons chopped shallot
  ½ cup dry sherry

   8 10-inch crepes
    Melted butter
  ½ cup grated Gruyère cheese
    Périgueux or mushroom sauce (use your favorite recipe)

Butter baking sheet and set aside. Melt 6 to 8 tablespoons butter in large skillet over medium-high heat. Add veal fillets in batches and sauté on both sides until nicely browned and almost cooked through, about 2 to 4 minutes. Season with salt and pepper to taste. Remove veal fillets from skillet; set aside and keep warm.

Add mushrooms and shallot to same skillet and sauté over medium-high heat, scraping up any browned bits clinging to bottom of pan, for 3 to 4 minutes. Add sherry and continue cooking, stirring constantly, until liquid is reduced, about 5 minutes.

Preheat oven to 400°F. Divide mushroom mixture evenly among crepes. Top each with veal fillet. Carefully fold crepe over meat. Brush each crepe on both sides with melted butter. Arrange seam side down on baking sheet. (Crepes can be assembled several hours ahead and set aside at room temperature.) Sprinkle top with cheese. Bake crepes until heated through, about 5 to 7 minutes. Serve hot. Pass sauce separately.

COTES DE VEAU POELE AUX MORILLES
(Veal Chops with Morel Sauce)

THE JOCKEY CLUB
WASHINGTON, D.C.

8 servings

  1½ ounces dried morels

    Flour
   8 center-cut veal chops
    Salt and freshly ground pepper
   5 tablespoons (⅝ stick) butter
   2 shallots, chopped

   6 tablespoons brandy
   6 tablespoons Madeira
   6 tablespoons dry white wine

   5 cups whipping cream
    Chicken bouillon cubes (optional)

    Chopped parsley (garnish)

Combine morels in large bowl with enough cold water to cover and let stand, changing water about 4 times until clear, about 6 to 8 hours. Drain well. Discard stems; pat caps dry.

Preheat oven to 350°F. Flour veal chops lightly and sprinkle both sides with salt and pepper. Melt 3 tablespoons butter in large heavy skillet over medium-high heat. Add chops in batches and cook on both sides until golden brown. Transfer chops to baking dish (reserve skillet) and roast 30 minutes, turning once. Transfer to heated serving platter and keep warm. Meanwhile, melt remaining butter in medium saucepan over medium-high heat. Add shallots and morels and sauté until all liquid is absorbed. Set aside.

Discard any fat from reserved skillet. Add brandy, Madeira and wine and cook over medium-high heat, scraping up browned bits, about 5 to 10 minutes. Add cream and continue cooking over medium-high heat until thickened. Season with salt and pepper to taste. (Add bouillon cubes for additional flavor, if desired.) Stir morels and shallots into sauce and cook 3 to 4 minutes.

Arrange chops on individual plates and pour on sauce. Garnish with chopped parsley. Serve at once.

COTES DE VEAU A LA CREME DE CIBOULETTE
(Veal Loin Chops with Cream and Chives)

LE FRANÇAIS
WHEELING, ILLINOIS

6 servings

   6 lean loin veal chops about 1½ inches thick (preferably first cut), trimmed of excess fat (bones Frenched)
    Salt and freshly ground pepper
   1 cup all purpose flour

   5 tablespoons (⅝ stick) butter, clarified

   1 cup dry white wine
  1½ cups whipping cream
   1 teaspoon reduced chicken stock
   3 tablespoons snipped fresh chives
   2 to 3 tablespoons (¼ to ⅜ stick) unsalted butter
    Juice of ½ lemon

Preheat oven to lowest setting. Season chops on both sides with salt and pepper. Dip in flour, shaking off excess.

Warm clarified butter in heavy 12-inch skillet over high heat until very hot. Add chops and sauté until richly browned, about 8 to 10 minutes per side, turning once and adjusting heat as necessary to prevent burning. Transfer to serving platter and keep warm in low oven.

Pour off any excess fat from skillet. Deglaze pan with wine. Boil over high heat until liquid is reduced to about ½ cup. Reduce heat to low, stir in cream and chicken stock and blend well. Add chives, remaining butter and lemon juice and bring sauce just to simmer. Pour sauce over chops and serve.

VEAL AMELIO

AMELIO'S
SAN FRANCISCO, CALIFORNIA

"My husband and I dined not long ago in an absolutely superb San Francisco restaurant called Amelio's. My husband had a veal dish he swears melted in his mouth."
—Sandra Deeny, Phoenix, Arizona

8 servings

> 2 **pounds veal fillet, cut into 1½-ounce pieces**
> **Flour**
> **Salt and pepper**
> 2 **tablespoons olive oil**
> 1 **cup (2 sticks) butter**
>
> 6 **tablespoons dry white wine**
> 1 **tablespoon lemon juice**
> 1 **pound fresh mushrooms, sliced**

Pound veal gently with wooden mallet. Sprinkle lightly with flour and salt and pepper to taste. Heat olive oil and 2 tablespoons butter in large skillet. When pan is hot, sauté veal on both sides without browning. Remove veal pieces and set aside, keeping them warm.

Add wine to pan and heat slightly. Add remaining butter and lemon juice. Sauté mushrooms briefly.

Place several veal slices on each plate and top with mushrooms and sauce.

VEAL JEANINE

CAFE MARTINIQUE
FORT LAUDERDALE, FLORIDA

"We recently enjoyed a house specialty made with Swiss cheese sauce, fresh mushrooms and red wine. Magnificent!"
—Sue Forman, Fort Lauderdale, Florida

6 to 8 servings

> 2 **cups grated Swiss cheese**
> 1 **cup béchamel sauce**
>
> 1½ **cups sliced mushrooms**
> 3 **tablespoons (⅜ stick) butter**
> ½ **cup Burgundy**
>
> 2½ **pounds veal, sliced ¼ inch thick, pounded thin**
> **Salt and freshly ground pepper**

Combine cheese and béchamel sauce in large non-aluminum saucepan. Heat slowly until cheese is completely melted, stirring occasionally; do not allow to boil.

Meanwhile, in medium skillet sauté mushrooms in 1 tablespoon butter, just until absorbed. Cool slightly; add mushrooms with wine to cheese mixture. Keep warm.

Heat remaining 2 tablespoons butter in large skillet over medium-high heat. Add veal in batches and sauté quickly until tender. Pour off fat. Return all meat to skillet, add sauce and heat through. Season with salt and pepper to taste. Transfer to platter and serve immediately.

VEAL SCALOPPINE

GIUSEPPE'S OLD DEPOT RESTAURANT
COLORADO SPRINGS, COLORADO

6 to 8 servings

> ¼ **cup olive oil**
> 1 **cup chopped onion**
> 1 **large garlic clove, minced**
> 1 **cup chopped green pepper**
> ½ **cup chopped celery**
> ½ **cup chopped parsley**
> 2 **medium bay leaves**
>
> 1 **16-ounce can tomatoes, undrained and chopped**
> 1 **cup tomato juice**
> 1 **6-ounce can tomato paste**
> 1 **4½-ounce jar mushrooms, undrained**
> 1 **cup hot water**
> 1 **tablespoon salt**
> 1 **to 1½ teaspoons pepper**
>
> ¼ **cup cherry wine or other sweet red wine**
> **Olive oil**
>
> 2 **pounds thin veal scallops (12 to 16 pieces)**
> **Cooked rice**

Heat ¼ cup oil in large saucepan. Add onion and garlic and sauté until soft. Stir in green pepper, celery, parsley and bay leaves. Cook, uncovered, over low heat until tender, about 5 minutes, stirring several times.

Blend in tomatoes, juice, tomato paste and mushrooms. Add water and simmer uncovered 30 minutes. Stir in seasonings and cook 15 minutes more, stirring occasionally. Remove bay leaves.

Preheat oven to 350°F. Stir wine into sauce. In large skillet, heat small amount of oil. Sauté veal scallops in batches 1 to 2 minutes on each side. Drain on paper towels. Place scallops in 9x13-inch baking dish. Pour sauce over meat. Cover and cook 30 minutes. Serve over rice.

May be made in advance and reheated.

VEAL CUTLETS POJARSKY

CATTAILS
PALM SPRINGS, CALIFORNIA

Chef Hinaman credits this dish to Frederic Farlow of Houston, Texas.

8 servings

  1 cup fresh breadcrumbs
½ cup half and half

  1 pound veal
  1 pound chicken breasts, skinned
    and boned

  1 teaspoon salt
½ teaspoon freshly ground pepper
  1 cup (2 sticks) butter, softened

  4 tablespoons (½ stick) butter
½ pound mushrooms, sliced
½ teaspoon salt
¼ teaspoon freshly ground pepper
    Juice of ½ lemon

  1 cup fine breadcrumbs

¼ cup dry white wine
  1 teaspoon arrowroot
  1 teaspoon water
  1 lemon, sliced (garnish)

Combine fresh breadcrumbs and half and half in small bowl and set aside to soak.

Meanwhile, grind veal and chicken through fine blade of grinder. Repeat. Transfer ground meat mixture to large bowl.

Squeeze excess moisture from breadcrumbs through tea cloth. Add breadcrumbs, salt and pepper to meat mixture. Stir in 1 cup butter 1 tablespoon at a time, blending well. Cover and refrigerate 1 hour.

Melt 2 tablespoons butter in medium skillet over medium heat. Add mushrooms and sprinkle with salt, pepper and lemon juice. Cover with buttered waxed paper and top skillet with lid. Steam mushrooms 4 to 5 minutes, shaking pan frequently to prevent sticking. Remove from heat. Strain liquid into small bowl and transfer mushrooms to another bowl. Set aside.

Roll meat mixture into 12-inch cylinder. Chill 15 minutes. Cut cylinder into 1¼-inch slices. Flatten and shape into choplike portions. Roll in fine breadcrumbs, coating completely. (Cutlets can be prepared ahead to this point and refrigerated.)

Melt remaining butter in large skillet over medium-high heat. Add cutlets and sauté 5 to 7 minutes per side. Set aside and keep warm. Deglaze pan with wine, scraping up any browned bits clinging to bottom. Add reserved mushroom liquid and arrowroot dissolved in water. Stir until sauce is thickened. Strain; return to skillet. Add mushrooms, salt and pepper, stirring to blend. To serve, spoon sauce onto heated platter. Arrange cutlets over sauce and garnish with lemon.

VEAL TYROLEAN

THE BIG CHEESE RESTAURANT
BALTIMORE, MARYLAND

6 servings

  2 pounds boned veal shoulder

¼ cup (½ stick) butter
½ cup brandy (100 proof)
½ cup seedless light raisins

½ cup finely chopped shallots

  3 tablespoons flour
  1 cup coffee
½ cup rich chicken stock
    Freshly ground white pepper

¾ cup sour cream
  2 teaspoons fresh tarragon, chopped, or
    1 teaspoon dried

    Stuffed Potatoes*

Preheat oven to 375°F. Remove membrane and sinew from veal. Cut meat into 1½-inch cubes.

In 10-inch skillet with lid, heat 2 tablespoons butter until very hot. Brown veal cubes few pieces at a time, removing when brown. When all veal is browned, return to skillet. Heat ¼ cup brandy, ignite and pour over meat. Soak raisins in remaining ¼ cup brandy.

Remove meat from skillet and set aside. Heat 2 tablespoons butter in skillet; add shallots and sauté gently 2 to 3 minutes. Remove from heat.

Thoroughly stir in flour; blend in coffee and chicken stock. Drain raisins and add brandy to sauce, reserving raisins. Return skillet to heat and stir until sauce boils. Season with white pepper to taste. Simmer a few minutes. Add veal and raisins. Cover with waxed paper and lid and bake until veal is tender, 1 to 1½ hours.

Remove veal from sauce with slotted spoon and pile in center of round, shallow earthenware dish. If sauce is too thin, reduce over medium-high heat until thickened. Carefully mix in sour cream and tarragon, but do not allow to boil. Pour sauce over veal. Serve with Stuffed Potatoes.

*Stuffed Potatoes

6 servings

  3 small Idaho potatoes
  3 egg yolks
  6 tablespoons (¾ stick) butter
    Salt and cayenne pepper
½ cup finely chopped onion

Preheat oven to 375°F. While veal is cooking, place potatoes in oven and bake until tender, 45 minutes to 1 hour. Cut potatoes in half lengthwise and scoop out pulp. Rub through fine strainer or ricer. Beat in yolks, butter, salt and cayenne to taste. Mix in onion. Carefully fill potato skins with potato-egg mixture. Smooth with spatula and score top with fork. Broil 1 to 2 minutes to brown.

BLANQUETTE DE VEAU WITH FRESH PASTA

RESTAURANT BOCUSE
LYONS, FRANCE

4 servings

    1 **pound large mushrooms, caps cut into
       ⅛-inch pieces (stems reserved)**
  ¾ **cup water**
    1 **tablespoon butter
       Pinch salt**

    2 **pounds veal shoulder, trimmed and cut
       into 1- to 1½-inch pieces
       Salt and freshly ground pepper**
    1 **cup dry white wine**
    2 **carrots**
    2 **leeks, with 2 inches of green, quartered
       and washed**
  ½ **medium onion**
    3 **to 4 sprigs tarragon**
    3 **sprigs thyme**
    1 **small celery stalk with leaves,
       coarsely chopped**
    1 **bay leaf**
    2 **to 3 garlic cloves, unpeeled**

    1 **pound baby carrots (or 4 carrots)
       halved lengthwise and cut into thirds**

    1 **cup whipping cream
       Salt**

    5 **egg yolks
       Fresh pasta***

Combine mushroom caps, water, butter and salt in medium saucepan. Cover and bring to boil over high heat. Remove from heat and drain well, reserving liquid. Set aside.

Sprinkle veal generously with salt and pepper. Transfer to 6-quart saucepan or Dutch oven. Add wine and enough water to cover and bring to boil over high heat, skimming any foam that accumulates on surface for first 5 to 7 minutes. Tie carrots, leeks, onion, tarragon, thyme, celery and bay leaf in cheesecloth and add to veal with reserved mushroom stems and unpeeled garlic. Reduce heat, cover and simmer until veal is tender, 50 to 60 minutes.

Meanwhile, blanch baby carrots in boiling water in medium saucepan until tender, about 3 minutes. Drain immediately and plunge into ice water to stop cooking process. Drain again.

Transfer meat to platter. Discard cheesecloth bag from stock. Increase heat to medium and reduce stock by ⅓. Strain stock into bowl, pressing vegetables with back of wooden spoon to extract as much liquid as possible. Return stock to saucepan or Dutch oven. Add reserved mushroom liquid and ½ cup cream. Cook over medium heat until reduced by another ⅓. Season with salt to taste. (Sauce can be prepared ahead to this point, covered and refrigerated up to 2 days. Rewarm slowly over low heat before serving.)

Beat egg yolks with remaining ½ cup cream in medium bowl until well blended. Whisk about 3 tablespoons of warm sauce into yolk mixture, then add mixture to sauce. Cook over medium heat, stirring constantly, until sauce coats spoon; do not boil. Return meat, carrots and mushrooms to pan, stirring into sauce. Cook until just heated through. Transfer to platter and serve immediately with pasta.

Fresh Pasta

4 to 6 servings

    3 **egg yolks**
    2 **eggs**
    2 **tablespoons whipping cream**
    1 **teaspoon salt**
    3 **cups all purpose flour
       Softened butter**

  ¼ **cup (½ stick) butter
       Salt**

Whisk egg yolks, eggs, cream and salt in large bowl. Mix in flour until dough leaves sides of bowl. Form into ball. Turn out onto lightly floured surface and knead about 10 minutes. Coat with softened butter to prevent drying. Cover and refrigerate 2 hours.

Roll dough out on lightly floured work surface until paper thin and translucent, stretching and sprinkling with additional flour to prevent sticking. Let dry for 30 minutes.

Roll dough up lengthwise and slice into thin strips. Unroll into rapidly boiling salted water and cook until al dente, about 3 to 4 minutes. Remove from heat and drain well. Rinse in cold water and drain again. Melt butter in large skillet over medium heat. Add pasta and toss until heated through. Season with salt to taste.

VEAL LIVER WITH APPLES AND ONIONS

KAHALA HILTON
HONOLULU, HAWAII

6 servings

    4 **to 6 tablespoons (½ to ¾ stick) butter**
    1 **large apple, quartered, cored and
       thinly sliced**
    1 **medium onion, thinly sliced**

  12 **3-ounce slices high quality veal liver
       Salt and freshly ground pepper
       Flour**
    2 **tablespoons light vegetable oil**
    3 **tablespoons chopped fresh parsley
       (garnish)**

Heat 2 to 3 tablespoons butter in medium skillet over medium heat. Add apple and onion and sauté until soft. Keep warm.

Sprinkle liver with salt and pepper. Dredge in flour, shaking off excess. Heat remaining butter with 2 tablespoons oil in large skillet over medium-high heat. Add liver and quickly sauté to medium-rare or medium. Transfer to heated platter, spread apples and onions over top and sprinkle with parsley. Serve immediately.

ITALIAN SAUSAGE ROLLED IN VEAL

CASA MARRA RESTAURANT
NEW HAVEN, CONNECTICUT

6 servings

>   3 hot Italian sausages, cut in half crosswise
>
>   6 boneless veal cutlets
>
>   2 tablespoons freshly grated Parmesan
>   cheese
>   2 tablespoons finely chopped fresh parsley
>   1 teaspoon fennel seeds, crushed
>   1 garlic clove, crushed
>   Flour
>
>   2 cups vegetable oil
>   6 ounces mushrooms, sliced
>
>   2 tablespoons (¼ stick) butter
>   1 cup dry sherry

Prick sausages all over with point of sharp knife. Transfer sausages to large skillet. Place over medium heat and fry until sausages are browned and cooked through, about 30 minutes. Drain on paper towels.

Pound cutlets so they are large enough to enclose sausage completely without overlap.

Combine cheese, parsley, fennel seeds and garlic in bowl and mix well. Divide among cutlets, spreading evenly. Place sausage along 1 edge of cutlet. Roll up and tie securely with string. Roll in flour, shaking off excess. Repeat procedure with remaining sausages and cutlets.

Heat oil in deep large skillet or deep fryer until hot (about 375°F). Add veal rolls and fry until golden brown. Drain on paper towels. Set aside and keep warm. Add mushrooms to hot oil and fry until browned, about 1 to 2 minutes. Remove with slotted spoon and drain well.

Melt butter in large skillet over medium-high heat. Add sherry and cook until thickened, about 5 to 10 minutes. Stir in mushrooms. Arrange veal rolls on platter and cover with sauce. Serve immediately.

OSSO BUCCO

FLAVIO'S
APOLLO, PENNSYLVANIA

6 to 8 servings

>   8 veal shanks
>   Salt and pepper
>   ½ cup flour
>   2 tablespoons olive oil
>   ¼ cup (½ stick) butter
>
>   1 large carrot, chopped
>   1 cup chopped onion
>   6 garlic cloves, peeled and minced
>   6 anchovy fillets, chopped

>   1 medium bay leaf
>   2 tablespoons chopped fresh parsley
>   3½ cups chopped fresh tomatoes
>   2 cups consommé
>   ½ cup brandy
>   ¾ cup cream sherry
>   3 small pieces lemon peel
>   3 small pieces orange peel
>
>   2 to 4 tablespoons cornstarch diluted in
>   equal amount of water (if needed)

Preheat oven to 350°F. Season veal with salt and pepper. Dredge in flour. Heat oil and butter in large skillet. Sauté veal until brown on each side. Remove to large baking dish.

Add carrot, onion and garlic to skillet and cook until onions start to brown. Remove from heat and add anchovies, bay leaf, parsley and tomatoes. Cook 5 minutes. Add consommé, brandy, sherry, lemon and orange peels. Adjust salt and pepper to taste. Discard bay leaf. Pour sauce over veal.

Cover baking dish and cook until well done, about 1½ hours. Remove from oven and transfer veal to serving platter. Keep meat warm.

Sauce should have consistency of heavy cream. If too thin, transfer to saucepan and thicken with cornstarch diluted in water. Cook for 5 minutes. Pour little sauce over veal and serve remaining sauce in sauceboat.

SWEETBREADS FINANCIERE

THE BALLARD STORE
SOLVANG, CALIFORNIA

4 servings

>   2 strips bacon, diced
>   1 tablespoon butter
>   ½ medium onion, chopped
>   1 garlic clove, minced
>   ½ cup sliced mushrooms
>   ¾ cup dry sherry
>   ¾ cup beef stock or consommé
>   2 tablespoons catsup
>   1 tablespoon Maggi seasoning
>
>   1 pound veal sweetbreads
>   1 celery stalk, chopped
>   ½ medium onion, chopped
>   1 bay leaf
>   Pinch thyme
>   1 lemon, halved
>
>   Flour
>   Salt and pepper
>   ¼ cup (½ stick) butter, melted

Cook bacon over medium heat until it begins to brown. Add 1 tablespoon butter, ½ onion and garlic and sauté until onion is translucent. Add mushrooms. When mushrooms are slightly brown, add sherry, beef stock, catsup and Maggi seasoning. Bring to simmer. Set aside.

Place sweetbreads in boiling salted water to cover with celery, remaining onion, bay leaf and thyme. Add juice of ½ lemon plus squeezed lemon ½. Poach gently 20 minutes. Drain and cool slightly. Remove all fat and membranes from sweetbreads. Transfer to plate, cover with another plate and place weight on top. Allow to stand for at least 1 hour (sweetbreads should be about 1 inch thick). Slice in ½.

Roll sweetbreads in flour seasoned with salt and pepper to taste and sauté in ¼ cup butter until lightly browned. Transfer to sauce, add juice of remaining ½ lemon and cook until sauce is reduced by ½. Serve immediately.

SWEETBREADS WITH MUSHROOMS

SAM'S GRILL
SAN FRANCISCO, CALIFORNIA

"When in San Francisco, I make it a point to have at least one meal at Sam's Grill. In my opinion it's one of the best restaurants anywhere. I am partial to their sweetbreads sautéed with fresh mushrooms."
—Carl Hyman, Carlsbad, New Mexico

6 to 8 servings

    2 pounds veal sweetbreads, well rinsed
    1 celery stalk, chopped
    ½ onion, chopped
    ½ lemon, sliced
    1 garlic clove, quartered
    6 peppercorns
    1 teaspoon salt
    1 bay leaf

    1 14¾-ounce can brown gravy

    3 tablespoons (⅜ stick) butter or margarine
    1 bunch green onions, chopped
    ½ pound mushrooms, sliced
    ½ cup Sauternes

Combine first 8 ingredients in large saucepan, add water to cover and simmer, uncovered, 20 minutes. Drain and immediately plunge sweetbreads into cold water to firm. When cool, drain again. Trim away tough membrane, tubes and connective tissue. Using fingers, gently break into small sections. Blot dry with paper towels.

Begin warming gravy over low heat.

Melt butter or margarine in large skillet over medium heat. Add sweetbreads and sauté until browned.

Add green onion and cook 2 minutes. Stir in mushrooms and cook 2 minutes more. Drain off remaining liquid. Reduce heat, add wine, cover and simmer 2 to 3 minutes. Uncover, add gravy and gently cook 5 minutes longer.

HASENPFEFFER

RIVERS END RESTAURANT
JENNER, CALIFORNIA

6 servings

    ¾ pound bacon, diced
    2 2½- to 3-pound rabbits, each cut into 6 pieces
      Salt and freshly ground pepper
      Flour

    1 medium onion, diced
    1 carrot, diced
    1 celery stalk, diced
    10 garlic cloves, minced
    2 cups chicken stock
    2 cups dry red wine
    2 tablespoons brandy
    1 teaspoon currant jelly
    1 bay leaf
    ½ teaspoon dried rosemary
    ½ teaspoon dried thyme

    2 tablespoons fresh lemon juice
    1 tablespoon cracked black pepper

Cook bacon in Dutch oven over medium heat until crisp. Remove bacon with slotted spoon and set aside on paper towel to drain; do not wipe out pan.

Sprinkle rabbit with salt and pepper to taste, then coat with flour, shaking off excess. Return Dutch oven to medium-high heat. When bacon fat is hot, add rabbit in batches and brown well on all sides. Remove rabbit from Dutch oven and set aside.

Add onion, carrot, celery and garlic to pan and sauté until browned, about 5 to 10 minutes. Stir in stock, wine, brandy, jelly, bay leaf, rosemary and thyme. Return rabbit and any accumulated juice to pan. Reduce heat and simmer until rabbit is tender, about 45 minutes.

Remove rabbit from sauce and keep warm. Strain sauce into casserole dish. Stir in lemon juice and pepper and bring to boil. Add rabbit and sprinkle with reserved bacon. Serve immediately.

LIGHT ENTREES

The late A. J. Liebling, in his classic 1960s memoir *Between Meals: An Appetite for Paris*, describes in detail the Homeric gustatory binges that were commonplace in French restaurants not very long ago. He also mentions, in passing, a current "fad" for serving something very light, such as a quiche, an omelet, perhaps some pasta, and "calling that a meal."

Well, the fad became a trend, and the trend has become something of a revolution. No longer do hosts and hostesses—and restaurateurs—feel it absolutely necessary to satiate their guests with multicourse, meat-heavy meals. Often a dinner consisting of only a light entree, a salad and a simple dessert is not only completely appropriate, but very welcome as well. These lighter main courses appeal not just to the figure-conscious diner; home cooks love them because they are simple to prepare, highly nutritious and easy on the budget.

The entrees that follow—all based on eggs, cheese, pasta or pancakes—suggest some delicious alternatives to the standing rib roast and *coq au vin*. Regardless of which came first, eggs are almost as adaptable as chicken and, with a little imagination, can become anything from *oeufs concorde* to a plump, satisfying omelet. Cheese is everyone's favorite, especially when it turns up in a quiche or as delicate *gnocchi*. Pasta, long mistakenly thought of as "heavy," is actually one of our lightest foods, and it can be served in more ways than there are Italians. And pancakes are no longer just a breakfast staple—just look at the number of creperies and pancake houses that have appeared in recent years.

Of course, any of these lighter entrees could, with a little adjustment, become part of a larger and more extravagant meal—one that Liebling would have approved of.

Tourte Milanaise from Michel Richard in Los Angeles (see page 147).

EGGS COMMANDER'S

COMMANDER'S PALACE
NEW ORLEANS, LOUISIANA

For each serving:

  2 **rusks**
  ½ **cup Commander's Sauce***
  2 **poached eggs**
  ¼ **cup Béarnaise Sauce****
  2 **2-ounce cooked Commander's
     Sausage patties*****
     Minced parsley

Arrange rusks on plate and top each with ½ Commander's Sauce. Place poached egg over sauce and top each with ½ Béarnaise Sauce. Place 1 sausage patty on either side of eggs. Sprinkle with parsley; serve immediately.

*Commander's Sauce

Makes 3 cups

  ¾ **cup (1½ sticks) butter**
  ¼ **cup all purpose flour**

  2 **cups chicken stock**
  2 **tablespoons pureed yellow onion**
  1 **tablespoon Chablis**
  1 **teaspoon Worcestershire sauce**
  ½ **garlic clove, minced**
  ½ **teaspoon salt**
  ½ **teaspoon freshly ground pepper**
     Pinch garlic powder

  6 **ounces smoked ham, finely chopped**
  3 **tablespoons minced white onion**

  ½ **cup whipping cream**

Make roux by combining ¼ cup butter and flour in small skillet over medium-low heat and stirring constantly until butter is melted and mixture forms smooth paste. Remove from heat and set aside.

Bring stock to boil in medium saucepan over medium-high heat. Reduce heat and simmer gently until reduced to 1 cup. Add pureed onion, Chablis, Worcestershire sauce, garlic, salt, pepper and garlic powder and blend well. Stir in roux and continue to simmer over low heat until mixture is consistency of slightly whipped cream, about 20 minutes.

Meanwhile, sauté ham and minced onion in small skillet just until onion is softened.

Remove sauce from heat and add ½ cup butter in chunks little at a time, whipping constantly with whisk. Gently stir in cream. Add ham and onion mixture and blend well.

**Béarnaise Sauce

Makes about 1½ cups

  1 **tablespoon white wine**
  1 **tablespoon dried tarragon leaves**

  4 **egg yolks**
     Juice of ½ lemon

  1 **tablespoon white wine**
  1 **teaspoon vinegar**
  1 **teaspoon Worcestershire sauce**
     Pinch cayenne pepper
  1 **pound (4 sticks) unsalted butter, melted**
     Salt (optional)

Heat 1 tablespoon white wine with tarragon in small skillet over medium-low heat until wine evaporates.

Combine yolks, lemon juice, 1 tablespoon white wine, vinegar, Worcestershire sauce and cayenne in top of double boiler over gently simmering water. Whip together with whisk until sauce begins to thicken. Add butter in slow steady stream, whisking constantly until sauce is creamy and thick. Stir tarragon mixture into sauce and blend well. Season with salt if desired.

***Commander's Sausage

Makes 12 to 14 patties

  ½ **pound finely ground veal**
  ½ **pound finely ground pork**
  ½ **pound finely ground beef**
  ½ **cup Creole Seafood Seasoning
     (see page 88)**
  6 **green onions, chopped**
  ½ **teaspoon fennel**
  ½ **teaspoon garlic powder**
  ½ **teaspoon freshly grated nutmeg**
     Dash thyme
     Salt and freshly ground pepper to taste

Combine all ingredients in large mixing bowl and blend well. Place on 12-inch length of aluminum foil and form into cylinder shape about 1½ inches in diameter. Chill in freezer until firm enough to cut without mashing, about 1 hour. Cut into 12 to 14 patties about ½ inch thick. Fry in skillet over medium-high heat until brown on both sides. Drain well on paper towels.

GUACAMOLE CON QUESO OMELETS

LA RANCHERITA
LA JOLLA, CALIFORNIA

"Our favorite omelet is a Mexican version created at La Rancherita—a melt-in-the-mouth combination of cheese, hot chili sauce and guacamole."
                    —Susan Littell, San Diego, California

6 servings

  1½ **pounds Monterey Jack cheese, shredded**
  6 **tablespoons (¾ stick) butter**
  12 **eggs**
     Guacamole*
     Salsa**

Divide cheese into 12 equal portions and set aside. For each omelet: Melt 1 tablespoon butter in 8-inch pan. When butter is bubbly, add 2 lightly beaten eggs and cook until almost set; sprinkle with portion of cheese. Fold omelet in ½ and slide onto oven-proof plate. Sprinkle with another portion of cheese and run under broiler until cheese is melted. Spread generously with Guacamole and serve immediately. Pass Salsa separately.

*Guacamole

  Juice of ½ lime
4 large avocados, peeled and seeded
1 medium green bell pepper, minced
1 large tomato, chopped
1 celery stalk, minced
½ onion, minced
⅓ cup chopped cilantro
2 tablespoons Salsa**
1 garlic clove, minced
½ teaspoon salt
⅛ teaspoon freshly ground pepper

Squeeze lime juice over avocados. Mash coarsely with fork. Add remaining ingredients. Taste and adjust seasoning.

**Salsa

2 8-ounce cans tomato sauce
½ cup chopped cilantro
3 jalapeño peppers, stemmed and minced
¼ medium onion, diced
2 tomatoes, diced
1 celery stalk, diced
1 tablespoon olive oil
2 garlic cloves, minced
1 dried small hot chili pepper, crushed
½ teaspoon salt
⅛ teaspoon freshly ground pepper
¾ cup (about) water

Combine all ingredients except water. Add water in steady stream until desired consistency is reached. Chill until ready to serve.

JOE'S SPECIAL

THE FIREHOUSE
SACRAMENTO, CALIFORNIA

"Such a versatile, adaptable dish for brunch, lunch or a late supper." —Mrs. John Burns, Galesburg, Illinois

6 servings

1 tablespoon butter
1 tablespoon olive oil
1 medium onion, chopped
1 cup chopped fresh mushrooms
1 pound ground sirloin
3 slightly beaten eggs
½ teaspoon granulated garlic
1 teaspoon oregano
1 teaspoon salt
1 teaspoon freshly ground pepper
6 cups coarsely chopped raw spinach

Melt butter and oil in large skillet. Add onion and sauté briefly. Mix in mushrooms and meat and cook until meat is brown. Add eggs and seasonings and stir over medium heat until eggs are almost cooked. Stir in spinach and cook few minutes longer, until spinach is barely wilted. Serve immediately.

KNEDLICKY S VAJICKY A PIVO
(Dumplings with Eggs and Beer)

MANKAS CZECH RESTAURANT, INVERNESS LODGE
INVERNESS, CALIFORNIA

"My husband and I just spent a delightful weekend at the Inverness Lodge. The restaurant serves some truly outstanding dishes. Our favorite was from the breakfast menu—a most unusual combination of dumplings, eggs and onions."
—Mrs. David A. Curry, San Leandro, California

Dumplings should be made the day before you plan to serve them. Accompany with toasted rye bread and Pilsner beer.

6 to 8 servings

Dumplings

4 cups all purpose flour
1 teaspoon salt
4 egg yolks
1 to 1½ cups milk

3 cups diced stale bread

3 quarts water
2 teaspoons salt
1 cup cracker crumbs or breadcrumbs

Place flour in medium bowl. Add salt, yolks and milk all at once and work together with wooden spoon until dough forms ball. Cover with plastic wrap and let stand at room temperature ½ hour.

Work in diced bread little at a time, kneading gently to distribute evenly throughout dough.

In large pot, bring water to boil. Add salt. Cut dough mixture into 3 equal sections and shape each into roll approximately 6 inches long by rolling in cracker crumbs or breadcrumbs. Gently place rolls in boiling water. Simmer, uncovered, for 1 hour.

Remove dumplings with slotted spoon. Allow to cool slightly before slicing into 1-inch pieces with sharp knife. Cool. Cover and refrigerate overnight.

Dumplings with Eggs

¼ cup (½ stick) butter
6 cups cold dumplings
1 medium onion, diced
½ teaspoon salt
¼ teaspoon pepper

12 eggs, well beaten

Melt butter in heavy 12-inch skillet. Add dumplings, onion, salt and pepper and sauté, turning frequently, until dumplings are evenly browned.

Pour eggs over mixture and continue to cook until eggs are set, stirring occasionally. Taste and adjust seasoning, if needed.

OEUFS CONCORDE
(Poached Eggs with Salmon and Caviar)

RESTAURANT BOCUSE
LYONS, FRANCE

4 servings

> **Butter**
> 4 **tablespoons crème fraîche**
> **Salt and freshly ground pepper**
> 16 **2x1x¼-inch pieces fresh salmon**
> **(about ½ pound)**
> 4 **eggs**
>
> 4 **teaspoons caviar**
> 2 **slices white bread (crusts trimmed),**
> **buttered, toasted and each cut**
> **into 6 strips**

Preheat oven to 350°F. Generously butter 4 ramekins and spoon 1 tablespoon crème frâiche in
bottom of each. Add salt and pepper to taste.

Season salmon with salt and pepper. Arrange 4
salmon slices in each ramekin over crème frâiche,
leaving open area in center. Break 1 egg into center
of each ramekin. Transfer dishes to shallow baking
pan. Add enough simmering water to pan to come
halfway up sides of ramekins. Cook over medium
heat until eggs are poached, about 2 to 3 minutes.
Cover pan with foil and bake 10 minutes.

Top each ramekin with 1 teaspoon caviar and serve
immediately with toast.

SPIEDINI DI MOZZARELLA
ALLA ROMANA

ANGELO OF MULBERRY STREET
NEW YORK, NEW YORK

4 to 6 servings

Sauce

> 2 **tablespoons (¼ stick) butter**
> 6 **tablespoons dry white wine**
> 1 **24-ounce can Italian plum tomatoes,**
> **drained and mashed**
> 2 **cups consommé**
> 2 **tablespoons fresh lemon juice**
> 2 **anchovy fillets, minced**
> 1 **tablespoon chopped parsley**
> 1 **teaspoon basil**
> **Salt and freshly ground pepper**

Spiedini

> 12 **slices white sandwich bread, crusts**
> **removed**
> 1 **pound mozzarella cheese slices**
>
> **Oil for deep frying**
> 1 **cup flour**
> 2 **eggs, lightly beaten**

For sauce: Melt butter in large skillet over low heat.
Stir in wine and tomatoes. Add remaining ingre-

dients and cook, uncovered, over medium-low heat
until thick, 30 to 40 minutes. Keep warm.

For spiedini: Cut each bread slice into 3 equal pieces.
Cut cheese into 27 slices approximately same size as
bread. Form sandwiches, alternating bread and
cheese, using 4 pieces of bread and 3 pieces of cheese
for each. Secure with toothpicks.

Heat oil to 375°F. Dip sandwiches in flour, then in
egg, then in flour again. Fry 2 at a time until golden
brown on all sides, about 4 minutes. Drain on paper
towels. Remove toothpicks and cut each sandwich
into thirds. Place in sauce, cover and cook 5
minutes. Serve hot.

ENGLISH-STYLE CHEESE STRATA

DAVID COPPERFIELD RESTAURANT
ARCADIA, CALIFORNIA

8 servings

> 1 **1½-pound loaf white bread, crust**
> **removed**
> 2 **pounds grated cheddar cheese**
> 10 **large eggs, beaten**
> 4 **cups milk**
> 1 **teaspoon dry mustard**
> 1 **teaspoon salt**
> 1 **teaspoon white pepper**
> 2 **teaspoons Worcestershire sauce**

Dice bread and mix with cheese. Set aside. Mix
together eggs, milk and seasonings. Add bread-
cheese mixture and mix well. Let stand for ½ hour.

Preheat oven to 350°F. Pour mixture into 9x13-inch
baking pan set in larger pan of hot water. Bake until
brown and puffy, about 45 to 50 minutes.

MOUSSAKA QUICHE

THE COTTAGE CREST
WALTHAM, MASSACHUSETTS

12 to 16 servings

> 2 **cups oil**
> 1 **medium eggplant, peeled and thinly**
> **sliced**
>
> 2 **cups thinly sliced onion**
> 6 **mushrooms, thinly sliced**
> 3 **cups cooked ground beef or lamb, or**
> **1½ pounds fresh lean ground beef**
> **or lamb, browned and drained**
> 1 **teaspoon dried crushed red peppers**
>
> 6 to 8 **eggs**
> 2 **cups milk**
> 4 **dashes hot pepper sauce**
> ⅓ **cup grated Parmesan cheese**
> ¼ **cup chopped chives**
> **Salt, pepper and garlic powder**
>
> 2 **9-inch unbaked pie shells**
> 3 **medium tomatoes, thinly sliced**

Heat oil in 10-inch skillet. Deep-fry eggplant slices until transparent and lightly browned, 2 to 3 minutes and place on paper towels to drain.

Drain oil from skillet, leaving thin coating on bottom. Sauté onion until almost soft, and remove to paper towels to drain. Sauté mushrooms until moisture evaporates; drain. Mix meat with pepper.

Preheat oven to 325°F. In large bowl, combine eggs, milk, pepper sauce, cheese and chives with salt, pepper and garlic powder to taste. Whip 3 minutes.

Place layer of eggplant in each unbaked pie shell. Follow with layers of mushrooms, onions, tomatoes and meat mixture. Continue layering until shells are ¾ full (do not pack down, as egg mixture must seep in). Divide egg mixture between quiches.

Place quiches on cookie sheet and bake in lower third of oven until custard is set, about 45 to 60 minutes. (If quiche starts to brown too fast before custard is done, cover with foil.)

MUSHROOM QUICHE

THE CASTLE
GRAND RAPIDS, MICHIGAN

6 to 8 servings

Crust

  1¼ cups whole wheat cracker crumbs
       (about 24 large crackers)
  ⅓ cup (¾ stick) butter, melted

Filling

  ¼ cup (½ stick) butter
  1½ pounds mushrooms, sliced
  4 green onions, chopped
  1 garlic clove, minced
  2 teaspoons oregano
  2 teaspoons basil
  1½ teaspoons salt
  1½ teaspoons freshly ground pepper
  1 teaspoon marjoram
  ½ teaspoon thyme
  ½ teaspoon dry mustard

  5 eggs
  1 cup half and half
  Juice and finely grated peel of ½ lemon

Topping

  1½ cups mayonnaise
  ⅓ cup half and half
  2 teaspoons dried dill (optional)

For crust: Combine crumbs and ⅓ cup butter in medium bowl and blend well. Pat into 9-inch pie plate. Chill while preparing filling.

For filling: Position rack in lower third of oven and preheat to 375°F. Melt ¼ cup butter in large skillet over medium-high heat. Add mushrooms, onions and garlic and sauté until liquid is evaporated, about 10 to 15 minutes. Stir in oregano, basil, salt, pepper, marjoram, thyme and mustard and cook 2 minutes. Let cool 5 minutes.

Combine eggs, half and half, lemon juice and peel in large bowl and beat well. Fold in mushroom mixture. Turn into prepared crust. Bake 25 minutes. Let cool slightly.

For topping: Combine mayonnaise, half and half and dill in small bowl. Spoon evenly over quiche. Continue baking until top is set, 20 to 25 minutes.

QUICHE LE GRANDE

EMBREE'S OLD TOWN RESTAURANT
GARLAND, TEXAS

8 servings

  ¼ cup (½ stick) butter
  1 small white onion, finely chopped

  2 eggs
  1½ cups half and half
  6 tablespoons freshly grated Parmesan
       cheese
  1 teaspoon freshly grated nutmeg
  Salt and freshly ground pepper

  1¼ cups chopped broccoli, blanched and
       well drained
  2 tablespoons (¼ stick) butter, melted
  ½ teaspoon dried basil
  ¼ teaspoon Worcestershire sauce
  ¼ teaspoon dried fines herbes
  ¼ teaspoon dried tarragon
  ⅛ teaspoon ground coriander
  ⅛ teaspoon ground cinnamon
  ⅛ teaspoon garlic salt
  ⅛ teaspoon ground cumin
  Dash paprika
  Pinch salt

  1 9-inch baked deep-dish pie shell
  1½ cups cooked turkey breast, cut into
       ½-inch cubes
  2 cups grated Swiss cheese

Position rack in center of oven and preheat to 350°F. Melt ¼ cup butter in small skillet over low heat. Add onion; cook until soft, 12 to 15 minutes. Set aside.

Beat eggs on high speed of electric mixer until light and fluffy. Reduce speed to medium and blend in half and half, ¼ cup Parmesan, nutmeg and salt and pepper to taste.

Combine broccoli, 2 tablespoons melted butter, basil, Worcestershire sauce, fines herbes, tarragon, coriander, cinnamon, garlic salt, cumin, paprika and salt in medium bowl and toss lightly until thoroughly mixed.

Sprinkle pie shell with remaining Parmesan. Add sautéed onion, spreading evenly. Arrange broccoli mixture over onion. Top with turkey. Cover completely with Swiss cheese. Pour in egg mixture to just below rim of pie shell.

Bake until quiche is set, about 50 minutes (filling will be slightly sticky). Let stand 15 to 20 minutes before serving.

QUICHE LORRAINE L'ESCOFFIER

L'ESCOFFIER, THE BEVERLY HILTON
BEVERLY HILLS, CALIFORNIA

"At a recent wine tasting I attended at The Beverly Hilton, an exceptionally creamy version of quiche lorraine was served."

—Peter Sonntag, Los Angeles, California

6 to 8 servings

   ¼ **pound slab bacon, cut into ¼-inch dice, cooked crisp and drained**
   1 **9-inch unbaked pie shell**
   ½ **pound Gruyère cheese, grated**
   5 **eggs**
   2 **cups whipping cream**
      Salt and freshly ground pepper
      Pinch freshly grated nutmeg

Preheat oven to 300°F. Sprinkle bacon over pie shell and top with cheese. Combine eggs and cream in medium bowl and whisk until well blended. Mix in seasoning. Pour over cheese. Bake until lightly browned, about 1 hour. Cut into wedges and serve.

SPINACH AND PISTACHIO QUICHE

JENNY'S
LAHASKA, PENNSYLVANIA

8 to 12 servings

   1 **10-inch unbaked pie shell**

   6 **eggs**
   1 **cup ricotta cheese**
   2 **cups whipping cream**
   1 **cup grated Swiss cheese**
   2 **tablespoons grated Parmesan cheese**
1½ **cups chopped, cooked spinach, loosely packed**
   ½ **cup shelled and chopped pistachios**
   2 **teaspoons salt**
1½ **teaspoons chopped fresh dill or 1 teaspoon dried dill**
   ½ **teaspoon white pepper**
   ½ **teaspoon sugar**
      Grated provolone and Swiss cheese (about 1 cup total) for topping
      Paprika

Preheat oven to 400°F. To prevent shrinking, prick bottom and sides of pie shell with fork or line with waxed paper and fill with rice. Bake 7 minutes. Remove from oven; reduce temperature to 350°F.

In large mixing bowl, combine all ingredients except cheese topping and paprika in order given, mixing well after each addition. Pour into partially baked pie shell and bake until firm, about 45 to 55 minutes. Top with grated cheeses and sprinkle with paprika. Return to oven until cheese melts.

TOMATO AND STILTON CHEESE TART

THE HOLE IN THE WALL
BATH, ENGLAND

6 to 8 servings

      Pastry for 10-inch pie shell
   1 **egg**
   1 **tablespoon cold water**

   2 **tablespoons minced shallots**
   2 **medium tomatoes, peeled, thinly sliced and well drained**
 12 **ounces Stilton cheese, crumbled**
   4 **large eggs, lightly beaten**
   2 **cups whipping cream**
   ¾ **teaspoon salt**
   ¼ **teaspoon ground pepper**

Preheat oven to 400°F. Fit pastry into 10-inch quiche dish or tart pan with removable bottom. Trim off excess dough by moving rolling pin over top of pan. Cut circle of parchment paper to fit bottom of pan and weight with dry beans or rice. Bake shell for 15 minutes. Remove paper and beans. Beat egg with cold water. Brush inside of shell with egg wash and return to oven for 2 minutes to seal.

Reduce oven temperature to 375°F. Sprinkle bottom of pastry with shallots and cover with tomato slices. Distribute cheese evenly over tomatoes. Combine 4 eggs, cream, salt and pepper and blend well. Strain through fine sieve and pour over tomatoes and cheese. (Shell will be very full.) Bake until puffed and lightly browned, 35 to 40 minutes. (Tart will be creamier if slightly underbaked.)

SPINACH AND MUSHROOM GATEAU

LA CREPERIE
MADISON, WISCONSIN

8 servings

Mushroom Filling

   2 **pounds mushrooms, sliced**
   3 **shallots, mashed**
1½ **pounds (3 8-ounce packages) cream cheese, softened**

Wine Mornay Sauce

   ¼ **cup (½ stick) butter**
   ¼ **cup chopped onion**
   ¼ **cup flour**
   ¼ **teaspoon each: salt, pepper and nutmeg**
1½ **cups milk, warmed**
   ½ **cup half and half, warmed**
   2 **tablespoons dry white wine**
   ½ **cup grated Swiss cheese**
   ¼ **cup freshly grated Parmesan cheese**

   2 **pounds fresh spinach, washed, dried and chopped**

25 8-inch crepes
1 pound Jarlsberg or Swiss cheese, very
thinly sliced
6 long bamboo skewers

For filling: Heat mushrooms in covered 10-inch skillet over medium heat until they exude moisture. Add mashed shallots and cream cheese. Heat, stirring constantly, until mixture is smooth. Set aside.

For sauce: Melt butter and sauté onion until translucent. Stir in flour to make roux. Add salt, pepper and nutmeg. Add warmed milk and half and half. Stir until sauce begins to thicken. Add wine and grated cheeses and stir continuously until sauce is smooth and heated through, but not too thick.

Steam spinach until limp. Drain well. Combine spinach and ½ cup Mornay Sauce in small bowl.

Preheat oven to 350°F. Oil baking sheet. Alternate crepe topped with mushroom filling and crepe topped with spinach filling and sliced cheese. Repeat for 25 layers, ending with crepe. Top with Mornay and final cheese slice. Secure crepes with skewers to prevent slipping during baking. Bake until Gâteau is golden brown, about 45 minutes. Let stand 5 minutes. Cut into wedges and serve with remaining Mornay Sauce.

VEGETABLE GATEAU

LE DOMAINE DE LA TORTINIERE
MONTBAZON-EN-TOURAINE, FRANCE

"While staying at Le Domaine de la Tortinière in Montbazon-en-Touraine, France, a highlight of our dining experience was a slice of 'the rainbow'—a marvelous pureed vegetable loaf."
—Carmen Fortenberry, Merritt Island, Florida

8 to 10 servings

¾ pound carrots, coarsely chopped
1 pound cauliflower, coarsely chopped
1 pound celery, coarsely chopped
3 tablespoons (⅜ stick) butter
3 small russet potatoes, peeled and
quartered
1 to 1½ cups water

9 eggs

2 tablespoons brown sugar
1¼ teaspoons salt
¾ teaspoon freshly ground white pepper
¼ teaspoon nutmeg
¼ teaspoon celery salt
    Boiling water

Lightly oil 9x5-inch loaf pan. In 3 medium skillets, separately sauté carrots, cauliflower and celery in 1 tablespoon butter each, just until they begin to brown. Add 4 potato quarters and ¼ cup water to each skillet. Cover and simmer just until tender, adding small amounts of water if necessary and stirring frequently to prevent scorching. Drain any remaining liquid.

Preheat oven to 350°F. Transfer contents of each skillet in separate batches to blender and puree as follows: To carrots add 3 eggs, brown sugar, ½ teaspoon salt and ¼ teaspoon pepper; to cauliflower add 3 eggs, ½ teaspoon salt, ¼ teaspoon pepper and nutmeg; to celery add 3 eggs, ¼ teaspoon salt, ¼ teaspoon pepper and celery salt.

Layer pureed vegetables in loaf pan with carrots on bottom, cauliflower in middle and celery on top. Set in larger pan and add boiling water to depth of 1 inch around loaf pan. Bake until edges begin to pull away from sides of pan, about 35 minutes. Cool to room temperature. Turn out onto serving platter and cut into uniform slices.

Seasonal vegetables may be substituted. Make your vegetable selection with varied colors in mind.

GYRO SANDWICH

JOURNEY'S END
MUNDELEIN, ILLINOIS

"Not long ago while traveling, we stopped for a sandwich and discovered the fabulous Gyro at a charming family restaurant and pub called Journey's End. We have not been able to find another sandwich that would begin to compare."
—C. Patricia Mellican, Galesburg, Illinois

The gyro (pronounced "yeé-ro") patties are of Greek origin, and very highly seasoned. The yogurt sauce is a cooling complement.

Makes 16 sandwiches

Gyro Patties

1¼ pounds lean ground beef
1¼ pounds lean ground lamb
¼ cup oregano
1½ tablespoons onion powder
1 tablespoon garlic powder
¾ to 1½ tablespoons freshly ground pepper
1 teaspoon thyme
¾ teaspoon salt

Yogurt Sauce

1 cup plain yogurt
¼ cup finely chopped cucumber
¼ cup finely chopped onion
2 teaspoons olive oil
    Garlic powder, salt and freshly ground
    white pepper

8 large pita bread rounds, cut in half
    Thinly sliced onion rings (garnish)

For patties: Preheat broiler or prepare barbecue. Combine ingredients lightly but thoroughly in large bowl. Shape into 16 thin patties and broil, turning once, until done as desired.

For sauce: Combine first 4 ingredients in small bowl. Add garlic powder, salt and pepper to taste.

To assemble sandwich, place 1 meat patty in each pita half and top with yogurt sauce and onion slices.

FEUILLETE DE LEGUMES AU COULIS DE HOMARD
(Vegetables in Puff Pastry with Lobster Sauce)

TAILLEVENT
PARIS, FRANCE

6 servings

Sauce Americaine

  ½ cup olive oil or vegetable oil
  2 tablespoons (¼ stick) butter
  1 live lobster (1½ to 2 pounds), cut into 8 pieces (tail cut into 4 pieces, body halved, claws left whole), tomalley reserved (optional)
    Salt
  ⅔ cup finely chopped onion
  ⅓ cup finely chopped carrot
  2 sprigs fresh thyme or ¼ teaspoon dried, crumbled
  1 parsley sprig
  1 bay leaf
  ½ cup dry white wine
  2 teaspoons chopped shallot
  ¼ cup brandy, heated
  1 cup tomato puree
  ½ cup fish stock
  3 tomatoes, peeled, seeded and chopped

  ½ teaspoon chopped fresh tarragon
  1 small garlic clove, crushed
    Freshly ground pepper

Puff Pastry

  1 pound homemade puff pastry or 1 17¼-ounce package puff pastry sheets

  1 egg mixed with 1 teaspoon water

Vegetables

  2 cups water
  6 large spinach leaves with stems
  ½ cup matchstick-cut carrots
  7½ cups (about) chicken stock or water
  ½ cup matchstick-cut zucchini
  ½ cup matchstick-cut green beans
  ½ cup matchstick-cut celery root
  ¾ cup cauliflower florets

Lobster Sauce

  3 egg yolks
  2 tablespoons fresh lemon juice
  ¼ teaspoon salt
  ⅛ teaspoon ground red pepper or freshly ground white pepper
  ½ cup (1 stick) unsalted butter, melted and sizzling hot
  ⅓ cup whipped cream

  2 tablespoons (¼ stick) butter
  6 cherry tomatoes, halved

For Sauce Americaine: Heat oil and 1 tablespoon butter in large heavy saucepan over medium-high heat until very hot. Add lobster pieces and salt and sauté, stirring frequently, until shells turn red, about 3 minutes. Reduce heat to low. Stir in onion, carrot, thyme, parsley and bay leaf. Cover and cook 5 minutes. Add wine, 1 tablespoon butter and shallot to saucepan. Pour brandy over and ignite, shaking pan until flame subsides. Stir in tomato puree, fish stock and tomatoes. Increase heat to medium-low, cover pan tightly and cook mixture 15 minutes.

Remove lobster from saucepan; remove meat from shell and set aside for garnish. Return shells to pan and cook 10 more minutes. Press mixture through fine sieve set over bowl, scraping underside of sieve frequently to extract all puree; discard shells and fibrous residue. Stir in tarragon and garlic. Taste and season with salt and pepper. Transfer sauce to clean saucepan and cook over medium-low heat until reduced to about 1½ cups. (Sauce Americaine can be made 1 day ahead and refrigerated. For heightened flavor, leave shells in sauce during refrigeration. Or, add reserved tomalley and 1 tablespoon butter after reducing, blending well. Do not heat sauce after adding tomalley.)

For puff pastry: Cut puff pastry sheets into 6 4x2½-inch rectangles. Sprinkle baking sheet with cold water. Transfer pastry to baking sheet. Refrigerate for at least 45 minutes.

Preheat oven to 425°F. Brush pastry with egg mixture; do not let any run down sides. Bake until puffed, brown and crisp, 25 minutes. Cool on rack.

When pastry is cool enough to handle, split in half horizontally. Scoop out and discard semicooked pastry from inside.

For vegetables: Bring water to boil in small saucepan. Add spinach and blanch 15 to 20 seconds. Remove with slotted spoon. Cut off stems, flatten and pat dry. Set aside. Cook carrot in 1½ cups chicken stock in medium saucepan over medium-high heat until crisp-tender. Remove with slotted spoon, drain well and set aside. Repeat with remaining vegetables, adding more stock as necessary.

For lobster sauce: Just before serving, combine yolks, lemon juice, salt and pepper in processor or blender and mix 5 seconds. With machine running, pour sizzling butter into egg mixture in slow steady stream (it should take about 15 seconds), mixing constantly until sauce thickens. Transfer to mixing bowl and cool 3 minutes. Slowly fold in whipped cream, blending gently but thoroughly. Carefully fold in ⅓ cup Sauce Americaine.

To assemble: Arrange bottom halves of puff pastry shells on individual plates. Cover with 1 spinach leaf. Melt 2 tablespoons butter in large heavy skillet over low heat. Add vegetables and toss gently until heated through. Spoon vegetables over spinach, dividing evenly among pastry shells. Arrange reserved lobster meat over vegetables. Nap with lobster sauce. Cover with top half of pastry shell. Garnish with cherry tomato halves and serve.

TAILLEVENT—A BALANCE OF TRADITIONAL AND NEW CUISINES

Sequestered in the rue Lamennais in the busy eighth *arrondissement*, Taillevent has been drawing seekers of fine food ever since it opened its doors in 1946. The founder, the late André Vrinat, established a reputation for quality that has been continued and even improved upon by his son, Jean-Claude, the current proprietor. Collaborating with Claude Deligne, the *chef de cuisine* since 1970, the younger Vrinat produces a menu that is always intriguing but never faddish. Specialties in a given season may include *cervelas de fruits de mer* (a sausage of shellfish, truffles and pistachios poached in wine), fresh duckling accented with either lemon or cassis, *panache d'agneau* (a combination of lamb, lamb kidneys and sweetbreads with a hint of tarragon), and an array of superb desserts. It is classic French cuisine infused with the best of the new ideas in the world of food. But, as Vrinat remarks, "If there is a new idea or dish, we will discuss it, test it, make changes, test again. If it works, we will use it—but only if it fits into our overall cuisine."

As befits a restaurant named for the first great French chef, Taillevent is strongly traditional in looks as well as taste. The setting of the two dining rooms is formal but not overpowering; wood-paneled walls and colorful paintings lend an air of understated conviviality that obviously suits the enthusiastic clientele.

There is only one seating for 80 at both luncheon and dinner, and a staff of almost 50 ensures that the service is every bit as good as the dishes that come from Chef Deligne's kitchen. "Excellent" is the mildest of the superlatives customarily applied to Taillevent, and that is reflected in its three Michelin stars.

TOURTE MILANAISE

MICHEL RICHARD
LOS ANGELES, CALIFORNIA

6 to 8 servings

   1 **pound puff pastry**

   1 **tablespoon oil**
   1 **tablespoon butter**
   1 **pound fresh spinach, blanched and well drained**
   2 **garlic cloves, minced**
   ¼ **to ½ teaspoon nutmeg**
      Salt and freshly ground pepper
   2 **large red peppers, cut into 1-inch pieces and blanched**

Omelets

   5 **eggs**
   2 **teaspoons chopped chives**
   2 **teaspoons chopped parsley**
   1 **teaspoon chopped tarragon or ½ teaspoon dried tarragon**
      Salt
   2 **tablespoons (¼ stick) butter**
   8 **ounces Swiss cheese, thinly sliced**
   8 **ounces ham, thinly sliced**

   1 **egg, beaten**

Lightly grease 8-inch springform pan. Roll out ¾

pastry ¼ inch thick and line bottom and sides of pan. Keep remaining pastry refrigerated.

Heat oil and butter in large skillet. Add spinach and garlic and sauté 2 to 3 minutes. Season to taste with nutmeg, salt and pepper. Remove from skillet. Add red peppers to skillet and sauté briefly. Remove from heat and set aside.

For omelets: Lightly beat eggs, herbs and salt to taste. In 7- to 8-inch skillet over medium heat, add 1 tablespoon butter and shake so butter coats bottom evenly. Pour in ½ egg mixture and stir briefly. As eggs start to set, lift edges so liquid can run under. When eggs are completely set, and top of omelet is no longer moist, shake pan and slide omelet onto warm plate. Repeat with remaining butter and egg mixture.

To assemble: Position rack in lower ⅓ of oven and preheat to 350°F. Layer ingredients in prepared pan in following order: 1 omelet, ½ spinach, ½ cheese, ½ ham and all red peppers. Repeat layering in reverse order, using remaining ingredients.

Roll remaining pastry ¼ inch thick. Cut out 8-inch circle. Place over omelet and seal well to pastry lining by pinching with fingers. With tip of knife, draw number of slices desired directly on pastry, or decorate with scraps of pastry. Brush with beaten egg. Place pan on baking sheet and bake until golden brown, about 70 to 75 minutes. Cool slightly. Release from pan and serve tourte warm, slicing with sharp, thin knife.

GABBY CRABBY
(Hot Crab Sandwich)

THE GREENERY RESTAURANT
OGDEN, UTAH

"We returned from a very pleasant vacation in Utah with good memories of several fine restaurants. One of our favorites was the Greenery, where we had a delicious baked crab sandwich."
　　　　　　　—Nancy Otka, North Branford, Connecticut

6 servings

- 1¼ **pounds king crabmeat, cut into large pieces**
- 1¼ **cups mayonnaise**
- 2 to 3 **green onions, chopped**
- ½ **head iceberg lettuce, chopped**
- 1 **tablespoon seasoning salt**
- ½ **tablespoon fresh lemon juice**

- 12 **tomato slices (about 2 large tomatoes)**
- 6 **English muffins, split, toasted and buttered**
- 12 **slices mozzarella cheese (about 9 ounces)**

Preheat oven to 350°F. Mix crab, mayonnaise, onions, lettuce, salt and lemon juice.

Place tomato slice on each muffin half. Arrange crab salad on top of tomato, dividing equally among sandwiches. Top each with slice of mozzarella.

Transfer to baking sheet and bake until cheese is lightly browned, about 15 to 20 minutes.

CHEYENNE CITY SANDWICH

LOCK, STOCK & BARREL
CLINTON TOWNSHIP, MICHIGAN

6 servings

- 3 **cups buttermilk**
- 2 **eggs, well beaten**
- 1 **teaspoon baking soda**
- 2¾ **cups all purpose flour**
- ¼ **cup sugar**
- 2 **tablespoons vegetable oil**
- 1 **tablespoon baking powder**
- 1½ **teaspoons salt**
- 1½ **teaspoons vanilla**

- 6 **thick slices Polish ham**
- 6 **thick slices cooked turkey breast**
- 6 **slices cheese (American, Muenster or Swiss)**
- 12 **thick slices egg bread**

- 6 **small metal or wooden skewers**

  Oil for deep frying
  Jam

In large mixing bowl, combine buttermilk, eggs and baking soda and blend well. Add next 6 ingredients

and beat until smooth. Refrigerate at least 1 hour. (Any remaining batter can be used for pancakes.)

To assemble each sandwich, layer 1 slice ham, turkey and cheese between 2 slices bread. Quarter sandwiches and stack 4 quarters side by side, piercing through with skewer to hold sections together.

Heat oil to 350°F. Dip each skewered sandwich into chilled batter, coating completely. Deep fry until golden brown, about 3 minutes on each side; do not crowd pan. Drain sandwiches briefly on paper towels. Serve with dollop of jam on the side.

MUSHROOM MADNESS

ROARING CAMP CAFE
OAKLAND, CALIFORNIA

6 servings

Marinade

- 1 **tablespoon red wine vinegar**
- 1 **tablespoon fresh lemon juice**
- 2 **teaspoons Dijon mustard**
- 1 **garlic clove, minced**
- ½ **teaspoon Worcestershire sauce**
  Dash hot pepper sauce
  Pinch dried oregano
  Pinch dried tarragon
  Salt and freshly ground pepper
- 3 **ounces olive oil**
- 1½ **pounds mushrooms, sliced**
- 1 **medium red onion, thinly sliced**

Curry Mustard Sauce

- 2 **tablespoons (¼ stick) butter**
- 2 **tablespoons all purpose flour**
- ¾ **cup milk**
- ½ **cup chicken broth**
- 2 **tablespoons dry sherry**
- 2 **teaspoons prepared mustard**
- 1 **teaspoon curry powder or to taste**
  Salt and freshly ground pepper

- 6 **slices seedless Russian rye bread**
- 3 **cups shredded Swiss cheese**

For marinade: Combine first 9 ingredients in large bowl; blend well. Whisk in olive oil. Add mushrooms and onion and toss lightly to coat. Set aside.

For sauce: Melt butter in small saucepan over medium heat. Stir in flour and blend well. Reduce heat to low and cook 2 minutes. Blend in milk, broth, sherry, mustard and curry powder. Bring to boil, stirring constantly. Remove from heat. Taste and season with salt and pepper.

To assemble: Preheat oven to 350°F. Arrange bread on baking sheet. Divide mushrooms evenly among slices, mounding slightly in center. Top each with about 3 tablespoons of sauce and sprinkle with ½ cup cheese. Bake until sandwiches are heated through, about 20 minutes.

CANNELLONI DEI PANZONI

OSTERIA DEI PANZONI
MONTREAL, QUEBEC, CANADA

8 to 10 servings

Filling

     4 tablespoons oil
 1½ pounds veal, cubed
     1 chicken leg, boned
     1 chicken liver

     2 medium onions, coarsely chopped
     4 stalks celery, coarsely chopped
     3 large carrots, coarsely chopped
     2 bunches fresh spinach, washed
        and trimmed
     1 cup canned peeled tomatoes, undrained
 ½ cup milk
        Salt and pepper to taste

Béchamel Sauce

 ¾ cup (1½ sticks) butter
     1 cup flour
     3 cups milk, warmed
        Salt and pepper
        Nutmeg

   24 to 30 crepes
     4 cups Italian meat sauce (homemade or
        commercial variety)
 ⅔ cup freshly grated Parmesan cheese

Heat 2 tablespoons oil in 12-inch skillet. Sauté veal, chicken and liver over medium-high heat until brown on all sides, about 10 to 15 minutes. Remove to 6- to 8-quart casserole or roaster.

Preheat oven to 300°F. To same skillet, add remaining oil and sauté onions, celery and carrots until they just begin to brown, about 10 to 15 minutes. Add spinach in 4 batches, allowing it to shrink down and cook after each addition. Combine vegetables with meat; stir in tomatoes, milk, salt and pepper. Cover and bake 3 hours. Remove lid and allow to cool slightly, about 20 to 30 minutes.

For sauce: While mixture is cooling, melt butter in small saucepan. Stir in flour to make roux. Add milk and season with salt, pepper and nutmeg. Set aside.

Run cooled meat/vegetable mixture through meat grinder or food processor. Reheat oven to 350°F. Grease 2 9x13-inch baking dishes.

Place 1 cup Béchamel and 1 cup meat sauce in each baking dish. Fill each crepe with heaping tablespoon of ground meat/vegetable mixture, roll up and place crepes in baking dishes as they are completed, seam side down. Top each casserole with equal amounts of remaining sauces. Sprinkle with Parmesan. Bake, uncovered, 20 minutes. Let set briefly before serving.

This recipe freezes well.

HAM PALACSINTAS

MAGIC PAN

"These crepes number among the most delicious foods I have ever tasted."
                —Meris Etienne, Tujunga, California

8 servings

Filling

     1 pound ham, ground
     1 cup sour cream
     2 eggs
 ½ teaspoon onion powder
     2 teaspoons Worcestershire sauce
        Salt and white pepper
 ¼ cup chopped black olives (optional)

     8 8-inch crepes

     3 eggs
     1 cup milk
        Cracker meal
        Oil for deep frying

        Mustard Sauce*

For filling: Mix ham, sour cream, eggs, onion powder, Worcestershire sauce, salt and white pepper to taste and black olives if desired.

Fill each crepe as follows: Spread filling on ½ crepe, forming rectangle 6 inches long and about 1½ inches wide. Fold filled ½ over to center line of crepe, covering filling. Roll up, pressing down lightly on edge so that it holds together and is slightly flattened.

Mix eggs and milk together. Dip filled crepes into egg mixture and drain. Roll in cracker meal. Heat oil in deep fryer to 350°F, and fry crepes until golden, about 1½ minutes. Serve with Mustard Sauce.

*Mustard Sauce

Makes 2 cups

     4 egg yolks
     1 teaspoon salt
 ⅛ teaspoon white pepper
     4 teaspoons vinegar
     2 cups salad oil
     1 tablespoon lemon juice
     4 tablespoons prepared mustard
     2 tablespoons honey

Place egg yolks in mixing bowl or blender. Beat lightly. Add salt, white pepper and vinegar. Blend thoroughly. Pour oil very slowly into eggs while beating continuously at medium speed. Add lemon juice, mustard and honey. Blend until well mixed.

PAELLA A LA VALENCIANA

EL FARO
NEW YORK, NEW YORK

"Greenwich Village is one of our favorite dining haunts. El Faro, a restaurant that specializes in Spanish cuisine, has a wonderful paella that we think would be fun to make for a party."
  —*Mr. and Mrs. J. Facciolo, Brooklyn, New York*

6 to 8 servings

    ½ cup olive oil
    1 3-pound chicken, cut into 16 pieces

    1 cup finely chopped onion
    ½ cup finely chopped green pepper
    1 ripe tomato, peeled and chopped
    1 tablespoon crushed garlic
    2 teaspoons salt or to taste
    ⅛ teaspoon oregano
    ⅛ teaspoon pepper
    1 small bay leaf
   20 petals of saffron or ½ teaspoon powdered
    1 tablespoon Spanish paprika

    3 cups hot water
    1 cup chicken broth
    4 cups raw rice

   12 clams, scrubbed
    1 pound shrimp, shelled and deveined
    1 pound scallops
    ½ pound Spanish sausage, sliced

    ½ cup cooked green peas (garnish)
       Pimiento (garnish)
    2 tablespoons dry Spanish sherry

Heat oil in paella pan or 12- to 14-inch skillet. Add chicken and sauté until brown on all sides, about 5 minutes. Remove from pan and set aside.

In same pan, sauté onion, green pepper, tomato, garlic, salt, oregano, pepper and bay leaf 2 minutes. Add saffron and paprika; cook, stirring, 1 minute.

Add hot water and chicken broth. Bring to boil and add chicken and rice. Cover and cook 10 minutes.

Place clams around edge of skillet, arrange shrimp and scallops on top of rice and distribute sliced sausage evenly over top. Cover and cook over low heat until rice is cooked, about 15 to 20 minutes.

Garnish paella with peas and pimiento and sprinkle with sherry.

LASAGNE VERDI ALLA BOLOGNESE

RISTORANTE DIANA
BOLOGNA, ITALY

12 servings

Ragù alla Bolognese

    2 tablespoons oil
    ½ cup minced pancetta

    ¼ to ½ cup minced onion
    2 tablespoons minced celery
    2 tablespoons minced carrot
    2 pounds lean ground beef
       Salt and freshly ground pepper
       Freshly grated nutmeg

    ¾ cup dry white wine
    3 tablespoons tomato paste
       Water

Lasagne Verdi

   3½ cups all purpose flour
    ¼ cup water
    2 tablespoons oil
    2 eggs
    ¼ to ½ cup cooked, drained and
       chopped spinach

Béchamel Sauce

    6 tablespoons (¾ stick) butter
    1 cup (scant) all purpose flour
    1 quart (4 cups) milk, heated to boiling
       Pinch salt
       Dash freshly grated nutmeg

       Lightly salted water
       Oil

    1 cup freshly grated Parmesan cheese
       Butter
       Chopped plain omelet
       Additional Parmesan (optional garnish)

For ragù: Heat oil in Dutch oven or large saucepan over medium-high heat. Add pancetta and cook until browned. Add onion, celery and carrot and continue cooking, stirring constantly with wooden spoon, until browned. Add beef, salt and pepper to taste and dust lightly with nutmeg. Continue cooking, stirring constantly, until meat loses all pink color, about 30 minutes.

Reduce heat to medium. Add wine and continue cooking, stirring occasionally, until wine has evaporated. Blend in tomato paste. Add water to cover all ingredients (about 2½ cups). Bring to boil, reduce heat and simmer uncovered about 45 minutes. Remove from heat.

For lasagne: Combine all ingredients and knead until smooth. Roll out on lightly floured surface to thickness of about ⅛ inch (or use pasta machine and roll quite thin). Cut into 5½- to 6-inch squares, rerolling scraps and cutting as many additional squares as possible.

For Béchamel: Melt butter in 3-quart saucepan over medium heat. Whisk in flour, blending well. Let cook several minutes, whisking constantly. Slowly whisk in boiling milk, blending until smooth. Add salt and nutmeg. Reduce heat to low and cook about 10 minutes, stirring constantly. Set aside.

Bring large quantity of lightly salted water to boil with small amount of oil in large pot. Add ½ pasta and cook quickly just until al dente, about 1 minute. Drain well. Lay on dish towels to dry. Repeat with remaining pasta.

To assemble: Preheat oven to 350°F. Generously butter 9x13-inch baking dish. Arrange layer of pasta in dish. Spread with about ⅓ Béchamel, then some of ragù. Sprinkle with about ⅓ cheese. Repeat. Add another layer of pasta, then remaining béchamel and cheese; dot with butter. Bake until hot and bubbly, about 40 minutes. Sprinkle with chopped omelet and serve immediately, accompanied by remaining ragù and additional Parmesan.

PAGLIA E FIENO
(Straw and Hay)

SAN MARCO RESTAURANT
NEW YORK, NEW YORK

6 servings

½ **pound thin green noodles (about ⅛ inch wide)**
½ **pound thin noodles (about ⅛ inch wide)**
½ **cup (1 stick) butter**
¼ **pound prosciutto, finely minced**
1 **10-ounce package frozen tiny peas, thawed**
1 **cup half and half**
½ **lightly beaten egg yolk**
1 **cup freshly grated Parmesan cheese
Pinch ground nutmeg**

Add noodles to large pot of rapidly boiling salted water. Return to boil and cook until al dente. Drain well. Transfer noodles to well-buttered 2-quart rectangular baking dish.

Preheat oven to 400°F. Melt butter in medium saucepan over medium-high heat. Add prosciutto and sauté 2 to 3 minutes. Reduce heat, stir in peas, half and half, egg yolk, ¾ cup Parmesan and nutmeg and blend well. Pour over noodles and toss. Sprinkle with remaining cheese. Bake until top is golden, about 8 to 10 minutes.

LINGUINE WITH BROCCOLI, CAULIFLOWER AND MUSHROOMS

SELENA'S
TAMPA, FLORIDA

"We recently visited Selena's, a unique little restaurant in a restored area of Tampa called Old Hyde Park. Their pasta dish with vegetables was such a treat!"
—*Jeane Emery, Tampa, Florida*

8 servings

1 **cup ricotta cheese**
⅓ **cup grated Romano cheese**
1 **teaspoon salt**
1 **medium head cauliflower, trimmed and cut into florets**
1 **bunch fresh broccoli, trimmed and cut into florets**

1 **cup olive oil**
6 **garlic cloves, minced**
1 **pound mushrooms, thickly sliced**
2 **teaspoons salt**
½ **teaspoon crushed red pepper**
1 **pound linguine
Grated Romano**

Combine ricotta and ⅓ cup Romano; set aside.

Bring large stockpot of water to rolling boil. Add salt, cauliflower and broccoli. Cover and return to boil. Uncover and cook until vegetables are crisp-tender, about 7 minutes. Remove vegetables with slotted spoon; reserve liquid for cooking linguine.

Heat olive oil and garlic in large skillet. When garlic is lightly browned, stir in mushrooms, salt and red pepper and sauté about 5 minutes. Stir in broccoli and cauliflower and continue cooking 10 minutes. If mixture becomes too dry, add some of reserved cooking liquid.

Bring cooking liquid to rapid boil, adding water if needed. Add linguine, stirring with fork to prevent sticking, and cook until al dente, about 10 to 12 minutes. Drain well. Reheat vegetable mixture; stir in linguine. Divide among shallow bowls and top with cheese mixture. Dust with more Romano.

PAGLIA E FIENO PAPALINA
(Straw and Hay)

ROMEO SALTA
NEW YORK, NEW YORK

6 servings

4 **to 6 tablespoons (½ to ¾ stick) butter**
1 **garlic clove**
1 **pound fresh mushrooms, sliced
Salt**
½ **pound prosciutto, minced**
1 **cup light cream**
8 **ounces fresh egg noodles**
8 **ounces fresh green noodles**
¼ **cup Parmesan cheese, grated**

Heat 2 to 3 tablespoons butter in deep frying pan; add garlic and sauté until browned. Remove garlic and add sliced mushrooms; sprinkle lightly with salt and sauté for 10 minutes.

In another pan, melt remaining butter and fry prosciutto until browned. Heat cream in top of double boiler. Keep all these ingredients hot.

Bring 2 large pots of salted water to boil and cook pastas separately until tender. If freshly made, they will be cooked almost as soon as water returns to boil. However, if using commercially made dried pasta, follow instructions on package. When noodles are tender but still firm, drain, turn into deep, heated serving dish and toss together. Toss noodles with mushrooms, prosciutto, cream, grated cheese. Serve immediately.

RAVIOLI AL BURRO

LUCIA'S ITALIAN RESTAURANT
FREMONT, CALIFORNIA

"One day on my lunch hour, I stopped in Lucia's Pizza Restaurant and found a bit of serendipity. I have returned many times, making the 20-mile jaunt from my home, for the special made twice monthly—homemade Ravioli al Burro. Our waitress told us it is a family recipe that is 150 years old."

—*Mrs. J. Golick, San Jose, California*

4 servings

Pasta

> 3 egg yolks
> 1 egg
> 2 tablespoons water
> 1 teaspoon olive oil
> ½ teaspoon salt
> 1¾ cups all purpose flour

Filling

> ½ pound ricotta cheese
> ⅛ pound (2 ounces) cream cheese, room temperature
> 1 pound Swiss chard, leaves only, or spinach, cooked, squeezed dry and finely chopped
>   Pinch salt and freshly ground pepper
> 2 eggs
> 2 cups grated Parmesan cheese
>
>   Melted butter
>   Minced garlic
>   Grated Parmesan cheese (garnish)

For pasta: Combine egg yolks, egg, water, oil and salt in medium bowl and mix thoroughly. Spoon 1½ cups flour into large bowl. Make well in center and add egg mixture. Stir with fork until flour is moistened and well mixed. Pat into ball.

Sprinkle remaining ¼ cup flour onto work surface. Knead dough until smooth and elastic, about 5 to 10 minutes (with pasta machine, kneading time will be less). Wrap in plastic; refrigerate until ready to use.

For filling: Combine ricotta cheese, cream cheese, Swiss chard or spinach, salt and pepper to taste in large bowl. Add eggs and 2 cups Parmesan cheese and blend well. Set aside.

To assemble: Flour work surface. Divide pasta in ½. Roll into thin large rectangle. Drop filling onto pasta by teaspoons, spacing 2 to 2½ inches apart. Dip pastry brush in water and moisten all area around filling. Roll remaining dough out into thin large rectangle. Position over filled sheet. Press together gently with fingertips, sealing firmly at edges and between filling. Cut into individual squares using ravioli cutter or small sharp knife.

Drop ravioli into boiling water. Cook 6 to 8 minutes. Drain well. Transfer ravioli to platter.

Combine butter and garlic to taste and pour over top. Garnish with Parmesan; serve immediately.

Tomato-meat sauce can be substituted for butter-garlic mixture.

SPAGHETTI PRIMAVERA

LE CIRQUE
NEW YORK, NEW YORK

6 to 8 servings

> 1 pound spaghetti
> 2 tablespoons (¼ stick) butter or oil
>
> 1½ cups coarsely chopped broccoli
> 1½ cups snow peas
> 1 cup sliced zucchini
> 1 cup baby peas
> 6 asparagus stalks, sliced
>
> 1 tablespoon olive oil
> 2 medium tomatoes, chopped
> 3 teaspoons minced garlic
> ¼ cup chopped parsley
>   Salt and pepper
>
> ¼ cup olive oil
> ⅓ cup pine nuts
> 10 mushrooms, sliced
> 1 cup whipping cream
> ½ cup Parmesan cheese
> ⅓ cup (¾ stick) butter
> ⅓ cup chopped fresh basil

Cook spaghetti with 2 tablespoons butter or oil in rapidly boiling water until barely tender.

Blanch broccoli, snow peas, zucchini, peas and asparagus in boiling water 3 to 4 minutes. Rinse in cold water and set aside.

In medium skillet, heat 1 tablespoon olive oil. Add tomatoes, 1 teaspoon garlic, parsley, salt and pepper to taste. Sauté 2 to 3 minutes. Set aside; keep warm.

Heat small amount of oil in large skillet and brown pine nuts. Add remaining oil and garlic, mushrooms, and blanched vegetables. Simmer few minutes. Add spaghetti, cream, Parmesan, butter and basil. Mix gently with fork. Top with sautéed tomatoes and serve immediately.

SPAGHETTI WITH ASPARAGUS

LANTERNA BLU
IMPERIA, ITALY

"While touring the areas of France and Italy that surround Monaco, we stopped for lunch at a unique and picturesque sidewalk cafe called Lanterna Blu. We

asked the congenial waiter to bring us 'the best spaghetti in the house.' The spaghetti with asparagus he brought was a totally new experience for us, and we have raved about it to our friends here in New England ever since."
—Mr. and Mrs. Donald N. Reed, Gorham, Maine

4 servings

- ¼ cup (½ stick) butter
- 1½ tablespoons olive oil
- ½ onion, thinly sliced
- 1 slice Parma ham, chopped
- ½ pound asparagus, cut into slivers
- ½ cup water
- 1 chicken bouillon cube or 1 teaspoon chicken stock base

- ½ pound thin spaghetti or vermicelli
- ½ cup half and half
- ¼ cup freshly grated Parmesan cheese
  Freshly ground pepper

Heat butter and oil in 1-quart saucepan over medium-high heat. Add onion and sauté until golden; do not brown. Add ham and sauté briefly. Add asparagus, water and bouillon cube. Reduce heat and simmer about 15 minutes.

Add spaghetti to large pot of rapidly boiling salted water and cook until al dente, about 5 to 6 minutes. Drain well. Return spaghetti to pot. Add asparagus mixture and half and half and cook over medium-low heat until warmed through. Top with Parmesan and pepper before serving.

TAGLIOLINI VERDI GRATINATI

HOTEL VILLA CIPRIANI
ASOLO, ITALY

6 servings

- 3½ to 4½ cups all purpose flour
- ½ pound spinach, cooked, drained, squeezed dry and finely chopped
- 4 eggs
- 1 teaspoon salt

- 4 to 8 ounces ham, thinly sliced and cut into strips
- ½ cup freshly grated Parmesan cheese
- ¼ cup (½ stick) butter, cut into small pieces
- ½ to ¾ cup béchamel sauce

Mound 3½ cups flour on work surface. Make well in center and add spinach, eggs, salt and few drops of water. Mix with hands, incorporating flour gradually, until dough forms ball, adding more flour as necessary to make dough moist but not wet. Divide into several workable pieces.

Working by hand or machine, roll and stretch dough into thin sheet. If working by hand, roll up dough jelly roll fashion. Cut into ¼-inch widths. Carefully

unroll pasta onto cloth or board and allow to dry completely. If using machine, allow dough to dry partially, about 1 hour. Set machine on narrow setting and cut dough. Separate pasta and allow to dry completely.

Cook dried pasta in 6 to 8 quarts boiling salted water until al dente, about 4 minutes. Drain well. Turn into ovenproof serving dish. Add ham and all but 2 tablespoons Parmesan. Dot with butter and toss lightly. Cover with béchamel, then sprinkle with remaining Parmesan. Preheat broiler. Place dish about 6 inches from heat until top is light brown, about 3 minutes.

CALZONE ROLANDI

PIZZA ROLANDI
COZUMEL, MEXICO

6 servings

Pizza dough

- 1 envelope active dry yeast
- 1½ cups warm water (105°F to 115°F)
- 4 cups all purpose flour
- 1 teaspoon salt
- ¼ cup olive oil

- 2 cups pizza sauce
- 1 pound mozzarella cheese, diced
- 1 cup sliced mushrooms
- 6 asparagus spears, cooked
- 6 egg yolks, lightly beaten
- 12 square slices boiled ham
  Salt and freshly ground pepper

  Olive oil
  Oregano

For pizza dough: Dissolve yeast in ¼ cup water and let stand 10 minutes to proof. Combine flour and salt in large bowl. Make well in center and pour in yeast mixture, remaining water and oil. Mix with fingers or fork until dough can be gathered into ball. Transfer to floured board and knead until smooth, shiny and elastic, about 15 minutes. Cover with plastic wrap and damp cloth and let rise in warm draft-free area until doubled, about 1½ hours.

Preheat oven to 500°F. Punch dough down and divide into 6 equal parts. Roll out 1 part at a time (keep remaining dough covered with damp cloth) into 10-inch round. Spread 1 tablespoon pizza sauce over half circle and sprinkle with ⅙ of cheese and mushrooms. Lay asparagus spear lengthwise over mushrooms and top with some of yolks. Cover with 2 squares ham and season with salt and pepper. Fold turnover fashion and pinch edges together to close. Repeat for each calzone.

Bake directly on oven racks until nicely browned, about 8 to 10 minutes. Brush each hot calzone with remaining pizza sauce and few drops of olive oil. Sprinkle with oregano and serve immediately.

QUESADILLAS

THE BISTRO GARDEN
BEVERLY HILLS, CALIFORNIA

"While sitting outside in the lovely patio of The Bistro Garden restaurant, we were surprised and delighted to find on the menu a Mexican specialty, quesadillas."
— Martha Hummer, Los Angeles, California

6 servings

    Oil
 1 medium onion, sliced
 3 cups shredded cooked chicken or beef
    Butter
 6 12-inch flour tortillas
 8 ounces Monterey Jack cheese, grated
12 strips canned green chilies
12 avocado slices
    Guacamole and green chili salsa

Heat oil in large skillet and sauté onion and chicken or beef until onion is golden brown.

Butter each tortilla and place 1 at a time on hot griddle, buttered side down; butter top. Layer cheese, chilies, avocado and onion-meat mixture in center of each tortilla. Fold in half and transfer to heated platter. Serve with guacamole and salsa.

GNOCCHI

GIAN MARINO'S
NEW YORK, NEW YORK

6 servings

 2 pounds White Rose potatoes, unpeeled, scrubbed
    Salt to taste
11 ounces all purpose flour (approximately 2⅓ cups)
 2 egg yolks
¼ cup (½ stick) butter, melted
    Freshly grated Parmesan cheese

Place potatoes in boiling salted water; cover and cook until tender. Drain. Peel and mash in large bowl until smooth. Add flour and salt. Beat in egg yolks and mix to firm doughy consistency.

Place small portion (about ½ cup) of dough onto floured surface and shape into finger-thick roll. Cut into pieces about 1 inch long. Form into crescent shapes and arrange on lightly floured board or table to dry while remaining dumplings are formed.

In large pan, bring salted water to boil; add gnocchi 1 at a time until bottom of pan is covered. When they rise to surface, remove with slotted spoon and drain well. Place in heated serving dish. Continue cooking remaining dumplings. Pour melted butter over and sprinkle with Parmesan.

These are also delicious with gravy or tomato sauce.

ORIGINAL DIRIGIBLE

CLAWSON'S
BEAUFORT, NORTH CAROLINA

"Last summer our family cruised the Intracoastal Water-way. We stopped overnight in the charming little town of Beaufort, North Carolina, where we had a superb meal at the waterfront restaurant, Clawson's. Each of us ordered a "dirigible"—a baked potato stuffed with various fillings. We voted the Original Dirigible our favorite."—Jane W. Craft, Manning, South Carolina

8 servings

 8 14- to 16-ounce baking potatoes
½ pound cooked turkey, cut into ½-inch cubes
½ pound cooked ham, cut into ½-inch cubes
½ pound medium-sharp cheddar cheese, cut into ½-inch cubes
½ pound provolone cheese cut into ½-inch cubes
 2 green peppers, seeded and chopped
 1 medium onion, chopped
½ cup (1 stick) butter or margarine, melted

    Sour cream and chives (garnish)
    Chopped crisply cooked bacon (garnish)

Preheat oven to 500°F. Scrub potatoes under cold running water. Place wet on baking sheet and bake until potatoes test done, about 75 minutes. Let potatoes cool until warm.

Combine turkey, ham, cheese, green peppers and onion in bowl and toss to mix. Cut potatoes lengthwise not quite in ½. Loosen pulp and remove ¼. Divide butter among potatoes and mix well. Mound with meat-cheese mixture. (At this point potatoes can be wrapped and refrigerated for 3 to 4 days before serving.)

Bake in 375°F oven until heated through and cheese is melted, or microwave on High about 5 minutes. Serve topped with heaping scoop of sour cream and chives and generous sprinkling of bacon.

JACKSON LAKE LODGE BLUEBERRY PANCAKES

JACKSON LAKE LODGE
GRAND TETON NATIONAL PARK, WYOMING

Makes about 20 pancakes

 1 cup all purpose flour
 1 cup whole wheat flour
 4 teaspoons baking powder
 1 tablespoon sugar
¼ teaspoon cinnamon
 2 cups milk

1 **egg, beaten**
¼ **cup vegetable oil**
Juice of ½ lemon
⅛ **teaspoon vanilla**
½ **cup drained canned blueberries**

Blueberries and powdered sugar (garnish)

Combine flours, baking powder, sugar, salt and cinnamon in large bowl and mix well. Stir in milk, egg, oil, lemon juice and vanilla; do not overmix. Gently fold in canned blueberries.

Preheat griddle or electric skillet to 400°F; grease lightly. Stir through batter several times. Using about ¼ cup batter for each (pancakes should be 3 to 4 inches in diameter), cook pancakes until done, turning once, about 3 to 4 minutes. Garnish with blueberries, sprinkle with sugar and serve.

SWISS APPLE PANCAKES

LA COSTA HOTEL AND SPA
CARLSBAD, CALIFORNIA

"My memory of apple pancakes was rekindled at La Costa Hotel, where Chef Willy Hauser prepares a family recipe for delicious buttery and caramelized pancakes."   —*Tina Hahn, Atlanta, Georgia*

Makes 8 to 10 6-inch pancakes

2 **cups flour**
2 **cups cold milk**
2 **eggs**
Pinch salt

¾ **cup (1½ sticks) butter, melted**
3 **medium apples, peeled, cored and sliced**
1 **cup sugar**
Sour cream and currant jelly

Combine flour, milk, eggs and salt and blend until smooth. Set aside.

For each pancake: Heat heavy 6-inch frying pan over medium heat. Add 2 tablespoons butter. When butter starts bubbling add enough batter just to cover bottom of pan. Cook until partially set but still a little liquid. Cover with apple slices. When bottom of pancake is brown use spatula to flip. Sprinkle browned side with about 1 tablespoon sugar. Add more butter and flip pancake again. Repeat until both sides are golden brown and sugar-glazed. Serve hot with sour cream and currant jelly.

WHOLE WHEAT PANCAKES

KUNG FOOD
SAN DIEGO, CALIFORNIA

Makes 12 large or 24 to 36 small pancakes

3 **large eggs**
2 **cups milk**
¼ **cup cold pressed safflower oil**
¼ **cup honey**

2½ **cups whole wheat flour**
5 **teaspoons baking powder**
2 **teaspoons ground coriander**
1 **teaspoon cinnamon**
1 **teaspoon ground nutmeg**
¼ **teaspoon salt**

1 **cup fresh or frozen blueberries (thawed if frozen) or ½ cup mixed chopped dates and walnuts**

In 8-cup bowl with lip for pouring, beat eggs with electric mixer 1 minute at medium speed. Add milk and continue mixing 1 minute. Add oil and honey.

Blend flour, baking powder, spices and salt. Add to egg mixture and combine well.

Heat griddle or 10-inch skillet. Grease lightly with safflower oil or butter. Pour out batter into rounds of desired size. While first side is cooking, place teaspoonful of blueberries or date-nut mixture in center of each pancake. When batter begins to bubble, turn pancake and cook until browned.

VEGETABLES

Nothing testifies more to the growing sophistication of restaurants in general than their presentation of vegetable dishes. Not too long ago, vegetables rarely even appeared on the menus of most restaurants. There might have been a line of fine print offering a "Choice of Vegetables," but that choice usually consisted of a baked Idaho potato, mushy carrots, or something green that was often unidentifiable, usually not fresh and always overcooked. A sensible customer ordered the potato and hoped that the chef would remember to bake it.

The fact that this is no longer the case can be credited to three influences: oriental cookery, the pioneering chefs of *nouvelle cuisine* and the general demand for healthier, more natural dishes. Chinese cooks have always used the freshest and best vegetables, no matter what the dish, and the stir-fry method of cooking them has come to be accepted as one of the best ways to retain each vegetable's texture and flavor. The *nouvelle* chefs married the most delicate sauces to lightly cooked vegetables, then took their lead from the Japanese in making each dish a treat for the eye as well as for the palate. And in a health- and diet-conscious society, vegetables are enjoying a new, long-deserved popularity.

Vegetables are not just side dishes anymore, either. Casseroles, vegetable cakes and tourtes, *gratins* and stir-fry medleys are easing their way into the entree column—even the humble potato is appearing in many fresh new guises.

When he was ninety years old, George Bernard Shaw attributed his longevity to the fact that he was a vegetarian. That may or may not have been true, but what is certain—to borrow a tag from a writer less well known—is that you don't have to be a vegetarian to love vegetables, especially as they appear in this collection.

Le Pâté de Poireau au Coulis de Tomate from Ernie's in San Francisco (see page 165).

BANANA FRITTERS

VINTON'S COUNTRY HOUSE
SHOHOLA, PENNSYLVANIA

"With the main course, Vinton's serves the most wonderful banana fritters instead of potatoes or rice."
—*Mrs. Michael Parmer, Port Jervis, New York*

Makes 16 to 18 fritters

  1½ **cups sifted flour**
  1½ **teaspoons baking powder**
  ½ **teaspoon salt**
  3 **tablespoons sugar**
  2 **eggs**
  2 **tablespoons milk**
  2 **tablespoons banana liqueur**
  2 **tablespoons brandy**
  1 **ripe banana, mashed**

  Solid vegetable shortening for deep fat frying

Sift first 4 ingredients together. Using electric mixer set at medium speed, individually add eggs, milk, liqueur, brandy and mashed banana in order given, mixing well after each is added.

Preheat shortening in deep-fat fryer to 375°F. Form fritters with tablespoon. Fry 6 at a time until fork inserted into fritters comes out clean, about 4 minutes. Drain on paper towels and serve immediately.

GLAZED CARROTS

SHANNON'S TABLE
SALEM, MISSOURI

"Our vacation in the Ozarks was enhanced by an exceptional dinner at Shannon's Table. We returned to the buffet line time after time for their marvelous glazed carrots."   —*Holly W. Whitcomb, Iowa City, Iowa*

4 to 6 servings

  1 **pound fresh carrots, peeled and cut into 2- to 3-inch pieces**
  1½ **cups orange juice**
  ½ **cup light brown sugar**
  1½ **tablespoons margarine**
  1 **tablespoon cornstarch**
  ¼ **cup cold water**
  Pinch ground ginger
  Mint leaves (garnish)

Steam carrots until just tender. Transfer to serving bowl and keep warm. Combine orange juice, sugar and margarine in saucepan and heat almost to boiling point. Dissolve cornstarch in water, stir in and cook until clear and thickened. Add ginger. Pour over carrots; toss to coat. Garnish with mint.

PUREED CARROTS

LE TALBOOTH RESTAURANT
DEDHAM, ENGLAND

3 to 4 servings

  1 **pound carrots, peeled and sliced**
  4 **tablespoons (½ stick) butter**
  ½ **teaspoon sugar**
  Salt and freshly ground pepper
  1 **tablespoon whipping cream**
  1 **tablespoon Madeira**

Combine carrots, 2 tablespoons butter, sugar, salt and pepper to taste in small saucepan. Add water to cover. Bring to boil, then reduce heat and simmer until carrots are tender when pierced with knife, about 5 to 10 minutes. Drain off excess liquid. Transfer carrots to blender or processor. Add cream, Madeira and remaining butter and puree until smooth. Taste and adjust seasoning.

HILDA CROCKETT'S CORN PUDDING

CHESAPEAKE HOUSE
TANGIER ISLAND, VIRGINIA

"Last year my mother-in-law visited the Chesapeake Bay area and discovered a corn pudding at the Chesapeake House that she still talks about."
—*Lesly Livengood, Indianapolis, Indiana*

6 to 8 servings

  ½ **to 1 cup sugar**
  3 **tablespoons cornstarch**
  2 **eggs**
  1 **1-pound can cream-style corn**
  1 **13-ounce can evaporated milk**
  Butter

Preheat oven to 350°F. Lightly grease 1½-quart baking dish. Combine sugar and cornstarch in medium bowl. Add eggs, corn and milk and mix well. Turn into baking dish and dot generously with butter. Bake until center of pudding is almost firm, about 1 hour.

JALAPENO CORN PUDDING

OLD PINEVILLE DEPOT RESTAURANT
CHARLOTTE, NORTH CAROLINA

"Take two natives of the state of Texas and a unique location in Charlotte, North Carolina, join them together and voilà—Jalapeno Corn Pudding, a wonderful combo of the Old West and the Deep South, served as a spicy side dish."   —*Marla Moore, Portland, Oregon*

9 to 12 servings

- 1½ cups creamed corn
- 1 cup yellow cornmeal
- 1 cup (2 sticks) butter, melted
- ¾ cup buttermilk
- 2 medium onions, chopped
- 2 eggs, beaten
- ½ teaspoon baking soda
- 1½ to 2 cups grated sharp cheddar cheese
- 3 jalapeño peppers (fresh or canned), diced

Preheat oven to 350°F. Grease 9-inch square baking pan. Combine first 7 ingredients in large bowl and mix well. Turn ½ batter into pan. Cover evenly with ½ of cheese, then peppers, then remaining cheese. Top with remaining batter. Bake 1 hour. Let cool 15 minutes. Cut into squares.

SZECHWAN DAN DAN NOODLE

YENCHING PALACE
WASHINGTON, D.C.

8 to 10 servings

- 5 tablespoons oil
- ¼ teaspoon red pepper
- ½ cup plus 2 tablespoons chunky peanut butter
- 3 to 4 tablespoons minced green onion
- 3 tablespoons soy sauce
- 2 tablespoons vinegar
- 1 to 2 teaspoons crushed garlic
- 1 teaspoon sugar
- ¼ teaspoon crushed Szechwan peppercorns*

- 1 pound Chinese egg noodles*
- 1 bunch spinach or watercress, parboiled and drained

Heat oil with red pepper. Combine with next 7 ingredients in small bowl; add water if thinner consistency is desired.

Cook noodles in boiling water until tender but still firm, checking frequently to avoid overcooking. Drain and transfer to serving bowl. Add spinach and sauce; toss lightly.

*Available in oriental markets.

FRIED MARINATED ONIONS

DEJA-VU
PHILADELPHIA, PENNSYLVANIA

4 to 6 servings

- 1 pound pearl onions, peeled
- 2 cups white vinegar
- 1 cup water
- 2 bay leaves
- 2 teaspoons dill seeds
- 2 teaspoons sugar

- Oil for deep frying
- ½ cup all purpose flour
- ½ cup toasted whole wheat breadcrumbs
- 2 to 3 egg yolks, beaten

Combine onions, vinegar, water, bay leaves, dill seeds and sugar in medium saucepan and cook over medium-high heat until onions are tender, about 5 to 10 minutes. Let cool. Transfer to bowl, cover tightly and refrigerate 48 hours.

Remove onions from marinade and drain on paper towels. Pour oil into large skillet to depth of 1 inch. Place over medium-high heat. Meanwhile, combine flour and crumbs in flat dish. Dip onions into egg yolks, then roll in flour mixture, covering completely. When oil is hot, add onions to skillet and fry until brown and crisp. Drain on paper towels. Serve immediately.

COLD EGGPLANT PROVENCALE

THE COACH HOUSE
NEW YORK, NEW YORK

10 to 12 servings

- 3 large eggplants, sliced into rounds ½ inch thick
- Salt

- 1 cup chopped fresh parsley
- 2 large onions, thinly sliced
- 6 large tomatoes, peeled and sliced
- 2 large garlic cloves, minced
- 2 celery hearts, finely chopped
- 2 teaspoons black currants
- 1 teaspoon dried basil
- 1 teaspoon crushed black peppercorns
- 1 teaspoon chopped capers

- Salt and freshly ground pepper
- 1 cup olive oil

- Lemon wedges (optional garnish)

Sprinkle eggplant slices generously on both sides with salt. Place in large colander, cover with weight and let stand about 45 minutes. Rinse thoroughly under cold running water; dry with paper towels.

Preheat oven to 275°F. Arrange ½ of eggplant in 11x15-inch baking dish. Sprinkle with about ½ of parsley. Arrange onions, tomatoes, garlic, celery, currants, basil, peppercorns and capers evenly over top. Season to taste with salt and pepper and sprinkle with remaining parsley. Top with remaining eggplant and pour olive oil evenly over. Cover tightly with foil and bake 4 hours. Remove foil and stir mixture well with long fork or spoon. Continue baking 1 hour. Let cool, then chill.

Let stand at room temperature 2 to 3 hours before serving. Garnish dish with lemon wedges if desired.

BLACK ANGUS POTATOES AU GRATIN

BLACK ANGUS RESTAURANT
YAKIMA, WASHINGTON

6 to 8 servings

   1½ pounds potatoes, unpeeled
       Salt

    2 tablespoons (¼ stick) butter
    2 tablespoons flour
   1½ cups hot milk
    ½ cup shredded sharp cheddar cheese
    1 teaspoon freshly grated Parmesan cheese
    1 garlic clove, minced
       Salt and freshly ground pepper

       Shredded cheddar, grated Parmesan and
       paprika (topping)

Boil potatoes in lightly salted water until tender. Cool, peel and cut into ¼-inch slices. Layer slices in buttered casserole.

Preheat oven to 350°F. Melt butter in medium saucepan and stir in flour until mixture is smooth. Gradually add hot milk, stirring constantly. Stir in ½ cup cheddar cheese, 1 teaspoon Parmesan cheese and garlic and continue cooking until cheese is melted. Season to taste with salt and pepper.

Pour over potatoes and sprinkle with additional cheddar, Parmesan and paprika. Bake 20 minutes. Place under broiler just until brown and bubbly. Serve immediately.

CROQUETTE POTATOES

FOULARD'S
HOUSTON, TEXAS

Makes about 8 dozen

    2 pounds baking potatoes, scrubbed
       Salt and white pepper
       Nutmeg
    2 large eggs, beaten
    3 to 4 tablespoons whipping cream

    2 tablespoons chopped onion
    1 tablespoon butter
    2 slices bacon, cooked, drained and
       crumbled
    2 1-ounce slices American cheese, minced
    2 teaspoons chopped chives or parsley
    2 large eggs, beaten
    ⅓ cup milk
    ½ cup flour
    3 cups soft breadcrumbs

       Oil

Preheat oven to 400°F. Bake potatoes until fork-tender, about 50 to 60 minutes. Cool slightly, scoop pulp into medium bowl and mash well. Season to taste with salt, pepper and nutmeg. Add 2 eggs and

enough cream to hold pulp together without letting mixture become too moist. If using electric mixer, be careful not to overblend.

Sauté onion in butter and stir in with bacon, cheese and chives or parsley. Form into cylinders about 1½x⅝ inches. Combine remaining eggs and milk. Coat cylinders in flour, then egg-milk mixture and breadcrumbs.

Preheat oven to 400°F. In deep fryer or skillet, heat oil to 375°F. Fry croquettes, being careful not to crowd, until evenly browned, about 3 to 4 minutes. Drain on paper towels. Place on cookie sheet and bake 8 to 10 minutes. Serve hot.

PAMELA BARRETT'S GARLIC POTATOES

ROBESTON HOUSE
PEMBROKESHIRE, WALES

"While visiting Great Britain my husband and I had occasion to dine at the Robeston House in Wales. This elegant 'country house' hotel, which cultivates its own vegetables in a walled kitchen garden, serves an exquisite dish of potatoes, garlic and cheddar."
—Mrs. Gary M. Banina, Hammond, Indiana

4 to 6 servings

   1½ pounds potatoes (about 3 medium),
       peeled

    ½ teaspoon salt
       Freshly ground pepper
   12 ounces cheddar cheese, grated
    ⅔ cup whipping cream
    4 garlic cloves, crushed

Combine potatoes in large saucepan with enough water to cover and bring to boil over high heat. Reduce heat and simmer until potatoes are tender, about 20 minutes. Drain well; let stand until cool.

Preheat oven to 350°F. Slice potatoes thinly and arrange in lightly buttered shallow baking dish. Sprinkle with salt and pepper. Top with ⅓ of cheese. Pour over ½ of cream. Top with ⅓ of remaining cheese. Pour over remaining cream and top with remaining cheese. Sprinkle garlic evenly over top. Bake until browned and crisp, about 40 minutes.

POMMES A L'AIL
(Garlic-Fried Potatoes)

AIR FRANCE

4 to 6 servings

   1½ pounds large firm potatoes
       Oil for deep frying
    1 egg
    1 garlic clove, minced

BEHIND THE SCENES AT THE JOCKEY CLUB

During the Kennedy administration it was *the* new restaurant: a political gourmet's social spot where White House and State Department brass and the president himself gathered along with gentlemen and their wives from nearby Embassy Row. Today, politicians have given way to a more social crowd. However, the scene and the atmosphere remain unchanged—the fine beamed ceilings, the dark oak paneling, the soft tavern lanterns that evoke an elegant old English inn. Handsome Remington bronzes and fresh flowers grace the arches that divide the large main room into cozy publike areas.

But what makes the atmosphere here so consistently convivial is the excellent service under the direction of Paul Delisle and the fine food under the sleeves-up supervision of Chef Jean-Claude and his youthful staff.

A morning tour through Jean-Claude's domain reveals an organized fever of activity. At the giant range is a huge braising pot with beef bones browning for stock, nine different sauces in bain-maries ready and holding and a ten-gallon pot simmering away with Ratatouille Niçoise. There are enormous tins of sliced, toasted French bread and pans of rock salt ready for Oysters Rockefeller. Beyond the main arena salads are prepared. Bakers' racks are filled with warm fresh croissants and pastries.

In the cold room are clams and oysters waiting to be shucked, a huge pot of cooling fish fumet and fresh fish, much of it air lifted from France. Prosciutto and peeled crescents of honeydew are assembled on chilled plates and avocados filled with chicken salad. Soon these will be wheeled to adjacent dining room service areas, ready for the first luncheon guests at noon. Most days, there are several lunch parties, and in the evenings, around 150 diners enjoy this landmark restaurant.

Peel potatoes and cut as for french fries. Heat oil to 370°F. Add few potato slices at a time and cook 5 minutes, moving them occasionally for even cooking. Drain well. Beat egg with garlic in large bowl. Increase oil temperature to 390°F and refry potatoes until browned and crisp. Drain well and add immediately to eggs, turning to coat evenly. Serve.

ASSIETTE DE LEGUMES CHAUDS
(Mixed Vegetable Platter)

THE JOCKEY CLUB
WASHINGTON, D.C.

6 servings

  2 **heads broccoli, broken into florets**
  1 **head cauliflower, broken into florets**
  2 **pounds carrots, sliced**
  2 **pounds green beans, trimmed and cut into 4-inch lengths**

  6 **artichoke bottoms**
  1 **pound red potatoes**

  4 **medium tomatoes, peeled and sliced**
    Hollandaise Sauce (see page 80)

Cook broccoli in boiling salted water in medium saucepan over medium-high heat until al dente, about 3 to 5 minutes. Remove with slotted spoon or strainer and immediately plunge into ice water to stop cooking process. Drain well. Repeat with all remaining vegetables except potatoes and tomatoes, cooking each in separate saucepan. Cooking time for cauliflower, about 3 minutes; carrots, about 5 minutes; green beans, about 3 minutes; and artichoke bottoms, about 5 minutes. Cook potatoes in boiling water until tender and drain well. Cut potatoes into ½-inch cubes.

Arrange vegetables in circle on large serving platter beginning with broccoli at outer edge, then tomatoes, potatoes, green beans and carrots. Mound artichoke bottoms and cauliflower in center. Serve with Hollandaise Sauce.

ROESTI POTATOES

KAHALA HILTON
HONOLULU, HAWAII

6 servings

- 8 slices bacon, finely chopped
- 2 large onions, minced
- 1 pound potatoes, shredded
  Salt and freshly ground pepper

Sauté bacon in large skillet until rendered. Add onion and sauté until soft. Add potatoes and fry until golden brown, about 15 to 20 minutes. Season with salt and pepper to taste.

STUFFED BAKED POTATOES

CANLIS'S
SEATTLE, WASHINGTON

"A baked potato is a baked potato, unless you've tried the memorable spuds served at Canlis's."
—*Diane Smyser Pledger, Annandale, Virginia*

4 servings

- 2 large baking potatoes
- ¼ cup sour cream
- 8 teaspoons freshly grated Romano cheese
- 4 slices bacon, crisply fried, drained and crumbled
- 4 teaspoons minced green onion
  Salt and freshly ground pepper

- 4 to 8 pats butter

  Minced fresh parsley and paprika (garnish)

Preheat oven to 425°F. Bake potatoes 45 minutes. Remove from oven and reduce heat to 350°F. Cut each potato in ½ horizontally and gently scoop pulp into small bowl; reserve skins. Add sour cream, 4 teaspoons cheese, bacon and onion to pulp and mix with fork until well blended but not mashed. Add salt and pepper to taste. Fill potato skins and sprinkle with remaining cheese. Bake until heated through, about 20 minutes.

Add 1 to 2 pats butter to each ½ and top with sprinkling of parsley and paprika.

PRUNE PUREE

RESTAURANT ANDRE DAGUIN, HOTEL DE FRANCE
AUCH, FRANCE

An excellent side dish with veal chops.

Makes about 2 cups

- 1 12-ounce box pitted prunes
  Dry white wine

- 1 tablespoon minced shallots
  Pinch salt
- 1⅓ cups whipping cream
- 1 to 2 tablespoons minced lemon zest (optional)

Combine prunes in nonaluminum saucepan with enough wine to cover and bring to boil. Reduce heat to low and add shallots and salt. Cover and cook 30 minutes, stirring occasionally. Remove lid and reduce any remaining cooking liquid to thick glaze.

Transfer prunes to food processor and puree. With machine running, add cream slowly. Taste and fold in zest if puree seems too sweet. Serve warm.

Prune puree can be prepared ahead and warmed over low heat just before serving.

SPICED RICE

FRIAR TUCK'S
NEVADA CITY, CALIFORNIA

6 to 8 servings

- ½ cup raisins, plumped in boiling water
- 2½ cups water
- 2 cups brown rice
- ¾ teaspoon cinnamon
- ¾ teaspoon nutmeg
- ¼ teaspoon salt
- ¼ cup (½ stick) butter
- 2 garlic cloves, crushed

Combine all ingredients except butter and garlic in medium saucepan and bring to rolling boil. Reduce heat, stir rice once (too much stirring will make rice gummy), cover and simmer until tender, about 45 minutes. Just before serving, melt butter with garlic and pour evenly over rice.

DIRTY RICE

VARGO'S
HOUSTON, TEXAS

8 to 10 servings

- 2 tablespoons (¼ stick) butter
- 1 tablespoon oil
- 1 cup ground yellow onion
- 2 cups ground chicken gizzards (some hearts and livers included)
- 2 cups rice
- 3 cups chicken broth
- 2 tablespoons minced green onion
- 2 tablespoons minced fresh parsley
- 1 to 2 garlic cloves, minced

Preheat oven to 350°F. Heat butter and oil in large ovenproof saucepan over medium-high heat. Add onion and sauté 4 to 5 minutes. Stir in gizzards and sauté until cooked. Blend in rice. Add broth, green onion, parsley and garlic and bring to boil. Cover and bake until liquid is absorbed and rice is tender, about 45 minutes.

BERGHOFF CREAMED SPINACH

THE BERGHOFF
CHICAGO, ILLINOIS

4 to 6 servings

   2 slices bacon, diced
   2 tablespoons (¼ stick) butter
1½ tablespoons flour
   1 cup half and half, scalding hot
   1 onion, diced
   1 tablespoon butter or oil
   4 bunches spinach, cooked and finely chopped
   ¼ teaspoon salt
   ⅛ teaspoon freshly grated nutmeg

Sauté bacon in medium saucepan until crisp. Reduce heat to medium-low and add 2 tablespoons butter. When melted, whisk in flour to make roux. Cook 2 minutes, stirring constantly. Slowly add hot half and half, whisking constantly until sauce is smooth and thickened. Simmer about 10 minutes, stirring frequently. Sauté onion in remaining butter or oil, add with remaining ingredients and heat through.

TOMATOES STUFFED WITH RICE

HOTEL HASSLER
ROME, ITALY

12 servings

 12 large firm tomatoes
    Salt

   1 bunch fresh parsley, stems removed
   ¼ cup chopped fresh basil leaves, lightly packed, or 1 tablespoon dried
   2 to 3 garlic cloves
   ⅔ cup long-grain rice (Italian preferred)
   ½ cup olive oil
   3 tablespoons freshly grated Parmesan cheese
   ⅛ teaspoon oregano
     Salt and fresly ground pepper to taste

Preheat oven to 350°F. Lightly oil baking dish and set aside. Slice tops from tomatoes and set aside. Remove pulp and press through fine sieve into large bowl. Sprinkle tomato cavities with salt and let stand 15 minutes.

Mince parsley, basil and garlic together. Add to tomato pulp with remaining ingredients and blend well. Fill tomatoes. Replace tops and transfer to

baking dish. Cover with foil and bake 1 hour, removing foil last 5 minutes. Serve tomatoes upside down, either warm or lightly chilled.

MIXED STEAMED VEGETABLE PLATE

THE NATURAL KITCHEN
TAMPA, FLORIDA

"My husband and I love natural food restaurants, our particular favorite being The Natural Kitchen. One exceptional item is the steamed vegetables 'all the way' (with a marvelous onion sauce and melted cheese)."
  —Barbara Carlin, Cleveland, North Carolina

Owner/Chef Robert Tutenberg suggests serving the steamed vegetables with brown rice and mild, white cheddar cheese. Any seasonal vegetables may be added or substituted.

6 to 8 servings

Sauce

   2 tablespoons peanut oil
   2 large Spanish onions, chopped
   ¼ cup whole wheat flour
   ¼ cup tamari*
   ¾ cup tomato juice
   ¾ cup purified water

Vegetables

   4 celery stalks, sliced in 1-inch pieces
   2 large zucchini or crookneck squash, sliced in 1-inch pieces
   2 large carrots, sliced in 1-inch pieces
   1 small head cauliflower, cut into florets
   1 small head broccoli, cut into florets
   ½ small head red cabbage, coarsely chopped
   ½ small head green cabbage, coarsely chopped
   2 large firm tomatoes, cut into wedges

For sauce: Heat 1 tablespoon oil in large skillet over medium-high heat. Add onions and sauté until tender. Reduce heat and add remaining oil. Slowly add flour, stirring constantly to avoid sticking, until all flour is thoroughly mixed with onions. Stirring constantly, slowly add tamari, tomato juice and water. Let simmer 30 minutes, stirring often.

For vegetables: Place all vegetables except tomatoes in large steamer or wok with rack and steam until just tender, about 25 to 30 minutes. Add tomatoes and steam 3 minutes more. Transfer to heated platter, pour sauce over and serve immediately.

Sauce Variations: Add chopped mushrooms when onions are tender (onions must be finely chopped in this case). If preferred, omit oil and substitute 1 tablespoon tamari and 1 tablespoon tomato juice. Add remaining soy and juice in order given. A good soup stock can be used instead of purified water.

*A low-salt soy sauce available at natural food stores.

MONTEREY JACK'S VEGETABLE BAKE

THE GARDEN POTPOURRI, MONTGOMERY MALL
BETHESDA, MARYLAND

6 to 8 servings

    2 tablespoons corn oil margarine
    ½ pound fresh broccoli, broken into
        florets, stems peeled and cut into
        ½-inch pieces
    1 to 2 tablespoons soy sauce
    1½ teaspoons minced fresh garlic
    1 teaspoon celery seeds
    ½ teaspoon dried dill
        Salt and freshly ground pepper
    ½ pound carrots, peeled and diced
    1 small onion, diced

    7 eggs
    1¼ cups milk
    1 pound Monterey Jack cheese, shredded

Melt margarine in medium skillet until foam subsides. Add broccoli stems and sauté briefly. Add soy sauce, garlic, celery seeds, dill and salt and pepper to taste. Cook over low heat about 5 minutes, stirring occasionally. Add carrots, onion and broccoli florets; cover and cook until tender, about 10 minutes, stirring occasionally.

Preheat oven to 350°F. Beat eggs and milk in large bowl. Add cheese and vegetables. Turn into lightly greased deep 3-quart baking dish. Place in large, shallow pan and add boiling water to depth of 1 inch. Bake until knife inserted in center comes out clean, about 50 to 60 minutes.

VEGETABLE CASSEROLE

NICOLE'S CAFE-BISTRO
TULSA, OKLAHOMA

"For those who like vegetables, the Vegetable Casserole served at Nicole's Cafe-Bistro in Tulsa is a deliciously different treat."
                    —*Mrs. Trueman Martinie, Joplin, Missouri*

12 to 16 servings

    2 medium eggplants, peeled and sliced
        crosswise into circles ½ inch thick
        Salt
    3 tablespoons oil (or more)

    2 large zucchini, sliced
    ½ pound mushrooms, sliced
    1 large green pepper, seeded and diced
    2 large tomatoes, sliced
    1 bunch fresh spinach, well washed and
        stems removed
    2 cups grated asiago or Parmesan cheese
    3 large tomatoes, chopped
        Oregano
        Salt and freshly ground pepper

Sprinkle eggplant generously with salt, place in colander and allow to stand at least 30 minutes. Rinse well and pat dry. Heat oil in large skillet. Sauté eggplant in batches until lightly browned, adding oil as necessary.

Preheat oven to 375°F. Layer ½ eggplant, zucchini, mushrooms, green pepper, sliced tomatoes, spinach, cheese and chopped tomatoes in greased 5- to 6-quart casserole (or 2 3-quart casseroles). Sprinkle generously with oregano, salt and pepper. Repeat layering with remaining ingredients. Bake, uncovered, until vegetables are tender, 30 to 40 minutes.

GOURMANDISE DE LEGUMES
(Rainbow of Four Vegetable Purees)

ERNIE'S
SAN FRANCISCO, CALIFORNIA

6 servings

    2 medium turnips, peeled and chopped
    2 large or 3 medium carrots, chopped
    1 bunch broccoli, florets only
        Salt and freshly ground white pepper

    1 pound fresh mushrooms, finely chopped
    1 tablespoon butter

Custard

    1 cup whipping cream
    1 egg
    2 egg yolks
    1 tablespoon fresh lemon juice
        Dash freshly grated nutmeg

    Hollandaise Sauce* (optional)

Cook turnips, carrots and broccoli separately in boiling salted water until very tender. Drain and dry on paper towels. Puree each in processor or blender until smooth. Return to pans and cook over low heat to remove any excess moisture. Measure 1 cup of each puree and season with salt and pepper to taste.

Squeeze mushrooms in corner of towel to remove excess moisture. Melt butter in skillet over medium heat. Add mushrooms and cook until almost black and moisture has evaporated. Measure 1 cup and season with salt and freshly ground pepper to taste.

For custard: Combine ingredients in medium bowl and beat just until smooth. Add about 2 tablespoons to turnip puree or just enough to make thick, smooth paste. Repeat with remaining vegetables.

Preheat oven to 350°F. Generously butter six ½-cup timbale molds or soufflé dishes. Using pastry bag fitted with ¼-inch plain tip (or 20-inch piece of parchment or heavy-duty foil shaped into cone), pipe turnip puree into each mold until ¼ full. Smooth surface with back of spoon and tap molds on counter to distribute puree evenly. Repeat procedure with carrots, then broccoli, and finish with mushrooms, smoothing and tapping molds after each is added.

Set in deep baking pan and add boiling water to come within ½ inch from top of molds. Cover with parchment or foil and bake 30 minutes. Remove from water bath and let stand 10 minutes. Invert onto plates and serve with Hollandaise Sauce.

Hollandaise Sauce

Makes about 1 cup

>   4 egg yolks
>   1 tablespoon lemon juice
>   ¼ teaspoon salt
>   Dash freshly ground white pepper
>   ½ cup (1 stick) butter, heated until sizzling
>   ½ cup Chablis or other dry white
>   wine, heated

Combine yolks, lemon juice, salt and pepper in blender and mix well. With motor on high, begin adding butter drop by drop, then in thin steady stream, and blend until sauce is thickened. Pour in wine and serve at once.

MIXED ORIENTAL VEGETABLES

TRUFFLES, HYATT REGENCY
CHICAGO, ILLINOIS

8 servings

>   1 head Chinese cabbage (bok choy),
>   chopped
>   ½ cup julienned carrots
>   2 cups fresh Chinese pea pods
>   3 tablespoons (⅜ stick) butter
>   3 tablespoons peanut oil
>   1 cup sliced fresh mushrooms
>   3 cups fresh bean sprouts
>   1 basket cherry tomatoes
>   4 ounces miniature canned corn
>   Dressing*

Sauté cabbage, carrots and pea pods al dente in butter and oil. Add mushrooms, bean sprouts, tomatoes, corn and dressing to taste. Simmer for 2 minutes, taking care that vegetables do not overcook. Serve immediately.

Dressing

Makes 1 quart

>   1 cup oyster sauce*
>   1 cup sugar
>   2 cups soy sauce
>   Salt and pepper

Blend all ingredients thoroughly. Adjust seasonings.

*Available in Chinese and specialty markets.

LE PATE DE POIREAU AU COULIS DE TOMATE
(Leek Pâté with Puree of Fresh Tomato)

ERNIE'S
SAN FRANCISCO, CALIFORNIA

8 servings

Pâté

>   12 to 14 large leeks, white and tender green
>   part only plus 6 outer leaves
>   2 quarts (8 cups) rich chicken stock
>   Bouquet garni (2 garlic cloves,
>   1 teaspoon dried thyme and 1 bay leaf
>   tied in cheesecloth bag)
>
>   4 envelopes unflavored gelatin

Sauce

>   ¼ cup (½ stick) unsalted butter
>   1 bunch celery, thinly sliced
>   1 small carrot, thinly sliced
>   1 small onion, thinly sliced
>   4 large tomatoes, peeled and seeded
>   1 tablespoon sugar
>   1 teaspoon minced parsley stems
>   ¼ teaspoon dried thyme
>   ¼ teaspoon crumbled bay leaf
>   Salt and freshly ground pepper
>
>   Watercress sprigs (garnish)
>   Tomato roses (optional garnish)

For pâté: Clean leeks thoroughly. Combine stock and bouquet garni in Dutch oven and bring to boil. Add leeks (including 6 reserved leaves) and cook until tender, about 10 to 12 minutes. Drain well; discard bouquet garni. Return 1 quart stock to pan (chill or freeze remainder to use as desired).

Sprinkle gelatin over warm stock and stir to dissolve. Return leeks to stock and mix well. Quickly drain leeks. Layer lengthwise into 12x4-inch enameled pâté pan or 9x5-inch glass bread pan or rectangular mold. When mold is about half full, wrap leek leaves into single cylinder and set in center of mold. Continue until mold is full.

Set weight on pâté and press to make leeks compact. Refrigerate until set.

For sauce: Heat butter in large skillet over medium heat. Add celery, carrot and onion and sauté lightly. Add tomatoes, sugar and herbs and simmer uncovered until mixture has thickened, about 20 minutes. Puree in blender or press through a strainer. Season with salt and pepper to taste. Chill.

To serve: Unmold pâté and slice ¼ to ½ inch thick. Spoon sauce on plates and top with slice of pâté. Garnish with watercress and tomato rose, if desired.

BREAD BASKET

Man may not live by bread alone, but there has never been a time when he would happily live without it. The fact that bread is an integral part of our lives is reflected in our very use of the word: Someone's "bread and butter" is his livelihood, and if we "take the bread out of his mouth," we are depriving him. We "cast bread upon the waters" when we do good deeds with no expectation of return, and whenever we sit down to a meal, we "break bread." Bread is so important that it is no surprise that, in today's slang, someone with "a lot of bread" is considered very rich.

In the form of simple flat cakes made of flour and water, bread has been around since prehistoric times, and these unleavened breads are still the standbys of many "peasant" cuisines. The ancient Egyptians are generally credited with discovering fermented bread, which resulted in the familiar leavened, or yeast-risen, loaf. (The Book of Exodus tells us that the Israelites, when fleeing Egypt, forgot to take yeast with them; hence the importance of unleavened bread in Jewish tradition.) By the late Middle Ages, salt, at first a luxury, was added to the dough, and bread began to take the forms we know best today—the *pains ordinaires* of every French home, restaurant and bread shop.

Breadmaking itself has enjoyed quite a renaissance of late, as more and more cooks discover the great and simple pleasure of working with dough—not to mention the wonderful, nostalgic aromas that emanate from the oven when the bread is baking. Today every cook worthy of the name has a few breads in his or her repertoire, from classic French and Italian breads to "quick" breads flavored with fruits, vegetables and spices, from tea breads to coffee cakes, from muffins to rolls to corn bread to fried bread. Most restaurants have at least one bread specialty, too—"baked fresh daily"—and some of the best are presented here.

WHOLE WHEAT BREAD

THE WINDOWS BAKERY AND CAFE
VICTORIA, TEXAS

Makes 1 9x5-inch loaf

  1¼ **cups warm water (105°F to 115°F)**
  1⅔ **cakes yeast**
   2 **tablespoons (¼ stick) butter**
   1 **tablespoon honey**
   1 **teaspoon salt**
   4 **cups whole wheat flour**
      Melted butter

Grease large bowl and set aside. Combine first 5 ingredients in mixing bowl. Gradually stir in flour until well blended. Turn dough out onto lightly floured surface and knead until smooth, about 10 minutes. Transfer to greased bowl, turning to coat all surfaces. Cover with damp towel and let stand in warm draft-free area until doubled, about 1 hour.

Oil 9x5-inch loaf pan. Punch dough down. Turn into pan. Cover and let stand in warm draft-free area until doubled in volume, about 45 minutes.

Position rack in center of oven and preheat to 375°F. Brush top of loaf with melted butter. Bake until tester inserted in center comes out clean, about 30 to 35 minutes.

PANACHE'S WHOLE WHEAT BREAD

PANACHE
SALT LAKE CITY, UTAH

Makes 3 9x5-inch loaves

   3 **cups rolled oats**
   3 **cups hot water**
   1 **cup molasses or honey (or combination)**
   1 **cup bran flakes**
   3 **tablespoons (⅜ stick) butter, bacon fat or margarine, room temperature**
   1 **tablespoon salt**

   1 **envelope dry yeast**
   1 **cup warm water (105°F to 115°F)**

   2 **cups whole wheat flour**
  10 to 12 **cups all purpose flour**

Generously grease large bowl and 3 9x5-inch loaf pans. Combine oats, hot water, molasses, bran flakes, butter and salt in another large bowl and blend well. Leave at room temperature until cool.

Combine yeast and warm water in small bowl and let stand until foamy and proofed, 5 to 10 minutes.

Stir yeast into oat mixture. Add whole wheat flour and mix well. Turn out onto lightly floured surface and gradually knead in all purpose flour until dough is firm, satiny and no longer sticky. Transfer to greased bowl, turning to coat entire surface. Let stand in warm draft-free area until doubled.

Punch dough down. Turn out onto lightly floured surface. Divide into 3 and shape into loaves. Transfer to prepared pans. Cover lightly and let stand in warm draft-free area until loaves are doubled.

About 15 minutes before baking, preheat oven to 350°F. Bake bread until well browned and loaves sound hollow when tapped, about 50 minutes. Remove from oven and cool slightly. Turn out onto rack and cool completely.

ALDERBROOK NORWEGIAN RYE BREAD

ALDERBROOK
BRUSH PRAIRIE, WASHINGTON

"Alderbrook—a garden restaurant built over and around Salmon Creek in Washington—serves an authentic Norwegian Rye Bread."
         —*Jean Staelman, Vancouver, Washington*

Makes 2 8-inch round loaves

   2 **envelopes dry yeast**
   2 **cups warm water (105°F to 115°F)**
  4½ **cups all purpose flour (or more)**
   1 **teaspoon sugar**

  1½ **cups rye flour**
   ⅔ **cup firmly packed dark brown sugar**
  3½ **tablespoons dark unsulfured molasses**
   3 **tablespoons (⅜ stick) butter, melted**
   1 **tablespoon finely grated orange peel**
   1 **teaspoon salt**
   1 **teaspoon vinegar**
      Pinch whole anise

      Vegetable shortening

Soften yeast in 1 cup warm water. Combine 1 cup flour and 1 teaspoon sugar in medium bowl. Add yeast mixture, stirring well. Let stand until foamy, about 5 minutes.

Stir in remaining warm water. Transfer mixture to large bowl. Add 3½ cups all purpose flour and remaining ingredients except shortening, stirring until thoroughly combined. Turn out onto well-floured surface and knead until dough is smooth and satiny, adding additional all purpose flour as necessary, about 25 to 30 minutes.

Lightly grease large bowl with shortening. Add dough, turning to coat all surfaces. Cover with towel and let rise in warm draft-free area until doubled, about 1 hour.

Turn dough out onto well-floured surface and knead until no longer sticky, about 10 minutes. Return to same bowl, coating top lightly with shortening. Cover and let rise until doubled, about 30 minutes.

Divide dough in ½. Shape each into 8-inch round loaf. Transfer loaves to baking sheet. Cover and let rise in warm area until doubled, about 30 minutes.

Preheat oven to 350°F. Bake loaves until lightly browned, about 25 to 30 minutes.

WILLOW INN WHOLE WHEAT BREAD

WILLOW INN
WAYNESBURG, PENNSYLVANIA

"Located in the southwest corner of Pennsylvania is an authentically restored 1816 brick farmhouse. This lovely place—where you dine by candlelight—is called Willow Inn. The owner-chef Ralph Wilson prepares everything himself—including marvelous Whole Wheat Bread."
—*Gayle Swanson, Morgantown, West Virginia*

Makes 1 9x5-inch loaf

> **Vegetable oil**
>
> **4 cups whole wheat flour**
>
> **2 envelopes dry yeast**
> **⅔ cup warm water (105°F to 115°F)**
> **⅓ cup honey**
>
> **1½ cups warm water (105°F to 115°F)**
> **¼ cup molasses**
> **½ cup wheat germ**
> **1 teaspoon salt**
> **½ cup vegetable oil**
> **Sugar**

Line 9x5-inch loaf pan with heavy-duty foil. Brush lightly with oil and set aside. Preheat oven to 250°F. Spread flour on baking sheet and bake 20 minutes.

Meanwhile, combine yeast and ⅔ cup warm water in small bowl and stir until yeast is dissolved. Add honey, mixing well. Let stand until yeast is foamy, about 5 minutes.

Blend remaining warm water with molasses in another bowl. Mix wheat germ and salt in large bowl. Stir heated flour into wheat germ mixture. Add yeast, molasses and ½ cup oil and mix well. Turn into prepared pan. Sprinkle top with sugar, patting with back of large spoon. Let stand in warm draft-free area until dough rises to top of pan (do not be concerned if it rises slightly above pan). Preheat oven to 375°F. Bake bread until tester inserted in center comes out clean, about 40 minutes. Let cool briefly in pan, then turn out onto wire rack.

TRAPP FAMILY LODGE LIGHT RYE BREAD

TRAPP FAMILY LODGE
STOWE, VERMONT

Makes 3 1-pound loaves

> **Yellow cornmeal**
> **1 envelope active dry yeast**
> **2¼ cups warm water (105°F to 115°F)**
>
> **4 cups bread flour**
> **2 cups dark rye flour**
> **1 tablespoon caraway seeds**
> **1 tablespoon salt**
> **1 tablespoon molasses**
> **1 tablespoon vegetable oil**

Egg Wash
> **1 egg**
> **¼ cup milk**
> **Pinch salt**

Lightly grease baking sheet and sprinkle liberally with cornmeal. Dissolve yeast in water and leave it to proof 10 minutes.

Combine remaining ingredients except Egg Wash in large bowl. Add yeast and mix thoroughly. Transfer dough to generously floured board and knead until no longer sticky, about 8 to 10 minutes. Place dough in greased mixing bowl and turn to coat entire surface. Cover and let rise in warm place until doubled, 45 minutes to 1 hour.

Punch dough down. Form into 3 loaves about 10 inches long and 3 inches across. Let rise on baking sheet 15 to 20 minutes.

Preheat oven to 400°F. Place large shallow pan half filled with water on lower rack. Combine ingredients for Egg Wash and brush on loaves. Bake 20 minutes, then brush again with wash and continue baking until loaves are golden brown and sound hollow when tapped, about 10 minutes.

MONTI'S ROMAN BREAD

MONTI'S LA CASA VIEJA
TEMPE, ARIZONA

Owner Leonard Monti's parents brought this recipe from Italy nearly 60 years ago.

Makes 1 8-inch round loaf

> **1½ cups warm water (105°F to 115°F)**
> **1 tablespoon sugar**
> **1 cake compressed yeast**
>
> **4 cups all purpose flour (or more)**
> **½ cup finely chopped onion**
> **2 teaspoons salt**
> **Oil**
> **1 teaspoon coarse salt**
> **Dried rosemary**

Combine water and sugar in large mixing bowl. Crumble yeast over, then stir well. Let stand until foamy, about 5 minutes.

Stir in 2 cups flour, blending well. Add another 2 cups flour, onion and 2 teaspoons salt. Transfer dough to well-floured board and knead until smooth, about 20 minutes, adding more flour as necessary to prevent sticking. Place dough in well-oiled bowl, turning to coat all surfaces. Cover with towel and let rise in warm draft-free area until doubled, about 1 hour.

Turn dough out onto oiled baking sheet. Shape into round loaf 1 inch thick. Let rise until dough is doubled, about 30 minutes.

Preheat oven to 400°F. Brush top of loaf lightly with oil. Sprinkle with coarse salt and rosemary. Bake until top is very lightly browned, 20 to 25 minutes. Serve bread warm.

POPPY SEED BREAD

THE SLOGAR
CRESTED BUTTE, COLORADO

Makes 2 9x5-inch loaves

    2½ cups sugar
    2½ cups oil
     2 cups evaporated milk
     5 eggs
    ½ cup milk
     5 cups all purpose flour
    4½ teaspoons baking powder
    ¼ teaspoon salt
    ½ cup poppy seeds
    2½ teaspoons vanilla

Preheat oven to 350°F. Generously grease 2 9x5x3-inch loaf pans. Combine first 5 ingredients in large bowl and mix on medium speed of electric mixer until well blended. Sift together flour, baking powder and salt. Blend into egg mixture on low speed. Add seeds and vanilla and beat until smooth. Turn into pans and bake until golden and bread tests done, 60 to 65 minutes.

POPPY SEED SWIRL BREAD

HERITAGE HOUSE
LITTLE RIVER, CALIFORNIA

Makes 2 loaves

     1 yeast cake
    ¼ cup lukewarm water

     1 tablespoon butter
     1 tablespoon shortening
     2 tablespoons sugar
     2 teaspoons salt
     1 cup scalded milk
     1 cup boiling water

     5 to 5½ cups all purpose flour

       Poppy Seed Filling*

       Melted butter
       Poppy seeds (optional)

Dissolve yeast in lukewarm water.

Combine 1 tablespoon butter, shortening, sugar, salt, milk and water in large mixing bowl. Cool to lukewarm. Add dissolved yeast.

Add 3 cups flour and combine thoroughly. Beat at high speed with electric mixer at least 3 minutes.

Dough Hook Method: Put mixture on dough hook and add 1 cup flour. Mix until blended. Add next cup of flour (or more, if needed) and mix until blended. Knead with dough hook until dough comes free from bowl and is no longer sticky. Place on lightly floured board and knead few strokes by hand; dough will be smooth and elastic.

Hand Method: Add 2 cups flour and mix thoroughly. Turn dough onto floured board and knead until dough is smooth and elastic.

Place dough in greased bowl, turn once, cover and let rise until doubled in bulk. Knead again, then let rest 5 minutes. Cut dough in ½. Roll 1 piece of dough on lightly floured board until about 2 inches thick. Spread ½ filling over surface; roll up dough starting on short side. Place in well-greased 9x5-inch bread pan. Roll second piece of dough, fill and roll and place in second bread pan. Let rise until doubled.

Preheat oven to 400°F. Bake 45 to 50 minutes. Brush with melted butter before removing from pans, and, if desired, sprinkle with few poppy seeds. Turn onto racks and cool.

*Poppy Seed Filling

Makes about ½ cup

     4 tablespoons poppy seeds
     2 tablespoons honey
     2 teaspoons sugar
    ⅛ teaspoon salt

     1 teaspoon lemon juice
     1 egg, lightly beaten

In saucepan, combine poppy seeds, honey, sugar and salt. Stir constantly and cook over low heat until hot, about 5 minutes.

Add lemon juice. Add a little hot mixture to beaten egg, continuing to beat egg while adding. Add egg mixture to hot mixture. Place over low heat and cook, stirring constantly, until thick. Cool thoroughly before using.

POPPY SEED BREAD

TERWILLIGER'S TAVERN
MONTGOMERY, OHIO

"Terwilliger's Tavern, a quaint little restaurant built in an 1804 saltbox cottage northeast of Cincinnati, serves a wonderful poppy seed bread that would make a tasty gift."   —Blanch Larva, Cincinnati, Ohio

Makes 2 9x5-inch loaves

     3 eggs
    ⅔ cup oil
    1¼ cups evaporated milk
     1 teaspoon vanilla
    2¼ cups sifted flour
    1½ cups sugar

¾ **cup poppy seeds**
4½ **teaspoons baking powder**

Preheat oven to 350°F. (If using glass loaf pans bake at 325°F.) Grease and flour 2 9x5-inch loaf pans. Lightly beat eggs in large mixing bowl. Add oil, milk and vanilla and beat well. Add dry ingredients and beat until smooth. Turn into pans and bake until toothpick inserted in center of loaves comes out clean. 45 to 50 minutes.

SALLY LUNN

GADSBY'S TAVERN
ALEXANDRIA, VIRGINIA

"On our vacation we lunched at historic Gadsby's Tavern, where George and Martha Washington once dined and danced. Accompanying the meal was a marvelous homemade Sally Lunn bread—served warm with plenty of butter."
—*Jaynene Ewing Mockus, South Euclid, Ohio*

10 to 12 servings

1 **cup milk**
½ **cup solid shortening**
¼ **cup water**
4 **cups flour, sifted**
⅓ **cup sugar**
2 **teaspoons salt**
1 **envelope dry yeast**
3 **eggs**

Generously grease 9- or 10-inch tube pan. Warm milk, shortening and water in small saucepan over low heat to 120°F (shortening does not have to melt). Combine 1⅓ cups flour, sugar, salt and yeast in large mixing bowl. Add warm milk mixture and beat at medium speed 2 minutes, scraping sides of bowl several times. Continuing to beat, gradually add ⅔ cup flour and eggs. When mixed in, beat at high speed 2 minutes. Add remaining flour and blend thoroughly. Cover bowl lightly and let dough rise in warm draft-free area (85°F) until doubled in bulk, about 1¼ hours.

Beat dough down with spatula or use lowest speed on mixer. Turn into baking pan. Cover lightly and let dough rise until increased in bulk by ⅓ to ½, about 30 minutes.

Meanwhile, preheat oven to 350°F. When dough has risen, bake 40 to 50 minutes. Carefully remove bread from pan and let cool slightly. Slice with serrated knife.

DILLY CHEESE BREAD

MISS DAISY'S TEA ROOM
FRANKLIN, TENNESSEE

Makes 1 9x5-inch loaf

3 **cups biscuit mix**
1½ **cups grated sharp cheddar cheese**
1 **tablespoon sugar**
1¼ **cups milk**
1 **egg, lightly beaten**
1 **tablespoon vegetable oil**
½ **teaspoon dill**
½ **teaspoon dry mustard**

Preheat oven to 350°F. Generously grease 9x5-inch loaf pan or 6-cup bundt pan. Combine biscuit mix, cheese and sugar in large bowl. Combine remaining ingredients in second bowl and mix well. Stir into dry mixture, blending thoroughly, then beat slightly to remove lumps. Turn into pan and bake until golden, 45 to 50 minutes.

GARLIC BREAD

KAVANAUGH'S SYLVAN LODGE
LAKE SYLVAN, MINNESOTA

"Kavanaugh's Sylvan Lodge is a small seasonal (just for the summer months) restaurant located in the beautiful resort area of Lake Sylvan. As soon as you are seated, they bring a basket of garlic bread. We always eat every bit and then get a second basket because it is so good."
—*Dorothy O. Cummings, Kearney, Nebraska*

Makes 1 9x5-inch loaf

1 **1-pound loaf frozen bread dough**

¼ **cup (½ stick) unsalted butter**
1 **tablespoon finely chopped fresh parsley**
1 **tablespoon beaten egg**
1 **teaspoon garlic salt**

Thaw bread just until it can be sliced, about 20 minutes. Cut into 15 pieces.

Melt butter in small saucepan over low heat. Remove from heat. Stir in parsley, egg and salt. Roll bread pieces into balls. Dip each into butter mixture, coating completely. Arrange in single layer in buttered 9x5-inch loaf pan. Let rise in warm draft-free area until doubled, about 2½ hours.

Preheat oven to 350°F. Bake until top is golden brown, about 25 minutes. Let cool slightly in pan before serving.

ELISE BOWEN'S LEMON BREAD

THE WILLIAMSVILLE INN
WEST STOCKBRIDGE, MASSACHUSETTS

"My husband and I have just returned from a delightful trip to the Berkshires, which included a stop at The Williamsville Inn. They serve a wonderful lemon bread." —Mrs. Leonard Sapoff, New York, New York

Makes 1 9x5-inch loaf

     1 **cup sugar**
    ½ **cup milk**
     6 **tablespoons (¾ stick) unsalted butter, room temperature**
     2 **eggs**
  1½ **cups all purpose flour**
     1 **teaspoon baking powder**
    ⅛ **teaspoon salt**
        Finely grated zest of 1 lemon (about 1 tablespoon)
        Lemon Glaze*

Preheat oven to 350°F. Grease and flour 9x5-inch loaf pan. Combine first 4 ingredients in medium bowl and mix well. Blend in dry ingredients and lemon zest. Turn into pan and bake 1 hour. Let cool slightly. Remove from pan and set on piece of foil. Pour hot Lemon Glaze slowly over surface. Let bread cool completely before slicing.

***Lemon Glaze**

    ½ **cup sugar**
    ¼ **cup fresh lemon juice**

Combine ingredients in small saucepan. Place over low heat; stir until sugar dissolves and glaze is hot.

OATMEAL RAISIN BREAD

RAGS N' ROSES
PROVINCETOWN, MASSACHUSETTS

Makes 1 9x5-inch loaf

     2 **cups whole wheat flour**
     2 **cups rolled oats**
     2 **cups buttermilk**
  1½ **cups raisins**
     1 **cup firmly packed light brown sugar**
     3 **eggs**
     2 **tablespoons baking soda**
     2 **tablespoons baking powder**

Preheat oven to 350°F. Generously grease 9x5-inch loaf pan. Combine ingredients thoroughly. Spoon into pan, filling just to ¾ full to allow for rising during baking. Bake until toothpick inserted in center of loaf comes out clean, about 1 hour. Remove from pan and place on wire rack to cool.

DEJA-VU NUT BREAD

DEJA-VU
PHILADELPHIA, PENNSYLVANIA

Makes 4 baguettes

  4¼ **cups warm water (105°F to 115°F)**
     3 **tablespoons dry yeast**
   11 **to 12 cups unbleached all purpose flour**

     5 **tablespoons (⅝ stick) butter**
     5 **tablespoons unrefined honey**

  1½ **cups whole wheat flour**
  1½ **cups wheat germ**
  1½ **tablespoons salt**
     1 **cup finely chopped walnuts**

     1 **egg white, lightly beaten**

Combine ¼ cup warm water and yeast in large bowl and stir until yeast is dissolved. Let stand until foamy and proofed, about 15 minutes. Stir in remaining warm water and 4 cups all purpose flour. Let stand in warm draft-free area until bubbly, about 10 to 15 minutes.

Meanwhile, melt butter with honey in medium saucepan over medium-high heat. Whisk until mixture swells and lightens. Set aside to cool.

Transfer yeast mixture to large bowl of electric mixer fitted with dough hook. Add honey mixture, 7 cups all purpose flour, whole wheat flour, wheat germ and salt and beat at medium speed until dough is smooth and elastic, about 10 minutes (or knead by hand 20 to 25 minutes), adding remaining 1 cup all purpose flour if necessary. Stir in walnuts. Cover and let rise in warm draft-free area until doubled, about 45 minutes.

Generously grease 4 18-inch baguette pans. Divide dough into 4 equal portions. Flatten 1 piece into rectangle. Fold long edge over ⅓. Fold over remaining long edge to form narrow rectangle. Pinch edges together to seal. Roll into 18-inch cylinder using rocking motion. Repeat with remaining pieces. Transfer to prepared pans seam side down. Let rise in warm draft-free area until doubled in volume, about 50 to 60 minutes.

Position rack in center of oven and preheat to 350°F. Set shallow pan of boiling water on lower rack. Bake loaves on center rack 50 minutes. Brush lightly with egg white. Continue baking until baguettes are brown and sound hollow when tapped on bottom, about 10 minutes. Remove loaves from pans and let cool on wire rack.

LIVERY STABLE STRAWBERRY BREAD

THE LIVERY STABLE
BOZEMAN, MONTANA

Makes 2 9x5-inch loaves

    2 cups frozen unsweetened whole
       strawberries
       Sugar

    3 cups plus 2 tablespoons all purpose flour
    2 cups sugar
    1 tablespoon cinnamon
    1 teaspoon salt
    1 teaspoon baking soda
 1¼ cups oil
    4 eggs, beaten
 1¼ cups chopped pecans

Place strawberries in medium bowl. Sprinkle lightly with sugar to taste. Let strawberries stand until thawed, then slice.

Preheat oven to 350°F. Butter and flour two 9x5-inch loaf pans. Combine flour, sugar, cinnamon, salt and baking soda in large bowl and mix well. Blend oil and eggs into strawberries. Add to flour mixture. Stir in pecans, blending until dry ingredients are just moistened. Divide batter between pans. Bake loaves until tester inserted in centers comes out clean, about 45 to 50 minutes. Let cool in pans on rack for 10 minutes. Turn loaves out and cool completely.

ZUCCHINI NUT BREAD

LA QUICHE
HOUSTON, TEXAS

Makes 2 8½-inch or 3 6-inch loaves

    5 eggs
    1 cup oil
    1 tablespoon fresh lemon juice
    2 teaspoons vanilla

    3 cups flour
 1½ cups sugar
    2 tablespoons cinnamon
    2 teaspoons baking powder
    2 teaspoons baking soda
    1 teaspoon salt
    ¾ pound zucchini, grated (about 2⅓ cups)
    ½ cup chopped walnuts
    ¼ cup dark raisins

Egg Wash

    1 egg
    ¼ cup milk

Preheat oven to 350°F. Grease and flour 2 8½-inch or 3 6-inch loaf pans.

In large mixing bowl, beat eggs, oil, lemon juice and vanilla until yellow and foamy.

In separate bowl, sift together flour, sugar, cinnamon, baking powder, soda and salt. Mix in zucchini, nuts and raisins. Gradually add to egg mixture, beating until smooth. Divide batter evenly between pans and bake until loaves begin to pull away from sides of pans, about 60 minutes.

Mix Egg Wash ingredients and brush over tops of loaves. Return to oven until toothpick inserted into center of loaf comes out clean, about 5 minutes.

CAPTAIN BUDDY'S PEPPERY HUSH PUPPIES

BUDDY'S SEAFOOD RESTAURANT
CHARLESTON, SOUTH CAROLINA

Use floury stone-ground cornmeal to keep the Hush Puppies light and hold them together as they fry. An electric wok works well for this recipe. Beer gives these puffs a light texture.

Makes about 6 dozen

    4 cups sifted stone-ground yellow
       cornmeal
    2 cups sifted self-rising cake flour
    1 tablespoon baking powder
 1¼ teaspoons salt
    ½ teaspoon baking soda
    2 to 2½ cups beer or milk
    1 medium onion, finely minced
    1 egg
    ¼ cup minced fresh parsley or parsley flakes
 1½ teaspoons freshly ground pepper

    3 quarts peanut oil

Sift cornmeal, flour, baking powder, salt and soda into large bowl. Make well in center. Add 2 cups beer or milk, onion, egg, parsley and pepper. Stir quickly until just combined; do not overmix. Add remaining ½ cup beer if batter is too thick; it should be consistency of porridge.

Preheat oven to 250°F. Heat oil in electric skillet, deep fat fryer or large saucepan to 365°F. Drop batter by rounded teaspoon into hot oil and fry, turning once, until richly browned, about 2 minutes per side. Drain on paper towels. Transfer to serving platter and keep warm in oven. Repeat with remaining batter. Serve hot.

CORN STICKS

THE COACH HOUSE
NEW YORK, NEW YORK

Makes about 20 5-inch corn sticks

> 4 cups cornmeal
> 3 cups all purpose flour
> 5 tablespoons sugar
> 2 tablespoons baking powder
> 1¼ teaspoons salt
> 4 eggs
> 3 cups milk
> 1 cup vegetable shortening, heated but not fully melted

Combine dry ingredients in large bowl. Add eggs 1 at a time, mixing well after each is added. Thoroughly blend in milk. Add shortening and mix well. Cover and refrigerate 1 hour.

Preheat oven to 500°F. Grease small corn stick molds (individual sections should measure 5x1½ inches) and set in oven until molds are very hot.

Using pastry bag without tip, quickly pipe batter into hot molds. Bake until tops are golden brown, about 10 minutes. Serve immediately.

NAAN BREAD

THE THIRD FLOOR RESTAURANT
HAWAIIAN REGENT HOTEL
HONOLULU, HAWAII

"Last year I had the pleasure of dining at The Third Floor Restaurant. Our pâté was served with a very unusual crackerlike bread made from yogurt and flour—I believe it was called Naan."
—Becky Bedell, Huntington Beach, California

Makes about 30 6-inch rounds

> 4 cups all purpose flour
> 1 tablespoon sugar
> 1 tablespoon baking powder
> 1½ teaspoons salt
> ¾ teaspoon baking soda
> ¾ cup milk
> ¼ cup plain yogurt
> 2 eggs
> 2 tablespoons oil

Combine dry ingredients in large bowl and blend thoroughly. Make well in center and add remaining ingredients. Mix until dough is somewhat sticky; add warm water if necessary. Turn onto floured board and knead until dough is elastic. Pinch off pieces about size of golf balls and place on large buttered pan. Cover with damp cloth and let rest 1 hour. (Dough may be refrigerated at this point for baking later.)

When ready to bake, preheat oven to 450°F. Pat balls into thin circles about 6 inches in diameter. Place on baking sheet and bake until bread puffs and is lightly browned, 2½ to 4 minutes. Serve hot.

OATCAKES

INVERARY INN
BADDECK, NOVA SCOTIA, CANADA

Oatcakes are best if baked a day before serving. Store in an airtight container.

Makes 4 to 5 dozen 3-inch squares

> 6 cups rolled oats
> 3 cups unsifted all purpose flour
> 1 cup sugar
> 1 teaspoon salt
> ½ teaspoon baking soda
> 2 cups vegetable shortening
> 5 tablespoons cold water
>
> **Whole wheat or graham flour**

Mix oats, all purpose flour, sugar, salt and soda together until evenly blended. Cut in shortening until mixture resembles coarse meal. Add cold water 1 tablespoon at a time, blending after each addition, until mixture easily forms ball.

Preheat oven to 375°F. Flour board with whole wheat or graham flour and form dough into 2 balls. Roll each into rectangle approximately ¼ inch thick. Cut into 3-inch squares and bake until slightly browned on top, about 15 to 20 minutes.

PANE PETITTO®
(Fried Bread)

PETITTO'S
WASHINGTON, D.C.

6 servings

> 1 envelope active dry yeast
> ½ cup warm milk (105°F to 115°F)
> 1½ cups warm water (105°F to 115°F)
> 3 tablespoons (⅜ stick) melted butter
>
> 3 teaspoons salt
> 6¼ cups sifted all purpose flour
>
> ½ cup all purpose flour
>
> **Oil**

Dissolve yeast in milk in small bowl and let stand until bubbly, about 10 minutes. Transfer to large mixing bowl. Gradually add water, butter and 2 teaspoons salt. Blend in sifted flour using electric mixer fitted with dough hook. Continue mixing and kneading until dough is smooth and elastic. (If mixing by hand, turn dough out onto lightly floured board and knead until smooth, 10 to 15 minutes.)

Divide dough into 6 equal pieces. Spread ½ cup flour mixed with remaining salt on board. Flatten each piece into 8-inch circle using heal of hand. Cover top and bottom of circles with waxed paper. Let stand in warm draft-free area until circles have tripled in volume.

Pour oil to depth of ½ inch into 10-inch skillet and heat to about 375°F. Fry circles 1 at a time until they just begin to brown. Turn and brown on other side. Remove from pan, drain off excess oil, wrap in heavy cloth napkin and serve immediately.

CHEESE BISCUITS

THE CAFE, LORD & TAYLOR'S
NORTHBROOK, ILLINOIS

Makes about 12 2-inch biscuits

  2   cups all purpose flour
  1   tablespoon plus 1 teaspoon baking
      powder
  1   teaspoon salt
  2   tablespoons vegetable shortening
  ¾   cup milk
  ¾   cup shredded sharp cheddar cheese

Preheat oven to 400°F. Sift dry ingredients into medium bowl. Cut in shortening using pastry blender or 2 knives. Add milk and toss mixture with fork just until moistened. Stir in cheese. Gently gather dough into ball. Transfer to lightly floured board and knead gently 5 to 8 times. Flatten dough into circle, then roll out to thickness of ½ inch. Cut into rounds using 2-inch biscuit cutter. Arrange rounds on baking sheet. Bake until biscuits are lightly browned, about 8 to 10 minutes.

SKYLINE'S APPLE MUFFINS

SKYLINE RESTAURANT
ORLANDO, FLORIDA

Makes 15 muffins

  ⅓   cup sugar
  1   tablespoon butter, room temperature
  1½ cups firmly packed brown sugar
  ⅔   cup vegetable oil
  1   egg
  1   cup buttermilk
  1   teaspoon baking soda
  1   teaspoon salt
  1   teaspoon vanilla
  2½ cups sifted all purpose flour
  1½ cups peeled apple, cut into ¼-inch dice
  ½   cup toasted chopped pecans

Preheat oven to 325°F. Grease and flour muffin pans. Combine sugar and butter in small bowl and mix until crumbly. Combine brown sugar, oil and egg in large bowl. In another bowl, combine buttermilk, soda, salt and vanilla. Blend flour into brown sugar mixture alternately with buttermilk mixture, stirring just until ingredients are combined; do not overmix. Fold in apple and pecans. Divide batter among muffin pans and sprinkle with sugar-butter mixture. Bake until toothpick inserted in center comes out clean, about 30 minutes.

NASHVILLE HOUSE FRIED BISCUITS

RAMADA INN
NASHVILLE, INDIANA

Makes about 4 dozen

  3½ teaspoons active dry yeast
  2   cups warm milk (105°F to 115°F)
  ¼   cup shortening
  3½ to 4½ cups flour
  2   tablespoons sugar
  2   to 3 teaspoons salt

      Oil for deep fat frying

Dissolve yeast in milk and let stand until foamy, about 10 minutes. Stir in shortening. Gradually add flour, sugar and salt and mix until smooth. Cover with damp towel and let stand in warm draft-free place until doubled, about 2 hours.

On lightly floured board roll dough into rectangle ¼ inch thick. Heat oil to 375°F. Cut dough with biscuit cutter and drop few at a time into oil. When biscuit is puffed and browned, turn to brown other side. Remove with slotted spoon, drain on paper towels and serve immediately.

Biscuits can be made ahead and reheated at 200°F for 5 to 10 minutes.

SCOTTISH SCONES

THE ABERFOYLE MILL
ABERFOYLE, ONTARIO, CANADA

This scone resembles a baking powder biscuit in flavor and texture.

Makes about 16 to 20 scones

  5¼ cups flour
  3   tablespoons baking powder
      Pinch salt
  ½   cup shortening
  5   tablespoons sugar
  1½ cups buttermilk

      Butter

Sift flour, baking powder and salt into large bowl. Rub shortening in with hands until mixture develops sandy texture. Make well in center; add sugar and buttermilk. Gradually stir flour mixture into center and mix lightly.

Roll out dough 1 inch thick on lightly floured surface. Cut scones with 2-inch round cutter. Place on ungreased cookie sheet and let stand 15 minutes. Preheat oven to 450°F.

Place second baking sheet of same size under first to prevent bottoms of scones from burning. Bake in top of oven until tops are golden brown, about 10 to 15 minutes. Let cool slightly. Serve warm with butter.

May be refrigerated and rewarmed before serving.

APPLE MUFFINS

THE HICKORY GROVE INN
COOPERSTOWN, NEW YORK

Makes 24 muffins

3½ cups all purpose flour
3 cups finely chopped peeled apples
2 cups sugar
1 teaspoon salt
1 teaspoon baking soda
1 teaspoon cinnamon
1½ cups vegetable oil
½ cup toasted chopped nuts
1 teaspoon vanilla

Preheat oven to 350°F. Grease and flour muffin pans. Thoroughly combine flour, apples, sugar, salt, soda and cinnamon in large bowl. Stir in oil, nuts and vanilla. (Batter will be stiff but might vary with type of apple used.) Divide batter among muffin pans, filling about ½ to ⅔ full. Bake until toothpick inserted in center comes out clean, about 30 minutes.

JULIUS STURGIS PRETZELS

STURGIS PRETZEL HOUSE
LITITZ, PENNSYLVANIA

Makes about 24 pretzels

Coarse salt
1 package dry yeast
1⅓ cups plus 2 tablespoons warm water
(105°F to 115°F)
⅓ cup firmly packed brown sugar
5 cups all purpose flour

Baking soda
Mustard (optional garnish)

Grease 2 baking sheets and sprinkle with coarse salt. Combine yeast and 2 tablespoons water in large mixing bowl and stir until yeast is dissolved. Add remaining warm water and brown sugar and mix well. Gradually add flour, stirring constantly until dough is smooth and no longer sticks to bowl.

Turn dough out onto lightly floured surface. Flour hands lightly. Knead dough until smooth and elastic. Divide dough in ½; cover ½ with plastic wrap while shaping remainder. Pinch off golf ball-size piece of dough and roll into cylinder about 14 inches long. Twist cylinder into pretzel shape and set aside. Repeat with all remaining dough.

Preheat oven to 475°F. Fill large skillet with water, adding 1 tablespoon baking soda for each cup of water. Bring to gentle boil over medium-low heat. Lower pretzel into skillet using spatula. Cook 30 seconds. Transfer to prepared baking sheet using slotted spoon. Repeat with remaining pretzels. Sprinkle generously with coarse salt. Bake until golden, about 8 minutes. Let cool slightly on rack. Serve warm with mustard for dipping if desired.

To reheat pretzels, cover loosely with foil and warm in 350°F oven 10 minutes.

THE BUTTERY CROISSANTS

THE BUTTERY
SANTA MONICA, CALIFORNIA

Richard E. Mynatt of The Buttery suggests that when making croissants at home you should make more than you need and freeze the remainder. It takes almost as much time for one dozen as two or three.

Makes about 3 dozen

3 envelopes dry yeast
7 tablespoons sugar
3 cups warm milk (105°F to 115°F)

2 pounds (about 8 cups) unbleached bread flour
1 cup plus 2 tablespoons pastry flour
1 tablespoon salt

2 cups (4 sticks) unsalted butter, room temperature

1 egg
1 tablespoon water

Combine yeast, sugar and milk and let stand until foamy, about 10 minutes.

Measure flours and salt into large bowl of electric mixer. Add yeast and beat at low speed just until ingredients are combined and dough is smooth and slightly sticky. Turn onto lightly floured baking sheet, cover with plastic wrap and chill 1 hour.

Dust work surface and dough with flour. Roll out dough into 36x12-inch rectangle, making sure corners are square. Brush off excess flour. Leaving 1-inch margin, spread ⅔ dough (24x12-inch portion) with butter. Fold unbuttered part over ½ buttered part, then fold over remaining buttered dough. (There will be 2 layers of butter and three layers of dough.) Press ends with rolling pin to seal. Place on lightly floured baking sheet, cover and return to refrigerator to rest 20 to 30 minutes.

Roll out dough again into 36x12-inch rectangle. Fold in thirds, cover and return to refrigerator to rest another 20 to 30 minutes. Repeat rolling, folding and resting 2 more times. After last folding, allow dough to rest in refrigerator 2 to 3 hours.

To shape croissants, remove dough from refrigerator and cut in ½ lengthwise; return ½ dough to refrigerator. Roll remaining dough on well-floured work surface until 10 inches wide and ¼ inch thick. Cut in ½ to make 2 pieces 5 inches wide.

Mark strips into 5-inch triangles. Cut precisely using pastry cutter or pizza wheel. Separate triangles and place on floured tray. Chill. Repeat procedure with remaining dough.

Line baking sheet with aluminum foil. Remove 3 or 4 triangles at a time from refrigerator and roll from broad base toward point, stretching as you roll and ending with point on top. Place dough on baking sheet and bend ends inward to form crescent shape. Repeat until baking sheet is filled. Lightly beat egg and water and brush over tops.

Let rise uncovered in warm place (area should not be so warm that butter runs out) until dough is doubled. (At this point croissants may be frozen. Allow to thaw 1½ to 2 hours before baking.)

Preheat oven to 450°F. Brush tops again with egg wash. Bake 1 sheet at a time until croissants are golden, about 10 minutes.

MRS. B.'s MOUNTAIN BRAN MUFFINS

TEA HOUSE IN THE CLOUDS
BANFF, ALBERTA, CANADA

"I have discovered the best bran muffins 7,500 feet above sea level in the Canadian Rockies!"
—Lupe Sterten, Manhattan Beach, California

Makes 18 muffins

    ½ cup firmly packed brown sugar
    ¼ cup shortening
    ¼ cup molasses
    2 eggs
    1 cup milk
    1½ cups bran
    1 cup all purpose flour
    1½ teaspoons baking soda
    ¾ teaspoon salt
    ½ cup raisins (optional)

Preheat oven to 400°F. Prepare muffin tins with paper liners. In medium bowl, cream sugar and shortening on low speed of electric mixer. Add molasses and eggs and beat well. Mix in milk, then bran. Sift together flour, baking soda and salt and stir in just until thoroughly blended. Fold in raisins if desired. Divide batter among muffin tins and bake for 15 minutes.

SWEET POTATO MUFFINS

CHRISTIANA CAMPBELL'S TAVERN
WILLIAMSBURG, VIRGINIA

Makes 24 muffins

    1¼ cups plus 2 tablespoons sugar
    1¼ cups mashed cooked sweet potatoes or yams (fresh or canned)
    ½ cup (1 stick) butter, room temperature
    2 large eggs, room temperature

    1½ cups flour
    2 teaspoons baking powder
    1 teaspoon cinnamon
    ¼ teaspoon nutmeg
    ¼ teaspoon salt
    1 cup milk

    ½ cup chopped raisins
    ¼ cup chopped walnuts or pecans
    ¼ teaspoon cinnamon

Thoroughly grease 24 muffin cups or prepare with paper liners. Preheat oven to 400°F.

Beat 1¼ cups sugar, sweet potatoes and butter until smooth. Add eggs and blend well.

Sift together flour, baking powder, spices and salt. Add alternately with milk to sweet potato mixture, stirring just to blend; do not overmix.

Fold in raisins and nuts. Spoon into muffin cups. Mix remaining sugar with cinnamon and sprinkle over muffins. Bake until muffins test done, about 25 to 30 minutes. Serve warm.

Muffins may be frozen and reheated.

SOUR CREAM COFFEE CAKE WITH PECAN TOPPING

RAMADA INN
SCOTTSBURG, INDIANA

8 to 12 servings

        Butter
    8 pecan halves

    1 cup (2 sticks) butter
    2 cups sugar
    2 eggs
    2 cups sifted cake flour
    1 teaspoon baking powder
    ⅛ teaspoon salt
    1 cup sour cream
    ½ teaspoon vanilla

Topping

    ½ cup chopped pecans
    2 tablespoons sugar
    1 teaspoon cinnamon

Generously coat 12-cup bundt pan with butter, placing little extra butter in each notch of pan. Press pecan half into each notch. Preheat oven to 350°F.

Cream 1 cup butter and sugar in large mixing bowl. Beat in eggs. Sift together flour, baking powder and salt. Add gradually to creamed mixture, blending well. Carefully fold in sour cream and vanilla.

For topping: Mix chopped pecans with sugar and cinnamon. Sprinkle 2 tablespoons in bottom of bundt pan. Cover with ⅓ cake batter, then alternate 2 tablespoons topping, batter, topping, batter, ending with topping. Bake until toothpick inserted in thickest part of cake comes out clean, about 55 to 60 minutes. Cool 10 minutes in pan, then turn out onto serving plate.

Note: Cake will have a dark outer crust.

CARROT MUFFINS

LOCK 24
ELKTON, OHIO

"Our family has been dining at Lock 24 for months. It's a 45-minute drive from our home, but their carrot muffins are well worth it."

—Arlene McMurray, Mineral Ridge, Ohio

Makes 2½ dozen muffins

    2 cups sugar
    1¼ cups oil
    4 eggs, lightly beaten
    3 cups all purpose flour
    2 teaspoons baking powder
    1 teaspoon baking soda
    ½ teaspoon salt
    2 cups grated carrots
    ½ cup chopped nuts
    ½ cup raisins (optional)

Preheat oven to 350°F. Grease muffin tin or prepare with paper liners. Beat sugar and oil in medium bowl. Blend in eggs. Sift flour, baking powder, baking soda and salt into another bowl. Gradually stir dry ingredients into oil mixture, blending well. Fold in carrot, nuts and raisins if desired. Spoon batter into tin, filling each cup ⅔ full. Bake until tester inserted in centers of muffins comes out clean, about 35 to 40 minutes. Serve warm.

BUTTERMILK COFFEE CAKE

THE GREEN HERON INN
KENNEBUNKPORT, MAINE

8 to 12 servings

    2½ cups all purpose flour
    1 cup sugar
    ¾ cup firmly packed brown sugar
    ¾ cup salad oil
    1 teaspoon nutmeg
    ¼ teaspoon salt
    ½ cup chopped walnuts
    ½ teaspoon cinnamon

    1 cup buttermilk
    2 eggs, lightly beaten
    1 teaspoon baking powder
    1 teaspoon baking soda

Preheat oven to 350°F. Grease 9x13-inch baking pan. Combine first 6 ingredients in large mixing bowl and blend well. Remove ½ cup of mixture and toss with walnuts and cinnamon in small bowl. Set aside to be used as topping.

To original mixing bowl, add buttermilk, eggs, baking powder and baking soda and blend thoroughly on medium speed of electric mixer. Pour into baking pan and sprinkle topping evenly over batter. Bake until cake tests done, about 30 minutes. Cool slightly on rack. Serve warm.

SOUR CREAM COFFEE CAKE

THE STOCKPOT
STOCKBRIDGE, MASSACHUSETTS

"The Stockpot, a delightful New England inn, serves, among other goodies, a sour cream coffee cake that is studded with nuts."

—Sylvia Rosenthal, New York, New York

10 servings

    3 cups all purpose flour
    1½ teaspoons baking powder
    1½ teaspoons baking soda
    ¼ teaspoon salt
    1½ cups (3 sticks) butter, room temperature
    1½ cups sugar
    3 eggs
    1½ cups sour cream
    2½ tablespoons vanilla

    ¾ cup firmly packed brown sugar
    ¾ cup chopped walnuts
    1½ teaspoons cinnamon
    2 tablespoons water
       Powdered sugar (garnish)

Preheat oven to 325°F. Butter 10-inch tube pan. Sift together first 4 ingredients; set aside. Combine butter and sugar in large bowl and beat until fluffy. Add eggs 1 at a time, beating well after each addition. Blend in sour cream and ½ tablespoon vanilla. Gradually add sifted dry ingredients and beat well.

Combine brown sugar, walnuts and cinnamon in small bowl. Turn ⅓ batter into prepared pan and sprinkle with ½ nut mixture. Repeat. Add remaining batter. Mix remaining vanilla with water and spoon over top. Bake 60 to 70 minutes. Cool 10 minutes before removing from pan (texture will be moist). Dust generously with powdered sugar.

BARBARA'S CINNAMON ROLLS

THE HOUSE OF EMBERS
LAKE DELTON, WISCONSIN

Makes 48 rolls

    ½ cup lukewarm water (105°F to 115°F)
    2 envelopes dry yeast
    1¾ cups plus 1 teaspoon sugar

    1½ cups milk
    6 tablespoons (¾ stick) butter
    2 teaspoons salt
    5½ to 6 cups all purpose flour
    2 eggs, beaten

    ½ to ¾ cup (1 to 1½ sticks) butter, melted
    1½ teaspoons cinnamon

Butter muffin tins; set aside. Mix together water, yeast and 1 teaspoon sugar in small bowl and let proof until foamy, about 10 minutes.

Combine milk, 6 tablespoons butter and salt in small saucepan. Place over medium heat and bring to boil, stirring occasionally. Pour into large mixing bowl. Add ¼ cup sugar and 4 cups flour 1 cup at a time, mixing thoroughly after each cup of flour is added. Add eggs and mix with dough hook on low speed 3 to 4 minutes. When dough has cooled to lukewarm, add yeast and remaining flour. Mix on medium speed 4 to 5 minutes, scraping sides of bowl several times.

Divide dough in ½ and roll into rectangular sheets ¼ inch thick. Brush surfaces with melted butter. Combine remaining sugar and cinnamon and sprinkle evenly over dough. Roll up each sheet tightly and lay seam side down. Slice into ½-inch rounds and place in muffin tins. Cover lightly and let rise in warm draft-free area until doubled in bulk.

Preheat oven to 400°F. Bake rolls until light golden brown, about 10 to 12 minutes.

FINISHING TOUCHES

There is an old story about Diamond Jim Brady, the famous *bon viveur* of the Gay Nineties. It seems that Brady arrived one evening at his favorite restaurant, Delmonico's, and proceeded to order—and consume—four dozen oysters, several squab, a whole turbot, and most of a leg of lamb with sundry vegetables. While he was taking a breather, a suitably impressed waiter trotted up to his table with an elegant tray of cheeses. Brady waved him away. "You tempt me," said Diamond Jim. "But I really must save a little room for dessert."

Saving room for dessert is a favorite pastime. The last course is always the most popular; it is the luxurious finish to any good meal, and it always carries with it a feeling of celebration. Like the flourish at the end of a symphony, dessert isn't strictly necessary—but everyone would miss it if it weren't there.

Dessert can be spectacular: The huge architectural marvels that Careme delighted kings with 150 years ago might seem a bit ostentatious today, but the ingenious creations of modern pastry chefs and *chocolatiers* still delight both the eye and the palate. Or it can be simple: It is hard to turn down the pies, puddings and cookies that are the heritage of generations of English and American home bakers. It can be large, like the fifty-foot-high layer cake that was served to the citizens of Philadelphia during the Bicentennial festivities. Or it can be small, like a perfect *petit four* or a tiny chocolate truffle.

The selection of restaurant specialties presented here includes almost every kind of dessert—tarts, souffles, mousses, *beignets*, strudels, puddings, myriad cakes and pies—but they all have one thing in common. They disappear in a hurry. . . .

Truffles (see page 223) and an edible chocolate serving container from the White House in Washington, D.C.

BEIGNETS DE POMMES

RESTAURANT BOCUSE
LYONS, FRANCE

4 servings

  1 **cup pastry flour**
  ¼ **teaspoon salt**
  3¼ **teaspoons sugar**
  7 **ounces beer**
  1 **egg**
  2 **tablespoons (¼ stick) butter,**
     room temperature

     Oil for deep frying
     Sugar
  3 **tablespoons Calvados**
  3 **Golden Delicious apples, peeled, cored,**
     seeded and cut into ½-inch rings

  1 **egg white**
     Powdered sugar

Combine flour, salt and ¼ teaspoon sugar in medium bowl. Mix in beer, blending well. Beat in egg. Blend in butter. Strain mixture into another bowl. Let batter stand at room temperature for about 2 hours.

Pour oil into large skillet or deep fat fryer to depth of 3 to 4 inches and heat to 375°F. Dust baking sheet with sugar, then drizzle with Calvados. Roll apple slices in sugar mixture, coating well.

Preheat broiler. Beat egg white in small bowl until foamy. Add remaining sugar and beat until stiff. Fold into batter (it will be thin). Dip apple slices into batter, shaking off excess. Add apples to hot oil in batches and fry on both sides until golden. Drain on paper towels. Dust with powdered sugar. Transfer to baking sheet. Caramelize beignets lightly under broiler and serve.

COLONY BAKED APPLES

COLONY STEAK HOUSE, HYATT REGENCY WAIKIKI
HONOLULU, HAWAII

6 servings

  4 **cups water**
  2 **tablespoons lemon juice**

  6 **large Washington or McIntosh apples**

  ½ **cup chopped macadamia nuts**
  ½ **cup seedless raisins**
  2½ **cups brown sugar**
  2 **cups apple juice**

  1 **cup (2 sticks) lightly salted butter,**
     softened
  ¼ **teaspoon cinnamon**

Combine water and lemon juice. Set aside.

Peel ¼ inch of skin from tops of apples. Remove core and seeds, being careful to leave bottoms intact. As each apple is peeled, dip in lemon and water.

Preheat oven to 350°F. Combine nuts, raisins and ½ cup brown sugar. Stuff into centers of apples. Place in deep baking dish. Add apple juice. Cover and bake until apples are soft, not mushy, about 50 to 60 minutes.

While apples are baking, whip butter with remaining brown sugar and cinnamon. Place in double boiler and cook over low heat about 20 minutes. Keep warm. When apples are done pour sauce over top. Cover and cook 5 more minutes. Serve warm or cold, as desired.

GERMAN-STYLE APPLE PANCAKE

FAR HORIZONS
LONGBOAT KEY, FLORIDA

"Each year when we come to Longboat Key, we enjoy eating at the Far Horizons restaurant. Their dessert menu includes an apple pancake that they serve with side dishes of syrup, cinnamon sugar and lingonberries."
—Suzanne S. Mahler, Dexter Village, Michigan

Chef Harold Wuelfrath, who created this recipe, urges those who feel adventuresome to substitute bananas for apples.

Makes 2 10-inch pancakes

Cinnamon sugar

  ½ **cup sugar**
  1 **tablespoon cinnamon**

  1 **cup all purpose flour**
  ½ **cup cold water**
  ¼ **cup vegetable oil**
  3 **tablespoons sugar**
  1 **teaspoon vanilla extract**
  ½ **teaspoon lemon extract**
  6 **eggs, room temperature**

  2 **apples**
  3 **tablespoons (⅜ stick) butter**
  2 **tablespoons (¼ stick) butter, melted**
     Syrup and lingonberries (optional)

For cinnamon sugar: Mix ½ cup sugar and cinnamon; set aside.

Combine flour, water, oil, remaining sugar and extracts in large bowl and blend well. Add 3 eggs and beat until smooth. Stir in remaining eggs and blend gently just until well combined.

Preheat oven to 400°F. Peel and core apples and cut into ¼-inch slices. Melt 1½ tablespoons butter in 10- to 11-inch skillet or omelet pan over medium-high heat. Add ½ fruit and sauté, turning once, until golden brown. Pour ½ batter over fruit and cook until set, about 2 minutes. Slide pancake onto large plate. Invert skillet over pancake and flip plate to return pancake to skillet. Continue cooking until underside is set, about 2 minutes. Slide pancake onto heatproof platter. Sprinkle with 1 tablespoon cinnamon sugar and drizzle with 1 tablespoon melted butter. Set aside. Prepare second pancake with remaining butter, fruit and batter. Bake pancakes 5 minutes. Serve immediately with remaining cinnamon sugar and side dishes of syrup and berries.

CANTON APRICOTS

NEW CANTON
WEST READING, PENNSYLVANIA

4 to 6 servings

   4 **cups water**
   ¾ **cup sugar**
   1 **pound whole fresh apricots**
   1 **teaspoon cinnamon**

Sauce

   2 **cups milk**
   1 **cup sugar**
   1 **teaspoon almond extract**

Combine water and sugar in medium saucepan and bring to boil over high heat. Reduce heat, add apricots, cover and simmer until slightly soft, about 5 minutes. Stir in cinnamon. Cool and chill.

For sauce: Combine ingredients in small pan and bring to boil over medium heat. Cool and chill several hours or overnight. Serve over apricots.

BANANA FRITTERS

TRADER VIC'S
SAN FRANCISCO, CALIFORNIA

4 to 6 servings

       Oil for deep frying
   ½ **cup milk**
   2½ **tablespoons flour**
   2 **tablespoons cornstarch**
   1 **tablespoon sugar**
   1 **egg, well beaten**
   ⅛ **teaspoon baking powder**
   1 **tablespoon melted butter**
   4 to 6 **ripe but firm medium bananas, cut into 1½- to 2-inch sections**
       Whipped cream

Preheat oil in wok, deep fryer or electric skillet to 375°F. Meanwhile, combine milk, flour, cornstarch and sugar in small bowl and blend well. Add egg and baking powder. Stir in butter, mixing well. Dip banana sections into batter and deep fry until golden brown, about 2 to 3 minutes. Remove with slotted spoon and drain on paper towels. Serve each portion on bed of whipped cream.

STRAWBERRIES SAM MALICK

THE BAKERY
CHICAGO, ILLINOIS

"The late Sam Malick, one of the all-time great restaurant personalities, once imparted to me this unforgettable piece of wisdom: 'Louis, it is an old saying that while some people complain about the holes in the cheese, others rejoice about the cheese around the holes.' When a California strawberry grower developed an extra large berry with a hole in the middle, many people in our industry objected to the hole. Remembering Sam Malick, I developed the following recipe."
   —Louis Szathmary, The Bakery, Chicago, Illinois

   1 **cup orange liqueur***
   1 **basket extra large strawberries**

Using plastic medical syringe with large needle, draw syringe full of liqueur. Insert needle very close to green hulls of strawberries until end of needle reaches cavity within berry. Gently but firmly push enough liqueur into cavity to fill it.

*Orange liqueur can be mixed with a little brandy for a slightly less sweet effect.

PEARS BELLE HELENE

RESTAURANT LA COCOTTE, HOTEL RICHMOND
COPENHAGEN, DENMARK

"When in Copenhagen we stayed at the Hotel Richmond, where we also dined—superb food. Our dessert one night was Pears Hélène, a simple but delicious dish. It would be an impressive touch for a home dinner party.
   —Mrs. R. Summitt, Hayward, California

4 servings

   1 **quart water**
   2½ **cups sugar**
   1 **vanilla bean, split**
   4 **pears, peeled**

   4 **ounces dark sweet chocolate**
   ½ **cup whipping cream**

       French vanilla ice cream

Combine water, sugar and vanilla bean in large saucepan and bring to boil. Add pears, reduce heat and cook gently until tender, about 30 minutes. Refrigerate pears in syrup for 24 hours.

Remove vanilla bean from syrup. Melt chocolate in heavy saucepan over low heat, stirring frequently until smooth and glossy. Scrape vanilla bean pulp into chocolate. Add cream and bring to boil, stirring constantly. Remove from heat.

To serve, place scoop of ice cream in dessert bowl. Place pear alongside ice cream and spoon chocolate sauce over top.

SYMPHONIE AU COULIS DE CASSIS
(Poached Pear with Charlotte and Sorbet)

TAILLEVENT
PARIS, FRANCE

6 servings

Pear Charlotte

- 2¼ cups water
- 1 cup sugar
- 4 to 5 large pears, peeled, halved and cored
- 1 tablespoon unflavored gelatin
- 4 to 5 tablespoons pear liqueur
- ¾ cup whipping cream, whipped

Poached Pears

- 4 12-ounce jars whole black currants in syrup, undrained and pureed* (reserve about 1 tablespoon whole currants for garnish)
- 6 medium pears, peeled (stems intact), cored from bottom and grooved on spiral (use zester)

    Sorbet (pineapple, cassis or other fruit flavor)
    Mint leaves (garnish)

For charlotte: Combine water and sugar in large saucepan over medium-low heat and cook until sugar is dissolved, swirling pan occasionally. Add pear halves and cook, turning frequently, just until tender. Drain well, reserving poaching liquid. Finely dice enough pear to equal ½ cup and set aside. Puree remaining pears in processor or blender until smooth and creamy. Transfer to bowl. Combine gelatin and 1 tablespoon reserved poaching liquid in small cup and stir until gelatin is dissolved. Add to hot pear puree, stirring thoroughly. Cool to room temperature; do not refrigerate. Stir in pear liqueur. Fold in whipped cream and diced pear. Spoon mixture into six ½-cup molds (or nine ⅓-cup dariole molds), smoothing top. Chill until set.

For poached pears: Combine pureed currants with whole pears in large saucepan and simmer over medium-low heat until tender, turning frequently to color pears evenly. Remove pears from puree using slotted spoon and drain thoroughly.

To assemble: Spoon puree onto individual dessert plates. Stand poached pear near center. Unmold charlotte to side of pear. Arrange 3 small scoops of sorbet in front. Garnish with mint leaves and reserved currants.

*Sweeten with additional sugar if desired.

BOCCONE DOLCE
(Sweet Mouthful)

GENOA
PORTLAND, OREGON

6 to 8 servings

- 6 egg whites, room temperature
  Pinch salt
- ¼ teaspoon cream of tartar
- 1½ cups sugar

- 6 ounces semisweet chocolate
- 3 tablespoons water

- 2½ to 3 cups whipping cream, whipped
- 1½ pints fresh strawberries, hulled and sliced lengthwise
- 6 to 8 large whole strawberries (garnish)

Preheat oven to 250°F. Beat egg whites with salt until foamy. Add cream of tartar and beat until soft peaks form. Gradually beat in sugar until meringue is stiff and glossy.

Line baking sheet(s) with waxed paper and trace 3 circles 8 inches in diameter. Evenly spread or pipe meringue onto circles. Bake 1 hour. Turn off heat and let meringues dry in oven for another hour. Remove from oven and carefully peel off waxed paper. Let cool completely on wire racks.

Melt chocolate with water in top of double boiler and stir until smooth. Spread over 2 meringue layers and let stand until set.

To assemble: Place 1 meringue circle chocolate side up on serving plate. Spread with ½-inch layer of whipped cream. Cover with about ½ sliced berries. Repeat with second chocolate-covered layer. Top with plain meringue and frost entire cake with remaining cream. Garnish with whole strawberries and refrigerate 24 hours.

Seasonal fresh fruit such as raspberries, blueberries or sliced peaches may be substituted.

JAPANESE STRAWBERRIES

THE COUNTRY HOUSE
KIMBERTON, PENNSYLVANIA

10 to 12 servings

   2 cups whole blanched almonds
1¾ cups plus 4 teaspoons sugar

   6 egg whites

   1 quart fresh strawberries, washed
     and hulled

     Coffee Icing*

   1 cup whipping cream
   ½ teaspoon vanilla

Line backs of 2 baking sheets with parchment paper.
Trace (do not cut out) 10-inch circle on each sheet.
Preheat oven to 300°F. Grind 1½ cups almonds and
1½ cups sugar in food processor or blender until
pulverized. Sift through coarse strainer.

Beat egg whites until stiff but not dry (do not over-
beat). Carefully fold in almond-sugar mixture.
Spread meringue onto paper circles. Bake 1 hour.
Lift carefully onto rack, remove paper and cool.

Increase oven temperature to 350°F. Spread
remaining ½ cup almonds on baking sheet and toast
in oven until golden, about 7 to 8 minutes. Allow to
cool, then grind coarsely.

Set aside 3 or 4 strawberries. Halve remaining
strawberries and place in bowl. Sprinkle with 2
tablespoons sugar and mix lightly.

Spread Coffee Icing on 1 meringue layer, coating
it completely.

Beat cream until stiff. Add remaining sugar and
vanilla. Spread on second meringue layer. Arrange
strawberries cut side up on cream. Place iced
meringue layer on top. Spread ground almonds
around sides, pressing into whipped cream and
icing. Decorate top with reserved whole strawberries. Refrigerate until serving time.

*Coffee Icing

10 to 12 servings

   1 cup powdered sugar
   4 teaspoons hot milk
   2 teaspoons instant coffee powder
   ¼ teaspoon vanilla

Mix all ingredients until smooth.

FRESH RASPBERRIES WITH GRAND MARNIER SAUCE

THE SWISS LAKEWOOD RESTAURANT & LODGE
HOMEWOOD, CALIFORNIA

8 to 10 servings

   ¾ cup sugar
   1 teaspoon cornstarch
   ¾ cup water
     Finely grated peel of 1 orange
     Finely grated peel of 1 lemon
   ½ vanilla bean, split lengthwise
   8 egg yolks, lightly beaten
   1 envelope (1 tablespoon) unflavored
     gelatin
   2 tablespoons cold water

   2 cups whipping cream
   ⅓ cup Mandarine Napoléon liqueur
   ⅓ cup Grand Marnier
   1 quart fresh raspberries

Combine sugar and cornstarch in top of double
boiler and mix well. Stir in ¾ cup water, orange and
lemon peels and vanilla bean. Set over simmering
water and stir constantly until mixture begins to
thicken, about 5 minutes. Stir small amount into
egg yolks, then add yolks to pan and continue
cooking, stirring constantly, until thickened, about
5 minutes. Stir in gelatin softened in cold water,
blending thoroughly. Remove from heat and strain
into large bowl. Cover and chill.

Whip cream until soft peaks form. Fold into chilled
mixture. Add liqueurs and stir until smooth.
Arrange raspberries in large glass serving bowl and
pour sauce over.

COLD LIME SOUFFLE

THE JOCKEY CLUB
WASHINGTON, D.C.

8 to 10 servings

   1 cup sugar
   ¼ cup water
   7 egg yolks

   ½ cup lime juice or to taste
   2 cups (1 pint) whipping cream, whipped

Combine sugar and water in medium saucepan and
cook over medium-high heat until candy thermometer registers 240°F (soft-ball stage). Mix egg
yolks in blender. With machine running at highest
speed, add sugar mixture in slow steady stream and
mix well. Transfer to large bowl of electric mixer
and beat at medium speed until cool.

Add lime juice to egg mixture and blend well.
Gently fold in whipped cream. (Add green food
coloring if more intense color is desired.) Pour
mixture into 8 to 10 small soufflé dishes and freeze
until serving time.

THE FROZEN LEOPARD

THE LEOPARD
NEW YORK, NEW YORK

10 to 12 servings

- **3 cups crushed macaroons**
- **1 cup sugar**
- **1 cup half and half**
  Pinch salt
- **3 cups whipping cream, whipped**
- **1 cup brandy**

Combine macaroon crumbs, sugar, half and half and salt in large bowl. Fold in whipped cream. Gradually fold in brandy. Spoon into individual dishes and place in freezer. About 15 minutes before serving, remove from freezer and let set at room temperature to partially thaw.

This may also be served chilled instead of frozen.

COFFEE CUP SOUFFLE

THE FOUR SEASONS
NEW YORK, NEW YORK

8 servings

Sugar

- **4½ tablespoons (little over ½ stick) butter**
- **4½ tablespoons all purpose flour**
- **1½ cups milk**
- **1 tablespoon instant coffee**

- **6 eggs, separated**
- **¼ teaspoon cream of tartar**
- **¼ teaspoon salt**
- **¾ cup sugar**

- **¼ cup coffee ice cream, softened**

Butter 8 10-ounce ovenproof mugs; dust lightly with sugar. Preheat oven to 425°F.

Combine butter and flour in small bowl and mix well. Combine milk and coffee in large saucepan and bring to boil. Reduce heat, add butter-flour mixture and stir constantly until thickened. Allow to cool.

Stir egg yolks into coffee mixture. In large bowl, beat whites until foamy. Add cream of tartar and salt and continue beating, adding sugar gradually, until stiff peaks form. Fold into coffee-yolk mixture.

Set aside ¼ cup mixture and fill coffee mugs ⅔ full with remaining mixture. Bake soufflés 15 to 20 minutes depending on whether soft or firm consistency is desired.

For sauce: Combine reserved soufflé mixture and ice cream. Serve soufflés immediately from oven, topping each with sauce.

FROZEN HAZELNUT SOUFFLE

COQUILLE ST. JACQUES
JENKINTOWN, PENNSYLVANIA

"The selection of desserts at Coquille St. Jacques restaurant is dazzling and it is difficult for me to decide which one to order. The most unusual is a Frozen Hazelnut Soufflé."
—Stuart Solomon, Cherry Hill, New Jersey

10 to 12 servings

- **1¾ cups sugar**
- **1 cup water**
- **9 egg yolks**
- **3 cups whipping cream, whipped**
- **1 cup blanched hazelnuts, toasted and finely chopped**
- **2 tablespoons Cognac**
- **2 tablespoons Frangelico liqueur**

Prepare 8-inch soufflé dish. Make collar by cutting piece of foil long enough to encircle dish with 2-inch overlap. Fold foil in ½ lengthwise, oil 1 side and place around dish, extending 4 inches above edge. Tie or tape firmly around edge of dish. Refrigerate until ready to fill.

Stir sugar and water in small saucepan until sugar is thoroughly moistened; then let boil without stirring for about 5 minutes. Meanwhile, place egg yolks in large mixer bowl and beat at medium speed until light and lemon colored. Increase speed to high and slowly pour in sugar syrup, beating until mixture is quite stiff and cool. Gently fold in 2½ cups whipped cream until completely combined. Fold in nuts, Cognac and liqueur. Spoon into soufflé dish. Cover with remaining cream. Refrigerate 6 hours or overnight. Remove foil collar and serve immediately.

FROZEN RASPBERRY SOUFFLE

THE ARGYLE
SAN ANTONIO, TEXAS

"During a visit to Texas I dined at The Argyle, a beautiful old ranch home now converted to a private club and restaurant. For dessert we were served a fabulous creation called Frozen Raspberry Soufflé."
—Tracie Weathermon, San Francisco, California

12 to 16 servings

- **12 egg yolks**
- **2¼ cups sugar**
- **1 cup pureed and strained fresh raspberries***
- **⅔ cup framboise**
- **2 cups whipping cream, whipped**

- **8 egg whites, room temperature**
  Pinch salt

- **Sweetened whipped cream and fresh raspberries (garnish)**
  Sabayon sauce or crème fraîche

LE FRANÇAIS—A GASTRONOMIC MIRACLE

Few restaurants in America have been so resoundingly acclaimed—and by the most discriminating critics—as Le Français in Wheeling, Illinois. Le Français owes its success to the genius and determination of Jean Banchet in the kitchen and to the warmth and concern of his wife, Doris, who welcomes the guests. The Banchets came to this country from France in 1972, when Jean was hired as executive chef of the Playboy Club in Lake Geneva, Wisconsin. After a year in that post, Banchet was ready to open his own restaurant.

Banchet is the first to arrive at the restaurant every day. After reviewing the produce that has arrived from his far-flung network of suppliers, he begins his 14-hour workday by planning the day's specials.

The formidable kitchen is large in proportion to the dining room. Massive stoves and ovens extend the length of the room, in two rows. At the end of each row is a huge vat—used early in the day to make stocks to enrich Banchet's sauces and later to blanch vegetables. "Some of the nouvelle cuisine restaurants don't make these rich stocks," Banchet says. "Then the sauces taste flat."

Watching Jean Banchet at work is an engrossing experience. He moves with a deftness and speed that are awe-inspiring, timing, stirring, tasting and all the while talking about how he creates new dishes. Because he likes to see what others do, he goes to France every year for an eating tour of the restaurants he has read about or heard about from friends. "When I come back I re-create some of the dishes I've eaten—not exactly, but along the same lines. In this profession, you are never finished learning."

Prepare 3-quart soufflé dish or mold with oiled aluminum foil collar extending about 4 inches above rim. Tie or tape securely.

In large bowl, beat yolks until thick and lemon colored. Add 1¼ cups sugar and beat until dissolved. Blend in raspberries. Transfer to double boiler, place over hot water and cook until custard coats metal spoon: do not allow to boil at any time. Strain into large metal bowl set over ice and stir until cool. Add framboise little at a time, blending thoroughly after each addition. Fold whipped cream into mixture.

In large bowl, beat egg whites with salt until soft peaks form. Gradually beat in remaining sugar 2 tablespoons at a time. Mix ⅓ whites into custard to loosen, then gently fold in remaining whites.

Pour into prepared dish, smooth top with spatula and freeze overnight. When firm, cover top with plastic wrap or foil.

Just before serving, remove foil collar and smooth sides with spatula. Garnish with whipped cream and fresh raspberries and accompany with cooled sabayon or crème fraîche.

This melts quickly so serve directly from freezer.

*Unsweetened frozen berries may be used if fresh are unavailable.

GRAND MARNIER SOUFFLES

LE FRANÇAIS
WHEELING, ILLINOIS

6 servings

> 6 teaspoons (¼ stick) butter, softened
> Sugar
>
> 6 eggs, separated
> ½ cup sugar
> ¼ cup fresh orange juice
> 3 tablespoons Grand Marnier
> 2 teaspoons finely grated orange peel
> 1 tablespoon fresh lemon juice
> Powdered sugar

Preheat oven to 450°F. Butter 6 individual soufflé dishes 4 inches in diameter, using 1 teaspoon for each. Dust each dish with sugar, shaking out excess.

Combine egg yolks, 7 tablespoons sugar, orange juice, liqueur and peel and whisk just until blended. Beat egg whites with 1 tablespoon granulated sugar until soft peaks form. Add lemon juice and blend thoroughly. Fold yolk mixture into whites. Spoon into soufflé dishes. Use thumb to make rim around outer edge of soufflés. Bake until puffed and browned, about 10 minutes. Remove dishes from oven. Sprinkle tops with powdered sugar, set dishes on napkin-lined plates and serve immediately.

PENINSULA HOTEL'S SOUFFLE GLACE GRAND MARNIER

THE PENINSULA HOTEL
KOWLOON, HONG KONG

10 servings

    5 eggs
    ½ cup plus 2 tablespoons sugar
    2 cups milk
      Lemon peel

    ½ cup Grand Marnier or to taste

    2 cups whipping cream

      Shaved chocolate and whipped cream (garnish)

Place eggs and sugar in bowl and beat well. Place milk in saucepan with ½-inch piece of lemon peel and bring to boiling point. Immediately remove milk from heat, remove peel and beat hot milk into sugar and egg mixture. Strain.

Place mixture in top of double boiler over hot water and cook until thick and smooth, stirring constantly. When it has cooled, beat with whisk or in blender until mixture resembles thick cream. Pour in Grand Marnier to taste.

Whip cream. Fold into mixture until well blended. Pour mixture into 1½-quart soufflé dish and refrigerate until set.

To serve, top with additional whipped cream and shaved chocolate if desired.

SALZBURGER NOCKERLN

HOTEL WINKLER
SALZBURG, AUSTRIA

4 servings

    3 tablespoons (⅜ stick) butter, room temperature
    4 tablespoons sifted powdered sugar
    2 tablespoons milk

    5 egg whites
    3 egg yolks
    1 teaspoon sifted flour
    1 teaspoon finely grated lemon peel
      Powdered sugar (garnish)

Preheat oven to 350°F. Combine butter, 1 tablespoon powdered sugar and milk in large oval baking dish. Place in oven just until butter melts. Remove from oven and spread mixture evenly over bottom.

Beat egg whites until foamy. Add remaining powdered sugar and continue beating until stiff peaks form. Lightly beat egg yolks in large bowl. Sprinkle with flour and lemon peel, then stir until well combined. Using rubber spatula, stir small amount of whites into yolks, then gently fold in remainder. Using large spoon, form mixture into 4 mounds in baking dish. Bake until lightly browned, 10 to 12 minutes. Dust with powdered sugar; serve.

ORANGE MARMALADE SOUFFLE

HYEHOLDE RESTAURANT
CORAOPOLIS, PENNSYLVANIA

6 to 8 servings

    ¼ cup Grand Marnier
    1 tablespoon fresh lemon juice
    3 teaspoons unflavored gelatin

    5 eggs, separated
    1 cup sugar
    ¾ cup fresh orange juice
    ⅓ cup orange marmalade
    ¼ teaspoon salt
    ½ teaspoon finely grated lemon peel

    1 cup whipping cream

Garnish

    ½ cup whipping cream
    2 teaspoons powdered sugar
    ½ cup mandarin orange segments, drained
      Grand Marnier Sauce*

Prepare 1-quart soufflé dish with lightly oiled 1-inch waxed paper collar. Set aside.

Combine Grand Marnier and lemon juice in small bowl. Sprinkle in gelatin; let stand until softened.

Combine egg yolks, ¾ cup sugar, orange juice, marmalade and salt in top of double boiler. Set over simmering water and cook, whisking constantly, until mixture thickens and coats spoon, about 5 minutes. Remove from heat. Stir in softened gelatin and lemon peel. Turn into large bowl. Let custard cool to room temperature.

Beat egg whites until foamy. Gradually add remaining ¼ cup sugar and continue beating until stiff peaks form. In another bowl, whip 1 cup cream until soft peaks form. Stir some of whites into cooled custard to lighten, then fold in remaining whites, blending well. Fold in whipped cream. Turn into prepared dish. Refrigerate until soufflé is firm and spongy.

For garnish: Whip remaining cream with powdered sugar until stiff. Spoon into pastry bag fitted with star tip. Pipe rosettes over top of soufflé. Decorate with mandarin orange segments and serve with Grand Marnier Sauce.

Grand Marnier Sauce

6 to 8 servings

    2 cups milk
    ¼ cup (½ stick) butter
    ⅔ cup sugar

    3 egg yolks, room temperature
    2 tablespoons cornstarch
    1 teaspoon vanilla
    ⅓ cup Grand Marnier
    ⅓ cup whipping cream

Combine milk, butter and ⅓ cup sugar in medium saucepan over medium heat and bring to boil, stirring occasionally.

Using electric mixer, beat yolks and remaining sugar in small bowl until thickened. Add cornstarch and continue beating until mixture is light and lemon colored. Gradually beat in enough hot milk to warm mixture slightly. Strain into remaining milk, whisking until blended. Place over medium heat and bring to boil. Remove from heat and stir in vanilla. Let stand until cool. Refrigerate until ready to serve. Just before serving, cook over low heat, stirring in liqueur and cream.

MOUSSE D'ASPERGE SUR TUILES AUX AMANDES
(Sweet Asparagus Mousse on Almond Cookies)

ERNIE'S
SAN FRANCISCO, CALIFORNIA

4 servings

    20 to 25 medium asparagus spears (fresh or frozen), tender part only
     6 tablespoons sugar
     1 tablespoon salt

     2 egg yolks
     ¾ cup (about) whipping cream (enough for 60/40 ratio with asparagus puree)

       Tuiles aux Amandes*

Cook asparagus in large pan of boiling water with 3 tablespoons sugar and salt until soft. Drain thoroughly on paper towels. Transfer to processor and mix until pureed. Return to saucepan and cook over very low heat, stirring constantly, until excess moisture is evaporated and puree is firm, about 10 minutes. Push through medium strainer; set aside.

Combine egg yolks with remaining sugar in top of double boiler. Set over simmering water and beat vigorously until very thick. Remove from water and continue beating until mixture is cool. Add puree and mix well.

Whip cream until stiff. Fold into asparagus mixture gently but thoroughly. Cover and chill mousse until ready to serve.

Spoon mousse into pastry bag fitted with ½-inch plain tip. Pipe down center of each tuile.

Tuiles aux Amandes

4 servings

    2¼ cups sliced almonds
     ¾ cup sugar
     ¼ cup all purpose flour
     3 egg whites
     ¼ cup (½ stick) unsalted butter, melted

Combine almonds, sugar and flour in bowl and mix well. Add egg whites and butter and blend thoroughly. Cover and refrigerate at least 1 hour.

Preheat oven to 350°F. Line baking sheet with heavy duty foil; butter generously. Drop batter by level tablespoons, leaving 5 to 6 inches between each cookie; spread batter evenly with spoon or fork. Bake until cookies are deep brown around edges and firm in center, about 12 to 15 minutes. Remove from oven and let stand 30 seconds. Lift carefully from sheet using spatula, invert tuile and curl around rolling pin or wine bottle. If cookies become too firm to curl, return briefly to oven. Store in airtight can in cool, dry area.

PALACE WHITE CHOCOLATE MOUSSE

THE PALACE
NEW YORK, NEW YORK

"A trip to New York City was made even more memorable by a visit to The Palace restaurant, where we had an exceptional dessert mousse made with white chocolate." —Steven W. Brown, Bristol, Rhode Island

Chef de cuisine Michel Fitoussi, who created this mousse, serves it in tuiles. He uses a cup or small flat-bottomed bowl to shape these thin almond cookies while still warm.

6 servings

    ¼ pound sugar cubes
    ¼ cup water
    ½ cup egg whites (from about 4 large eggs), room temperature
    1 pound imported white chocolate, cut into very small cubes

    2 cups whipping cream, well chilled

      Strawberry Sauce*
      Mint leaves (garnish)

Combine sugar cubes and water in saucepan and bring to boil, stirring or shaking pan occasionally until sugar melts. Cook without stirring until syrup reaches hard ball stage (255°F on candy thermometer). Whip egg whites to form soft peaks, then reduce speed of mixer and slowly add syrup. Beat in chocolate pieces (they will melt partially). Cool to lukewarm.

Whip cream until stiff and fold into mousse. Chill for at least 4 hours.

To serve, place Strawberry Sauce on chilled dessert plate (or in tuile cup), then top with mousse. Garnish with 1 or 2 mint leaves and pass remaining sauce separately.

Strawberry Sauce

6 servings

    2 pints strawberries, washed and hulled
    2 tablespoons imported kirsch
    1 tablespoon sugar
      Pinch salt

Puree strawberries. Stir in remaining ingredients. Cover and chill thoroughly.

CHOCOLATE MOUSSE

L'ESCARGOT ON MICHIGAN
CHICAGO, ILLINOIS

8 servings

> 1 8-ounce package semisweet chocolate
>
> ½ cup sugar
> ½ cup water
>
> 5 egg yolks, beaten
>
> 1 tablespoon unflavored gelatin
> 2 tablespoons dark rum
>
> 5 egg whites
> ½ teaspoon cream of tartar
> ¼ teaspoon salt
> 2 cups whipping cream, whipped

Melt chocolate over very low heat and mix until smooth. Cool in large bowl.

Mix sugar and water together in small saucepan. Boil until transparent and syrupy, about 3 to 5 minutes. Cool slightly.

Slowly pour syrup in very thin stream into egg yolks, beating vigorously with whisk.

Soften gelatin in rum. Add to warm egg-sugar mixture, blending well. Gradually stir into melted chocolate with whisk. Allow to cool.

Whip egg whites with cream of tartar and salt until stiff and glossy. Fold into chocolate along with whipped cream. Spoon into 2-quart soufflé dish or 8 individual dessert dishes. Refrigerate until ready to serve, at least 4 hours.

CHOCOLATE MOUSSE AU PROVENCE

AU PROVENCE RESTAURANT
CLEVELAND HEIGHTS, OHIO

8 to 10 servings

> 6 ounces semisweet chocolate
> 2 ounces unsweetened chocolate
> 2 cups whipping cream
>
> 7 egg whites, room temperature
> 1 cup superfine sugar
> 7 dried jumbo apricots, finely chopped
> 2 teaspoons grated orange rind
> ½ tablespoon instant coffee powder
>
> Peppermint-Chocolate Leaves (garnish)*

Place semisweet and unsweetened chocolate in top of double boiler over hot water until just softened (chocolate must not be hot). Whip cream until it begins to thicken. Add softened chocolate and continue whipping until stiff.

Whip whites until they form soft peaks. Gradually add sugar and beat until stiff. Fold into chocolate mixture. Carefully fold in apricots, orange rind and coffee powder.

Spoon into individual soufflé dishes or custard cups and chill at least 4 hours. Arrange Peppermint-Chocolate Leaves on top just before serving.

*Peppermint-Chocolate Leaves

8 to 10 servings

> 3 ounces semisweet chocolate
> 3 drops peppermint extract
> Rose leaves (or any small, shiny leaves)

Melt chocolate; add peppermint extract and mix thoroughly. Wash and dry leaves. Brush chocolate on shiny side of leaves, being careful not to get chocolate on opposite side. Place on baking sheet lined with waxed paper and refrigerate until chocolate is set. With cool hands, carefully peel leaf from chocolate. Refrigerate until mousse is ready to serve. Can be stored in refrigerator several weeks.

MARQUISE AU CHOCOLAT ET A LA PISTACHE
(Chocolate Marquise with Pistachio Cream)

TAILLEVENT
PARIS, FRANCE

8 servings

> 8 ounces semisweet chocolate, cut into small pieces
> 1 cup plus 2 tablespoons powdered sugar
> ¾ cup (1½ sticks) unsalted butter, cut into ½-inch pats
> 5 eggs, separated
> ¾ cup unsweetened cocoa powder
>
> Dash salt
> Dash cream of tartar
> ¾ cup whipping cream
>
> Crème Anglaise à la Pistache*

Melt chocolate in heatproof bowl set over simmering water (maintain simmer). Add sugar and mix well. Stir in butter 1 piece at a time and blend well. Remove bowl from over water and add egg yolks 1 at a time, mixing well after each addition. Beat in cocoa. Let cool 5 minutes, stirring frequently.

Beat egg whites with salt and cream of tartar until stiff peaks form. Gently stir ⅓ of whites into chocolate mixture, then fold remaining whites into chocolate mixture; do not beat. Whip cream to soft peaks. Carefully fold whipped cream into chocolate mixture until well blended. Pour into 9x5-inch glass loaf pan or 1½-quart mold (do not use metal). Chill at least 12 hours.

Just before serving, moisten kitchen towel with hot water. Wrap towel around pan or mold and invert onto platter. Slice marquise into serving portions. Transfer to individual dessert plates. Spoon crème anglaise around slices. Serve immediately.

Crème Anglaise à la Pistache

Makes about 2 cups

- 7 egg yolks
- ½ cup sugar
  Pinch salt
- 2 cups milk
- 1 1-inch piece vanilla bean, split
  and scraped

- 12 ounces unsalted pistachio nuts, shelled
- ¼ cup pistachio liqueur

Combine yolks, sugar and salt in large bowl and beat until thick and pale lemon colored, 1 to 2 minutes. Scald milk with vanilla bean in nonaluminum saucepan. Remove vanilla bean and set aside. Slowly beat 1 cup milk into yolk mixture. Return yolk mixture to milk in saucepan, whisking constantly. Add reserved vanilla bean. Cook over medium heat, stirring constantly, until custard thickens; do not boil. Pour into processor or blender.

Meanwhile, boil pistachios in enough water to cover until soft, about 3 to 5 minutes. Drain well. Peel off skins. Pat dry with paper towel. Add to custard. Pour in liqueur and mix until smooth. Refrigerate until ready to use. Press custard through fine sieve before serving.

COCONUT MOUSSE PISTACHIO

TRADER VIC'S
SAN FRANCISCO, CALIFORNIA

9 to 10 servings

- 2 cups (1 pint) half and half
- 1 cup coconut syrup
- 3 egg yolks, lightly beaten
- 1½ tablespoons (1½ envelopes)
  unflavored gelatin
  Pinch salt

- 3 egg whites
- 1 tablespoon sugar
- 3 ounces (6 tablespoons) pistachio nuts,
  crushed
- 9 to 10 slices pound cake, ½ inch thick
  Whipped cream flavored with coconut
  syrup (garnish)
  Toasted shredded coconut (garnish)

Combine first 5 ingredients in large heavy-bottomed saucepan. Place over medium heat and stir constantly until gelatin is dissolved. Pour into medium bowl and place in larger bowl filled with ice. Chill until thick, 20 to 30 minutes, stirring frequently.

When mixture is thick, beat egg whites until stiff peaks form. Gradually add sugar and beat until stiff. Carefully fold into gelatin mixture; fold in nuts. Pour into 9 or 10 4-ounce molds and place 1 slice pound cake atop each, trimming to fit. Chill until firm, at least 2 hours. Unmold onto serving dishes and top with whipped cream and toasted coconut.

LEMON MELTING MOMENTS

PROOF OF THE PUDDING
NEW YORK, NEW YORK

8 to 10 servings

- 1 pint (2 cups) whipping cream
- ½ cup superfine sugar
  Juice of 4 lemons
  Grated zest of 2 to 4 lemons
- 2 tablespoons condensed milk
- 8 to 10 fresh strawberries (garnish)

Combine all ingredients except berries in large, well-chilled mixing bowl and beat until very thick. Divide among parfait glasses and chill until ready to serve. Top each with strawberry before serving.

ROSE MOUSSE

DEJA-VU
PHILADELPHIA, PENNSYLVANIA

6 servings

- ½ cup fresh orange juice
- ½ cup firmly packed brown sugar
  (turbinado)
- 1 tablespoon dried rose hips (with
  some leaves)
- 1½ teaspoons sweet white wine (preferably
  Johannisberg Riesling)
- 1½ teaspoons unflavored gelatin
- ¼ cup orange flower water
- 1 teaspoon natural orange food coloring*

- 2 cups whipping cream

  Petals and leaves from 6 roses or
  mint leaves (garnish)

Combine orange juice, brown sugar, rose hips, wine, gelatin, orange flower water and food coloring in medium saucepan and bring to slow boil over medium heat, stirring constantly until gelatin is dissolved, about 10 minutes. Strain mixture into small bowl. Set bowl in large bowl filled with ice cubes and whisk mixture frequently until cool and slightly thickened, about 3 minutes. Set aside.

Whip cream in large bowl until stiff. Gently fold in orange mixture. Spoon mixture into ½-cup ramekins or soufflé dishes. Tap dishes lightly on counter to remove air bubbles. Cover with plastic wrap and refrigerate overnight.

To serve, run sharp, thin knife around molds. Invert onto individual plates. Garnish with rose petals and leaves or mint leaves.

*Available at natural food stores.

THE COACH HOUSE BREAD AND BUTTER PUDDING

THE COACH HOUSE
NEW YORK, NEW YORK

10 servings

    12 or 13 slices French bread cut ½ inch
       thick, crusts trimmed
     3 to 4 tablespoons (⅜ to ½ stick) unsalted
       butter, room temperature
     5 eggs
     4 egg yolks
     1 cup sugar
    ⅛ teaspoon salt

     4 cups (1 quart) milk
     1 cup whipping cream
     1 teaspoon vanilla

       Powdered sugar
       Fresh raspberries, pureed and strained

Preheat oven to 375°F. Butter one side of each slice of bread; set aside. Beat eggs, yolks, sugar and salt in large bowl until thoroughly combined; set aside.

Combine milk and cream in saucepan and heat until scalded. Gradually stir hot liquid into egg mixture. Blend in vanilla.

Layer bread buttered side up in 2-quart soufflé dish, cutting slices as needed to fit dish and fill spaces evenly. Strain custard over top. Add boiling water to depth of about 1 inch in roasting pan. Set soufflé dish in pan and bake until knife inserted in center comes out clean, about 45 minutes. Remove from roasting pan and sprinkle pudding generously with powdered sugar. Run under broiler until glazed. Serve warm with raspberry puree.

INDIAN PUDDING YESTERYEAR

YESTERYEAR
KANKAKEE, ILLINOIS

6 servings

     1 quart (4 cups) milk
    ¼ cup cornmeal
    ½ cup unsulphured molasses
    ¼ cup sugar
     1 tablespoon butter
     1 teaspoon ground ginger
     1 teaspoon salt
    ½ teaspoon cinnamon
    ½ teaspoon nutmeg
       Vanilla ice cream

Preheat oven to 275°F. Scald milk in top of double boiler set over simmering water. Slowly stir in cornmeal, blending well. Cook 20 minutes, stirring occasionally. Add next 7 ingredients. Transfer to well-buttered 1½-quart casserole. Bake 3 hours, stirring once after 1½ hours. Serve warm with vanilla ice cream.

SCIENCE HILL INN BREAD PUDDING

SCIENCE HILL INN
SHELBYVILLE, KENTUCKY

6 to 8 servings

     3 tablespoons (⅜ stick) butter, melted
     8 slices homemade bread
     4 cups milk
    1½ cups sugar
     4 large eggs
    ⅓ cup golden raisins
       Bourbon Sauce* (optional)

Preheat oven to 350°F. Pour melted butter into 12x8x2-inch baking pan. Tear bread into small pieces and place in large mixing bowl. Add milk and soak 5 minutes. Combine sugar, eggs and raisins and mix well with bread and milk. Pour into prepared pan and bake 1 hour. If desired, serve with Bourbon Sauce.

Bourbon Sauce

6 to 8 servings

    ½ cup (1 stick) butter
     1 cup sugar
    ¼ cup water
     1 egg, beaten
    ⅓ cup bourbon whiskey

Melt butter in small saucepan over medium heat. Add sugar and water and cook, stirring constantly, 2 minutes. Gradually add butter and sugar to egg, beating constantly. Slowly stir in bourbon.

MARY MAC'S PRESIDENT'S PUDDING

MARY MAC'S TEA ROOM
ATLANTA, GEORGIA

"I am a flight attendant for a major airline. On a recent layover in Atlanta, someone recommended a restaurant called Mary Mac's Tea Room, and am I glad they did! The finale to an exceptional Southern meal was a dessert called President's Pudding."
—Linda Dente, Fort Lauderdale, Florida

     2 3-ounce packages cream cheese,
       room temperature
     1 cup powdered sugar
    ½ cup peanut butter
    ¾ cup milk
    ¾ cup whipping cream, whipped
     6 to 8 baked individual tart shells
       Chopped peanuts (garnish)

Beat cream cheese, sugar and peanut butter in large bowl until smooth. Add milk, beating until well combined. Gently fold in whipped cream. Divide among tart shells. Top with nuts. Freeze until firm.

PLYMALE BREAD PUDDING

PLYMALE COTTAGE
JACKSONVILLE, FLORIDA

12 to 15 servings

>   9 slices whole wheat bread (including
>   heels and crusts), broken into pieces
>   6 cups evaporated milk
>   4 eggs
>   ½ cup sugar
>   ½ cup firmly packed brown sugar
>   2 teaspoons cinnamon
>   ½ teaspoon salt
>   ¼ teaspoon nutmeg
>   1 cup drained crushed pineapple
>   1 to 2 bananas, cut into pieces
>   ½ cup raisins
>   Whipped cream (garnish)

Preheat oven to 375°F. Butter and flour 9x13-inch baking dish. Combine first 8 ingredients in large bowl and let stand 30 minutes. Stir in pineapple, bananas and raisins. Turn into prepared dish and bake until almost set (center will still be soft), about 30 minutes; do not overbake. Cool and serve with whipped cream.

RICE, RAISIN AND RUM PUDDING

SHERWOOD INN
SKANEATELES, NEW YORK

12 servings

>   6 tablespoons converted rice
>   1 cup cold water
>   ½ cup raisins
>   ¼ cup dark rum
>
>   6 cups whipping cream
>   1½ cups sugar
>   12 egg yolks
>   1 tablespoon vanilla
>   Nutmeg

Combine rice and cold water in small saucepan. Bring to boil, reduce heat and simmer 12 to 15 minutes. Remove from heat, cover and let stand 1 hour. Drain any remaining liquid. Add raisins and rum and let stand 1 to 3 hours at room temperature.

Preheat oven to 325°F. Place 2 level tablespoons rice mixture in each of 12 6-ounce custard cups.

Mix cream and sugar in large saucepan and heat, stirring constantly, until just below boiling point. In large mixing bowl, gently beat egg yolks. Add cream and sugar mixture little at a time, mixing gently. Blend in vanilla. Pour over rice in custard cups. Sprinkle with nutmeg. Place cups in pan of hot water (water should come halfway up sides of cups) and bake until knife inserted in center comes out clean, about 1¼ hours. Serve cold or at room temperature.

OZARK PUDDING

MARSHALL FIELD'S
CHICAGO, ILLINOIS

Ozark Pudding is reported to have been the late President Harry Truman's favorite dessert.

4 servings

>   ⅓ cup all purpose flour
>   1¼ teaspoons baking powder
>   ⅛ teaspoon salt
>   1 egg
>   ¾ cup sugar
>   ½ cup peeled chopped apple
>   ½ cup chopped nuts
>   1 teaspoon vanilla
>   1 cup whipping cream, whipped, or
>   vanilla ice cream

Preheat oven to 325°F. Butter 1-quart casserole or soufflé dish. Sift together flour, baking powder and salt. Beat egg and sugar until light and fluffy. Add flour mixture and blend well. Fold in apple, nuts and vanilla. Spoon into prepared dish and bake 30 minutes. Serve pudding warm with whipped cream or ice cream.

KING'S ARMS TAVERN RAISIN RICE PUDDING

KING'S ARMS TAVERN
WILLIAMSBURG, VIRGINIA

8 to 9 servings

>   4 cups milk
>   ¼ cup converted rice
>
>   4 whole eggs
>   ½ cup sugar
>   1½ teaspoons lemon extract
>   1½ teaspoons vanilla
>   1 tablespoon melted butter
>
>   1 teaspoon nutmeg
>   ¾ cup light raisins

Bring 3 cups milk and rice to boil over direct heat. Lower heat and cook, covered, until rice is tender, about 15 to 20 minutes. Remove from heat.

Preheat oven to 350°F. Beat eggs well. Add sugar, beating continuously. Add remaining milk, lemon extract, vanilla and butter.

Combine rice and milk with egg mixture and pour into well-buttered 8x8-inch pan. Sprinkle with nutmeg. Place pan in larger pan, taking care that sides of smaller pan do not touch larger pan. Bake until custard begins to set, about 30 minutes. Stir in raisins and continue baking until knife inserted in center of custard comes out clean, about 15 minutes. Remove from oven and set custard pan on cake rack. Cool slightly before refrigerating.

FLAN

TALK OF THE TOWN RESORT HOTEL
ARUBA, NETHERLANDS ANTILLES

6 servings

>   1 **cup sugar**
> ¼ **cup water**
>   **Pinch cream of tartar**
>
>   3 **eggs, room temperature**
>   1 **teaspoon vanilla**
>   1 **teaspoon grated lemon peel**
>   2 **cups hot milk**

Combine ½ cup sugar and water in heavy small saucepan and bring to boil, shaking pan occasionally, until sugar is dissolved. Add cream of tartar. Boil until syrup turns golden brown, about 10 minutes. Divide among 6 custard cups; swirl to coat sides with syrup.

Preheat oven to 300°F. Beat eggs in small bowl using electric mixer. Add remaining sugar, vanilla and lemon peel and continue beating until well combined. Slowly add hot milk, stirring until most of foam has dissipated. Divide among cups and arrange in shallow baking dish. Add boiling water to come halfway up sides of cups. Bake until knife inserted in center comes out clean, about 1 hour. Remove from baking dish and let cool. Refrigerate until ready to serve. Just before serving, dip cups briefly into hot water and invert custard onto individual plates.

CREME BRULEE

THE TARRAGON TREE
MEYERSVILLE, NEW JERSEY

6 to 8 servings

>   1 **quart whipping cream**
> ¼ **cup sugar**
>   1 **tablespoon vanilla**
>   **Pinch salt**
>   8 **egg yolks**
>
>   **Dark brown sugar**

Preheat oven to 350°F. Combine first 4 ingredients in heavy saucepan and warm slowly over low heat until cream is scalded (180°F to 185°F), stirring occasionally. Meanwhile, beat yolks in stainless steel bowl until lemon colored. Very slowly pour hot cream into yolks; do not beat or mixture will foam. Pour into individual 6-ounce ramekins, 6- to 8-cup pie plate or shallow 2-quart casserole. Place in larger baking pan. Fill pan with hot water so water comes halfway up custard container. Bake until knife inserted 1 inch from edge of custard comes out clean (center will be soft), about 25 to 30 minutes. Remove custard from water bath and allow to cool, then cover and refrigerate overnight.

Preheat broiler. Sift brown sugar to depth of ¼ inch evenly over top of custard. Place custard under broiler 6 to 8 inches from heat. Watch carefully as sugar will melt in 1 to 2 minutes; do not let burn. If broiler is uneven, turn ramekin or casserole. When sugar is melted, return immediately to refrigerator. Serve very cold. (Crust will hold 4 to 6 hours.)

GRAND MARNIER CREAM

THE TARRAGON TREE
MEYERSVILLE, NEW JERSEY

"On a recent foggy drive through the Hopatcong Mountains in New Jersey, we came upon a most delightful restaurant, The Tarragon Tree. Although each course of the dinner was superb, we found the desserts to be especially memorable."
>   —*Fred Rosenfeld, Princeton Junction, New Jersey*

4 to 6 servings

> ¾ **cup water**
> ¾ **cup sugar**
>
>   8 **egg yolks**
> ⅓ **cup Grand Marnier**
>
>   1 **cup whipping cream**

Combine water and sugar in heavy 1-quart saucepan and stir to dissolve sugar. Bring to boiling point over high heat and let syrup boil without stirring for exactly 5 minutes.

Meanwhile, beat egg yolks with electric mixer until thick and lemon colored. Carefully add hot syrup in thin stream, continuing to beat until cool. Add Grand Marnier.

In separate bowl, whip cream until thickened but not stiff. Fold ½ cream into yolk mixture, then fold in remaining cream. Pour into dessert glasses or serving bowl, cover and freeze until ready to serve.

WHISKEY SABAYON

SOUPÇON
CRESTED BUTTE, COLORADO

"I recently had dinner at a tiny, exquisite restaurant in Crested Butte. For dessert I was served a bread pudding with a delicious whiskey sabayon."
—Irene T. Woodall, Boulder, Colorado

Makes about 1¾ cups

 1 **egg**
 ½ **cup superfine granulated sugar**
 ½ **cup (1 stick) butter**

 ¼ **cup dry sherry**
 ¼ **cup bourbon**

Mix egg and sugar in 1-quart enamel or stainless steel saucepan. Melt butter in separate pan. Place egg-sugar mixture over low heat and whip until sugar melts and sauce is thick, about 4 minutes.

Remove mixture from heat and add butter in steady stream, whisking continuously. Return to heat and whisk until sauce is fairly thick, about 1 minute. Add sherry and bourbon and whisk until light, creamy and coats wooden spoon, about ½ minute.

OEUFS A LA NEIGE

RESTAURANT BOCUSE
LYONS, FRANCE

4 to 6 servings

 2 **cups milk**
 1 **vanilla bean, split**
 6 **egg yolks**
 1½ **cups plus 3 tablespoons sugar**

 6 **egg whites**

 6 **tablespoons water**

Bring milk and vanilla bean to boil in large saucepan over medium-high heat. Whisk yolks and ¾ cup sugar in large bowl (or use electric mixer) until thickened, about 2 minutes. Skim foam from milk. Gradually whisk into yolks. Return mixture to saucepan and cook over medium-high heat, whisking constantly, until custard thickens and coats wooden spoon, about 8 minutes. Strain custard into bowl and let cool.

Beat whites in large bowl until foamy. Add 3 tablespoons sugar and continue beating until stiff peaks form. Fill large saucepan ¾ full of water and bring to very gentle simmer over low heat. Mound whites into large puffs with serving spoon. Transfer to simmering water (in batches if necessary) and poach puffs, turning over with slotted spoon, until slightly resistant when pressed, about 1 to 2 minutes. Remove with slotted spoon; drain on towel.

Combine remaining ¾ cup sugar with water in small saucepan. Place over high heat and bring to boil. Let boil, without stirring, until syrup is medium brown and caramelized. Set pan in ice water until syrup is cool. Remove and let stand at room temperature. Do not refrigerate.

To serve, spoon custard into shallow bowls, arrange meringue puffs over top and drizzle with caramel.

CREPES AMBROSIA WITH STRAWBERRIES AND ICE CREAM

ERNIE'S
SAN FRANCISCO, CALIFORNIA

2 servings

 2 **2½-inch scoops vanilla ice cream**

 12 **fresh strawberries, stems removed**
 ½ **orange, seeds removed**
 1 **tablespoon sugar**
 1 **to 2 tablespoons Grand Marnier**

 2 **teaspoons crushed toasted almonds**

 2 **6-inch dessert crepes**
 1 **tablespoon Cognac**

Using back of spoon, make indentation on top of each scoop of ice cream. Return to freezer with 2 dessert plates.

Place 8 strawberries in sauté or crepe pan. Add orange cut side down. Sprinkle berries with sugar and cook over low heat until sugar is dissolved, about 10 minutes. Squeeze orange into pan to release juice; discard orange and stir sauce until thoroughly blended. Increase heat to high, add Grand Marnier to pan and crush berries in liqueur. Cook, stirring constantly, until reduced and thickened. Remove from heat and keep warm.

Sprinkle chilled dessert plates with almonds. Set ice cream in center. Place 2 strawberries on either side.

Add crepe to sauce and turn quickly to coat on both sides. Lift carefully and drape over ice cream, pushing into indentation with back of spoon. Heat Cognac, ignite and add to pan; ladle sauce over crepes and serve.

FRIED ICE CREAM

SPRUCE POND INN
STOWE, VERMONT

10 servings

Cream Puff Shells

    1 cup water
    ½ cup (1 stick) butter
  1½ cups all purpose flour
    5 eggs, room temperature

  1½ quarts (about) vanilla ice cream, firmly frozen

Beer Batter

    2 cups all purpose flour
  12 ounces flat beer
    2 eggs, room temperature

     Oil for deep frying
     Pure maple or raspberry syrup

For shells: Preheat oven to 350°F. Lightly grease baking sheet. Bring water to boil in medium saucepan. Add butter and let melt. Add flour, stirring quickly until dough forms ball. Transfer to mixing bowl. Using electric mixer at medium speed, add eggs 1 at a time, beating thoroughly after each addition. Spoon 1½- to 2-inch mounds onto baking sheet or fill pastry tube with dough and mound onto sheet. Bake until golden brown, about 40 minutes. Let cool completely in draft-free area.

Slice partway through each shell and fill with ice cream. Wrap each puff with foil and freeze until solid, at least 1 hour.

For batter: Combine flour, beer and eggs in medium bowl and mix well.

Heat oil to between 350°F and 375°F. Dip frozen puffs in batter and deep fry until golden brown. Quickly drain on paper towels. Place each puff in individual serving dishes and pour syrup on top. Serve immediately.

WALNUT CREAM DESSERT

CAFE AT BON APPETIT
PHILADELPHIA, PENNSYLVANIA

Makes 10 servings

    4 egg yolks
    1 cup sugar
    1 tablespoon flour
    1 tablespoon arrowroot
    ¾ cup whipping cream
    ¾ cup milk
    3 tablespoons kirsch

    1 cup (2 sticks) butter, room temperature
    2 cups walnuts, toasted and finely chopped
     Chocolate Sauce*

Line 8-inch soufflé dish with plastic wrap, letting excess extend over edge; set aside.

Combine yolks, ¼ cup sugar, flour and arrowroot in medium saucepan. Whisk in cream, milk and kirsch. Place over medium heat and whisk constantly until mixture has thickened. Let mixture stand until completely cooled.

Beat butter and remaining sugar together in medium bowl until light and fluffy. Fold in walnuts and cooled yolk mixture. Turn into mold. Cover and refrigerate 6 hours or overnight. Remove from refrigerator and unmold. Serve immediately with Chocolate Sauce.

*Chocolate Sauce

10 servings

    ¼ cup (½ stick) butter
    ½ cup unsweetened cocoa
    ½ cup sugar
    ½ cup whipping cream

Melt butter in medium saucepan over medium heat. Reduce heat and whisk in cocoa and sugar. Gradually add cream, stirring constantly until mixture is smooth and heated through. Serve warm.

ESPRESSO ICE CREAM

RESTAURANT LA RESIDENCE
CHAPEL HILL, NORTH CAROLINA

"When my parents were vacationing in the South recently, they raved about the wonderful food served at the Restaurant La Résidence in Chapel Hill. I would love to surprise them with the special espresso ice cream that they enjoyed so much."

    —Lois Powers, Independence, Ohio

Makes 2 quarts

  1¾ cups half and half
    2 tablespoons instant coffee
    9 egg yolks
    ⅛ teaspoon salt
    ¾ cup sugar
  1½ cups whipping cream
    6 tablespoons (¾ stick) unsalted butter

    1 tablespoon vanilla
    ¼ cup ground espresso coffee

Scald half and half with instant coffee in small saucepan. Beat egg yolks with salt in large bowl, gradually adding sugar until mixture is light and fluffy. Slowly add hot half and half, beating constantly. Transfer to heavy saucepan and cook over medium heat, stirring constantly, until mixture thickens and almost reaches boiling point. Blend in cream and butter. Let cool.

Stir in vanilla. Strain. Pour into ice cream freezer and churn until desired consistency. Fold in espresso. Allow to set up in ice cream freezer (or regular freezer) for about 30 minutes before serving.

TRUFFLE ICE CREAM

RESTAURANT ANDRE DAGUIN, HOTEL DE FRANCE
AUCH, FRANCE

Makes about 2 quarts

- 4 **cups milk**
- 1 **vanilla bean, split**

- 10 **egg yolks**
- 1 **cup sugar**

- 1 **6½-ounce tin truffle juice***

- 3 **black truffles, cut into very
  small matchsticks**

Combine milk and vanilla bean in heavy-bottomed 2½-quart saucepan and bring to boil over low heat, stirring frequently with wooden spoon.

Beat yolks in large bowl with electric mixer until well blended. Gradually add sugar, beating constantly, until mixture falls from beaters in ribbons.

Remove vanilla bean from milk and set aside. Gradually add hot milk to yolk mixture in steady stream, beating constantly. Scrape seeds from vanilla bean and blend into yolk mixture. Stir in truffle juice, blending thoroughly.

Transfer to heavy-bottomed saucepan and cook over low heat, stirring constantly with wooden spoon, until mixture thickens and coats spoon. Do not boil or eggs will curdle. Strain custard into glass or metal bowl set in larger bowl filled with ice cubes. (This will stop cooking process.) Cover and let cool, stirring frequently. Add truffles. Place in ice cream maker and process according to directions.

*Available in specialty food stores.

GRAPEFRUIT SHERBET

THE PENINSULA HOTEL
KOWLOON, HONG KONG

"At The Peninsula hotel, they make a very light grapefruit sherbet that they serve in a grapefruit shell in a bowl of crushed ice, and they top it with a bit of gin. It is marvelously refreshing on a hot day."
—Frank Edwards, Buford, Georgia

6 servings

- 1 **cup sugar**
- ½ **cup water**

- 2 **cups fresh grapefruit juice**
- 1½ **tablespoons fresh lemon juice**
- 1½ **tablespoons egg white**
- 3 **grapefruit, halved, pulp and pith
  removed
  Gin to taste**

Combine sugar and water in saucepan and bring to boil, shaking pan gently until sugar is dissolved. Let cool completely.

Stir in grapefruit juice, lemon juice and egg white. Turn into ice cream freezer and mix until thickened. Pipe into grapefruit shells using pastry bag fitted with rosette tip. Freeze if not serving immediately. Just before serving, drizzle gin over sherbet.

GRANITE AU CHAMPAGNE

DOMAINE CHANDON
YOUNTVILLE, CALIFORNIA

For dessert, scoop into a glass filled with the same sparkling wine. May be served as a between-course cooler, garnished with berries.

Makes about 1 quart

- 1 **bottle brut Champagne**
- ½ **cup sugar or to taste**
- 1 **teaspoon kirsch**

Combine all ingredients quickly, blending only until sugar is dissolved; do not overmix or wine will lose its effervescence. Pour into shallow pan and freeze until firm. To serve, scrape ice to form ball of desired size for individual serving.

BISQUE TORTONI

SPERANZA ITALIAN RESTAURANT
CAYCE, SOUTH CAROLINA

12 to 14 servings

- 2 **egg whites**
- 2½ **cups whipping cream, well chilled**
- ¾ **cup powdered sugar**
- ½ **teaspoon vanilla**
- ½ **teaspoon rum extract
  Crushed coconut macaroons (garnish)**

Prepare muffin tin with paper liners. Beat egg whites until stiff peaks form. Hold in refrigerator. Using chilled beater and bowl, whip cream until slightly stiff. Add sugar, vanilla and rum extract and whip until cream holds peaks. Fold in egg whites. Pipe into paper liners and immediately place in freezer. Garnish with macaroon crumbs.

ALMOND CAKE AFTER LISBON'S TAVARES RESTAURANT

TAVARES
LISBON, PORTUGAL

12 servings

      3 eggs
  1½ cups sugar

  1½ cups whipping cream
    1 teaspoon vanilla
    ¾ teaspoon almond extract
    ¼ teaspoon salt

  1½ cups sifted cake flour
    2 teaspoons baking powder
    1 cup ground almonds

      Sauce*
    3 ounces whole blanched almonds,
      lightly toasted

Preheat oven to 350°F. Beat eggs until lemon-colored. Gradually add sugar, beating until mixture is light and fluffy.

Whip cream with vanilla, almond extract and salt in large mixing bowl until nearly stiff.

Sift together flour and baking powder. Fold egg mixture into whipped cream. Gradually fold in flour mixture and ground almonds.

Line 3 buttered 8-inch round layer cake pans with waxed paper; butter top of paper. Divide batter into pans, smoothing tops. Bake until cake springs back when lightly touched with fingertip, about 25 to 30 minutes. Cool in pans 5 minutes, then turn out onto racks to finish cooling.

Place 1 cake layer on serving plate. Spread top evenly with ¼ sauce. Repeat with second layer. Top with third layer, spreading remaining sauce over top and partly down sides of cake. Decorate with whole almonds.

Can be made ahead and chilled, but bring to room temperature before serving.

*Sauce

12 servings

    1 cup sugar
    6 tablespoons water

    6 well-beaten egg yolks

Combine sugar and water in heavy saucepan. Boil just until sugar dissolves. Allow to cool slightly.

Beating vigorously, pour syrup in thin stream into well-beaten egg yolks. Pour mixture back into saucepan and cook over low heat, stirring constantly, until slightly thickened and completely blended, about 15 minutes; do not let it boil. Strain into shallow platter and allow to cool.

CARROT CAKE

SOUPERB SALADS
SACRAMENTO, CALIFORNIA

16 to 20 servings

Cake

    2 cups sugar
  1½ cups vegetable oil
    3 eggs
    2 teaspoons vanilla
  2¼ cups all purpose flour
    2 teaspoons cinnamon
    2 teaspoons baking soda
    1 teaspoon salt
    2 cups shredded carrots
    2 cups flaked coconut
    1 8-ounce can crushed pineapple, drained
    1 cup chopped walnuts (optional)

Frosting

    6 ounces cream cheese, room temperature
    ½ cup (1 stick) melted butter
    ¼ cup milk
    2 teaspoons vanilla
    ¼ teaspoon salt
    3 to 4 cups powdered sugar

For cake: Preheat oven to 350°F. Generously grease 9x13-inch baking pan.

Combine sugar, oil, eggs and vanilla in large bowl and blend using wooden spoon. Stir in flour, cinnamon, soda and salt and mix well. Fold in carrots, coconut, pineapple and walnuts. Pour into prepared pan. Bake until tester inserted in center comes out clean, about 50 minutes. Let cool in pan 5 minutes. Invert onto rack and let cool.

For frosting: Combine cheese, butter, milk, vanilla and salt in medium bowl and blend well using electric mixer. Beat in enough powdered sugar to make mixture spreadable. Frost top and sides of cooled cake.

BUTTER BRICKLE TOASTED PECAN CAKE

TIMBER RIDGE COUNTRY CLUB
MINOCQUA, WISCONSIN

8 servings

    3 tablespoons (⅜ stick) butter
    1 cup chopped pecans

    ⅔ cup butter, room temperature
  1⅓ cups sugar
  1½ teaspoons vanilla
    2 eggs
    2 cups sifted cake flour
  1½ teaspoons baking powder
    ¼ teaspoon salt
    ⅔ cup milk
      Butter Pecan Cream Cheese
      Frosting*

Preheat oven to 350°F. Grease and flour 3 8x1½-inch cake pans; set aside. Combine 3 tablespoons butter and pecans, spread evenly on baking sheet and toast until deep golden brown, stirring several times, 10 to 15 minutes. Let cool. Keep oven at 350°F.

Cream ⅔ cup butter. Gradually add sugar and beat until light and fluffy. Add vanilla. Beat in eggs 1 at a time, beating well after each addition. Sift dry ingredients and add alternately with milk, beating well after each addition. Fold in 1 cup toasted pecans (save remainder for frosting). Divide batter among pans and bake until toothpick comes out clean, about 30 to 35 minutes. Cool 10 minutes. Gently remove from pans and cool completely before frosting. Store in refrigerator after frosting.

*Butter Pecan Cream Cheese Frosting

8 servings

- 1 8-ounce package cream cheese, room temperature
- ¼ cup (½ stick) butter, room temperature
- 1 pound powdered sugar
- 1 teaspoon vanilla
- ⅓ cup chopped pecans

Cream cheese and butter. Add sugar and vanilla and beat until smooth. Stir in toasted pecans.

CHOCOLATE CAKE

THE COACH HOUSE
NEW YORK, NEW YORK

Prepare 2 or 3 days before serving.

16 to 20 servings

Cake

- 4 cups all purpose flour
- 1½ cups (3 sticks) unsalted butter, room temperature

- 1 pound bittersweet chocolate
- ¼ cup water
- 2 teaspoons salt

Filling

- 1 quart whipping cream
- 1½ pounds bittersweet chocolate

  Powdered sugar and chocolate curls (decoration)

For cake: Combine flour and butter in large bowl and mix with fingertips until consistency of coarse oatmeal; do not let butter melt and become oily.

Melt chocolate in saucepan over very low heat. Add water and salt and beat until smooth. Make well in flour mixture. Pour in chocolate and mix lightly but thoroughly. Divide dough into 3 parts and wrap each in waxed paper. Refrigerate dough until firm, about 20 minutes.

Preheat oven to 350°F. Place 1 piece of dough between 2 sheets of waxed paper and roll into large circle about ⅛ inch thick. Lift off top sheet of paper and use sharp knife to cut circle 9 to 10 inches in diameter; remove excess dough. Carefully invert circle onto ungreased baking sheet and remove remaining paper. Bake 15 to 18 minutes. Working carefully, loosen pastry with spatula and slide onto heavy duty foil to cool. Repeat with rest of dough.

For filling: Place cream in large bowl and set in larger bowl or sink on bed of ice. Melt chocolate in heavy saucepan over very low heat or hot water. Whip cream until stiff, then fold in chocolate, mixing gently but thoroughly.

To assemble: Carefully slide one cake layer onto serving plate. Spread ½ filling over top. Repeat with second layer and remaining filling. Top with last layer. Sprinkle with powdered sugar and garnish with chocolate curls. Refrigerate for 2 to 3 days.

About 2 hours before serving, remove cake from refrigerator; while still cold, slice with serrated knife.

THE BRICKERVILLE HOUSE CHOCOLATE CAKE

THE BRICKERVILLE HOUSE
LITITZ, PENNSYLVANIA

10 to 12 servings

- 2 cups sugar
- 3 large eggs
- 1¼ cups oil
- 4 teaspoons vanilla

- 1⅓ cups boiling water
- 1 cup unsweetened cocoa
- 1⅓ teaspoons baking soda
- 1⅓ teaspoons baking powder
- ⅔ teaspoon salt
- 2⅓ cups unsifted all purpose flour

Peanut Butter Frosting

- 1 pound sifted powdered sugar
- ½ cup creamy peanut butter
- ¼ to ⅓ cup milk

Preheat oven to 350°F. Generously grease 2 9-inch round cake pans; set aside. In large mixing bowl, beat sugar and eggs until creamy. Blend in oil and vanilla and beat 2 minutes.

Combine boiling water and cocoa; add to egg mixture and blend thoroughly. Stir in soda, baking powder and salt. Add flour and beat until mixture is thoroughly blended and smooth.

Pour into prepared pans and bake 25 to 30 minutes. Remove from oven and let stand 5 minutes in pans, then turn onto racks. Let cakes cool completely before frosting.

For frosting: Combine sugar, peanut butter and ¼ cup milk in mixing bowl. Beat until smooth and creamy, adding more milk if necessary.

CHOCOLATE SOUFFLE ROLL

THE WHITE HOUSE
WASHINGTON, D.C.

This is a creation of Albert Kumin, formerly pastry chef at the White House in Washington, D.C. Since this recipe makes two cakes, you can freeze one for use later. Since center-of-oven rack placement is all-important, it would be best to bake both cakes at once in 2 ovens. However, if you have only 1 oven, bake them separately.

10 to 12 servings

16½ ounces sugar
  4 ounces (½ cup) water

 15 egg whites

2½ ounces semisweet chocolate, melted
1¾ ounces unsweetened chocolate, melted
  4 egg yolks
1½ ounces warm water

1½ ounces all purpose flour
1¼ ounces cornstarch

    Crème Ganache*

    Buttercream**

    Chocolate Sheets***

Position rack in center of oven and preheat to 400°F. Line 2 10x15-inch jelly roll pans with parchment paper. Combine 13 ounces sugar and 4 ounces water in small saucepan over medium-low heat and begin bringing to boil, stirring gently until sugar is dissolved (try not to splash sides of pan).

Meanwhile, on medium high speed beat egg whites, gradually adding remaining sugar, until stiff. When syrup registers 237°F on candy thermometer, remove from heat and beat into egg whites in slow steady stream. Continue beating until cool.

Blend chocolates, egg yolks and warm water in large mixing bowl. Stir about 1 cup meringue into chocolate mixture to loosen, then fold in remainder.

Sift together flour and cornstarch. Gradually resift into meringue mixture, folding them together gently but thoroughly.

Divide mixture between prepared pans, spreading evenly to edges. Bake until set, about 25 minutes; do not overbake. Let cool in pans.

Lightly grease 2 sheets of waxed paper long enough to accommodate roulades. Turn cakes out onto waxed paper and let cool completely. Spread thin layer of Crème Ganache over 1 cake. Spread small amount of Buttercream over Crème Ganache. Roll lengthwise like jelly roll. (Freeze second cake.) Spread remaining Buttercream over top and sides and coat with Chocolate Sheets.

*Crème Ganache

10 to 12 servings

  6 ounces semisweet chocolate

  1 cup whipping cream
 ¼ cup (½ stick) unsalted butter

Cut chocolate in ½-inch pieces and melt in double boiler over warm water.

Meanwhile, combine cream and butter in heavy-bottomed saucepan and bring to boil over medium heat, stirring lightly to blend ingredients. Remove from heat and gently stir in melted chocolate. Set in pan of ice water and stir gently as mixture thickens (do not whip; Ganache should be a dark color; whipping makes it lighter).

**Buttercream

 ½ cup egg whites (about 4 large eggs)
1½ cups plus 2 teaspoons superfine sugar

  1 cup (2 sticks) unsalted butter, room temperature

1½ to 2 tablespoons kirsch or to taste

Combine egg whites and sugar in large mixing bowl. Place in double boiler over hot, not boiling, water and stir until sugar is dissolved and whites are warmed. Remove from water and beat to thick meringue. Reduce speed; beat until cool.

Add butter 1 tablespoon at a time and beat until very smooth and creamy. If Buttercream curdles, place over low heat for 5 or 6 seconds, just long enough to start melting on the sides (it may look worse before it looks better). Beat vigorously with whisk until mixture thickens and glistens.

Lightly cover Buttercream and let stand at cool room temperature. When ready to use, add kirsch to taste.

***Chocolate Sheets

 12 ounces semisweet chocolate
  4 ounces glucose, room temperature

    Powdered sugar

Cut chocolate into ½-inch pieces. Melt ½ chocolate over hot water. Blend in ½ glucose. Let stand at room temperature about 30 minutes.

Turn onto work surface and knead 2 to 3 minutes to make smooth consistency suitable for rolling. (If not using immediately, wrap in plastic to prevent drying and let stand at room temperature.)

Sprinkle work surface lightly with powdered sugar. Divide chocolate into 2 pieces. Using rolling pin, flatten each piece into rectangle about 3 inches wide. Run each piece smoothly through electric pasta machine. (You may find this easier with an assistant.) Refrigerate until ready to use.

***Chocolate Sheets (alternate method)

  1 12-ounce package semisweet chocolate chips
 ¼ cup (½ stick) unsalted butter
 ¼ cup light corn syrup

Combine chocolate, butter and corn syrup in top of double boiler. Set over hot water, lay paper towel over top of pan and cover with lid (this will absorb any condensation). Remove from heat.

When chocolate is melted, mix until smooth. Using a spatula, spread chocolate about ⅛ inch thick onto waxed paper, getting as close to edge as possible. Refrigerate until firm.

HOT N' GOOEY CHOCOLATE CAKE

TAMBORINE
CHICAGO, ILLINOIS

10 to 12 servings

> ½ cup plus 1 tablespoon vegetable oil
> 4 eggs
> 1 cup sugar
>
> 1 cup cake flour, sifted
> ½ cup cocoa
> 2 teaspoons baking powder
> ⅛ teaspoon baking soda
> ½ cup milk
> 1 teaspoon vanilla
>
> **Hot Fudge Sauce***
> **Whipped cream (garnish)**

Preheat oven to 350°F. Grease and flour 9-inch tube pan or bundt pan, shaking out excess. Beat oil, eggs and sugar, using medium speed of electric mixer until mixture is light and lemon colored.

Resift flour with cocoa, baking powder and soda. Add to egg mixture with milk and vanilla. Beat at low speed until blended.

Pour into prepared pan. Bake until toothpick inserted in center of cake comes out clean, about 1 hour. Cool 10 to 20 minutes in pan. Invert onto platter. Serve warm with Hot Fudge Sauce and whipped cream.

*Hot Fudge Sauce

10 to 12 servings

> 4 1-ounce squares unsweetened
>   baking chocolate
> 2 tablespoons (¼ stick) butter
> ⅓ cup strong black coffee
> ⅓ cup boiling water
> 2 cups sugar
> ¼ cup corn syrup
> 1 tablespoon rum

Melt chocolate in top of double boiler set over gently simmering water. Add butter and stir until melted. Pour in coffee and water, stirring constantly until well combined. Blend in sugar and corn syrup. Transfer mixture to small saucepan. Cover and boil, without stirring, 3 minutes. Reduce heat and cook, uncovered, without stirring, 2 minutes. Remove from heat and stir in rum. Serve immediately.

COCONUT CAKE

HOTEL LUZ
GRANADA, SPAIN

"On a holiday trip to Spain last summer, I enjoyed a buffet luncheon at the Hotel Luz in Granada. Among the desserts was a coconut cake enclosed in a puff pastry that was the most delicious cake I have ever tasted."
—W. Gillespie Milwain, Bardwell, Kentucky

8 to 10 servings

> 1 pound puff pastry dough
>
> 4 eggs
> 1½ cups superfine sugar
> 4½ cups finely grated unsweetened coconut*
> 1 tablespoon melted butter
> 1½ teaspoons vanilla
>
> ⅔ cup apricot preserves
> ½ cup whipping cream

Place rack in lower ⅓ of oven and preheat to 350°F. Lightly grease 8-inch springform pan. Roll pastry to ¼-inch thickness and line bottom and sides of pan with dough; trim edges with sharp knife.

Beat eggs in large mixing bowl until thoroughly blended and foamy. Add sugar gradually and continue beating until very light, about 2 to 3 minutes. Blend in coconut, butter and vanilla. Spoon into pastry-lined pan. Place on baking sheet, preferably one with sides, and bake until golden brown, about 60 to 70 minutes.

Remove from oven and cool slightly. Release from pan and cool completely. Decorate top of cake with rim of apricot preserves. Whip cream and add in dollops over top and around bottom edges.

*Also called macaroon coconut; available at natural food stores.

PINEAPPLE NUT CAKE "1902"

GRANNY'S SANDWITCHERY AND GOURMET DINING
PARKERSBURG, WEST VIRGINIA

12 to 15 servings

> 2 eggs
> 2 cups sugar
> 1 teaspoon vanilla
> 2 cups flour
> 2 teaspoons baking soda
> 1 cup crushed pineapple
> 1 cup coarsely chopped walnuts
>
> **Cream Cheese Icing***

Preheat oven to 350°F. Beat eggs, sugar and vanilla until sugar is dissolved. Beat in flour, baking soda and pineapple. Fold in walnuts.

Pour into greased and floured 13x9x2-inch pan. Bake until firm, about 50 to 60 minutes. Turn out onto cake rack to cool. When completely cool, spread with icing.

*Cream Cheese Icing

12 to 15 servings

> 1 8-ounce package cream cheese
> ½ cup (1 stick) butter
> 1½ cups powdered sugar
> 1 teaspoon vanilla

Mix cream cheese and butter together until well blended. Add powdered sugar and vanilla and beat until creamy.

DOME CAKE LENOTRE
(Boule de Neige)

PRE CATELAN
PARIS, FRANCE

6 to 8 servings

Cake

    5 eggs, separated
    ⅔ cup sugar
    1 cup flour

Dessert Syrup

    ⅓ cup sugar
    6 tablespoons water
    2 tablespoons liquor such as kirsch, rum,
       Grand Marnier or 2 tablespoons water
       mixed with ½ teaspoon vanilla or
       coffee extract

Mousse Cafe

    ⅔ cup milk
    1½ cups plus 3 teaspoons sugar
    ¼ vanilla bean
    1 tablespoon instant coffee powder or
       espresso powder

    7 medium egg yolks

    2 tablespoons water
    2 medium egg whites

    2 cups (1 pound) butter, room
       temperature

    1 to 1¼ cups grated or shaved
       semisweet chocolate

       Powdered sugar

For cake: Position rack in lower ⅓ of oven and preheat to 350°F. Grease and lightly flour shallow 2-quart brioche bowl or 1½-quart dome-shaped mixing bowl 6½ inches in diameter.

Place yolks in medium bowl. With electric mixer at medium speed, gradually beat in all but 1½ tablespoons sugar. Continue beating until thick, very pale and mixture forms thick ribbon, about 3 minutes. Using spoon, carefully stir in flour, working mixture as little as possible to incorporate.

In separate bowl, beat egg whites for 1½ minutes using electric mixer at high speed. Add remaining 1½ tablespoons sugar; beat until stiff and glossy.

Carefully fold whites into batter. Pour batter into prepared bowl to within 1 inch of top (2-quart bowl will accommodate all of batter). Bake until lightly browned, about 45 to 50 minutes, checking cake after 45 minutes. (Toothpick inserted in center of

cake should be sticky but not wet.) Remove from oven and cool in bowl 30 to 45 minutes. Invert onto rack, remove bowl carefully and cool completely.

For syrup: Combine sugar and water in small saucepan and bring to boil, stirring with wooden spoon until sugar is dissolved. Remove from heat and cool completely. Blend in flavoring.

For mousse: Combine milk, ½ cup sugar, vanilla bean and coffee powder in small saucepan. Bring to boil, stirring occasionally until sugar is dissolved. Reduce heat, cover and keep hot.

Beat yolks with ½ cup sugar until mixture whitens and forms ribbon.

Remove vanilla bean from milk mixture. Gradually pour hot milk into yolks, beating constantly with whisk. Strain mixture through chinois or sieve into saucepan. Bring to boil, whisking constantly. Remove from heat, transfer to large mixer bowl and beat until cool.

Combine ½ cup plus 1 teaspoon sugar and 2 tablespoons water in small saucepan. Cover and cook over medium-high heat until mixture registers 250°F on candy thermometer. Beat egg whites with remaining 2 teaspoons sugar until foamy. Add syrup in slow steady stream and beat until cool.

Cream butter in large bowl until very soft. Slowly blend in milk mixture. If this mixture appears not to be blending well (or curdling), beat rapidly with large rubber spatula or whisk until smooth (mixture must be smooth before meringue is added). Gently and thoroughly fold in meringue.

To assemble: Cut cardboard circle ½ inch larger than bottom of cake. Trim any brown crust from top of dome using serrated knife. Slice cake horizontally into 4 layers, each approximately 1 inch thick. Place bottom layer on cardboard. Line up remaining layers on counter.

Using pastry brush or large paint brush, lightly paint tops of all layers with Dessert Syrup. Cover bottom layer with about ⅓ Mousse Cafe, using spatula to spread evenly. With spoon, sprinkle with some of chocolate. Top with next layer, syrup side down. Brush top with additional syrup and cover with some of Mousse. Sprinkle with chocolate. Repeat procedure with next layer, then add last layer dome side up, painting generously with syrup. Cover entire cake with remaining mousse, spreading thickly and evenly to edge so no cardboard shows and retaining dome shape.

Carefully set cake on inverted round cake pan to elevate slightly. Sift powdered sugar over entire cake, covering thickly. Heat skewer or wire hanger over direct heat. Sear sugar from center outward in spoke pattern. Transfer to serving plate. Chill.

CHOMEUR

CHEZ HELENE
VENICE, CALIFORNIA

"When I lived in Los Angeles, I often stopped for lunch at Chez Hélène, a charming French cafe. The luncheon menu featured a delicious dessert called Chomeur. Now that I live 3,000 miles away, I find myself missing that dessert." —Adrianne DeCarolis, Denville, New Jersey

Chomeur is a type of pudding-cake, baked in a rich caramel sauce.

4 to 6 servings

- 1½ **cups light brown sugar, firmly packed**
- ½ **cup milk**
- 3 **tablespoons (⅜ stick) butter, chilled, cut into bits**

- 1 **egg, lightly beaten**
- 4 **tablespoons sugar**
- 4 **tablespoons (¼ stick) butter, melted**
- ½ **cup milk**

- 1 **cup flour**
- 1 **teaspoon baking powder**
- 1 **teaspoon vanilla**
   Whipping cream (garnish)

Preheat oven to 350°F. In 1-quart ceramic or glass baking dish, combine sugar and milk. Add chilled butter to complete sauce ingredients.

In mixing bowl, combine egg, sugar and melted butter. Add remaining milk and stir well.

Sift together flour and baking powder and mix into egg-milk mixture. Add vanilla and mix until batter is smooth. Spoon batter into sauce in baking dish; do not mix or smooth out batter. Bake until cake is puffed and golden and knife inserted into cake comes out clean, about 50 minutes. Serve directly from baking dish, spooning sauce over individual servings, and top with cream.

COURT CAKE

PORT BAKEHOUSE
PORTLAND, MAINE

The recipe is an old family favorite given to owner Leslie Burnett by her grandmother when the Port Bakehouse first opened.

10 to 12 servings

- 1 **cup (2 sticks) butter, room temperature**
- 2 **cups sugar**
- 2 **eggs**
- 3 **cups all purpose flour**
- 1 **teaspoon salt**
- 1 **teaspoon mace**
- 1 **teaspoon nutmeg**

- ½ **teaspoon baking soda**
- 1 **cup milk**
- 1 **tablespoon vinegar**
- ½ **cup chopped walnuts**
- ½ **cup raisins**
   Finely grated peel of 2 oranges
   Orange Glaze* or powdered sugar

Preheat oven to 350°F. Grease and flour 9-inch springform pan. Cream butter and sugar until light. Beat in eggs. Sift dry ingredients and add alternately with milk soured with vinegar, beginning and ending with dry mixture. Generously flour nuts, raisins and orange peel and fold into batter. Turn into pan and bake until toothpick comes clean, about 80 minutes. When cake is cool, spread with Orange Glaze or sprinkle with powdered sugar.

*Orange Glaze

Makes 1½ cups

- 1¼ **cups sifted powdered sugar**
- ¼ **cup orange juice**
- 1 **teaspoon vanilla**

Blend ingredients in small bowl.

KEY LIME CAKE

PIGEON HOUSE PATIO
KEY WEST, FLORIDA

12 to 15 servings

- 1⅓ **cups water**
- 2 **cups all purpose flour**
- ⅔ **teaspoon salt**
- 1 **teaspoon baking powder**
- ½ **teaspoon baking soda**
- 1 **3-ounce package lime-flavored gelatin**
- 5 **eggs**
- 1⅓ **cups cooking oil**
- ¾ **cup orange juice**
- ½ **teaspoon vanilla**
- 1 **teaspoon lemon extract**

- ⅓ **cup Key lime juice***
- ⅓ **cup powdered sugar**

   Whipped cream (garnish)
   Lime slices (garnish)

Preheat oven to 350°F. Place dry ingredients into mixing bowl. Add eggs, oil, orange juice, vanilla and lemon extract. Beat until well blended. Pour batter into 9x13x2-inch pan; bake 25 to 30 minutes.

Remove cake from oven. Let stand in pan until almost cool, about 15 minutes. Prick cake all over with fork. Drizzle thoroughly with lime juice mixed with powdered sugar. Cover and refrigerate.

To serve, cut into squares, top with whipped cream and garnish with lime slices.

*If Key limes are unavailable, use regular limes.

JAMAICAN MYSTERY CAKE

WELLFLEET OYSTER HOUSE
WELLFLEET, MASSACHUSETTS

"The Wellfleet Oyster House serves a cake called Jamaican Mystery Cake. The mystery is how did the recipe for such a sensational cake end up in New England?" —Jennifer Benjamin, Boston, Massachusetts

Owner Nonie Castelo says the recipe has been in the family of Captain Reuben Baker for over three generations. His grandfather, Captain L. D. Baker, successfully imported bananas from his plantations in Jamaica to his home in New England in the 1800s.

Makes 8 to 10 servings

Cake

    ½ cup (1 stick) butter, room temperature
    1¼ cups sugar
    2 eggs
    2 cups sifted flour
    2 teaspoons baking powder
    ½ teaspoon salt
    ½ cup milk
    3 ripe small bananas, mashed
    ¾ cup toasted chopped walnuts

Icing

    1 cup (2 sticks) butter, room temperature
    1 cup sugar
    3 eggs
    2 teaspoons instant coffee dissolved in
       ¼ cup coffee liqueur

    1 banana
    1 ounce (2 tablespoons) Grand Marnier
    ½ cup toasted chopped walnuts (garnish)

For cake: Preheat oven to 350°F. Cream butter and sugar in mixing bowl. Add eggs 1 at a time, beating well after each addition. Sift together dry ingredients and add to butter mixture alternately with milk, beginning and ending with dry ingredients. Fold in mashed banana and walnuts.

Pour into greased 9x5-inch loaf pan and bake until toothpick inserted in center comes out clean, about 1 hour. Let cool in pan 5 minutes; invert on cake rack to cool.

For icing: In small bowl of electric mixer, cream butter and sugar at medium speed. Using high speed, add eggs 1 at a time, beating well after each addition. Blend in dissolved instant coffee mixture.

To assemble: Slice cake in ½ lengthwise. Place bottom layer cut side up on cake platter. Slice banana and arrange evenly over cake. Sprinkle with Grand Marnier. Spread ½ icing over bananas. Add top layer and frost top only with remaining icing. Garnish with walnuts. Refrigerate.

HONEY CAKE

NEVELE COUNTRY CLUB
ELLENVILLE, NEW YORK

Makes 1 9x5-inch loaf

    1 cup honey
    1 cup unpacked brown sugar
    2 eggs
    ½ cup oil
    ½ cup coffee
    ⅛ teaspoon baking soda
       Pinch salt
    3 cups rye flour
       Pinch cloves
       Pinch allspice
       Pinch cinnamon
    ½ cup toasted coarsely chopped walnuts

Preheat oven to 325°F. Grease and flour 9x5-inch loaf pan. Blend first 7 ingredients with mixer at low speed, about 2 minutes. Add remaining ingredients except walnuts and mix on medium speed until smooth, about 5 minutes. Blend in nuts. Turn into loaf pan and bake until toothpick inserted in center comes out clean, about 1½ hours. Cool 10 minutes. Remove from pan and cool completely on wire rack.

PECAN ROLL WITH CHOCOLATE WHIPPED CREAM

VINCENT'S RESTAURANT
BOSTON, MASSACHUSETTS

6 to 8 servings

Cake

    4 large eggs, separated
    1 cup sifted powdered sugar
    2 cups ground pecans*

Filling

    1 cup whipping cream
    3 tablespoons sugar
    2 teaspoons cocoa
    ½ teaspoon vanilla
       Powdered sugar

For cake: Preheat oven to 400°F. Butter 11x16-inch jelly roll pan. Line with waxed paper. Butter paper and set pan aside.

In medium bowl, beat yolks and powdered sugar until thick and lemon colored. Fold in pecans. Beat whites until stiff but not dry. Fold ¼ whites into yolk mixture to loosen texture, then gently fold in remaining whites. Spread evenly into prepared pan. Bake until cake is lightly browned and springs back when touched on surface, about 15 to 20 minutes.

Remove pan from oven and turn cake onto sheet of waxed paper. Lift pan from cake with small spatula. Do not remove waxed paper. Roll cake lengthwise and allow to cool completely.

For filling: Combine cream, sugar, cocoa and vanilla. Chill at least 30 minutes. Beat cream mixture until it forms firm but not stiff peaks. Unroll cake and carefully peel off waxed paper. Spread roll with whipped cream and roll up again. Place on serving platter seam down. Sprinkle with powdered sugar.

*Roll may also be made with almonds, walnuts or hazelnuts.

TIVOLI RUM CAKE

TIVOLI RESTAURANT
PITTSBURGH, PENNSYLVANIA

8 to 10 servings

Cake

    8 **eggs**
    1 **cup sugar**
  1¼ **cups flour**
   ¼ **cup cornstarch**
     Pinch finely grated lemon peel

Filling

    8 **egg yolks**
    1 **cup sugar**
    2 **tablespoons plus 2 teaspoons cornstarch**
   ¼ **teaspoon vanilla**
     Pinch salt
    4 **cups milk**

Rum Syrup

  1½ **cups water**
   ½ **cup sugar**
    2 **strips of lemon peel**
    3 **ounces (6 tablespoons) rum**

    1 **cup whipping cream**
   ¼ **cup toasted almonds (garnish)**

For cake: Preheat oven to 350°F. Grease and flour 3-inch-deep 9-inch springform pan. Combine eggs and sugar in large mixing bowl. Set over simmering water and stir until heated through, about 1 to 2 minutes. Remove from water and beat with electric mixer until stiff, about 10 minutes. Fold in flour

sifted with cornstarch until completely blended. Stir in grated peel. Turn into pan and bake until toothpick inserted in center comes out clean, about 30 to 40 minutes. Let cool in pan 5 minutes. Remove sides of pan and invert cake onto rack to cool.

For filling: Combine yolks and sugar in medium saucepan. Gradually add cornstarch, vanilla and salt. Scald milk and add gradually, whisking constantly until well blended. Cook over very low heat, stirring constantly until thickened and smooth, about 5 minutes. Let cool.

For syrup: Combine water, sugar and lemon peel in medium saucepan. Bring to boil, shaking pan occasionally until sugar is dissolved. Boil 5 minutes. Let cool completely, then stir in rum, blending well.

To assemble: Split cake into 3 layers. Place bottom layer cut side up on platter. Paint with syrup to coat evenly. Spread with ½ filling. Add middle layer and paint with syrup. Cover with remaining filling. Add last layer cut side down.

Whip cream until stiff. Pipe over top and sides of cake. Garnish with almonds.

SUMMER FOOL

CARL ANDERSEN'S CHATAM
LOS ANGELES, CALIFORNIA

6 servings

    2 **cups whipping cream**
    2 **tablespoons sugar**

    1 **sponge cake, 8 inches round, 2 inches high**
    1 **cup currant jelly, whipped thin for spreading**
    4 **cups thinly sliced peeled peaches**
    4 **cups thinly sliced strawberries**
     Additional whipped cream (garnish)

Whip cream and sweeten with sugar.

Slice sponge cake into 4 layers ½ inch thick. Place 1 slice in bottom of glass bowl. Spread with ¼ whipped currant jelly. Arrange layer of peaches on top of jelly, followed by layer of strawberries and layer of whipped cream. Continue layering until all ingredients have been included, ending with fruit.

Using pastry bag, decorate top of dessert with additional whipped cream.

DACQUOISE

THE COACH HOUSE
NEW YORK, NEW YORK

10 to 12 servings

Meringue

 5 egg whites, room temperature
⅛ teaspoon cream of tartar
 1 cup sugar
 1 cup plus 1 tablespoon ground
   toasted almonds
 3 tablespoons cornstarch

Buttercream

½ cup sugar
⅓ cup water
 5 egg yolks
 2 tablespoons Grand Marnier
   Scant ¾ teaspoon decaffeinated
   coffee powder
 1 cup (2 sticks) unsalted butter, cut into
   small pieces

 2 tablespoons powdered sugar (garnish)

For meringue: Position rack in center of oven and preheat to 225°F. Beat egg whites in large bowl until foamy. Add cream of tartar and beat briefly. Gradually add ¾ cup sugar and continue beating until stiff peaks form. Combine remaining ¼ cup sugar with almonds and cornstarch and mix well. Fold into meringue gently but thoroughly.

Generously butter large baking sheets. Sprinkle with flour, shaking to coat entire surface evenly; shake off excess. Trace 3 9-inch circles on sheets. Spoon meringue into pastry bag fitted with ½-inch plain tube. Starting at center, pipe meringue in spiral to cover circles completely. Bake until meringues are pale brown and have shrunk slightly at edges, about 55 minutes. Gently lift meringues onto racks and let cool completely in draft-free area.

For buttercream: Combine sugar and water in heavy small saucepan. Place over low heat and let cook without stirring until syrup reaches 234°F on candy thermometer (soft-ball stage). Meanwhile, beat yolks with electric mixer until thick, pale yellow and ribbon is formed when dropped from side of spoon. Beating constantly, gradually add syrup in thin steady stream. Add Grand Marnier and coffee powder and mix well. With mixer on high speed, add butter in small pieces and beat until it forms smooth peaks. Cover and cool in refrigerator.

To assemble: Place 1 meringue on serving plate. Spread some of buttercream evenly over top. Add second meringue, pressing gently into filling, and spread with buttercream. Top with last meringue, pressing gently, and frost top and sides with remaining buttercream. Chill at least 1 hour before serving. Sieve powdered sugar over top and cut into wedges with serrated knife.

REVANI WITH ORANGE

MYCONOS
YARMOUTHPORT, MASSACHUSETTS

"On a visit to Cape Cod we stopped at a wonderful Greek restaurant in Yarmouthport, run by the charming Chalpara family. I especially enjoyed an unusual cake dessert called Revani, one of their family secrets."
—Florence Sabatini, Beverly, Massachusetts

Makes 18 to 24 pieces

½ cup (1 stick) butter, room temperature
½ cup sugar
½ cup farina
 3 eggs, well beaten
½ cup all purpose flour
 1 tablespoon baking powder
⅛ teaspoon salt
¼ cup orange juice
   Zest of ½ orange, minced
½ cup finely chopped almonds

Syrup

1½ cups water
1½ cups sugar
 1 thick lemon slice

   Whipped cream and fresh strawberries
   (garnish)

Preheat oven to 350°F. Lightly grease 9-inch square baking pan. Cream butter and sugar in large mixing bowl. Gradually beat in farina. Add eggs 1 at a time, beating well after each addition. Sift together flour, baking powder and salt and add alternately with orange juice and zest. Stir in almonds. Turn into prepared pan and bake until center of cake springs back when lightly touched and top is golden brown, about 30 minutes.

For syrup: Combine water, sugar and lemon slice in medium saucepan. Bring to boil, stirring until sugar is dissolved, and boil 15 minutes. Cool slightly before pouring slowly over cake (leave cake in pan).

When cake is completely cool, cut into diamond-shaped pieces. Serve garnished with whipped cream and strawberries.

HAZELNUT DACQUOISE

WINDOWS ON THE WORLD
NEW YORK, NEW YORK

10 to 12 servings

Meringue

    8 large egg whites
    ½ teaspoon cream of tartar
    2 cups sugar
    ½ pound shelled hazelnuts, toasted
        and ground

Buttercream

    1½ cups (3 sticks) butter, room temperature
    3 cups sifted powdered sugar
    4 large egg yolks
    ¼ cup almond liqueur
    2 tablespoons strong brewed espresso

For meringue: Cut out 3 waxed paper circles 8 inches in diameter. Place on 2 greased cookie sheets and thoroughly grease paper; set aside. Arrange oven racks in upper and lower thirds of oven.

In large mixing bowl, beat egg whites and cream of tartar until foamy. Gradually add sugar tablespoon at a time beating until stiff peaks form. Fold hazelnuts into egg whites.

Preheat oven to 250°F. Using pastry bag fitted with tip ¾ inch in diameter, pipe out spiral design beginning in center of each waxed paper circle, making sure that meringue completely covers paper without any openings. Bake until meringues are firm but still white, about 35 to 40 minutes. Turn off heat and leave meringue circles to dry with door closed, about 1 hour.

Remove meringues from oven and carefully peel away waxed paper. Using serrated knife or kitchen shears, trim uneven edges of meringues, reserving all crumbs for sides of meringue.

For buttercream: Cream butter, 2 cups powdered sugar and egg yolks. Add liqueur and espresso, beating until thick and creamy. Add remaining powdered sugar and blend thoroughly.

To assemble: Select most perfect meringue for top and set aside. Place 1 meringue circle on serving platter. Spread with about ¼ buttercream. Repeat with second layer. Place third meringue on top, spreading ¼ buttercream over sides only. Sprinkle meringue crumbs on sides. Decorate top edge of dacquoise with remaining buttercream, using pastry tube fitted with star tip.

Refrigerate few hours before serving. To help prevent cracking, slice dessert with serrated knife. Do not cut into wedges. Instead, cut in ½, then proceed with straight slices.

HOULIHAN'S APPLE STRUDEL PIE

HOULIHAN'S OLD PLACE RESTAURANT & BAR
MANY LOCATIONS

"Friends and I searched for a new and different restaurant in Denver. We came up with Houlihan's Old Place and were completely happy with the choice. Our dessert was unforgettable . . ."
—Bonnie Smith, Denver, Colorado

6 to 8 servings

    6 or 7 green tart apples (preferably
            Greening or Pippin)
            Juice of ½ lemon, strained
    ¾ cup sugar
    ¼ cup firmly packed light brown sugar
    ¼ cup dark currants
    1 tablespoon all purpose flour
    1 teaspoon cinnamon
    ½ teaspoon nutmeg
    2 tablespoons cold water
    1 tablespoon butter, melted and cooled
    1 9- or 10-inch unbaked pie shell

Topping

    ⅓ cup (¾ stick) butter, room temperature
    ¼ cup all purpose flour
    ¼ cup sugar
    ¼ cup firmly packed light brown sugar
    ½ teaspoon cinnamon
    ¼ teaspoon nutmeg

Glaze

    ½ cup powdered sugar
    1 to 2 tablespoons strained fresh
            lemon juice

Preheat oven to 425°F. Peel and slice enough apples ¼ inch thick to make 6 cups. Toss in large bowl with lemon juice. Add sugars, currants, flour and spices. Toss lightly to distribute evenly. Add water and butter and toss. Pile evenly into shell.

For topping: Using 2 knives, cut butter into flour until mixture is crumbly. Gently mix in sugars and spices. Pile lightly over apples, covering top completely. Bake 10 minutes. Reduce heat to 325°F and continue baking 1 hour. Remove pie from oven and allow it to cool slightly.

For glaze: Combine ingredients and mix until smooth. Drizzle over warm pie.

Cool completely before serving.

CRANBERRY-APPLE PIE

MARION'S PIE SHOP
CHATHAM, MASSACHUSETTS

6 servings

- 4 tart medium apples, peeled, cored and sliced
- ½ cup water

- 1¾ cups sugar
- 2 tablespoons cornstarch
- ¼ teaspoon salt
- 2½ cups whole cranberries (fresh or frozen)
- 2 tablespoons grated orange peel
- 3 tablespoons (⅜ stick) butter

  Pastry for double-crust 9-inch pie (shell and lattice top)

Combine apples and water in large saucepan. Place over medium heat and cook, uncovered, until apples are slightly soft, about 5 to 8 minutes.

Preheat oven to 425°F. Combine sugar, cornstarch and salt and blend thoroughly into apples. Add cranberries, grated orange peel and butter. Cook, uncovered, over medium heat until cranberries start to pop, about 5 minutes.

Spoon into pie shell, top with lattice crust and bake 20 minutes. Reduce heat to 350°F and bake until top is deep golden brown, about 25 minutes. Serve warm or at room temperature.

RED LION INN APPLE PIE

RED LION INN
VAIL, COLORADO

"For the past two winters our family has skied at Vail, where we always take the opportunity to dine at the Red Lion Inn. We're looking forward to the Red Lion again this year, especially the marvelous apple pie with almonds and raisins."
—Mrs. Robert Brail, Longwood, Florida

8 servings

- ½ pound puff pastry dough
- 3 large tart red apples, peeled and thinly sliced

- 1¼ cups water
- ¾ cup plus 2 tablespoons sugar
- 2 tablespoons cornstarch

- ¾ cup graham cracker crumbs
- ½ cup (1 stick) butter, room temperature
- 6 tablespoons dark raisins
- ¼ cup blanched sliced almonds
- 1 tablespoon fresh lemon juice
- ¼ teaspoon vanilla
  Pinch each: cinnamon, mace and nutmeg

Grease 10-inch pie plate. Roll pastry ⅛ inch thick and fit into plate, cutting off excess with knife. Arrange apples over pastry.

Place rack in middle of oven and preheat to 400°F. Combine 1 cup water and ¾ cup sugar in small saucepan and bring to boil over medium heat, stirring until sugar dissolves, then boil 10 minutes without stirring. Add cornstarch dissolved in remaining water and stir constantly until thickened. Pour over apples.

Thoroughly combine crumbs, butter, raisins and almonds. Mix in remaining ingredients and sprinkle evenly over apples. Bake 15 minutes; cover with foil and bake 30 minutes longer. Serve warm.

LA TARTE TATIN
(Caramelized Apples on Puff Pastry)

ERNIE'S
SAN FRANCISCO, CALIFORNIA

4 servings

- ½ pound puff pastry (fresh or thawed frozen)

- 1 cup sugar
- ¼ cup water
- 5 pounds Golden Delicious apples, peeled, cored, quartered and tossed with lemon juice

- ½ teaspoon cinnamon
- ¼ cup (½ stick) unsalted butter, melted

  Sugar

For pastry: Preheat oven to 300°F. Roll pastry ⅛ inch thick. Cut into circle 1 inch larger than diameter of 1-quart soufflé dish. Transfer to baking sheet, prick with fork and bake 30 minutes. If not quite browned, increase heat to 350°F and continue baking until nicely colored. Let cool on wire rack.

Heat oven to 350°F. Combine ½ cup sugar with water in 8-inch skillet and cook, swirling pan frequently, until caramelized. Pour into 1-quart soufflé dish. Begin adding apples, arranging vertically (fill dish as compactly as possible since fruit will shrink during baking). Lay remaining apples (or as many as possible) on top.

Sprinkle with remaining ½ cup sugar and cinnamon. Pour melted butter evenly over top. Cover with foil, making several slits to allow steam to escape. Lay piece of foil on lower oven rack to catch any juices that might overflow. Bake, basting frequently, until apples are tender, about 1½ hours. Remove from oven and cool 15 minutes. Carefully pour off juices into 8-inch skillet and boil over medium-high heat until reduced and caramelized.

L'Escargot on Michigan, Chicago, 190
Le Francais, Wheeling, 70, 87, 112, 131, 132, 187
Marshall Field's, Chicago, 193
The Plantation, Moline, 25
Sully's, Kankakee, 19
Tamborine, Chicago, 201
Truffles, Hyatt Regency, Chicago, 165
Yesteryear, Kankakee, 192

INDIANA
Cafe Johnell, Ft. Wayne, 100
Harrison's, Indianapolis, 15
Le Petit Cafe, Bloomington, 109
Mama Lou's Pie Kitchen, Innkeeper's Square, Clarksville, 215
Patchwork Quilt Country Inn, Middlebury, 96
Ramada Inn, Nashville, 175
Ramada Inn, Scottsburg, 177

IOWA
Embassy Club, Des Moines, 14
Ox-Yoke Inn, Amana, 212

KANSAS
Dragon Inn, Overland Park, 14

KENTUCKY
Ninth Street House, Paducah, 48
Science Hill Inn, Shelbyville, 192
610 Magnolia, Louisville, 222

LOUISIANA
Brennan's, New Orleans, 26
Commander's Palace, New Orleans, 32, 40, 88, 92, 102, 140
Jacques', Sheraton Baton Rouge Hotel, Baton Rouge, 26

MAINE
The Firepond, Blue Hill, 38
The Green Heron Inn, Kennebunkport, 178
Julie's Ristorante, Ogunquit, 119
The Kennebunk Inn 1799, Kennebunk, 211
Port Bakehouse, Portland, 203

MARYLAND
The Big Cheese Restaurant, Baltimore, 134
Dockside Murphy's, Salisbury, 81
The Garden Potpourri, Montgomery Mall, Bethesda, 164
New Williamsburg Inn, White Marsh, 80
San Francisco East Company, Bethesda, 213

MASSACHUSETTS
Ahmed's/Henri IV, Cambridge, 106
Brax Landing, Harwich Port, 40
Cafe at the Mews, Provincetown, 85
The Cafe Budapest, Boston, 41
Cafe in the Barn, Seekonk, 57
The Captain's Chair, Hyannis, 4
The Castle Restaurant, Leicester, 48
Chillingsworth, Brewster, 49
The Cottage Crest, Waltham, 142
Crumble Station, Sudbury, 223
The Dolphin Inn, Taylors Point, Buzzards Bay, 13

The Houndstooth, Boston, 31
Lee Ann's, Lexington, 220
Marion's Pie Shop, Chatham, 208
Martha's Restaurant, Edgartown, 103
Myconos, Yarmouthport, 206
Poor Richard's Buttery Restaurant, Provincetown, 22
The Proud Popover, Boston, 58
Rags n' Roses, Provincetown, 172
The Red Lion Inn, Stockbridge, 47
Ship Ahoy, Essex, 224
The Stockpot, Stockbridge, 178
Vincent's Restaurant, Boston, 204
Wellfleet Oyster House, Wellfleet, 204
The Williamsville Inn, West Stockbridge, 172
The Woodbox, Nantucket, 64

MICHIGAN
Big Daddy's Den, Saline, 118
The Castle, Grand Rapids, 143
Complete Cuisine, Ltd., Ann Arbor, 106
Frankenmuth Bavarian Inn, Frankenmuth, 221
Lock, Stock & Barrel, Clinton Township, 148
Second Chance, Ann Arbor, 35
The Shaker Good Room, Spring Lake, 210

MINNESOTA
Kavanaugh's Sylvan Lodge, Lake Sylvan, 171
Les Quatre Amis, Northfield, 18
Lowell Inn, Stillwater, 119
Michaels Restaurant, Rochester, 33, 90
The Phoenix, St. Paul, 17
Tom Bell's Townhouse, Albert Lea, 36

MISSOURI
Frolics Restaurant, Kansas City, 215
Shannon's Table, Salem, 158
Trader Vic's, Kansas City, 23
Vintage 1847 Restaurant, Stone Hill Winery, Hermann, 129

MONTANA
The Livery Stable, Bozeman, 173

NEVADA
The Beef Baron, Las Vegas, 8
The Carson City "Nugget" Steak House, Carson City, 55
Chateau Vegas, Las Vegas, 37
Cosmo's Underground, Las Vegas, 79

NEW HAMPSHIRE
Blue Strawbery Restaurant, Portsmouth, 130
Dana Place Inn, Jackson, 100
Deacon Brodie's Tavern, Dublin, 126

NEW JERSEY
Delicious Orchards, Colts Neck, 209
The Jane Dooner Restaurant, Englewood, 91
Le Delice, Whippany, 105
The Salt Box Restaurant, Ocean City, 209
The Seasonings Cafe, Clinton, 13
Talk of the Town, Hillsdale, 86
The Tarragon Tree, Meyersville, 194

NEW MEXICO
Casa Vieja, Corales, 6
La Dona Luz, Taos, 100
Villa de Don Peralta, Taos, 10

NEW YORK
Angelo of Mulberry Street, New York, 142
Asa Ransom House, Clarence, 46
Benihana, New York, 92
Bird & Bottle Inn, Garrison, 76
Blu Adriatico, Flushing, 72
Brown's Hilltop Tavern, Stone Ridge, 224
The Butcher Block, Plattsburgh, 30
Cafe Geiger, New York, 120
The Canteen Restaurant, Chittenango, 55
Castle Restaurant, Olean, 59
The Coach House, New York, 36, 71, 89, 116, 124, 159, 174, 192, 199, 206
Crystal Room, Tavern on the Green, New York, 216
El Faro Restaurant, New York, 48, 150
The Four Seasons, New York, 186
Gian Marino's, New York, 154
The Hickory Grove Inn, Cooperstown, 176
Homowack, Spring Glen, 11
Indian Oven, New York, 53
Joy Garden, New York, 105
J. P.'s Porterhouse Too, Latham, 121
L'Aiglon, New York, 5
La Mascotte, Commack, 84
La Rive, Catskill, 4
Le Cirque, New York, 152
The Leopard, New York, 186
Mandarin Inn, New York, 130
Nevele Country Club, Ellenville, 204
Once Upon a Stove, New York, 122
Oyster Bar & Restaurant, New York, 9, 30, 65, 84, 212
The Palace, New York, 189
Proof of the Pudding, New York, 191
Romeo Salta, New York, 151
The Russian Tea Room, New York, 38
San Marco Restaurant, New York, 151
Sherwood Inn, Skaneateles, 193
65 Irving Place, New York, 210
Tavola Calda da Alfredo, New York, 16
Tino's, New York, 12
Twin Bridge Junction, Ferndale, 123
Waldorf-Astoria, New York, 99
Windows on the World, New York, 57, 207

NORTH CAROLINA
Balentines of Cameron Village, Raleigh, 213
Berry's, Winston-Salem, 55
Clawson's, Beaufort, 154
Jared's, Ashville, 56
Old Pineville Depot Restaurant, Charlotte, 158
Restaurant la Residence, Chapel Hill, 196
The Sea Ranch, Kill Devil Hills, 79
Winslow's Dining at Minnie Cole's, Cashiers, 78

OHIO
The Apple Tree, Xenia, 53
Au Province Restaurant, Cleveland
    Heights, 190
D'Amicos, Medina, 56
The Golden Lamb Inn, Lebanon, 58
Lock 24, Elkton, 178
The Meadows, Middletown, 57
Pigall's French Restaurant,
    Cincinnati, 108
Terwilliger's Tavern, Montgomery, 170
Wine Merchant, Akron, 33

OKLAHOMA
Legend's, Norman, 219
Nicole's Cafe-Bistro, Tulsa, 164

OREGON
Belinda's, Portland, 219
The Chowderhead, Gold Beach, 77
Genoa, Portland, 184
Horst Mager's Der Rheinlander,
    Portland, 65
The Pantry Restaurant, Portland, 33
Salishan Lodge, Gleneden Beach, 49
Zapata's Mexican Restaurant,
    Portland, 102

PENNSYLVANIA
The Black Angus Country Inn,
    Glenmoore, 18
Bogart's, Philadelphia, 130
The Brickerville House, Lititz, 199
Brookside Country Club, Macungie, 79
Cafe at Bon Appétit, Philadelphia, 196
Carmassi's, Pittsburgh, 17
Changing Scene Ltd., Walnutport, 118
The Commissary, Philadelphia, 212
Coquille St. Jacques, Jenkintown, 186
The Country House, Kimberton, 185
Déjà-Vu, Philadelphia, 4, 111, 125, 159,
    172, 191
Fisher's of Bucks, Cornwell Heights, 72
Flavio's, Apollo, 136
Glass Kitchen at the Willows,
    Lancaster, 215
Hyeholde Restaurant, Coraopolis, 188
Jenny's, Lahaska, 144
Johnny Lounder's Restaurant,
    Pittsburgh, 8
Kanpai Japanese Restaurant,
    Pittsburgh, 59
Kaufmann's Restaurants,
    Pittsburgh, 215
L'Auberge, Strafford, 83
Milos Country House, Pottstown, 97
New Canton, West Reading, 183
Pump House Inn, Canadensis, 93

Saladalley, Philadelphia, 43
Sturgis Pretzel House, Lititz, 176
Tivoli Restaurant, Pittsburgh, 205
Tramp's, Pittsburgh, 61
Under the Blue Moon, Philadelphia, 220
University Inn, Pittsburgh, 61
Vinton's Country House, Shohola, 158
Willow Inn, Waynesburg, 169

RHODE ISLAND
Classic Restaurant, Providence, 100

SOUTH CAROLINA
Buddy's Seafood Restaurant,
    Charleston, 81, 173
Greylogs, Caesar's Head, 44
McCabe's, Charleston, 61
The Side Porch, Ltd., Lancaster, 214
Speranza Italian Restaurant, Cayce, 197

TENNESSEE
Chattanooga Choo-Choo,
    Chattanooga, 26
Miss Daisy's Tea Room, Franklin, 171
The Orangery, Knoxville, 221

TEXAS
The Argyle, San Antonio, 186
Arthur's, Dallas, 13
El Mirador Restaurant, San Antonio, 32
Embree's Old Town Restaurant,
    Garland, 143
Foulard's, Houston, 160
Hilltop Herb Farm, Cleveland, 64
Humphrey's, Houston, 211
La Quiche, Houston, 173
The Old House on Mockingbird,
    Dallas, 218
Vargo's, Houston, 162
Webb's Cove, Seabrook, 217
Westin Galleria Hotel, Houston, 44
The Windows Bakery and Cafe,
    Victoria, 168

UTAH
The Greenery Restaurant, Ogden, 148
Panache, Salt Lake City, 168
The Roof, Salt Lake City, 132

VERMONT
Arlington Inn, Arlington, 26
Cafe Shelburne, Shelburne, 55
The Common Man, Warren, 107
The Inn at the Mountain, Stowe, 59
Needle in a Haystack, Montgomery
    Center, 19
Spruce Pond Inn, Stowe, 196
Trapp Family Lodge, Stowe, 169
Victoria's, Randolph, 214

VIRGINIA
Chesapeake House, Tangier Island, 158
Chowning's Tavern, Williamsburg, 22
Christiana Campbell's Tavern,
    Williamsburg, 177

Gadsby's Tavern, Alexandria, 171
Half Way House, Richmond, 27
Hollymead Inn, Charlottesville, 18
King's Arms Tavern, Williamsburg, 193
Ming Gate, Hampton, 101
Raleigh Tavern Bakery,
    Williamsburg, 223

WASHINGTON
Alderbrook, Brush Prairie, 168
Black Angus Restaurant, Yakima, 160
Canlis's, Seattle, 162
Green Lake Grill, Seattle, 125
Mirabeau Restaurant, Seattle, 73
Soupourri, Seattle, 36

WEST VIRGINIA
Granny's Sandwitchery and Gourmet
    Dining, Parkersburg, 201
Yellow Brick Bank Restaurant,
    Shepherdstown, 59

WISCONSIN
The House of Embers, Lake Delton, 178
La Creperie, Madison, 144
Timber Ridge Country Club,
    Minocqua, 198

WYOMING
Alpenhof, Jackson Hole, 7
Jackson Lake Lodge, Grand Teton
    National Park, 154
Lake Yellowstone Hotel, Yellowstone
    National Park, 78

U.S. Virgin Islands
Bluebeard's Castle Hotel, St. Thomas, 24

Wales
Robeston House, Pembrokeshire, 160

West Indies
Admiral's Inn, Antigua, 25
Bagatelle Great House, St. Thomas,
    Barbados, 24
Bahamas Princess Hotel, Freeport,
    Bahamas, 22
Da Luciano, Christ Church Parish,
    Barbados, 24

Many Locations
Houlihan's Old Place Restaurant &
    Bar, 207
Magic Pan, 34, 149
Neiman-Marcus, 58, 212

Miscellaneous
Air France, 160
Stella Solaris, Sun Line Cruises, 122

CREDITS

The following restaurants contributed material to this book:

The Abbey
The Aberfoyle Mill
Admiral's Inn
Adriano's Ristorante
Ahmed's/Henri IV
Air France: Michel Martin, chef
Alderbrook
Alpenhof
Amelio's
Angelo of Mulberry Street
Anne Menna's
The Annex
The Apple Tree
The Argyle
Arlington Inn
Arthur's
Asa Ransom House
Au Province Restaurant
Au Relais: Harry Marsden,
  chef-owner
The Back Porch Cafe
Bagatelle Great House:
  Mr. Blackman, head bartender
Bahamas Princess Hotel
The Bakery: Louis Szathmary,
  chef
Balentines of Cameron Village
The Ballard Store
Bastille Brasserie Parisienne
Beamreach Restaurant
Beaver Club, The Queen
  Elizabeth Hotel
The Beef Baron
Beethoven Restaurant
Belinda's
Belvedere Restaurant & Cabaret
Benihana
The Berghoff
Bernard's
Berry's
The Big Cheese Restaurant
Big Daddy's Den: Don Clawe,
  chef
Bird & Bottle Inn
The Bistro Garden
The Black Angus Country Inn
Black Angus Restaurant
Blackhawk Restaurant
Blackrock Castle
Blu Adriatico
Bluebeard's Castle Hotel: recipe
  compliments of Mr. Monroe
  Trotman
Blue Coat Inn
Blue Fox
Blue Strawbery Restaurant
Bogart's
Brax Landing
Brennan's
The Brickerville House
Brookside Country Club: Tom
  Brownlee, executive chef
Brown's Hilltop Tavern: The
  Brown Family
The Brownstone
Buddy's Seafood Restaurant
The Butcher Block
The Buttery, Key West, Florida
The Buttery, Santa Monica,
  California: Richard E. Mynatt
The Cafe, Lord & Taylor's
Cafe at Bon Appétit
Cafe at the Mews
The Cafe Budapest
Cafe Geiger
Cafe in the Barn
Cafe Jonell
Cafe Martinique: Jim Caron, chef
Cafe Shelburne
Can Can Parisien Bistro
Canlis's
The Canteen Restaurant

Cantina Los Tres Hombres:
  Everett Wooden, chef-owner
Capability Brown Restaurant
Captain Jon's
The Captain's Chair
Carl Andersen's Chatam
Carmassi's: Mrs. Evelyn
  Carmassi
The Carson City "Nugget"
  Steak House
Casa Juanita
Casa Maria Restaurant
Casa Vieja
The Castle, Grand Rapids,
  Michigan
The Castle Restaurant, Leicester.
  Massachusetts
Castle Restaurant, Olean,
  New York
Cattails: Ken Hinaman,
  chef-owner
Changing Scene Ltd.
Chateau Vegas
Chattanooga Choo-Choo
Chesapeake House
Chez Hélène
Chez Paul
Chillingsworth
The Chowderhead
Chowning's Tavern
Christiana Campbell's Tavern
Chuck's Steak House
The Church Restaurant
Classic Restaurant
Clawson's: Bill and Candy
  Rogers
The Coach House: Leon
  Lianides, owner; Roul
  Santana, chef
Coconut Willie's, Fontainebleau
  Hilton
Colony Steak House, Hyatt
  Regency Waikiki
Commander's Palace: Ella
  Brennan, owner
The Commissary
The Common Man
Complete Cuisine, Ltd.: Nancy
  Ciupek Kozak, chef
Cosmo's Underground
The Cottage Crest
The Country Frenchman
The Country House
Crumble Station
Da Luciano
D'Amicos
Dana Place Inn: Betty and
  Malcolm Jennings, innkeepers
Daphne and Victor's
Dar Maghreb
David Copperfield Restaurant
Deacon Brodie's Tavern
Debauchery
Déjà-Vu: Salomon Montezinos,
  chef-owner
Delicious Orchards
Dockside Murphy's
The Dolphin Inn
Domaine Chandon: Philippe
  Jeanty, chef; Edmond
  Maudière, owner
Don Hernando's
Dragon Inn
Dunain Park
The Elegant Attic
El Faro Restaurant
El Mirador
El Tio Pepe
Embassy Club

Embree's Old Town Restaurant
Empress of China
Ernie's: Roland and Victor
  Gotti, owners; Jacky Robert,
  chef
Far Horizons: Harold Wuelfrath,
  chef
The Farmer's Daughter
  Restaurant
The Firehouse
The Firepond
Fisher's of Bucks: Anthony
  Colasante, chef
Flavio's: Flavio, chef
Forest Restaurant, Harrah's
  Hotel/Casino
Foulard's
Four Ambassadors
Fournou's Ovens
The Four Seasons
Frankenmuth Bavarian Inn
Friar Tuck's
Frolics Restaurant
Gadsby's Tavern
The Gallery Restaurant
The Garden Natural Foods
  Restaurant
The Garden Potpourri,
  Montgomery Mall
Genoa
Gepetto's Tale of the Whale
Geppetto's
Gian Marino's
Giuseppe's Old Depot
  Restaurant
Glass Kitchen at the Willows:
  P.E. Neuber
The Golden Lamb Inn
Granny's Sandwitchery and
  Gourmet Dining: Mrs.
  Constance Harris, chef,
  owner, pastry cook
The Great Mexican Food and
  Beverage Company
The Greenery Restaurant
The Green Heron Inn
Green Lake Grill: Karl Beckley,
  chef-owner
Gregory's Restaurant
Greylogs
Gus's Clam House: Gus Stingo,
  president; Tony Stingo, chef
Half Way House
Harpoon Henry's Restaurant
Harrison's
Heritage House
The Hickory Grove Inn
Hilltop Herb Farm
The Hole in the Wall
Hollymead Inn
Homowak
Horst Mager's Der Rheinlander
Host International Restaurant:
  Leo Stronk, chef
Hôtel de Crillon: Jean-Paul
  Bonin, chef
Hotel Gran Capitan
Hotel Hassler
Hotel Inter-Continental: Werner
  Boettner, executive chef
Hotel Luz
Hotel Villa Cipriani
Hotel Winkler: Dick Bes,
  manager
Houlihan's Old Place Restaurant
  & Bar
The Houndstooth
The House of Embers: Barbara
  Obois
Humphrey's
Hyeholde Restaurant
Il Giardino
India House
Indian Oven
The Inn at the Mountain
Inverary Inn

The Iron Gate
J's
J. P.'s Porterhouse Too
Jackson Lake Lodge
Jacques', Sheraton Baton Rouge
  Hotel
The Jane Dooner Restaurant:
  Ray Kaminski, chef
Jared's
Jenny's: Bruce Scheeler, chef
The Jockey Club: Paul Delisle,
  director; Jean-Claude Galan,
  chef
Johnny Lounder's Restaurant
Journey's End
Joy Garden
Julie's Ristorante: The Marott
  Family
Kahala Hilton
Kanpai Japanese Restaurant
Kaufmann's Restaurants
Kavanaugh's Sylvan Lodge
The Kennebunk Inn 1799:
  Gerald Goodwin, chef
King's Arms Tavern
Kingston Harbour Yacht Club
Kung Food
La Casita
La Costa Hotel and Spa: Willy
  Hauser, chef
La Creperie
La Cuisine Restaurant
La Dolce Vita
La Dona Luz
La Famiglia
La Familia Restaurant: Lisa
  Habib
La Grotta Ristorante Italiano
L'Aiglon
Lake Yellowstone Hotel
La Mascotte
Lanterna Blu
La Quiche
La Rancherita
La Rive
L'Auberge: Helen Sigel Wilson
Laurita's
Le Cellier
Le Cirque
Le Club
Le Delice: John Foy, chef-owner
Le Domaine de la Tourinière
Lee Ann's
Le Français: Jean Banchet
Legend's
Lehr's Greenhouse Restaurant
Leith's Restaurant
The Leopard
Le Petit Café: Marina Ballor,
  chef; Patrick Fiore, owner
L'Escargot on Michigan
L'Escoffier, The Beverly Hilton:
  Raymond Dreyfus, chef
Les Frères Troisgros: Jean
  Troisgros
Les Pastoureaux
Les Provinces
Les Quatres Amis
Le St. Germain
Le Talbooth Restaurant
Little's
The Livery Stable
Lock, Stock & Barrel
Lock 24: Arlene Pugh
Longhi's Cafe
Lowell Inn: Arthur and Maureen
  Palmer, owners
Lucia's Italian Restaurant
Lung Kee Restaurant
Magic Flute Restaurant
Magic Pan, Inc.
Mama Lou's Pie Kitchen,
  Innkeeper's Square

The Mandarin: Cecilia Chiang, owner
Mandarin Inn
Mankas Czech Restaurant, Inverness Lodge
Marion's Pie Shop
Marshall Field's
Martha's Restaurant
Mary Mac's Tea Room
Max's Son
McCabe's
The Meadows
Michael's Canoga Inn
Michaels Restaurant: The Pappas family, owners
Michel Richard: Michel Richard, chef
Michi Dining Room: Hara, chef; special thanks to Mrs. Phillip Blumer of Midland, Michigan
Milos Country House
Ming Gate
Mirabeau Restaurant
Miss Daisy's Tea Room
Monti's La Casa Vieja: Leonard Monti, owner
Mount Kenya Safari Club
Muckamuck Restaurant
Myconos: The Chalpara family
The Natural Kitchen: Robert Tutenberg, chef-owner
Needle in a Haystack
Neiman-Marcus
Nevele Country Club
New Canton
New Otani Hotel
New Williamsburg Inn
Nicole's Cafe-Bistro
Nimble's
Ninth Street House
Oak Creek Owl
Old Bridge Hotel
The Old House on Mockingbird
Old Pineville Depot Restaurant: Jim and Holly Bunting, owners
Once Upon a Stove
Operakallaren: Tore Wretman, chef-owner
The Orangery: Mary Davis, pastry chef
Orient Express
Osteria dei Panzoni
Ox-Yoke Inn
Oyster Bar & Restaurant: Jerome Brody, owner
The Palace: Michel Fitoussi, chef
Panache
The Pantry
Patchwork Quilt Country Inn
The Peninsula Hotel

Pepin
Petitto's
Petri's
The Phoenix
Pigall's French Restaurant
Pigeon House Patio
Pittypat's Porch
Pizza Rolandi
The Plantation
Plantation Gardens
Plymale Cottage
Polaris Lounge
Poor Richard's Buttery Restaurant
Port Bakehouse: Leslie Burnett, owner
Porthole Eating-House
Pousada de Santa Maria
Pré Catelan: Gaston Lenôtre
Prince of Wales Grille, Hotel del Coronado
Proof of the Pudding: Richard Burns, executive chef
The Proud Popover
The Public House
Pump House Inn
Rags n' Roses
Raleigh Tavern Bakery
Ramada Inn, Nashville, Indiana
Ramada Inn, Scottsburg, Indiana
Rasa Sayang Hotel
The Red Lion Inn, Stockbridge, Massachusetts
Red Lion Inn, Vail, Colorado
The Red Onion
Restaurant André Daguin, Hôtel de France: André Daguin, chef-owner
Restaurant Bocuse: Roger Jaloux, chef de cuisine
Restaurant Boyer
Restaurante Solar do Lorento
Restaurant La Cocotte, Hotel Richmond
Restaurant la Residence
Richard's Restaurant
Ripe Tomato Restaurant
Ristorante Diana: Athos degli Esposti
Ristorante Torino
Rivers End Restaurant: Wolfgang Kraminski, chef
Roaring Camp Cafe
Robaire's: Robert Robaire
Robeston House
Romeo Salta
Ronnie's: Larry Leckart, owner
The Roof: Roger Cortello, chef
The Russian Tea Room
Saladalley: Elizabeth Rozen, soup expert
Salishan Lodge
Salmagundi
The Salt Box Restaurant
Salty Pelican Bay Garden
Sam's Grill

San Francisco
San Francisco East Company
San Marco Restaurant
Sawmill Depot
Science Hill Inn
The Sea Ranch
The Seasonings Cafe
Second Chance: Ollie Kiesel, chef
Selena's
The Shaker Good Room: Yvonne Way
Shannon's Table
Shepherd Restaurant
Sherwood Inn: Phillis Lipe, baker
Ship Ahoy
Siamese Princess
The Side Porch, Ltd.
610 Magnolia
65 Irving Place
Skyline Restaurant
The Slogar
Snobs
Sonesta Beach Hotel
Soupçon
Souperb Salads
Soupourri
Spago: Wolfgang Puck, chef-owner
Speranza Italian Restaurant
Spruce Pond Inn
Stella Solaris, Sun Line Cruises
The Stockpot
Sturgis Pretzel House: Julius Sturgis
Sully's
The Sun Dial
The Swiss Lakewood Restaurant & Lodge
Ta-Boo Restaurant
Taillevent: Claude Deligne, chef; Jean-Claude Vrinat, owner
Talk of the Town
Talk of the Town Resort Hotel
Tambo de Oro: Rinse Jan de Koning and Toni Griffin, chefs
Tamborine
The Tarragon Tree
Tavares
Tavern on the Green, Crystal Room
Tavola Calda da Alfredo
Tea House in the Clouds: Mrs. Ruth Brewster, baker

Ten Downing
Terwilliger's Tavern
The Third Floor Restaurant, Hawaiian Regent Hotel: Ram Arora, Indian chef
Three Dolphin Inn
Tiddy Dols Eating House: John Campbell, director
Timber Ridge Country Club: Carol Meade, pastry chef
Tino's
Tivoli Restaurant
Tom Bell's Townhouse
Tortilla Flats at the Wharf
Trader Vic's Restaurants: Victor J. Bergeron
Tramp's
Trapp Family Lodge: Marshall Faye, chef
Truffles, Hyatt Regency
Twigs, The Capital Hilton
Twin Bridge Junction: Jonathan Sunshine
Under the Blue Moon
University Inn
Vargo's
Victoria's
Villa de Don Peralta
Vintage 1847 Restaurant, Stone Hill Winery
The Vintage Press, Inc.
Vinton's Country House
Waldorf-Astoria: Arno Schmidt, chef
The Waterfront Restaurant
Webb's Cove
Wellfleet Oyster House
Westin Galleria Hotel
The White House: Albert Kumin, former pastry chef
The Williamsville Inn
Willow Inn: Ralph Wilson, chef-owner
The Windows Bakery and Cafe
Windows on the World
The Wine Cellar
The Wine Cellar Restaurant
Wine Merchant: John Piscazzi, owner
Winslow's Dining at Minnie Cole's: Winslow Jones, chef
The Woodbox
Yacht Harbor Restaurant: Geoffrey Arakawa, chef
Yamato
Yang Tze
Yellow Brick Bank Restaurant: Marianne Pernold
Yenching Palace
Yesteryear
Youngberg's: Patience Cryst, pastry chef
Zapata's Mexican Restaurant: Lucia, chef